Learn, Teach...

Succeed...

FTCE ELEMENTARY EDUCATION K-6

FLORIDA TEACHER CERTIFICATION EXAMINATIONS

Online Diagnostic
Plus TestWare® on CD

Rhonda Atkinson, Ph.D.
Professor of Education
Valencia College
Orlando, Florida

Nancy Ann Tattner, Ph.D.
Associate Professor
Daytona State College
Daytona, Florida

Betty Nielsen Green, Ph.D.
TESOL Educator
Daytona State College
Daytona, Florida

Research & Education Association

Visit our Educator Support Center: www.rea.com/teacher

Updates to the test and this book: www.rea.com/FTCE/ElemEdK6.htm

Research & Education Association
61 Ethel Road West
Piscataway, New Jersey 08854
E-mail: info@rea.com

**Florida FTCE Elementary Education K–6
with TestWare® on CD-ROM, 2nd Edition**

Library of Congress Control Number 2011941435

ISBN-13: 978-0-7386-1008-5
ISBN-10: 0-7386-1008-9

The competencies presented in this book were created and implemented by the Florida Department of Education and Pearson Education, Inc. For further information visit the FTCE website at *www.fl.nesinc.com*.

REA® and TestWare® are registered trademarks
of Research & Education Association, Inc.

A12-0101

About the Authors

Rhonda Atkinson, Ph.D., curriculum and instruction, with her background in reading and psychology, brings to her work an extensive understanding of how people learn. She has applied this knowledge to a variety of content areas and learner needs, and is an expert in instructional design.

After earning her doctorate from Louisiana State University, Dr. Atkinson went on to become a faculty member and administrator in post-secondary education programs in Louisiana, Missouri, and Florida. Along the way, she has created courses and workshops to meet different content and learner needs in online, face-to-face, and hybrid formats.

She has also developed educational materials for Northrop Grumman, the Institute for Healthcare Advancement, Novartis, the Public Broadcasting Corporation, the Louisiana Office of Elder Affairs, the Louisiana Office of Nutrition Education, and the Louisiana Department of Education.

Dr. Atkinson is the co-author of seven college textbooks—many of them in multiple editions—in reading and learning strategies. She currently serves as a professor of education at Valencia College, Orlando, Florida, where she teaches undergraduate education courses in student success and technology as well as post-graduate certification courses in education.

Nancy Ann Tattner, Ph.D., has been an educator for the past 28 years. She earned her Bachelor of Arts degree in Montreal at Loyola College in 1969. In 1973 she earned her Diploma in Education from McGill University. While in Montreal, she taught sixth grade for 5 years and second grade for one year.

Through1976 to 1986, she was a stay-at-home mother, raising her two children. She re-entered the teaching profession in 1986 after relocating to Daytona Beach, Florida. In Daytona she taught kindergarten, 4th grade and 5th grade.

When asked to be interim principal of a private K-8 school, she returned to school to earn a Master's degree in Educational Leadership from Nova Southeastern University (MS 1995). She then continued her studies to pursue a doctorate and graduated in December of 1998 from the University of Central Florida.

Under her leadership as principal, her school was named a Blue Ribbon School in 2006. Today, as an associate professor at Daytona State College, her mission is to prepare future teachers with the knowledge and skills to be effective, passionate teachers of tomorrow.

Betty Nielsen Green, Ph.D., was educated in Europe and in the United States. She holds degrees from University of Central Florida (B.A. 1985- Ed.D. 1994) and an M.S. in Education and TESOL from NOVA Southeastern University. Currently she works at Daytona State College where she teaches the TESOL anchor courses in an ESOL and Reading infused Education Program.

Prior to working at the college she was the Supervisor of Foreign Languages for 17 years at the Volusia County School District. Dr. Green is a linguist and speaks several languages fluently and dabbles in many more.

About Research & Education Association

Founded in 1959, Research & Education Association is dedicated to publishing the finest and most effective educational materials—including software, study guides, and test preps—for students in middle school, high school, college, graduate school, and beyond.

Today, REA's wide-ranging catalog is a leading resource for teachers, students, and professionals.

We invite you to visit us at www.rea.com to find out how "REA is making the world smarter."

Acknowledgments

In addition to our authors, We would like to thank REA's Larry B. Kling, Vice President, Editorial, for supervising development; Pam Weston, Publisher for setting the quality standards for production integrity and managing the publication to completion; John Paul Cording, Vice President, Technology, for coordinating the design, and development of REA's TestWare®; Kathleen Casey, Senior Editor, for project management and editorial preflight review; Alice Leonard, Senior Editor, and Diane Goldschmidt, Managing Editor, for post-production quality assurance; Heena Patel, software project manager, for her software testing efforts; Christine Saul, Senior Graphic Artist, for cover design; and Transcend Creative Services, for typesetting this editon.

Contents

Chapter 1: Passing the Examination   1

About This Book 1
About the Test. 2
How to Use This Book and TestWare® 4
Format of the Test. 5
Sample Formatted Questions 6
Answer Explanations for Sample Questions 9
Content of the Test 11
About the Subject Area Reviews in This Book 11
Scoring the Test 12
Studying for the Test 12
Before the Test 13
During the Test 14
Test-Taking Tips 14
FTCE: K–6 Study Schedule 15
After the Test 16

Diagnostic Test Online at *www.rea.com/FTCE/FTCE-K6/*

Chapter 2: Language Arts and Reading   17

Competency 1: Knowledge of the Reading Process .17
Competency 2: Knowledge of Literature and Literary Analysis. 36
Competency 3: Knowledge of the Writing Processes and Applications 55
Competency 4: Knowledge of Reading Methods and Assessment. 63
Competency 5: Knowledge of Communication 73
Competency 6: Knowledge of Information and Media Literacy. 79

Chapter 3: Social Science   87

Competency 7: Knowledge of Time, Continuity, and Change 87
Competency 8: Knowledge of People, Places, and Environment 143
Competency 9: Knowledge of Government and the Citizen 149
Competency 10: Knowledge of Production, Distribution, and Consumption 161
Competency 11: Knowledge of Instruction and Assessment of the Social Sciences 165

Chapter 4: Music, Visual Arts, Physical Education, and Health — 173

Competency 12: Knowledge of Skills and Techniques in Music and Visual Arts 173
Competency 13: Knowledge of Creation and Communication in
Music and Visual Arts 179
Competency 14: Knowledge of Cultural and Historical Connections in
Music and Visual Arts 182
Competency 15: Knowledge of Aesthetic and Critical Analysis of Music and Visual Arts . . . 193
Competency 16: Knowledge of Appropriate Assessment Strategies in
Music and Visual Arts 195
Competency 17: Knowledge of Personal Health and Wellness. 202
Competency 18: Knowledge of Physical, Social, and Emotional Growth and Development . . . 209
Competency 19: Knowledge of Community Health and Safety Issues 221
Competency 20: Knowledge of Subject Content and Appropriate Curriculum Design 231

Chapter 5: Science and Technology — 235

Competency 21: Knowledge of the Nature of Matter 235
Competency 22: Knowledge of Forces, Motion, and Energy. .238
Competency 23: Knowledge of Earth and Space 250
Competency 24: Knowledge of Life Science 263
Competency 25: Knowledge of the Nature of Science 273
Competency 26: Knowledge of the Relationship of Science and Technology. 277
Competency 27: Knowledge of Instruction and Assessment 279

Chapter 6: Mathematics — 283

Competency 28: Knowledge of Numbers and Operations 283
Competency 29: Knowledge of Geometry and Measurement. 301
Competency 30: Knowledge of Algebra 316
Competency 31: Knowledge of Data Analysis 322
Competency 32: Knowledge of Instruction and Assessment 325

Practice Test — 331

Answer Sheet 333
Practice Test 335
Answer Key 374
Answer Explanations 377

Index — 392

Installing REA's TestWare® — 404

Passing the Examination

About This Book

REA's *FTCE Elementary Education K–6* test preparation is comprehensive and designed to assist you in getting certified to teach in Florida. To enhance your chances of success in this important step toward your career as a teacher in Florida elementary schools, this test guide:

- Summarizes the content for a quick review

- Provides sample questions in the actual test format

- Offers tips and strategies for successfully passing the test

- Presents an accurate and complete overview of the FTCE K–6

- Provides a diagnostic test to help you pinpoint your weaknesses

- Provides one true-to-format full-length practice test for rehearsal before your test date

This guide is the result of extensive research. The editors considered the most recent test administrations, other test guides, and professional standards; they also researched information from the Florida Department of Education, professional journals, textbooks, and journals in the field.

In addition to guiding your preparation for certification, recertification, out-of-field certification, or multiple certifications, this REA test prep is a valuable resource for college and university personnel and in-service trainers. They will find the book helpful as they construct help sessions and recommend resources for a test candidate. The guide may even suggest topics or content to include in a college course syllabus.

Although our book is intended to help you succeed on the FTCE K–6, you should not consider it a replacement for any college course, a duplicate of the actual test, or a complete source of subject matter to master. Like knowledge itself, the FTCE K–6 can change.

This book includes the best test preparation materials based on the latest information available from test administrators. The number and distribution of questions can vary from test to test. Accordingly, prospective examinees should pay strict attention to their strengths and weaknesses and not depend on specific proportions of any subject areas appearing on the actual exam.

About the Test

Who Must Take the Test?

Individuals take the FTCE K–6 to obtain a temporary certificate (nonrenewable and valid for three school years) or a professional certificate (Florida's highest educator certificate, renewable and valid for five school years). To obtain either certificate, a prospective teacher must demonstrate mastery of subject matter knowledge, as indicated by a passing score on the FTCE K–6.

People taking the test include (1) individuals seeking initial teacher certification in Florida, (2) educators with temporary certificates who want professional certificates, and (3) educators who are making changes in their teaching career. You are eligible to take the test if you are:

- enrolled in a college or university teacher education program at the bachelor's or master's degree level,

- teaching with provisional certification, or

- making a change in your teaching career.

What If I Do Not Pass the Test?

If you do not achieve a passing score on the FTCE K–6, don't panic! Instead, as a serious test taker, plan to retake the test after waiting at least 31 days. The waiting period enables you to do additional work to improve your score on the next test. Remember, a low score on the FTCE is not an indication that you should change your plans about a teaching career.

Who Designs the Test?

The Florida Department of Education, together with the Evaluation Systems group of Pearson Education, Inc., develops and administers the FTCE K–6. The test reflects modifications the Florida Legislature has made to the program of testing required for teacher candidates, who must demonstrate mastery of subject matter in areas covered by the certification.

A diverse committee developed the FTCE K–6. The specialists on the committee came from within the state and included teachers, supervisors, and college faculty with expertise in the content areas. Recommendations by professional organizations, content area experts, and teachers' unions assisted in the selection of committee members.

The committee identified the information for inclusion on the FTCE K–6 and validated the content. To develop the test, the committee used reviews of the literature, surveys of and interviews with teachers, pilot tests, and their own expertise. They designed and implemented a validation process to ensure that the content and difficulty level of the test are appropriate.

About Computer-Based Testing

The FTCE K-6 is offered only on computer, at flexible times and locations throughout the year. Minimal computer and typing skills are required to complete the computer-based tests. You need to be comfortable with a Windows environment, using a mouse (including clicking, double-clicking, dragging, and scrolling), and typing at a rate that will allow you to complete the assignment in the allotted time (approximately 30 words per minute). In computer-based testing, examinees complete the tests by selecting answers on-screen to multiple-choice questions and typing or recording a response to a performance assessment component.

When Should I Take the FTCE K–6?

Most candidates for teacher certification take the test just before or after graduation. Some institutions have rules about the dates by which students must take and pass the examination. Consult the rules of the college where you are enrolled to determine if any stipulations exist.

The Florida Department of Education establishes the tests you must take for certification and the deadlines by which you must complete the tests for certification purposes. For instance, if you have a temporary certificate, it is good for only three years; if you do not take and pass the required FTCE K–6 within the period that the state sets, your certificate can lapse.

Several websites, phone numbers, and addresses help you stay up-to-date with information about the FTCE K–6. You can contact the Florida Department of Education as follows:

> **FTCE/FELE Customer Service**
> Evaluation Systems
> Pearson
> P.O. Box 660
> Amherst, MA 01004-9018
> Phone: (413) 256-2893
> Web site: *www.fldoe.org/*

In addition, these websites provide useful information:

- The FTCE Home Page: *www.fldoe.org/asp/ftce*.
- Certification Examinations for Florida Educators: *www.cefe.usf.edu/*

Is There a Registration Fee?

To take the FTCE K–6, you must pay a registration fee. Payment must be by personal check, money order, cashier's check, or credit card (Visa or MasterCard). Cash is not accepted. For information on the current test rules, regulations, and fees, contact the Florida Department of Education or go to the websites listed above.

How to Use This Book and TestWare®

The following sections outline ways you can use this study guide and take the practice tests to help you prepare for the FTCE K–6.

Apart from the book itself, we give you an online diagnostic test, and a CD-ROM with a full-length practice test. **We strongly recommend that you begin your preparation with online diagnostic test which will pinpoint your weaknesses making it easier to focus your study.** After some studying, then take the practice test on CD-ROM. The software provides the added benefits of instantaneous, automatic scoring and enforced time conditions. What's more, its powerful diagnostic component provides performance percentages for individual competencies, allowing you to manage your study time efficiently and effectively.

How Do I Begin Studying?

1. Review the organization of this test preparation guide.

2. Follow the "FTCE K–6 Study Schedule" presented at the end of this chapter. The schedule is for a seven-week independent study program, but you can condense or expand the schedule according to the time you have available.

3.   Take the Online Diagnostic Test at *www.rea.com/FTCE/ElemEdK6.htm* and begin by reviewing those competencies where you are weak.

4.   Review the section of this chapter titled "Format of the FTCE K–6," which provides the format of items on the sample test and a replica of the real test.

5.   Review the suggestions for test-taking presented later in this chapter.

6.   Pay attention to the information about the competencies and skills, content, and topics on the test.

7.   Spend time reviewing topics that warrant more study.

8.   Take the Practice Test and study those competencies that your test scores indicate need more review.

9.   Follow the suggestions presented later in this chapter for the day before and the day of the test.

Thoroughly studying the subject reviews in Chapters 2 through 6 of this guide will reinforce the basic skills you need to do well on the exam. Taking the practice test under timed, simulated testing conditions will help you become familiar with the format, and question types characteristic of the actual test.

When Should I Start Studying?

It is never too early to start studying for the Elementary Education K–6 test. (Actually, you started preparing when you began your first college course.) The earlier you begin using this guide, however, the more time you will have to sharpen your skills. Do not procrastinate! Cramming is not the most effective way to study; it does not give you the time you need to think about the content, review the competencies, and practice the test. It is important, however, to review the material one last time the night before the test administration.

Format of the Test

The Elementary Education K-6 test requires all morning and most of the afternoon to complete; test takers get a lunch break between the two parts. The morning test is about 135 minutes, and the afternoon test is 125 minutes. The total test-taking time is, therefore, 260 minutes (4 hours, 20 minutes). Adding the tutorial time and the lunch break, the total examination period is 330 minutes. The Elementary Education K-6 is the only subject area test that you cannot take on the same day as another test (e.g., the Professional Education Test).

You should have plenty of time to complete the Elementary Education K-6 during the examination period, but you will need to be aware of the amount of time you spend on each question. You do not want to find you have run out of time before you finish all the questions. You'll want to set a steady pace when answering the questions. Using the practice tests will help you establish a rhythm.

Each of the roughly 225 questions has four answer options: A, B, C, and D. Individual test items require levels of thinking, ranging from simple recall to evaluation, analysis, and problem solving. The questions, however, are all in multiple-choice format. To complete the FTCE K–6 in the allotted 260 minutes, you should allow yourself about one minute for each test question.

Sample Formatted Questions

There are several types of questions on the Elementary Education K-6 exam. The types are (1) scenario; (2) direct question, command, and sentence completion; (3) graphs and maps; (4) graphics; and (5) word problems. Following are definitions of each type of question and examples for practice.

I.   **Scenario.** You must examine a case study, scenario, or problem, answer the question, diagnose the problem, or suggest the best course of action from the provided options.

    1.   A student describes an analysis of a recent presidential address for the class. The teacher replies, "You have provided us with a most interesting way of looking at this issue!" The teacher is using

        (A)   simple positive response.

        (B)   negative response.

        (C)   redirect.

        (D)   academic praise.

    2.   While waiting for students to formulate their responses to a question, a student blurts out an answer. The teacher should

        (A)   ignore the answer entirely.

        (B)   respond immediately to the student's answer.

        (C)   silently acknowledge the student's response and address the response after someone else has answered the question.

        (D)   move on to another question without comment.

II. **Direct question, sentence completion, and command.** The examinee must choose the option that best answers the question, best completes the sentence, or best responds to the command given. With the direct question, there is actually a question mark as punctuation in the question stem. The examinee answers the question.

3.   Which of the following is a trait of effective professional development?

(A)   A continuous plan of lifelong learning

(B)   Activities developed solely by the principal

(C)   A one-hour stand-alone workshop

(D)   A totally theory-based program

4.   What is one way of incorporating nonperformers into a discussion?

(A)   Ask a student to respond to a previous student's statement.

(B)   Name a student to answer a question.

(C)   Only call on students with their hands raised.

(D)   Allow off-topic conversations.

III.   With the sentence completion, there is a portion of the sentence omitted. The test-taker chooses the best answer to finish the statement declaratory sentence.

5.   Teachers convey emotion through

(A)   body language, eye contact, and verbal cues.

(B)   verbal contact and cues.

(C)   voice levels.

(D)   the way they listen.

IV.   With the command, the word *you* is understood. The test-taker is given a direction to follow.

6.   Identify the type of traditional literature that serves to explain why a phenomenon or phenoma occur(s).

(A)   Fable

(B)   Fairy tale

(C)   Myth

(D)   legend

V.   **Graph or map.** Identify or interpret a graph or map by choosing the response that best answers the question.

7.   The following graph shows sales totals for each region of the state in thousands of dollars; the graph shows the totals by yearly quarters.

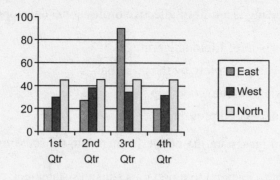

The region with the largest total sales for the year is the

(A) East.

(B) North.

(C) West.

(D) South.

VI. **Graphics.** Choose the response that best answers a question about a number line, a geometric figure, a chart, a graph of lines or curves, or a table–but not the typical maps and graphs of the previous question type.

8. Troubled by what seems to be an increase in gang-type activity among increasingly younger children, Bill wants to find out what his students think and know about gangs. He wants to learn the most he can about the students' thinking on this topic in the least amount of time. He wants all students to have the chance to share what they think and know, yet he also wants to maximize interaction among students. The students will spend the entire morning reading, talking, and writing a group report about this subject. Which of the following seating arrangements would best help Bill meet his objectives?

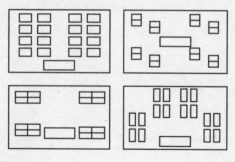

(A) The upper-left diagram

(B) The lower-left diagram

(C) The upper-right diagram

(D) The lower-right diagram

VII. **Word problem.** Apply mathematical principles to solve a real-world problem.

9.   Examine the following addition problems worked by an elementary school student. Analyze what error pattern the student's work is exhibiting. If the student worked the problem 88 ± 39 using the error pattern exhibited here, what answer would the student give?

$$
\begin{array}{cccc}
74 & 35 & 67 & 56 \\
+\ 56 & +\ 92 & +\ 18 & +\ 97 \\
\hline
1{,}210 & 127 & 715 & 1{,}413
\end{array}
$$

$$
\begin{array}{r}
88 \\
+\ 39 \\
\hline
1117
\end{array}
$$

(A)   127   (C)   51

(B)   131   (D)   1,117

Answer Explanations for Sample Questions

1.   (D)

Academic praise, response D, is composed of specific statements that give information about the value of the object or about its implications. A simple positive response, as in option A, does not provide any information other than the praise, such as the example, "That's a good answer!" There is nothing negative (choice B) about the teacher's response. A redirect (choice C) occurs when a teacher asks a student to react to the response of another student. The correct answer is D.

2.   (C)

If the teacher ignores the answer entirely, choice A, or moves on to another question, choice D, it devalues the student's response. If the teacher responds immediately to the digression, choice B, the disruptive behavior has been rewarded. Therefore, the correct answer is C.

3.   (A)

Effective professional development is not a one-time workshop, nor can it be satisfied within a specified amount of time, option C. To effect growth in children, teachers must grow and develop as well, response A. This learning must extend throughout the teacher's career and beyond. In addition, effective professional development relies on meeting the needs of those involved and therefore cannot be dictated solely by one individual, response B. Finally, in addition to being theory and research-based, the learning gained from professional development activities must be practical and applicable, as respresented by option D. Otherwise, the learning cannot be used at the school site, and the training is rendered useless. The correct answer is, therefore, option A.

4.   (A)

Nonperformers are students who are not involved in the class discussion at that particular moment. Asking students to respond to student statements, answer choice A, is the only option that describes a way of incorporating nonperformers into a class discussion.

5. (A)

Even without saying a word, teachers can communicate a variety of emotions with their body language, eye contact, and verbal cues, response A. Smiles, verbal cues (such as the intonation of voice), movement, posture, and eye contact with students can convey enthusiasm. Body language can even convey that teachers are actively listening to their students by maintaining eye contact and leaning into the conversation.

6. (C)

A myth, option C, is an explanation for something that a person does not understand; examples are stories about why a rabbit has a short tail, why the camel has a hump, and why there are certain patterns (constellations) in the night sky. A fable, response A, is a story that teaches a moral and that may have animals acting like people. A fairy tale, response B, is a story that often has stereotyping, magic, and good winning out over evil. A legend, response D, often has some elements of truth, but the person, place, or thing becomes exaggerated. For example, there is a fountain in St. Augustine, but it does not provide eternal youth; there was a lumberjack, but he did not have a blue ox and was not a giant (Paul Bunyan). Therefore, option C is the best answer.

7. (B)

To figure out the answer to any question involving the bar graph, you need to look at the graph carefully. The numbers on the left of the graph in this question are in increments of 20, which would be $20,000; these large increments make it difficult to get a precise answer. The first reaction is that the east might be the correct answer. The largest bar is in the color for the east. If you look more closely, however, you see that during the first quarter, the sales in the east were $20,000; sales were about $28,000 during the second quarter. The third quarter sales in the east, answer choice A, amounted to about $90,000; added to the $20,000 for the fourth quarter, you get a total of about $148,000. The totals for the north, response B, were $42,000, $42,000, $42,000, and $42,000; this gives a total of $168,000. The sales for the west, option C, are $30,000, $38,000, $37,000, and $25,000; that gives a total of $130,000. The reader has no idea of sales figures for answer choice D, the south.

8. (B)

Placing the students in small groups in which they meet face to face, answer choice B, will allow Bill to maximize the students' interaction while giving each student the maximum opportunity to speak. Placing students in the traditional rows facing the front discourages student interaction and minimizes each student's opportunity to speak, choice A. Although placing students in pairs maximizes each student's opportunity to speak, it limits the sources of interaction; each student can share thoughts with only one other student, choice C. In contrast, a group of four allows the student to interact as part of three dyads, two triads, and a quadrant. When placing the students in cooperative groups, it is wise to arrange the desks within the physical space of the classroom in such a way that each group's talking does not distract the members of other groups, response D.

9. (D)

You should note that the student is failing to carry in both the ones and tens places. 56 + 97 is being treated as 5 + 9 and 6 + 7. The two answers are then combined for a total of 1,413. Choice A presents the correct answer to the addition problem and therefore does not exhibit the error pattern. Choice C exhibits switching from addition to subtraction ($9 - 8 = 1$) and ($8 - 3 = 5$). Also, the child subtracts the top number from the bottom one in the first step. In choice B, the child subtracts 8 from 9, and also 3 from 8, and then adds to the 8 in the tens place. Only choice D illustrates the pattern of recording the sum and not carrying.

Content of the Test

The FTCE K–6 comprises five subject areas, with competencies (areas of content knowledge) under each subject:

- Language Arts and Reading: 6 competencies

- Social Science: 5 competencies

- Music, Visual Arts, Physical Education, and Health: 9 competencies

- Science and Technology: 8 competencies

- Mathematics: 5 competencies

The Florida Department of Education has identified skills related to each competency. These competencies and skills are the basis for the Elementary Education K–6 exam. You can use these competencies and skills as an inventory of information to consider when preparing to take the test. The subject area reviews, competencies, and skills in Chapters 2 through 6 of this guide will help you prepare for the Elementary Education K–6 test.

About the Subject Area Reviews in This Book

The subject area reviews in Chapters 2 through 6 of this book will help you sharpen the basic skills you will need when you take the test. In addition, the reviews provide you with strategies for attacking the test questions. Each teaching area has its own chapter; subtopics in each chapter include the competencies within the subject area and information on the skills within the competencies.

Your education has already provided much of the information you need to score well on the Elementary Education K–6 exam. Education classes and internships have given you the know-how to make important decisions about situations that teachers face. The review material in this book will help you fit the information you have already acquired into specific competency components. Reviewing class notes and textbooks and using the competency and skill reviews in this book will provide excellent preparation for passing the test. Each subject area review includes a competency statement and a list of the associated skills.

Another important part of the book is the practice test which will help develop your test-taking skills. Although the review sections and the practice test will help prepare you for the Elementary Education K-6 exam, this guide is not an all-inclusive source of information or a substitute for course work. The sample test items cannot be exact representations of questions that actually appear on the test.

Scoring the Test

How Do I Score the Practice Tests?

There are about 225 questions on the Elementary Education K–6 exam. The exact number of questions varies with different administrations of the test and therefore the number necessary for a passing score varies. Generally, a passing score on the test is 65 percent correct. In other words, if the test you take has 225 questions, you need to answer roughly 146 questions correctly to achieve a passing score. The passing score for each of the practice tests in this guide is also 65 percent.

If you do not achieve a passing score on the practice test in this guide, you should pay particular attention to the questions you answered incorrectly, note the types of questions you missed, and reexamine the corresponding review section. After further study, you might want to retake the practice test.

When Will I Receive My Score Report?

Unofficial score reports are available through the FTCE website after 5:00 p.m. on the day of the test. Official score reports will be posted to your account (as a PDF file) at approximately 10:00 p.m. eastern time approximately 3 weeks after you take your test. The Bureau of Educator Certification will receive an electronic copy of the score report. A copy of the score report will go to one Florida college or university and/or one school district if you so requested. Additional copies are $10.00 each.

Studying for the Test

Choose a study time and study place that suit the way you live and learn. Some people set aside a certain number of hours every morning to study; others choose to study at night before going to sleep. Busy test candidates study at random times during the day: while waiting in line for coffee, while eating lunch, or between classes. Only you can determine the study plan that is best for you.

It is important to study consistently and to use your time wisely. After you work out a study routine, stick to it. It is crucial not to wait until the last minute and not to cram.

When you take the practice test in this book, observe the time constraints and try to simulate the conditions of the actual test as closely as possible. Turn off the television, the phone, and the radio. Sit down at a table in a quiet room, free from distraction.

After you complete the practice test, calculate your score. Keeping track of your scores will enable you to gauge progress and discover general weaknesses in particular sections.

Reviewing thoroughly the explanations to the questions you answered incorrectly and noting the reasons for the correct answers will help you gain mastery. Give extra attention to the review sections that cover areas of difficulty you have noted, and gradually build skills in those areas.

It is important to concentrate on just one problem area at a time; a good way to do this is by studying the questions you missed and the explanations of why those answers are inappropriate. Study the corresponding chapter for additional information. Giving extra attention to competencies and skills related to your areas of weakness is an effective learning tool and will help increase your knowledge and confidence in subject areas that initially gave you difficulty.

Using note cards or flashcards to record facts and information for future review is a good way to study and keep the information at your fingertips in the days to come. You can easily pull out the small note cards and review them at random moments: during a coffee break or meal, on the bus or train as you head home, or just before falling asleep. Using the cards gives you essential information at a glance, keeps you organized, and helps you master the materials. Ultimately, you gain the confidence you need to succeed.

To create you own eFlashcards visit the FTCE site at *www.rea.com/ftce*.

Before the Test

If the test center is not located in a familiar area, you might want to make a trial run to ensure that you do not get lost and that there are no detours. It is always a good idea to check your registration slip to verify the time and place. Before leaving for the test center, be sure you have your admission ticket and two forms of identification. Both forms of identification must be valid, unexpired, and printed in English. The first must be government-issued and have a photograph and signature (e.g. driver's license, state-issued ID, US Military ID, or passport). The second form of identification must have either a photo or signature (e.g., Social Security card or student ID). You may not enter the test center without proper identification.

It is helpful to arrive at the test center early, in fact, you must report to the test center 30 minutes before your appointed time. This allows you some time to relax, and avoid the anxiety that might come with a late arrival.

You should plan what to wear ahead of the test day. It is important to dress comfortably and in layers; that way you can remove a sweater or add a jacket if the room is too hot or too cool. Dressing in layers ensures that the room temperature will not divert your concentration while taking the test.

You should wear a watch to the test center. However, you cannot wear a watch that makes noise because it can disturb the other test takers. You cannot bring cell phones, electronic devices, paper, dictionaries, textbooks, notebooks, calculators, briefcases, or packages. Food, drinks, cigarettes, and other smoking implements must also remain at home.

During the Test

The Elementary Education K-6 exam requires 260 minutes to administer. You will have a lunch break during the test. To maintain test security, test takers and the proctor must follow certain procedures. Once you enter the test center, you must follow all the rules and the instructions that the proctor gives. Test takers who do not do so risk dismissal from the test and having their test scores canceled.

After being seated for your computer-based test, you will complete a tutorial. The tutorial demonstrates how to move from question to question, how to mark and change answers, and how to go back and review previously answered or skipped questions.

Test-Taking Tips

Here are ways you can get ready to take the Elementary Education K-6 exam:

Tip 1.   Become comfortable with the format. Use the diagnostic and practice tests to simulate the conditions under which you will be taking the actual test, try to stay calm, and pace yourself. In fact, after simulating the test only once, you will boost your chances of doing well and will be able to sit down for the actual test with much more confidence.

Tip 2.   Read all the possible answers. Even if the first response appears to be the correct answer, the savvy test taker will read all the choices and not automatically assume that the first is the best answer. Read through each choice to be sure that you are not making a mistake by jumping to conclusions.

Tip 3.   Use the process of elimination by going through each answer to a question and discarding as many of the answer choices as possible. For instance, if you eliminate two of the four answer choices, the chances of getting the item correct have increased because you have only two choices left from which to make a guess—a 50-50 chance of choosing the correct answer.

Tip 4.   Never leave a question unanswered. It is better to guess than to leave a question blank.

Tip 5.   Work quickly and steadily when taking the test. The actual test consists of roughly 225 questions, and you will have 260 minutes to complete the test. Therefore, you will need to work at a constant pace over a long period of time. Wearing a watch and referring to the time occasionally will help you gauge the time left. Remember, you will need to allow about a minute for each question.

Tip 6.   Do not focus on any one question too long. Don't second guess yourself.

Tip 7.   Take the practice test in this guide to help you learn to budget the precious time allotted for the test session.

Tip 8.   Study the directions and the format of the test. Familiarizing yourself with the directions and format of the test will not only save time but also alleviate anxiety and the mistakes caused by being anxious.

FTCE K–6 Study Schedule

The following study schedule allows for thorough preparation to pass the Elementary Education K–6 exam. The course of study suggested here is seven weeks, but you can condense or expand your preparation program to match the time you have available for study. In any case, it is vital that you adhere to a structured plan and set aside ample time each day to study. Depending on your timeframe, you might find it easier to study throughout the weekend and during the week. No matter what timetable you plan, the more time you devote to studying for the test, the more prepared and confident you will be on the day of the actual test.

Week 1.   Take the diagnostic exam online at *www.rea.com/FTCE/ElemEdK6.htm.* The score will indicate your strengths and weaknesses. Make sure that you take the test under simulated exam conditions and observe the time guidelines. After taking the test, review the explanations, particularly for the questions you answered incorrectly.

Week 2.   Review the explanations for the questions you missed, and choose the review sections in the chapters that will provide information in your areas of weakness. Useful study techniques include highlighting key terms and information; taking notes on the material in the review sections as you work; and putting new terms and information on note cards to help you retain the content.

Weeks 3 and 4.   Reread the note cards you created in preparation for the test, look through your college textbooks, and read over your class notes from past courses. In addition, you may find it helpful to re-read the competencies and skills that the test emphasizes; a summary of this information is in the review sections of this guide. This is the time to consider any other supplementary materials that your counselor or the Florida State Department of Education suggests. (Be sure to review the website for the Florida Department of Education at *www.fldoe.org/.*)

Week 5.   Begin to condense your notes and findings. A structured list of important facts and concepts—based on the FTCE K–6 competencies and skills and written on index cards—will help you as you review for the test.

Week 6.   Have a relative, friend, or colleague quiz you using the index cards you created the previous week. Take the practice test on CD-ROM, adhering to the time limits and replicating actual testing conditions as closely as possible. Review the explanations for both the incorrectly and correctly answered questions.

Week 7.   Review your areas of weakness using study materials, references, and notes. This is a good time to retake the practice test on CD-ROM.

After the Test

When the time is up, the proctor will dismiss all the people taking the test. You are then free to go home and relax—a well-deserved treat!

Language Arts and Reading

Competency 1: Knowledge of the Reading Process

Knowledge of the development of reading is critical for the teacher who provides reading instruction, as is knowledge of the processes through which readers obtain meaning from text. The focus of Competency 1 is the reading process.

Skill 1.1: Identify the Processes, Skills, and Phases of Word Recognition That Lead to Effective Decoding

Skill 1.2: Identify Instructional Methods for Promoting the Development of Decoding and Encoding Skills

As discussed in this section, many different processes, skills, and phases of word recognition contribute to effective decoding and encoding.

Alphabetic Principle

The alphabetic principle is also referred to as graphophonemic awareness. This term refers to the understanding that written words are composed of letters and groups of letters that represent the sounds of spoken words.

Researchers at University of Oregon's Center on Teaching and Learning indicate that the alphabetic principle is composed of two parts:

1. *Alphabetic Understanding* is the knowledge that words are composed of letters that represent sounds.

2. *Phonological Recoding* is the recognition of systematic relationships between letters and phonemes (letter–sound correspondence) that allows one to retrieve the pronunciation of unknown printed words or to spell words.

Increasing phonological awareness occurs as children learn to associate the roughly 44 speech sounds in the English language with their visual representations. Children learn to pronounce these 44 sounds as they begin to talk. Because the English alphabet consists of only 26 letters, there will not be an exact one-to-one correspondence between letters and sounds. The 26 letters are combined in many different ways to reproduce the needed sounds.

Children in the early grades often create invented spellings when they try to write by applying their understanding of spelling rules. They soon realize that it is difficult to write and to decode many common words. As children progress through the grades, their spellings usually become more conventional.

Phonemic Awareness

Phonemic awareness is the ability to discern the phonemes in spoken language. Phonemes are distinct language sounds, not to be confused with the number of letters. For example, the word "dog" has three phonemes, as does the word "back."

Phonemic awareness should be developing in kindergarten and first grade. Initially, beginning readers must master the skill of segmentation (i.e., the ability to divide words into their constituent phonemes), and segmentation in turn supports phonemic awareness and then the ability to relate sounds and letter patterns.

The "Just Read, Florida" Reading Formula

Florida's reading formula is summarized as follows: 5 + 3 + ii + iii = No Child Left Behind. Following is an explanation of each part of the formula:

1. The "5" refers to the five components of reading identified by the National Reading Panel on the basis of a substantial review of research:

    • *Phonemic Awareness* (the ability to hear and identify individual sounds in spoken words).

    • *Phonics* (knowledge of the relationship between written letters and the sounds of spoken language).

- *Fluency* (the capacity to read text accurately, quickly, and expressively).

- *Vocabulary* (knowledge of the words needed to communicate effectively).

- *Comprehension* (the ability to understand and gain meaning from what has been read).

2.   The "3" in the formula refers to three types of assessment that should be used to promote reading instruction:

- *Screening*, to identify children as early as possible who struggle with reading.

- *Diagnosis,* to understand which specific skills need to be supported for a struggling reader.

- *Progress Monitoring*, to determine whether a student's instructional program is effectively supporting reading.

3.   The "ii" in the formula is an abbreviation that indicates an emphasis on initial instruction as the first line of defense against reading difficulties. Initial instruction should be explicit and systematic.

4.   The "iii" in the formula reflects an emphasis on immediate intensive intervention for struggling readers. The interventions are individualized on the basis of assessment and regularly monitored. The goal is to increase the number of instructional interventions available to these children.

Phonics

The most commonly used method of teaching reading in the United States from colonial times through the 1920s was the phonics method. Other reading methods—the sight-word method, the modified alphabet approach, and the whole language approach, for example—came into being after the 1920s, but phonics is still an important part of reading instruction in the United States.

The phonics method of teaching reading emphasizes the association between the grapheme (the written symbol) and the phoneme (the speech sound). The phonics method attempts to relate spelling rules to this process.

William Holmes McGuffey and Rudolf Flesch were early proponents of the phonics method. McGuffey produced his series of reading books in 1836. The McGuffey Readers used phonics while teaching morals to students; in other words, these books were a cultural force, not just reading textbooks. By 1920, sales of McGuffey Readers had reached 122,000,000. In 1955, Flesch wrote a book called *Why Johnny Can't Read—And What You Can Do About It* to warn parents that the reason many children cannot read is that the schools were not using the phonics approach.

Advantages of Phonics Method

Phonics is a skills-based approach. Several advantages of the phonics method are readily apparent:

1. Phonics gives children tools for decoding, or figuring out, how to read and pronounce words that they do not immediately recognize.

2. Because the phonics approach involves phoneme–grapheme associations, auditory learners—those who learn best through the sense of sound—often prefer to read using phonics. Auditory learners can usually hear a sound and associate it easily with its printed symbol.

3. The emphasis of phonics on sound–symbol relationships allows phonics readers to transfer their skills to spelling. Spelling involves associating sounds with letters; in a sense it is the opposite of phonics, which associates symbols with sounds.

4. Phonics readers often turn out to be good spellers.

At its January 1997 meeting, the board of directors of the International Reading Association (IRA) released a position statement entitled "The Rule of Phonics in Teaching Instruction." The key assertions of this statement are that phonics is an important component of beginning reading instruction, that primary teachers value and teach phonics, and that effective phonics is integrated into the total language arts program.

Disadvantages of Phonics Method

There are disadvantages to the phonics method as well:

1. Visual learners may not read well by means of the phonics method.

2. Rules of phonics do not hold true for all of the words that early readers encounter. Although scholars disagree about the exact percentages, not many grapheme-phoneme generalizations hold true in more than 50 percent of cases in reading materials for the primary grades.

3. Some students become confused when they learn a phonics rule and then encounter frequent exceptions; inconsistencies pose a problem for them, in other words.

4. Some educators, though not all, question whether skills such as phonics are essential to reading in the first place.

Methods of Phonics Instruction

To help children learn phonics, many teachers find certain techniques for teaching the method helpful. Students should have opportunities to practice phonics rules and generalizations in context, and instructors should make every effort to illustrate the transfer of the phonics rules and generalizations to everyday materials and to other subjects. **Analytic phonics** (phonics taught in context with actual materials), as opposed to **synthetic phonics** (phonics taught in isolation from meaningful books and materials, often using worksheets), seems to be the more helpful technique. This point is noted in "Becoming a Nation of Readers" (1986), in which the Commission on Reading emphasizes the role of phonics as an essential strategy for beginning reading. In this report, teachers are encouraged to use a systematic approach and present the skills in meaningful sentences, passages, and materials, not just as words in isolation.

Other reports stress the importance of phonics in any reading program, even if the emphasis of the program is on whole language.

Teachers can introduce a phonics rule or generalization as it appears, but such an incidental approach does not ensure that all students meet and practice the most frequently encountered phonics rules. A structured, systematic, sequential program of phonics helps ensure that readers have at their disposal an arsenal of skills to decode new words and spell them correctly. Such a plan of presenting the rules and regulations of phonics can help eliminate gaps in students' word attack skills.

A word of caution for teachers of phonics is that in the beginning, students may read slowly. When students begin to commit high-frequency words to memory, however, reading speed and, in turn, comprehension will increase. Knowledge of letters and letter sounds is an early source of support. Another technique that will help the child in decoding unknown words is analyzing the structure of the words, or structural analysis, as discussed below.

Word Structure

Breaking a word into its parts, or syllables, is called structural analysis. By dividing a word into its syllables and sounding out these smaller parts, students are often able to pronounce longer, unknown words that they previously did not recognize. There are many rules for dividing words into syllables; some of these rules are widely consistent across words, while other rules are not.

Children do not work with all the rules for structural analysis in the early years. Most children work primarily with adding word endings to words that are already a part of their sight vocabulary or word families. Some of the endings that children encounter first are the suffixes: *-ed, -s, -es,* and *-ing.* Experts have pointed out that six suffixes are responsible for a large percentage of structural variance across words: *-ed, -s, -er, -ly, -est,* and *-ing.*

Young children are constantly encountering new words. Even though some texts try to limit the new words a child meets at a given time (controlled vocabulary), most children do not experience such a protected environment. Some of the words a child sees may not be those in the list of sight words the child already knows. It is important for the child to have some **word attack skills** for deciphering new, unknown words.

Examples of Simple Structural Analysis

Separating the prefix and/or the suffix from the root word is an example of structural analysis. After separating these word parts, the child may be able to sound out the word. Examples include "untie" (un-tie), "repeat" (re-peat), and "ringing" (ring-ing).

Another important rule for structural analysis is the compound word rule. With this rule, the child divides a compound word into its parts. The child and the teacher can work together to sound out each part. Examples include "cowgirl" (cow-girl) and "baseball" (base-ball).

Two essential rules for structural analysis are the *v/cv* and the *vc/cv rules*. Teachers introduce these rules and encourage the students in the later stages of reading development to employ these attack skills. To use the rules successfully, the child must first determine if each letter in a word is a vowel (v) or a consonant (c). The child can write the label over each letter in the word. Looking for the *v/cv* or *vc/cv* pattern, the child separates the word at the appropriate place.

Examples of the *v/cv* rule are "oven" (o-ven) and "body" (bo-dy). Examples of the *vc/cv rule* are "summer" (sum-mer) and "igloo "(ig-loo).

Examples of Complex Structural Analysis

Rules of structural analysis such as the following are complex, useful, and best for older readers:

1. When *-le* comes at the end of the word and a consonant comes before it, the consonant goes with the *-le*, as in the words "purple" (pur-ple) and "bubble" (bub-ble). (An exception to this rule occurs when the word contains a *ck*, because one would not separate the *c* and the *k*, as in the word "pick-le".)

2. *-ed* forms a separate syllable if *d* or *t* comes before the *-ed*, as in "skidded" (skidd-ed) and "misted" (mist-ed).

Contextual Clues

As children progress in their skills and confidence, teachers might encourage them to use picture clues and previously read materials to predict what word would make sense in a particular context. To help children make their predictions, the teacher can give them a clue, like the first sound of the word. Another way a teacher can provide contextual clues is to mask words or portions of words with a "magic window"—a sturdy piece of cardboard with a small rectangle cut out of the center. The magic window allows the teacher to single out a letter or syllable for the children to consider. The teacher can also cover up words or parts of words on a transparency or PowerPoint slide.

Language Cues

The technique of using all the language cueing systems together is important to reading comprehension. Following are the three major types of language cues:

1. *Syntactic cues.* Syntax refers to the rules that govern word order and placement in sentences. Attention to syntax can increase reading comprehension. Syntactic cues include the order of words, as well as the way the words function in a phrase, sentence, or passage. To take just one example, the first three words in the sentence "Mary sees a dog" provide the reader with the grammatical cue that the final word is an object.

2. *Morphemic cues.* Morphemes are the elements of words that contribute to their meaning. For example, the word "walked" consists of two morphemes—the verb "walk" and the suffix "*ed*," which indicates a completed action. Phonics for students in upper grades focuses on multiple syllable words that contain morphological elements such as prefixes, suffixes, and derivations. These three elements affect both pronunciation and spelling.

3. *Semantic cues.* Semantic cues consist of "hints" within the sentence and/or broader passage that point to the meaning of a particular word. For example, the first three words in the sentence "Mary holds a book" tell the reader that the final word must be an object that is small enough to be held.

Phonemes and Graphemes

Phonemes and graphemes are crucial to reading and writing. A child who does not know the word "phone" but knows that the letters *ph* often sound like the letter *f* and knows that the sound of a phone is a ring may be easily able to figure out the word in the sentence "I heard the phone ring."

Through demonstration, invitation, and discussion, the teacher can help children confirm or correct as they read, monitor understanding during the reading process, and review and retain information after the reading is complete.

Although views about the development of reading vary from source to source, most experts agree that it is imperative for teachers to scaffold, or support, children of all ages. **Scaffolding** includes demonstrating, guiding, and teaching; the amount of support the teacher provides should be tailored to the individual child. According to one analysis, as students assume more and more responsibility, scaffolding declines from modeled to shared, interactive, guided, and then independent levels of support.

Stages of Reading Development

Martha Combs and others note three stages of development in reading, during which the necessary extent of scaffolding declines.

1. *Emergent reading stage.* A child at this stage is making the transition from speaking only to writing and reading as well, with support from others. Reading might involve predictable books that initially are at the child's frustration reading level, but, as the child practices, the books are increasingly at the child's instructional level and, eventually, at the independent level. Shared reading and interactive writings, which the child composes and the teacher records, provide practice and build confidence.

2. *Developing reading stage.* During this stage, the child (usually a middle-first- to late-second-grade student) becomes more independent in reading. The child's texts should now include many decodable words—i.e., words that follow regular patterns and have predictable sounds, such as "man," "tip," and "me." By practicing decoding skills while reading, the child gains confidence.

3. *Transitional reading stage.* A child who is a transitional reader usually has an instructional reading level of second grade or beyond. Ideally, the child spends much time with independent-level and instructional-level materials. The teacher is still there to help the child, but the child can refine old skills and practice new skills.

Reading Strategies

Looking at strategies used by proficient readers helps teachers make skillful choices of activities to maximize student learning in subject area instruction. Anne Goudvis and Stephanie Harvey offer the following list:

1. *Activating prior knowledge.* Readers pay more attention when they have a personal relationship to the text. Readers naturally bring their prior knowledge and experience to reading, but they comprehend better when they can think about connections between the text, their lives, and the larger world.

2. *Questioning.* Questioning is a strategy that helps keep readers engaged. When readers ask questions, whether during the reading or in advance, they are better able to refine their understanding as they read and confidently create meaning from texts. Asking questions is at the heart of thoughtful reading.

3. *Visualizing.* Active readers create visual images based on the words they read in the text. These created pictures can enhance their understanding, particularly if they are visual learners.

4. *Drawing inferences.* Inferencing takes place when readers go beyond the information given in the text in order to make a judgment, discern a theme, or speculate about what is to come. Drawing inferences is essential to making predictions while reading, and predictions in turn support the reading process.

5. *Determining important ideas.* Thoughtful readers grasp essential ideas and important information when reading. Readers must differentiate between less important ideas and key ideas that are central to the meaning of the text. This is a relatively advanced skill that develops gradually.

Additional Strategies

Following are some additional strategies that help readers of different levels:

- *Synthesizing information.* Synthesizing involves combining new information with existing knowledge to form an original idea or interpretation. Reviewing, sorting, and sifting important information can lead to new insights that change the way readers think about texts.

- *Repairing understanding.* If confusion disrupts meaning, readers need to stop and clarify their understanding. Readers may use a variety of strategies to "fix up" comprehension when meaning goes awry. One of the simplest of these strategies is simply rereading a key passage.

- *Confirming.* During reading and afterwards, students can confirm the predictions they originally made. There is no wrong answer. One can confirm negatively or positively, because the goal is simply to determine whether or not an initial prediction was correct.

- *Using parts of books.* Students should use different parts of books—including charts, diagrams, indexes, and the table of contents—to improve their understanding of the reading content.

- *Reflecting.* An important and useful strategy for readers is to reflect on what they have just read. Reflection can be merely entertaining whatever thoughts come to mind, or it can be more formal, as in a discussion or a journal-writing exercise.

Skill 1.3: Identify the Components of Reading Fluency

The National Reading Panel (2000) defines fluency as "the ability to read text quickly, accurately, and with proper expression." These are interrelated skills. The ability to read with proper expression is dependent on quickly grasping the meaning of text, and the ability to grasp the meaning is in turn dependent on the ability to quickly and accurately decode the words.

Automaticity

Just as fluency relies on comprehension, so it also sustains comprehension. A fluent reader is able to recognize words automatically, on the first attempt, and focus on the broader meaning of a passage rather than concentrating on decoding individual words.

Automatic word recognition can be thought of as a continuum that begins with the slow, struggling word recognition of a beginning reader and extends to the rapid, effortless word recognition of the skilled reader. Readers progress gradually along this continuum as a result of both instruction and practice.

Prosody

Prosody refers to the rhythm, stress patterns, and intonations of speech. Expressive reading reflects skillful use of prosody. A fluent reader is able to stress key words, introduce pauses in appropriate places, raise or lower his/her pitch appropriately, and in many other ways bring a written passage to life when reading out loud.

Skill 1.4: Identify Instructional Methods for Developing Reading Fluency

An instructor can teach reading strategies explicitly to students in a carefully orchestrated manner, as follows:

1. The teacher should initially model the strategy, explain it, and describe how to successfully apply the strategy. It will help if the teacher "thinks aloud" while modeling the strategy for students.

2. The teacher should then practice the strategy with the students. It is important to scaffold the students' attempts and support their thinking by giving feedback during conferencing and classroom discussion. In this case, it helps if the students "think aloud" while practicing the strategy.

3. Next, the teacher should encourage the students to apply the strategy and should offer them regular feedback.

4. Once the students clearly understand the strategy, they should apply it on their own in new reading situations. Here the teacher may need to ensure that the reading material is at the students' level of reading mastery. While monitoring students' understanding, the teacher should become aware of students' thinking as they read and as obstacles and confusions derail their understanding. The teacher can suggest, teach, or implement strategies to help students repair meaning when it breaks down. Teachers need to explicitly teach students to be aware of their extent of understanding, to check for misunderstandings, and to use reading comprehension strategies to create meaning from text. In particular, teachers can explicitly teach students the following monitoring and repair strategies:

    • Track your understanding with sticky notes, writing, or discussion.

    • Notice when you lose focus.

    • Stop and go back to clarify thinking.

    • Reread to enhance understanding.

    • Read ahead to clarify meaning.

    • Identify and articulate what is confusing or puzzling about the text.

- Recognize that all of your questions have value.

- Develop the disposition to question the text or author.

- Think critically about the text and be willing to disagree with its information or logic.

- Match the problem in understanding with the strategy that will best solve it.

Graphic Organizers

Depending on the situation, instructors may use the strategies described above in any subject area. In addition, the effective teacher can use graphic organizers such as these:

1. ***Double-entry journals,*** in which the student enters direct quotes from the text (with page numbers) in the left column and enters in the right column "thinking options," such as "This is important because," "I am confused because," or "I think this means."

2. ***Venn diagrams*** (two overlapping concentric circles), in which the student compares two items or concepts by placing specific criteria or critical attributes for one in the left circle, for the other in the right circle, and attributes or characteristics that are shared by the two in the overlapping section in the center.

3. ***Webs,*** in which the student charts out a concept or section of text in a graphic outline. The web begins with the title or concept written in the middle of the page and branches out in web fashion. Students note specific bits of information on strings of the web, and arrows or other kinds of lines can be used to indicate connections between bits of information.

These and many other **graphic organizers** can help students gain understanding of a text by making it more visual and concrete. Manipulating information in written text can help students understand it more clearly.

Skill 1.5: Identify Instructional Methods and Strategies for Increasing Vocabulary Acquisition

Teaching vocabulary across the content areas is important to instruction in language arts as well as in other subjects. Teachers identify important vocabulary words in their units and often single out those words for their students to study.

Vocabulary instruction consists of more than memorizing definitions, however. Effective teachers employ many strategies to increase the vocabulary of their students. These teachers post new words on a "word wall" as reminders of the new vocabulary words. They develop lessons about idioms, the use of dictionaries and glossaries, multiple meanings of words, figurative meanings, and categories of words such as antonyms, synonyms, and homonyms.

Effective vocabulary instruction includes efforts to make connections with the backgrounds of the students. Repeating vocabulary words and using them in meaningful sentences, as well as encouraging independent reading, will also enhance students' vocabulary development.

Children acquire vocabulary best when the teacher explains the meanings of new words in context. Children should have ample opportunities to review and use newly acquired vocabulary words, especially across different contexts. Shared reading is also particularly useful in vocabulary development.

Skill 1.6: Identify Instructional Methods and Strategies for Facilitating Students' Reading Comprehension

As discussed below, a teacher might encourage higher-level thinking skills in the classroom through activities like mapping or webbing, study plans like the SQ3R, puzzles, riddles, think-alouds, and programs like the Tactics for Thinking program (which provides activities for all levels of comprehension) adopted by South Carolina.

Mapping and Webbing

Story mapping or webbing helps students think about a reading passage and its structure. Some typical devices in narrative fiction that might be useful on a story map include setting, stylistic devices, characters, and plot.

Study Plans

The teacher can acquaint students with several plans to help them with subject-area reading. Many of these plans already exist, and the teacher and the students can simply select the plan(s) that works best for them with various subjects. Students may use mnemonic devices, or memory-related devices, to help them remember the steps in reading a chapter effectively.

SQ3R

Students often use study plans like the SQ3R, which consists of the following steps:

1. *Survey (S).* Before reading a passage, the student should look over the passage and consider some questions, such as: Are there illustrations, charts, or diagrams? Are there chapter or section headings? Are some words in bold type?

2.   *Question (Q).* Before reading, the student can also devise some questions that the passage will probably answer. If an assigned passage is accompanied by questions, the student can look over these questions, as they will serve as a guide to the passage.

3.   *Read (R1).* The student now reads the passage to answer the questions that he/she formulated.

4.   *Recite (R2).* The student attempts to answer orally or in writing the questions that he/she formulated.

5.   *Review (R3).* The student reviews the material to double-check the answers generated for his/her original questions.

There is some disagreement among experts about whether students typically use study plans, even when instructed. Some argue that even though an instructor may try to teach the "formula" for reading and studying a passage by having a class memorize the steps and practice the procedure several times, the SQ3R plan is difficult even for junior high school students. Others assert that the SQ3R plan is easily used by fifth graders.

PROVE

Experts point out that many students create their own self-directed reading strategies, such as the PROVE strategy, which consists of five parts:

1.   *Purpose.* Establish a purpose or create questions to guide your reading.

2.   *Read.* Read the passage to try to achieve the purpose or answer the questions.

3.   *Organize.* Create an outline of what you read, and link details to main ideas.

4.   *Vocabulary.* Note any new vocabulary or concepts that you encounter.

5.   *Evaluate.* Determine whether you achieved your purpose.

Puzzles, Riddles, and Think-Alouds

Students can practice their thinking skills by solving puzzles and riddles alone, in small groups, or as a class with the teacher helping in the modeling process.

Skill 1.7: Identify Essential Comprehension Skills

Comprehension skills allow readers to grasp the basic meaning of a text, to evaluate the text, and to identify information such as main ideas, supporting details, and authorial perspective. To help students develop comprehension skills, teachers should consistently emphasize meaning-making in the classroom and focus on the four levels of comprehension: *literal*, *interpretive*, *critical*, and *creative*.

The Literal Level of Comprehension

The literal level of comprehension, the lowest level of understanding, involves reading and understanding exactly what is on the page. Students may be asked to report facts or details directly from the passages as they read. For example, a teacher can work with students as they make their own playdough, using the recipe as a means to practice authentic reading. The teacher might question the students on the literal level as they mix their ingredients. Here are some sample questions:

- *Factual question*: How much salt do you add to the mixture?

- *Sequence question*: What is the first step in making the playdough?

- *Contrast question*: Do you add more or less salt than you did flour?

The Interpretive Level of Comprehension

The interpretive level of comprehension requires students to read between the lines. At this level, students must explain figurative language, define terms, and answer interpretive or inferential questions. Asking students to figure out the author's purpose or the author's point of view, to discern the main idea of a passage, or to identify missing information in the passage, are examples of inferential questions. Inferential questions may require students to draw conclusions, generalize, speculate, anticipate, predict, and/or summarize. For example, here are some interpretive questions the teacher could ask at the cooking center while students are making playdough:

- *Contrast*: How is the dry measuring cup different from the liquid measuring cup? Why are they different?

- *Deriving meaning*: What does the term "blend" mean?

- *Purpose*: What is the purpose of making playdough at home? Why would you want to make playdough instead of buying it?

- *Cause and effect*: Why do the directions say to store the playdough in a covered, air-tight container?

The Critical Level of Comprehension

The critical level of comprehension requires a high level of understanding, as students must judge the passage they have read. Having students determine whether a passage is true or false, decide whether a statement is a fact or an opinion, detect bias, or judge the qualifications of the author for writing the passage are examples of using the critical level of comprehension. Here are some examples of questions the teacher could ask students as they make playdough to encourage their thinking and understanding at the critical level:

- *Checking author's reputation*: The recipe for the playdough comes from a book of chemistry experiments. A chemist wrote the book. Do you think that a chemist would be a good person to write about playdough? Why or why not?

- *Responding emotionally*: Do you prefer to use the playdough we made in class or the playdough that the local stores carry? Why?

- *Judging*: Do you think that the recipe for playdough that is on the recipe card will work? Why or why not?

The Creative Level of Comprehension

The creative level of comprehension reflects the highest level of understanding. As with the critical level of comprehension, the student must read beyond the lines. In this case, the student generates ideas about an original course of action. The teacher may not want to stifle creativity by saying one action is better than another. For instance, the class may find that not long after making a batch of playdough, the material has become stiff and difficult to work with. With guidance from the teacher, the students can consult the original directions for making playdough for clues as to whether anything can be done to make the stiff playdough more pliable.

Skill 1.8: Identify Appropriate Uses of Multiple Representations of Information for a Variety of Purposes

Charts, tables, graphs, pictures, and print and nonprint media are examples of materials writers use to present information. It is not unusual to find literally hundreds of graphic aids in a single textbook. Because printing a book is expensive, the reader should immediately realize that visual presentations are more than just trimmings. Rather, their purpose is to present information and to encourage interpretation.

A graphic can expand a concept, serve as an illustration, support a point, summarize data, organize facts, add a dimension such as humor to the content, compare information, demonstrate change over time, or otherwise extend information in the text. Graphics can also arouse and sustain interest, although the very features that do so may also prove distracting in some cases. The questions that teachers use to guide student reading can positively impact students' ability to focus on and clarify the information derived from graphics.

Many students initially skip over graphic aids or give them a cursory look. These students may not have been taught how to use multiple representations of information, in which case they will not appreciate how the graphics may extend the text. Even students who have some training in the use of graphic information may not be able to transfer that knowledge to other content areas, or they may have trouble going from print to graphics and back to print.

Teachers can help students use multiple representations of information by means of open-book and guided reading. Making use of overhead projectors or PowerPoint presentations can be helpful, as can pausing a video to discuss a particular graphic.

Skill 1.9: Identifying Strategies for Developing Critical-Thinking Skills Such As Analysis, Synthesis, and Evaluation

A number of strategies are available to teachers for developing critical-thinking skills in the context of reading and reading instruction. Many of these strategies are informed by Bloom's Revised Taxonomy, an approach to classifying types of reasoning that is well known among educators.

Bloom's Revised Taxonomy of Educational Objectives

In 1956, Benjamin Bloom headed a group of educational psychologists who developed a classification of intellectual behavior important to learning. During the 1990s, a former student of Bloom's updated the taxonomy to reflect its relevance to the 21st century learning environment. The most significant change Lorin Anderson and his colleagues developed was the use of verbs instead of nouns to describe the different levels.

Bloom describes six levels of comprehension in his taxonomy. Each level depends on the one(s) below it. Although the higher levels in particular involve critical thinking, the teacher may wish to nurture development at all levels.

Bloom's Taxonomy is a way of classifying levels of critical thinking generally; here it is described with respect to reading in particular.

1. *Remembering*: This level concerns the literal representation of information in a text. Words that often elicit recall or memory answers include who, what, when, and where.

2. *Understanding*: This level concerns the meaning of both the literal and figurative information of what is read.

3. *Applying*: This is a higher-level category, and demonstrates the ability to apply what is read to a new or different situation. For example, after reading a story about how a school raised money for playground equipment, the students could discuss some ways that they might improve their own playground.

4. *Analyzing*: This level concerns the ability to analyze the parts or components of what is written. For example, students might examine a menu and identify members of particular food groups.

5. *Evaluating*: This level involves putting information together in new, creative ways of synthesizing knowledge. For example, after reading a story about numerous difficulties experienced at another school, the students might try to identify the fundamental problems.

6. *Creating*: This level involves making value judgments and very often involves the question "Why?" or a request to "Justify your answer." For example, students

might judge whether a theme developed in a passage is fact or opinion and, if it is an opinion, whether it appears to be accurate or not, biased or not, and so on.

Assessing Comprehension

A commonly used device for assessing comprehension is the oral or written question. A question may be **convergent**, which means that only one answer is correct, or **divergent**, which means that more than one answer is correct. Many tests include a combination of question types.

Another device for checking comprehension is a *cloze test*, a passage with omitted words that the test taker must supply. The test maker must decide whether to require the test taker to supply the exact word or to accept synonyms. If meaning is the intent of the exercise, the teacher might accept synonyms and not demand the surface-level constructs, or the exact word.

Comprehension can also be tested by examining how quickly a student reads, since the slow reader who must analyze each word does not comprehend as well as the fast reader. This is a far-from-infallible method, however, as some students read quickly without a deep grasp of the material, while others can be described as slow but methodical, with good comprehension. Thus, it is best to combine measures of reading speed with measures of comprehension. A teacher might ask students to read a passage and record their reading times. Then the teacher might give the students a quiz on the passage. This approach will allow the teacher to identify each reader's strengths and weaknesses.

Skill 1.10: Identify Instructional Methods to Teach a Variety of Informational and Literary Text Structures

As described below, informational writing and literary text commonly use several patterns of organization or structure: *descriptive writing, ordered list, sequence, cause and effect, comparison, contrast, chronological order*, and *problem and solution*.

Descriptive Writing

To set the scene for a novel or to describe a place in a geography text, for example, a writer often uses descriptive writing. Typically, the writer of fiction describes a time and place. Descriptions should encourage readers to feel some kind of connection to the information. Descriptive writing is usually in paragraph form and thus differs from the ordered lists and sequences described below.

Ordered List

The ordered list is typical in content-area textbooks. Using an ordered list, the author can present facts and information more quickly and concisely than is possible using the paragraph format. Text clues of an ordered list structure include numbers, bullets, letters, or word clues such as "first," "second," and so on.

Sequence

Sequence organization can occur in both fiction and nonfiction writing. A writer can organize a sequence to suit the purpose of the text—for instance, in alphabetical order, order of occurrence, or geographical placement. A reader who quickly determines the sequence will comprehend the material more readily. A perceptive reader watches for word clues that indicate sequence.

Cause and Effect

Cause-and-effect writing presents causes and their effects, but not necessarily in that order. A writer might decide, for example, that presenting the effect and then discussing the cause is the most effective way to present the material. In a social studies text, for instance, the writer might mention the American Revolution first and discuss the causes afterward; an alternative structure, however, would be to give the causes first and show how they led to the American Revolution. Teachers can guide students to watch for key words that indicate the cause-and-effect structure, including "because," "resulting in," "why," "consequently," and so on.

Comparison

Comparison writing occurs when the writer explains the similarities or differences between two or more things. When the focus is on similarities, the reader can identify this type of writing by looking for cue words such as "alike," "same as," and "similar to." When the writer intends to identify differences, the cue words that a reader can watch for include "alternatively," "on the other hand," and "opposite of."

Chronological Order

History books, biographies, and other kinds of narratives often relate their information in the order in which they happened, or chronological order. Words like "first," "next," "then," and "last" may serve as cues to readers that the organization is chronological.

Problem and Solution

Some writers structure their material according to a problem-and-solution organization. The writer states the problem and then offers one or several solutions without analysis of likely effectiveness.

Skill 1.11: Identify the Content of Emergent Literacy

Emergent literacy, a term coined by Marie M. Clay, consists of reading-related knowledge and skills that children develop prior to formal instruction in reading. Educators thus often associate emergent literacy with children up to about age 5. Children are exposed to a print-rich environment from an early age through the books, magazines, advertisements, and other sources of print they encounter at home, in daycare or preschool, and on outings. Through this exposure, they learn something about reading without actually being able to read. Following are a few examples of what they learn:

- Print differs from other visual patterns.

- Books contain print.

- Readers glean information from print.

- Print can be translated into speech.

- Reading follows certain conventions (e.g., in the U.S. book pages are turned from left to right, and print runs from left to right).

It is important for children's interest in reading- and literacy-related activities to be supported at this time, as **emergent literacy** is considered the foundation of later reading.

Some experts suggest that emergent literacy is a transitional period without sharp boundaries, during which a child gradually transforms from a nonreader to a beginning reader; others suggest that emergent literacy is a stage reflected in a particular set of skills, i.e., reading readiness. In either case, emergent literacy is understood to develop at individual rates. This raises the question of when children can be considered ready for formal reading instruction. Some educators suggest that if a child is not ready to read, the teacher should focus on instilling readiness. Others declare that the teacher should not begin formal reading instruction until the child is ready.

Many educators take the position that certain criteria should determine whether or not a child is ready for reading instruction. As discussed below, these criteria include being able to identify the parts of a book, indicate the directionality of print, and recognize that there is a connection between spoken and written words.

Parts of Books

Marie Clay developed a formal procedure for sampling a child's reading vocabulary and determining the extent of a child's print-related concepts. For instance, her assessment checks whether a child can find the title of a book, show where to start reading it, and locate the last page or end of the book. These components may differ from those typically considered essential before children can begin to read, like discriminating between sounds and finding likenesses and differences in print. A teacher or parent might hand a book to a child in a horizontal position with the back of the book facing the child. The adult would then ask questions like, "Where is the name of the book?" "Where does the story start?" "If the book has the words *the end*, where might I find those words?"

Directionality of Print

Another critical pre-reading skill is being able to indicate the directionality of print. The reader in the U.S. must start at the left side of the page and read to the right. This skill is not inborn but rather acquired, as some languages require the reader to progress from right to left (e.g., Hebrew), both left to right and right to left (e.g., some ancient Greek texts), or top to bottom (e.g., some Japanese texts).

To teach left-to-right directionality, the teacher can place strips of masking tape on the child's desk, study center, or table area. One strip is placed where the left side of the book or writing paper would be, while another strip indicates the right side of the book or writing paper. The child then colors the left side green and the right side red. The teacher helps the child use this device as a clue to remember on which side to begin reading or writing and reminds the child that green means "go" and red means "stop." Ideally, the teacher should use similar strips on the chalkboard or poster paper to model writing from left to right.

Children can also remember on which side to begin reading by holding up their hands with their thumbs parallel to the floor. The left hand makes the shape of the letter L, for "left," the side on which to begin reading. Another way a teacher can help children who are having trouble distinguishing left from right, or which side to begin reading and writing, is to point to sentences while reading from a big book or writing on the board; observing the teacher do this can help children master print directionality. Books that are 18 × 12 inches or larger are designed for this purpose and are effective with groups of children. Teachers or parents can also model directionality by passing their hands or fingers under the words or sentences as they read aloud.

Speech-to-Print Match

Being able to recognize the connection between the spoken word and the written word is part of children's emerging reading and writing skills. During the emergent literacy period, children begin to understand that the printed word represents speech, or can be examined and "turned into" speech. Shared reading can help children gain this understanding. As an adult reads aloud, children can join in with words, phrases, repetitions, and sentences they recognize. In this way, they begin to make the connection between words printed in the book and the words they and the adult are saying.

Competency 2: Knowledge of Literature and Literary Analysis

The power and versatility of language is reflected in literature. Novels, poetry, plays, essays, and other forms of literature are objects of study in their own right as well as a means of learning important information and ideas. The focus of Competency 2 is on the elements of literature and literary analysis.

Skill 2.1: Identify Characteristics and Elements of a Variety of Literary Genres

Following is a partial list of some of the main types of literary genres. These genres overlap somewhat, in that a particular text may represent more than one type.

Traditional Literature consists of stories that are passed down from one group to another over time. These stories include folk tales, legends, fables, fairy tales, tall tales, and myths.

Fantasy comprises stories with impossible elements such as talking animals or magical events.

Science Fiction is a type of fantasy that relies heavily on scientific and technological themes.

Realistic Fiction consists of stories in which the plots, characters, and settings could plausibly be observed in real life.

Historical Fiction consists of stories set in particular places and times in the past. The characters may be fictional, real, or a combination of the two.

Mysteries are suspenseful stories about puzzling events that are not understood until the end of the story.

Novels, Short Stories, and other forms of fiction are discussed below.

Nonfiction

Informational Texts provide facts about any of a variety of topics (sports, animals, science, history, careers, travel, geography, space, weather, and so on).

Biographies are written by authors who are describing the lives of others.

Autobiographies are stories that people write about their own lives.

Many approaches to writing straddle the distinction between fiction and nonfiction. For example, satire can be fictional or nonfictional. The purpose of satire is to expose, ridicule, and denounce undesirable attitudes and practices. Satirists use hyperbole, irony, and direct attacks on their targets. In the case of non-fictional satire, the actual people, attitudes, or social practices that are the target of the satire are identified. In fictional satire, a story is told in which the identities of the actual targets are more or less concealed.

Novels

A novel is a form of fiction that presents an extended prose narrative. Over the past 600 years, the novel has developed into many special forms. Classifications by subject matter include the *detective novel*, the *psychological novel*, the *historical novel*, the *regional novel*, the *picaresque novel*, the *Gothic novel*, the *stream-of-consciousness novel*, the *epistolary novel*, and so on. These terms are not exhaustive or mutually exclusive. Approaches to novelistic writing include *realism*, *romanticism*, *impressionism*, *expressionism*, *naturalism*, *neoclassicism*, *modernism*, *post-modernism*, and others.

There are many events in a long narrative. The main events comprise the **plot**. However, subplots often parallel or serve as counterpoints to the main plot line and enhance the central story. Minor **characters** sometimes have essentially the same conflicts and goals as the major characters, but the consequences of the outcomes seem less important. Sometimes the parallels involve reversals of characters and situations, creating similar yet distinct differences in the outcomes. Nevertheless, seeing the parallels makes understanding the major plot line less difficult.

Novels may be divided into chapters, or into books or parts, with chapters as subsections. Readers should make note of these divisions, and determine the relationships between them. Some writers, such as John Steinbeck in *The Grapes of Wrath*, use intercalary chapters, which alternate between the main story and peripheral or parallel stories. In such cases, the reader should note the organization and the interrelationships between alternating chapters.

Plots cannot happen in isolation from characters, and the interplay of plot and characters determines, in large part, the theme of the story. A distinction can be made between a *topic* and a *theme*.

- The topic of a story can be expressed as a phrase, such as "the prevalence of inhumanity" or "the unpredictability of fate."

- A theme turns a topic into a statement, such as "People's inhumanity toward each other is barely concealed by civilization" or "Humans are helpless in the unpredictable hands of fate." Although many writers deal with similar topics, their themes vary widely.

The relationship between plot, character, and theme is evident in the fairy tale "The Ugly Duckling." The plot of this story turns on the transformation of the main character into a beautiful swan. The duckling did nothing to merit his inherent ugliness and yet, outcast and lonely, he did not curse his fate. Nor did he gloat or seek revenge on those who had rejected him when he finally became beautiful. Rather, he eagerly joined the other members of his flock, who greatly admired his beauty. Some of the themes that are explored include the virtues of being patient and the tendency for social groups to reject those who are different from them while accepting those who resemble them.

Short Stories

Differing from traditional short fiction, such as the parable, fable, or folktale, the modern short story emphasizes character development through scenes rather than summary statements. In a successful short story, the elements of plot, character, setting, style, point of view, and theme all work toward a single unified effect. Unlike the novel, which has time and space to develop characters and interrelationships, the short story must rely on flashes of insight and revelation to develop plot and characters. The "slice of life" in a short story is of necessity much narrower than that in a novel; the time span tends to be much shorter and the focus much tighter.

Poetry

Poetry involves the innovative, often figurative use of language to stimulate thoughts and feelings in the reader. The poet pays close attention to the sounds and rhythms of language in order to create poetic effects, although not all poems rhyme or have a consistent, predictable rhythm.

Poems help the reader see things from a different perspective. For example, William Wordsworth's poem "Daffodils" presents the reader with a unique description of common flowers, comparing them to stars and then to dancing creatures: "Continuous as the stars that shine / And twinkle on the Milky Way, / They stretch'd in never-ending line / Along the margin of a bay: /Ten thousand saw I at a glance, / Tossing their heads in sprightly dance."

If poets enhance our power of sight, they awaken the other senses as well. In "Snake," the reader can hear Emily Dickinson's serpent in the repeated "s" sound of the lines: "A narrow fellow in the grass / occasionally rides....His notice sudden is. // The grass divides..."

Many children respond favorably to the poetry of nursery rhymes, ball-game chants, jump-rope patterns, and so on, owing to the pleasing sounds. Adults, too, read poetry for its sound, as well as its emotional appeal and, often, its deeper meaning.

Rhyme Schemes

In poetry, a stanza is a grouping of lines with a metrical order. Often, a poem has a repeated rhyme that is referred to as the rhyme scheme. Letters are used to represent repeating sounds, and the entire group of letters represents the rhyme scheme. For example, the following stanza from one of Lord Byron's poems is labeled with the letters "a" and "b" to indicate the rhyme scheme:

When a man hath no freedom to fight for at home,	a
Let him combat for that of his neighbors;	b
Let him think of the glories of Greece and of Rome,	a
And get knocked on the head for his labors.	b

The rhyme scheme can thus be described as *abab*. This simple rhyme scheme and the simple, almost bouncy rhythm deliberately clash with the tone of the poem, which is sarcastic and cynical.

The most common type of rhyme is the end rhyme. As illustrated by the previous excerpt, end rhyme occurs when words rhyme at the ends of certain lines. Another type of rhyme, known as internal rhyme, occurs when there is at least one rhyming word within the line. Byron created an internal rhyme in the second line of the stanza with his use of the words "combat" and "that." The first and third lines are called masculine rhyme, because they rely on one-syllable words. (Masculine rhymes also occur when the final, rhymed sound is a stressed syllable, as in "account" and "dismount.") Feminine rhyme

is illustrated by the second and fourth lines of the excerpt, in that two syllables of each word rhyme, and the final syllable is unstressed.

Poetic Terms

Following are a few of the many specific terms used in descriptions of poems.

Alliteration is the repetition of initial consonant sounds across neighboring words or syllables, as in the "d" sounds in "A damsel with a dulcimer."

Apostrophe is the direct address of someone or something that is not present. For example, many odes begin by addressing the subject of the ode, as in Keats' "Ode on a Grecian Urn," which begins with a reference to the urn: "Thou still unravished bride of quietness."

Assonance is the repetition of vowel sounds across neighboring words or syllables. For example, in Poe's "The Raven," the line "the silken sad uncertain rustling of each purple curtain" reflects assonance in the words "uncertain," "purple," and "curtain." (Alliteration is reflected in the words "silken" and "sad.")

Bathos is a deliberate anticlimax, often used to draw attention to a falseness, as for example in Alexander Pope's "Rape of the Lock": "Here thou, great Anna! whom three realms obey, Dost sometimes counsel take—and sometimes tea."

Chiasmus is a figure of speech in which the second half of a phrase reverses the first half, as for example: "Do we eat to live, or live to eat?"

Conceit is an elaborate metaphor, often extended across several lines or the entire poem.

Dead metaphors are those that have lost their freshness due to overuse, such as "beat around the bush."

Elision is the deletion of a vowel or syllable to suit the rhythm of a poem. An example would be the current American pronunciation of "vegetable," which treats the word as if it has three syllables.

Enjambment is the breaking of a sentence or grammatical unit across lines of poetry. (The alternative is the end stop, in which the end of a line corresponds to the end of the sentence or grammatical unit.)

Feet are the basic units of meter in poetry. Ordinarily, feet consist of two or three beats, each of which can be stressed or unstressed. For example, the iamb is a two-beat foot consisting of an unstressed syllable followed by a stressed one. The phrase "I think I know" comprises two iambs.

Homonyms are words that have the same pronunciation but different spellings and meanings, as in the words "son" and "sun." Homonyms can be contrasted with homophones, which share the same pronunciation and spelling (e.g., "pole" in the sense of a long cylindrical object, and "pole" in the sense of one end of the globe).

Hyperbole is extreme exaggeration, often used for the purpose of dramatic or ironic effect. Hyperbole can be contrasted with understatement, which also conveys dramatic or ironic effects.

Kennings are phrases composed of two nouns that stand for a different noun, as in the example of "whale-road," used to describe the ocean.

Leitmotivs are themes that run through poems.

Litotes is a form of ironic understatement in which something is affirmed by denying its opposite. For example, when Homer describes Achilles as neither unthinking nor unseeing, the meaning is that Achilles is actually thoughtful and perceptive.

Metonymy is the substitution of something closely related to a word for the word itself, as in the example of "the crown" used in place of the name of a specific monarch.

Onomatopoeia is the use of words whose sounds resemble the object being described, as in the use of the word "buzz" to describe bees or "z's" to describe snoring.

Paradox is a situation, action, or statement that appears to be contradictory or false but ultimately makes sense. The phrase "The pen is mightier than the sword" is not true, literally speaking, but it is sensible if understood to mean that communication is more powerful than conflict and war. A paradox based on two contradictory adjacent words, such as "sweet sorrow," is an oxymoron.

Parallelism is the use of repeated phrases that are similar in structure and meaning, as in a succession of lines that begin "I have seen..."

Pathos is a sense of sympathy or pity on the part of the reader. The term is also used to describe elements of a poem that create these feelings.

Purple patch is excessively florid writing.

Refrains are lines that are repeated throughout poems, such as "Sweet Thames! run softly, till I end my song" in Spenser's "Prothalamion."

Synechdoches are words that consist of a part or subset of a larger thing being named. An example would be the use of "hands" to describe sailors.

Forms of Poetry

There are two general forms of poetry: open and closed.

1. *Open-form poetry,* or free verse, has no set rules regarding number of lines, rhyme scheme, or meter.

2. *Closed-form poetry* follows conventions governing the number of lines, the rhyme scheme, and the meter. The poet using closed form will not deviate from the recognized form, unless the deviation contributes to the impact of the poem. Among the types of closed-form poetry are sonnets, epics, ballads, odes, villanelles, sestinas, and blank verse.

Other Forms of Literature

Other forms of literature include plays, which, like novels, short stories, and poems, can be considered fictional. Essays, in contrast, are a form of nonfiction, and thus require a different perspective from the reader. Essays tend to present a relatively direct account of the writer's opinion on a specific topic. Depending on the type of essay, the reader may become informed (expository essay), provoked (argumentative essay), convinced (persuasive essay), enlightened (critical essay), or acquainted with the writer (autobiographical essay).

Skill 2.2: Identify the Terminology and Appropriate Use of Literary Devices

Following are some examples of concepts used in the discussion of literary devices.

Theme

The theme is the main point of a story. Three of the most common themes in traditional literature can be called the survival of the unfittest theme, the picaresque theme, and the reversal of fortune theme.

*   *The survival of the unfittest theme* involves characters who face life-threatening situations yet manage to survive. Examples include the 18th century classics *Gulliver's Travels* and *Robinson Crusoe*.

*   *The picaresque theme* features a roguish character (*picaro* is Spanish for "rogue"). Typically lowborn but clever, the rogue wanders in and out of adventures that take place at all social levels. Often punctuated by humor, picaresque stories are often intended to convey social satire. Examples include the classics *Don Quixote*, *Tom Jones*, and *Moll Flanders*.

*   *The reversal of fortune theme* concerns the changing circumstance of a character or characters. Examples include the classics *Heidi* and *The Old Man and the Sea*.

Plot

In most fictional genres, including novels, short stories, and plays, the plot is one of the most important characteristics. The events of the plot may or may not occur in chronological order. In some narratives, the plot carries the reader from the present to the past by means of a flashback. In other narratives, there may be hints of future events expressed by means of foreshadowing.

Plots can be described as either progressive or episodic:

- *Progressive plots* are observed when the reader must finish reading the entire work to find out how key developments in the plot are resolved.

- *Episodic plots* are observed when units in the narrative, such as chapters, constitute complete stories unto themselves.

Conflict is essential to interesting plots. The conflict can be with self, others, society, or nature. For example, in *Where the Lilies Bloom*, Vera and Bill Cleaver present a family of children who are fighting society and its rules in order to remain together. In *The Chocolate War*, the main character, Jerry, faces conflicts with himself as well as with the rest of the school community over whether to sell chocolate.

A plot will also be interesting if there is an element of suspense, such that the reader is unaware of the outcome of the story until the end. For instance, in *The Island of the Blue Dolphins*, the reader does not know until the end of the book whether the main character, Karana, will stay on the island.

Sensationalism is when the plot turns on a series of exciting and unusual events. *Hansel and Gretel* is an example of sensationalism in traditional literature, in that the plot turns on the abandonment of children, the prospect of their being eaten by a witch, and so on.

The plot of a narrative leads to a denouement or the ending of the narrative. There are two types. A closed denouement occurs when all of the reader's questions about the plot are answered, while an open denouement occurs when key questions are unanswered.

Setting

Narratives in every genre of fiction and most genres of nonfiction present a setting. The setting—the time and place of a narrative—may be realistic or fictional, unusual or ordinary. In addition, settings may either be backdrop or integral.

- *A backdrop setting* is not essential to the plot. For example, the setting in many of the Nancy Drew books is a backdrop setting because the plot could have unfolded in almost any American city.

- *An integral setting* is essential to the plot. In *The Life of Pi*, the story would not make sense unless most of the events took place out on the open ocean.

Settings can also be used in a symbolic way. In *Lord of the Flies,* the setting of the island has symbolic importance to the themes Golding develops about human nature. Being remote from civilization, the island becomes a stage where "human nature" gradually expresses itself.

Characterization

Characterization is an essential part of any narrative. Following are some key distinctions in the treatment of characters:

1. *Round versus flat.* A round character is fully developed, meaning that much is known about the character's external and internal life. A flat character is not extensively developed; consequently readers know little about him or her.

2. *Dynamic versus static.* A dynamic character undergoes some kind of change during the course of the story. Static characters do not change in significant ways.

3. *Protagonist versus antagonist.* In a narrative, the protagonist struggles for someone or something, while the antagonist is the enemy or rival that the protagonist is struggling against.

Stock characters exist because the plot demands them. For instance, the ball scene in *Cinderella* must include many men and women who do nothing more than attend the dance.

A character can be a stereotype, without individual characteristics. For instance, in many fairy tales, the oldest daughter is ugly and mean, while the youngest daughter is beautiful—outside and inside. A sheriff in a small southern town, a football player who is all brawn, a librarian clucking over her prized books, or the cruel commandant of a prisoner-of-war camp might all be stereotypic.

Characters often serve as foils for other characters, serving to help the reader see the novel's other characters more clearly. A classic example is in Mark Twain's *The Adventures of Tom Sawyer.* Tom is the romantic foil for Huck Finn's realism. In Harper Lee's *To Kill a Mockingbird*, Scout serves as the naive observer of events that her older brother, Jem, comes to understand from the perspective of the adult world.

Some characters are allegorical, standing for qualities or concepts rather than for actual personages. In C. S. Lewis's *The Lion, the Witch, and the Wardrobe*, the Lion stands for goodness rather than representing a specific lion.

The Revelation of Characters

Writers use a variety of means to reveal characters to the reader:

1. The writer may tell the reader directly about the character.

2. The writer may describe the character in his or her natural surroundings.

3. The writer may show the character in action.

4. The writer may provide examples of the character's distinctive manner of speaking.

5. The writer may reveal the inner thoughts and feelings of the character.

6. The writer may describe the character's outward appearance.

7. The writer may quote others from the story discussing the character.

8. The writer may show how others react to the character.

Stereotyping in Characterization

Whatever methods are used to reveal character, the careful writer avoids stereotyping. Stereotyping is typecasting someone by characteristics such as nationality, religion, size, age, or gender. In traditional literature, for example, female characters engage in less critical problem solving, lead more placid lives, and depend on males for support and survival, particularly in times of crisis.

Some teachers who discover stereotyping in a juvenile book may wish to exclude it from the required reading lists for their classrooms. Other teachers may make a point of including such books as a way of helping students become aware of stereotyping and encouraging students to critically evaluate what they read.

Motifs

Skilled writers often employ motifs to help unify their works. A motif is a story detail or element that recurs throughout the work and helps convey the theme. The Nancy Drew books, for example, rely on motifs such as lonely roads, ticking clocks, shadows, and empty houses. These motifs help convey to the reader the challenges and perhaps even dangers facing the detective as she tries to solve the mystery.

Motifs can also be used in a symbolic way. For example, in William Golding's *Lord of the Flies*, Piggy loses one of the lenses of his glasses and later must function without glasses at all. This loss of insight on the part of a relatively wise character is symbolic of the loss of insight and wisdom in the midst of the growing chaos on the island.

Style

Stories can be differentiated according to their plots, characters, topics, themes, motifs, and settings, as well as by the style of the writing. Stylistic differences are easy to spot when comparing relatively diverse writers such as Jane Austen (formal and mannered), Mark Twain (casual and colloquial), and Ernest Hemingway (spare and driven).

Style is conveyed by many characteristics of a narrative, including the following:

- Word choice
- Syntax
- Rhythm
- Imagery
- Relative mix of narrative and dialogue
- Choice of narrative voice
- Level of detail
- Diction
- Use of humor, irony, and/or sarcasm
- Use of parody and/or satire

Figurative Language

Figurative language includes the use of similes, metaphors, and personification.

1.   *A simile* is a description that uses words such as "like," "than," or "as" to point out a similarity. For example, by saying that Mark looks like a pile of rumpled sheets early in the morning, one creates a simile comparing Mark's appearance to that of the sheets.

2.   *A metaphor* is a description of something in different terms. For example, by saying that someone is an old bear when it comes to the topic of money, one creates a metaphor suggesting that the person is grumpy and, perhaps, cautious about money.

3.   *A personification* is a type of metaphor in which human characteristics are given to inanimate objects. For example, by saying that the sun came close and rested its warm arms on my shoulders, one creates a personification in which the sun is given human qualities.

Traditional Children's Fiction

Based on its content, narrative fictional literature for children can be described as either traditional or modern.

Traditional children's literature consists of ancient stories passed from generation to generation by word of mouth. Eventually writers, such as Joel Chandler Harris, the Grimm brothers, and Charles Perrault, recorded the stories for other generations.

There are six types of traditional fiction, each of which possesses characteristics that set it apart from the others.

1. *Parables.* A parable is a story that is realistic and imparts a moral lesson. The story is didactic because it teaches something about morality. Unlike the fable, the parable could be, but is not necessarily, true. Well-known biblical parables include "The Prodigal Son" and "The Good Samaritan."

2. *Fables.* The fable is a nonrealistic story with a moral. Animals are often the main characters in fables. Aesop, a Greek slave supposedly born around 600 BCE, is often associated with the fable. Some of the best-known fables attributed to him are "The Fox and the Crane," "The Fox and the Crow," and "The Fox and the Grapes."

3. *Fairy Tales.* Although not every fairy tale includes a fairy among its cast of characters, the element of magic is necessary to this type of traditional children's literature. Most fairy tales follow a certain pattern and may present an "ideal." For instance, fairy tales like *Cinderella*, *Snow White*, and *Rapunzel* convey a message about the "proper" woman. According to these tales, the ideal woman is beautiful, kind, and long-suffering; she waits for her prince to come and save her from any disappointment or disaster that may occur.

Some writers, like Nathaniel Hawthorne, use the term "wonder tales" to refer to stories with magical elements. Examples of magic often appear in the characters of witches, wizards, and talking beasts. The use of the "magic three" is another frequent feature of the fairy tale; for instance, there are often three wishes, three attempts at achieving a goal, or three siblings.

Another characteristic of the fairy tale is that the listener or reader knows that good will always triumph over evil. A child may be frightened by witches, wicked ogres, and evil forces, but he or she learns that the protagonist of every fairy tale eventually manages to "live happily ever after."

Stereotyping is another characteristic of the fairy tale. As soon as the storyteller says the word "stepmother," for instance, the listener knows that the woman is "wicked," while the word "prince" is often used to indicate a young, handsome, and "good" man who rides a white horse (at least metaphorically).

4. *Folktales.* Folktales use simple language distinctive to the group in which the stories originated. The stories are intended primarily for entertainment. For example, "noodlehead stories" are folktales with a humorous bent. These stories feature one or more characters whom the reader or listener can easily outsmart. The humor of the story is in the ridiculous antics of a character that makes the listener or reader feel superior.

5. *Myths.* Myths are stories, often involving supernatural forces, that attempt to explain natural phenomena. Greeks, Romans, Norse peoples, and Native Americans, for example, developed myths about gods and heroes that account for thunder, fire, changes in weather, and the "movements" of the sun. Myths may explain events as fundamental as the creation of humanity as well as relatively minor phenomena such as why leopards have spots or rabbits have small tails.

6. *Legends.* Legends are stories—usually exaggerated—about real people, places, and things. George Washington, for instance, was a real person, but because there were no silver dollars minted during the American Revolution, it would have been impossible for him to have tossed a silver dollar across the Potomac, as described in a popular legend. Paul Bunyan may have been an actual logger or lumberjack, but it is doubtful that he owned a blue ox or had a pancake griddle large enough for his cook to skate across.

Modern Children's Fiction

The categories of traditional children's fiction apply to some of the modern works that are available. In addition, modern children's fiction can be classified into various, somewhat overlapping, categories. Following are four of the many categories that could be identified:

1. *Realist novels.* A realist novel may take place in any city or country or even on another planet. In each case, one of the author's goals is to convince the reader of the reality of the setting. Likewise, anyone can serve as a main character, and the author attempts to convince the reader that the character is believable.

2. *Romances.* As one of many genres of young adult fiction, the romance presents an idealized view of life. The characters and the setting are idealizations of real life. An ocean cruise in a romance novel might, therefore, involve characters who are young, good-looking and rich, and the weather would be clear and pleasant for the entire cruise. If a character did not match the others in appearance or affluence, or if the weather was terrible for part of the cruise, these deviations from the ideal would be used to advance the plot. The outsider would be accepted for his or her inner qualities, or the storm would provide an opportunity for one or more characters to demonstrate their courage.

3. *Confessions.* In a confession, a central character reveals personal thoughts and ideas. In Laura Ingalls Wilder's books, for example, the reader knows exactly what

the main character, Laura, is thinking, without being privy to the thoughts of others, such as Laura's sister.

4. *Satires.* As noted earlier, satire is a vehicle for social criticism. In a Menippean satire, the reader is shown the world through the eyes of another. For example, in Roald Dahl's *Charlie and the Chocolate Factory,* the reader sees the world and some of its flaws through Charlie's eyes.

Skill 2.3: Identify and Apply Professional Guidelines for Selecting Multicultural Literature

Literature for children is a window through which they view the world. For this reason, it is desirable for children's literature to reflect the diversity of the world's peoples—young and old, rich and poor, male and female, and so on. According to Denise Ann Finazzo, guidelines for selecting literature should ensure that the content enables the reader to recognize the following:

*   The likenesses and differences of various groups.

*   The cultural contributions of all citizens of the Earth.

*   The sense of pride that all people have as members of a family, a community, and a world.

*   The need to understand ourselves and others.

*   The opportunity to view others and ourselves as realistically and objectively as possible.

The oral traditions of the world's cultures are rich, and, with the advent of moveable type, many fables, fairy tales, parables, folktales, and myths became available in print. Researching the origin of this traditional literature reveals both culturally specific tales as well as those that are shared in variant forms across cultures. In China, for example, Cinderella's slipper is made of fur, not glass, and Red Riding Hood is Lon Po Po.

Multiculturalism and Cultural Pluralism

Multiculturalism concerns the possibility of many cultures combining to form a better society. Multiculturalism reflects both assimilationism and pluralism.

1. *Assimilationism* is the view that promotes a "national culture" and considers cultural differences as potentially problematic until people become part of the national culture.

2. *Pluralism* holds that in a functional society, cultural differences should be not only tolerated but encouraged.

The teacher who subscribes to multiculturalism combines some elements of both assimilationism and pluralism into the curriculum, positing the existence of a shared cultural identity among members of a society that does not require individuals to give up their distinctive cultural heritage.

Promoting Multiculturalism

An educator can promote multiculturalism in the classroom by emphasizing the following:

- The existence of many cultures in the world.
- The extent of diversity in American culture.
- The influence of other cultures on American society.
- The specific origins of rhymes, stories, games, riddles, and so on.

Children's literature of the current era contains ample evidence of stories, games, and riddles from many cultures and has begun to explore the origins of the literature. The variety of books and materials available each year is beginning to represent the many cultures of the world.

The Example of African American Children's Literature

An important consideration when selecting multicultural literature is that children's books often reflect the social norms of their times. The history of African American children's literature is one of many examples that illustrate the point.

Most senior adults in America can remember only three main children's books printed before the 1940s in which African Americans were portrayed as the main characters. The various editions of those books—*Uncle Remus Stories*, *Little Black Sambo*, and *Epaminondas and his Auntie*—did not always present the main characters in a favorable light, and the stereotyping in each presented an unfavorable image of the African American to the young reader or listener. These books clearly promoted a prejudicial point of view; no books with African Americans as positive role models existed at the time.

At the same time, a few books written during the late 1940s broke the traditional mold. *Two Is a Team* by Lorraine and Jerrold Beim shows two boys playing together. The two children are almost identical in size, facial features, interests, and even hair styles, but they differ in that one of the boys is "shaded" a somewhat darker color than the other. This book illustrates the idea that people are the same inside even though they might be different in color outside. Another book with a similar message is *Bright April*, by Marguerite deAngeli. April is a member of a Brownie troop who is almost identical in needs, interests, and physical appearance to the other girls in the troop, other than having darker skin. Although both books focus on similarities among people, deAngeli also refers to some of the racial problems of the era. Finally, a book for older readers, *Call Me Charley* by Jesse Jackson, conveys the discrimination that Charley encounters from his peers and from adults. Charley's quiet resignation and his father's acceptance of their lot are often points of discussion among students today.

During the 1950s, some children's books reflected interest in racial balance and institutional change. Books with African Americans as main characters, as well as interactions between African American and white characters, became more common. Some of these books faced racial controversies directly from the African American point of view. Even so, the authors often resolved the problems of racism too quickly and easily.

By the 1960s, most schools began to acknowledge racial and ethnic differences among people in their experiences, literatures, histories, and traditions. The view of America as a melting pot was beginning to change for some people to the view of America as a salad bowl. Change came slowly, however. In a 1965 "Saturday Review" article, Nancy Larrick expressed her fear that even though the curriculum was changing, students were still experiencing the "All-White World of Children's Books." Even though more books with African Americans as main characters were appearing on children's bookshelves at this time, the words often did not indicate the race of the characters. Books such as *The Snowy Day, Roosevelt Grady,* and *Mississippi Possum* received criticism "for 'whitewashing' blacks and attempting to make everyone the same. By contrast, *Stevie* was praised for capturing distinctive qualities of the African American experience.

Books published after the sixties, like *Shawn Goes to School* and *Cornrows* depict the uniqueness of the African American culture. Characters in these books are individuals; their facial features and the color of their skin emphasize their distinctiveness. Instead of trying to make all the characters look alike except for "shading," the books emphasize differences and encourage pride in self and family.

Use of Multicultural Literature

Cultural pluralism involves the acceptance of the distinctive characteristics of all cultures, including one's own. Teachers can heighten students' appreciation of cultural pluralism through literature-related activities such as the following:

1. Give students the opportunity to examine a situation through several viewpoints. For example, *Faithful Elephants* requires the reader to consider war through its impact on animals, particularly the animals in Japan. *Sadako and the Thousand Paper Cranes* enables the reader to consider war through the eyes of an innocent child. *Maniac Magee* asks the reader to consider prejudice in America through a child's eyes.

2. Invite members of the class and community to share their diverse backgrounds.

3. Establish a cooperative work environment in the classroom and school.

4. Explore the history of rhymes, riddles, superstitions, customs, symbols, chants, songs, foods, dances, and games reflecting a variety of different cultures.

5. Identify and read authors who describe different cultures.

6. Compare and contrast the "melting pot" view with the "salad bowl" view of American society.

7.   Study successful individuals who represent various cultural groups.

8.   Engage in culturally specific activities after reading stories of other cultures. For example, experiment with writing Haiku or make origami cranes after reading *Sadako and the Thousand Paper Cranes* or experiment with rope rhymes after reading Eloise Greenfield's poem "Rope Rhyme."

Exceptionalities and Children's Literature

Schools have progressed from ignoring children with special needs, to isolating children with special needs in special schools, to providing separate classrooms for these students within public schools, to mainstreaming the students into regular classrooms, and finally to including those with exceptionalities in the "regular" class. Because biases and prejudices sometimes exist as a result of or even before inclusion, teachers must help construct a working environment that meets each student's basic needs, including a feeling of belonging, a feeling of safety, and a place where each student feels loved and accepted.

Children's literature can show others how it feels to be different in some way and can emphasize that everyone has the same basic needs. For instance, "Crow Boy" helps students understand what it is like to be excluded because of being "different." "The Flunking of Joshua T. Bates" explores the impact that failing a class has on a student. "Discoveries" provides numerous biographical sketches of successful people who are deaf. The book establishes effective role models, discourages labeling, and presents individuals who have overcome obstacles in their lives.

Bibliotherapy—giving the right book to the right child at the right time or treating problems with books—can be helpful in constructing a cooperative classroom. Students might read and discuss books such as *I Have a Sister; My Sister Is Deaf* or *The Summer of the Swans*, which concern deafness and academic problems, respectively. These books and others can serve as springboards for discussions of exceptionalities.

Multicultural Poems and Poets

Teachers can include poetry of all cultures in their classrooms. For example, Cynthia Rylant has written many poems on growing up in the Appalachian Mountains. Charlotte Pomerantz writes about her winters in Puerto Rico. Louise Bennett writes of Jamaica. Javaka Steptoe emphasizes the African American experience. The Japanese Haiku is a type of poetry that is particularly suited to the elementary classroom because of its brevity.

Sexism

Despite Title IX and substantial publicity on the topic, students and teachers sometimes witness or perpetuate sex discrimination in educational settings. To keep students from taking discrimination for granted, it is helpful to raise their consciousness about sexism in American society.

Useful activities in this regard include role playing, having students look at key situations through several viewpoints, inviting successful community members of both sexes to visit the classroom, establishing a cooperative work environment in the classroom, and exploring the contributions of males and females in history. Books like *Focus on Women* provide activities, biographical sketches, and insight into the contributions of women to America.

Exploring the contributions of individual women to society is another valuable tool in handling sexism. One of many examples is *Harriet Quimby: America's First Lady of the Air*. When coupled with the suggested activities in the accompanying activity book, the class can engage in lively discussions and learning experiences.

Another helpful tool is recognizing that sexism may play a role in older children's books that are still used in educational settings. In the early 1970s, Suzanne Czaplinski conducted a study of picture books that won the Caldecott Medal. The researcher counted each appearance of a male or female in the text and in the pictures and calculated the number of males and females in each. Among Czaplinski's findings were that males outnumbered females both in the text (65% vs. 35%) and in the pictures (63% vs. 37%). Surprisingly, the percentage of females in the books decreased from 1950 (51%) through the 1960s (23%).

To find out if there had been changes since Czaplinski's study, Davis and McDaniel conducted a study with the help of their students based on the prediction that females would appear more frequently in Caldecott Medal winners after 1972, the year that Congress passed Title IX as part of a federal law to promote (if not guarantee) sex equity in education. Furthermore, sex discrimination was an emerging political issue in American life, feminism was on the rise, publishers were issuing guidelines for sex-neutral language, and women were outpacing men in college (and professional) school admissions as well as in academics. Surely, Caldecott winners from 1972 through 1997 would reflect a quarter century of social change.

When Davis, McDaniel, and their students compared their results to the earlier study conducted by Czaplinski, they discovered the following:

- There was very little change in the percentage of male vs. female characters in the text of Caldecott winners from 1972 through 1997. The percentages were 61% vs. 39%, respectively, as compared with Czaplinski's finding of 65% vs. 35%.

- There was also very little change in the percentage of males vs. females in the pictures of Caldecott winners from 1972 through 1997. The percentages were 65% vs. 35%, respectively, as compared with Czaplinski's finding of 63% vs. 37%.

- In the 1990s, 39% of characters in Caldecott winners were females, a slight decrease from the 1980s.

- The percentage of females appearing in texts of Caldecott winners never exceeded that of the decade of the 1950s, when 51% of the characters were females.

Davis, McDaniel, and their students were perplexed that the decade of the 1950s remains the golden era for representation of females in the text of Caldecott winners. The findings show that, in some ways, sexism is still a part of children's literature. The mere awareness of this fact can raise teachers' and students' consciousness and serve a purpose. The informed teacher can help make students aware of sex discrimination, modify the curriculum, and teach acceptance of others.

Skill 2.4: Identify Appropriate Techniques for Encouraging Students to Respond to Literature in a Variety of Ways

Some students spontaneously connect with literature, while others make connections only after some degree of scaffolding and encouragement. The following eight comprehension strategies may not only help students understand what they read but also promote thoughtful and useful responses to the reading:

1. *Predicting.* Making predictions requires readers to develop informed guesses about what will happen; they can then determine whether their predictions were accurate or not.

2. *Connecting.* Making connections requires readers to relate texts to their own lives, to the world, and to other materials.

3. *Visualizing.* Visualization requires students to create mental images of what they are reading.

4. *Questioning.* Questioning activities require students to answer literal, interpretive, critical, and creative questions that they ask themselves or that their teachers might ask.

5. *Identifying.* Identification requires students to recognize major points of information as they read, such as plot, topic, and theme.

6. *Summarizing.* Summarization requires students to restate key points in concise summaries, reports, dioramas, posters, plays, or other forms of expression.

7. *Monitoring.* Monitoring is performed by teachers and the students themselves to ensure that the latter understand what they are reading and can use the appropriate techniques (decoding, context clues, picture clues, sight words, etc.) if they are having difficulty.

8. *Evaluating.* Evaluation activities require students to think about and evaluate what they read as well as the experience of reading.

Competency 3: Knowledge of the Writing Process and its Application

The development of reading and writing are closely linked. As a result, instruction in one area necessarily involves skills and experiences of relevance to the other area. The focus of Competency 3 is on the writing process.

Skill 3.1: Demonstrate Knowledge of the Developmental Stages of Writing

For many years, educators believed that reading preceded writing in the development of literacy. This belief has changed recently. Emergent literacy research indicates that learning to write is an important part of the process by which a child learns to read.

Stages of Writing

As children begin to name letters and read print, they also begin to write letters and words. Writing development seems to occur at about the same time as reading development. Just as change has marked educators' beliefs about reading instruction and the way that reading develops, change has also marked the methods and philosophies behind the teaching of writing in the schools.

Children seem to progress through certain stages in their writing. Although many authorities have examined the stages of writing development, Alexander Luria presents the most thoroughly elaborated model. He cautions, however, that the stages are not entirely a function of age. Luria explains that it is not uncommon to find children between ages 3 and 6 who are the same age but two to three stages apart in their writing. He also notes that children do not advance systematically through the stages. At times, a child may regress or "zigzag." At other times, the child may appear to remain at one level over a relatively lengthy period without progress or regression to an earlier stage. Here is a summary of Luria's stages in the development of writing:

- *Stage 1:* The undifferentiated stage from ages 3 to 5 is a period that Luria defines as a prewriting or pre-instrumental period. The child does not distinguish between marks written on a page. The marks (i.e., writing) seem merely random to the child and do not help the child recall information.

- *Stage 2:* The differentiated stage from about age 4 or 5 is when the child intentionally builds a relationship between sounds and written expression. For instance, the child represents short words or short phrases with shorter marks and longer words, phrases, or sentences with longer marks. The child might use dark marks to help remember a sentence like "The sky was dark." Making such marks is an example of mnemonics, or associating symbols with information. It is not writing in the conventional sense, but nonetheless an important transition to writing.

- *Stage 3:* The pictographic stage from ages 4 to 6 represents an important development in the understanding of writing as a conceptual act. In this stage, specific marks consistently stand for specific words, in a pictorial way.

- *Stage 4:* In the final stage, children recognize that written marks are representations of words and that there is a one-to-one correspondence between specific sets of marks and specific words.

Skill 3.2: Demonstrate Knowledge of the Writing Process

In the early 1970s, teachers were very concerned with spelling and punctuation in students' papers. The teacher did all the "correcting" and watched carefully for grammatical, spelling, and punctuation errors. In the late 1970s, many writing experts argued that students' compositions were too dull. The schools began to foster creative writing and encouraged teachers to provide students with regular opportunities to do so. However, many teachers began to view creative writing activities as lacking in structure. Process writing has since become a popular alternative to unstructured writing. The stages of process writing are often described as follows:

1. *Prewriting Stage.* During the first stage of the writing process, students begin to collect information for the writing that they will do. The student selects a topic, considers the audience and purpose, and begins brainstorming lists of events, experiences, and/or key details. The student will also engage in organizational activities.

2. *Drafting Stage.* During this stage, the student begins to compose. The student should ask whether the writing fits the intended audience and purpose. The class resembles a laboratory at this point. Students may consult with one another and use various books and materials to create their drafts. At this stage, the students should not worry about spelling and mechanics.

3. *Revising Stage.* During the revising stage, the student will polish and improve the composition. The student can continue to ask whether the writing fits the audience and purpose, whether his or her thoughts and feelings are conveyed, whether the organization is appropriate, and whether the composition flows smoothly when read aloud.

4. *Editing Stage.* During the editing stage, students correct their own writing as well as the works of others. After self-evaluations, as well as evaluations and constructive criticism from classmates and teachers, the students rewrite their compositions.

5. *Publishing.* In some classes the students publish their own works and even have an author's chair from which they can share some things about themselves, discuss their writing process, and read their compositions aloud. Research studies suggest that the most effective writing process includes at least the pre-writing, composing, revising, and editing stages.

Skill 3.3: Identify Characteristics of the Modes of Writing

Writers choose their mode of writing based on the kind of impact they hope to have on their audiences. Writing can serve many different authorial needs, including narration (personal and fictional), description, exposition, persuasion, and speculation. Students need to be aware of, and to practice, these modes of writing.

Personal Narrative

The purpose of a personal narrative is to entertain or interest the reader. A personal narrative is a fictional or nonfictional account of an individual's feelings and experiences. The narrative may recount an incident or series of incidents or simply convey the writer's impressions pertaining to a certain topic. Personal narratives typically use first person and relate events in chronological sequence.

In creating personal narratives, students are likely to make use of time-order words, such as: *before, first, next, then, later, last, finally, yesterday, today, tomorrow,* and so on.

Fictional Narrative

A fictional narrative is a story that is created from the writer's imagination. A fictional narrative typically contains an interesting beginning, middle, and end. The narrative will be based on a plot, with a problem that is solved at the end. Included as well are a description of a setting and some extent of dialogue that can enliven the narrative.

In creating fictional narratives, students may benefit from using dialogue words, such as: replied, murmured, stammered, cried, exclaimed, shouted, whispered, babbled, remarked, and so on.

Descriptive

The purpose of descriptive writing is to provide information about a person, place, thing, event, or idea. Descriptive writing can be fiction or nonfiction. E. B. White uses description when he relates what the barn is like in *Charlotte's Web*; the book itself is fiction, however. Realtors use vividly descriptive writing when they advertise a house in a local newspaper; the general reader expects the description of the house to be nonfiction.

Expository

The purpose of expository writing is to present information about a topic in a clear and organized way. Expository writing introduces a main idea and develops the idea by means of additional detail. Sources may be included, and a conclusion will be drawn on the basis of the details provided.

A piece of expository writing may intend to introduce a topic, draw a comparison, or provide an evaluation. While the expository essay may have narrative elements, the storytelling aspect is secondary to the main purpose of providing descriptions and explanations. Textbooks are typical examples of expository writing.

Persuasive

The purpose of persuasive writing is to convince the reader of something, such as the merits of an idea or the accuracy of an opinion. Persuasive writing is prevalent in newspapers and magazines, as well as on the Internet. The persuasive writer may be trying to promote (or denigrate) a political candidate, praise (or condemn) an entertainer, or marshal support for (or against) a scientific theory.

Persuasive writing usually states an opinion, supports the opinion with evidence and argumentation, and encourages the reader to embrace the opinion. The structure may be very formal, with elaborated arguments and counterarguments, or relatively casual and anecdotal.

Speculative

Speculative writing explores ideas in a provisional way rather than explaining them, as in expository writing, or attempting to convince the reader of their merits, as in persuasive writing. Speculative essays are often meditative and develop more than one point. The main theme may not be as focused or clear-cut as that of an expository essay. The writer may deal with ideas in an associative manner and "play" with ideas by means of a relatively loose organizational structure.

Skill 3.4: Select the Appropriate Mode of Writing for a Variety of Occasions, Purposes, and Audiences

The writer must consider the audience, the occasion, and the purpose when choosing the mode of writing.

Audience

The teacher can designate an audience for students' writing. Knowing who will read their work allows students to think about modifying the writing to suit their intended readers. For instance, a fourth-grade teacher might suggest that the class take their compositions about a favorite animal to second graders and allow the younger children to read or listen to the works. The fourth graders will realize that they need to employ simple vocabulary, to avoid grammatically complex sentences, and to use manuscript rather than cursive when they write for their younger audience. The fourth graders would produce somewhat different compositions for the teacher or an administrator at a local zoo.

Occasion

The occasion also has an impact on the elements of the writing. The language of a piece of writing should fit the occasion. Formal writing is needed for formal occasions, while a casual tone is suitable for casual occasions. Young writers will learn that particular words may have certain effects, such as evoking sympathy or raising questions about an opposing point of view. Students can work together and/or work with their teachers to think about the kinds of language and organization that are suitable for each occasion.

Purpose

As noted earlier, the purpose of a piece of writing helps to determine the mode (narrative, expository, descriptive, persuasive, or speculative) as well as other aspects of the writer's language. Students will learn about the differences between writing a business letter, a communication with the residents of a retirement center, and a thank-you note to parents, for example.

In selecting the mode of writing as well as the content, the writer might ask the following:

- How interested is the audience in the topic?

- How controversial or emotionally charged is the topic?

- What would the audience need to know to understand you or to be persuaded your position?

- What is the audience most likely to disagree with?

- What common knowledge does the audience share with you?

- What background information do you need to share with the audience?

The teacher might wish to have the students practice selecting the mode and the language by adapting forms, organizational strategies, and styles for different audiences and purposes.

Skill 3.5: Identify Elements and Appropriate Use of Rubrics to Assess Writing

A rubric is a kind of checklist that includes values associated with each item on the list. To construct a rubric, a teacher will most probably make use of the lesson objectives. Students should receive an explanation of the rubric before starting to work on a writing assignment, and they can use the rubric for guidance while they are preparing the assignment. The teacher can then use the rubric to evaluate students' work after they have completed the assignment.

A well-planned rubric should explain each requirement or element in an assignment and summarize the criteria by which the quality of student work on each element is judged. In this way, students will know what is expected of them and how they will be evaluated.

Skill 3.6: Demonstrate Knowledge of Writing Conventions

Skill 3.7: Identify Instructional Methods for Teaching Writing Conventions

Conventions are commonly accepted rules of appropriate behavior. With respect to writing, students must learn the conventional rules for spelling, capitalization, punctuation, and so on. Writing conventions also pertain to organization, length, format, and genre-specific words such as "sincerely yours." Although advanced writers may flout conventions to make a point or create a certain effect, students must master the basic conventions first before diverging from them.

Spelling

Although the orthography (i.e., rules linking sounds to their representations in letters) of the English language is highly irregular, there are also orthographic conventions, or spelling rules, that provide guidance to budding writers. Following are a few of these conventions:

1. "i" comes before "e" except after "c" or in words with the long "a" sound, such as "neighbor" or "weigh."

2. "Sh" is used to represent the soft "sh" sound at the beginning of a word or end of a syllable, but not at the beginning of a syllable after the first one in a word. (In such cases, "ti," "si," or "ci" are used. Thus, we write "shoe" and "dish," and also "lotion," "tension," and "social.")

3. "E," "i," or "y" may make a "c" or "g" soft. An "e" at the end of a word makes the "c" or "g" before it soft (e.g., "rice" or "change"). The "e" remains when adding suffixes that begin with "a" or "o" (e.g., "changeable").

4. All syllables contain a vowel. Thus, we find a silent "e" at the ends of words such as "apple" and "bottle."

5. At the end of a one-syllable word that has a single vowel, the letters "f," "l," and "s" are often doubled. Thus, we have words such as "puff," "wall," and "grass."

6. The words "all," "full," and "till" are written with only one "l" when combined with another syllable (as in the case of "almost," "wonderful," and "until").

Steps for Learning to Spell a New Word

Following are the steps of a simple strategy that may be helpful to students as they learn how to spell new words:

1.   Look at the word you want to spell.

2.   Spell it aloud while pointing at or touching each letter.

3.   Write the word and say each letter as you write it.

4.   Close your eyes and try to see the word in your mind.

5.   Practice spelling the word from the picture in your mind.

6.   Repeat until the word is firm. Then try spelling it backward from the picture in your mind.

Capitalization

Following are some of the conventions governing the capitalization of words in English:

1.   The first word of a sentence should be capitalized. Example: *There are seven days in a week.*

2.   The first word of a direct quote should be capitalized. The second part of an interrupted quotation should not be capitalized. Example: *"Let's go to a party," she suggested, "and stay out until midnight."*

3.   When the second part of a quotation is a new sentence, put a period after the interrupting expression and capitalize the first word of the new sentence. Example: *"We aren't able to go," said Jenny. "We have to attend another engagement."*

4.   Capitalize all words in a letter's greeting, as well as the first word in the closing of the letter (e.g., *Sincerely yours*).

5.   Capitalize the names of people and the initials that stand for their names. In some cases, their titles should be capitalized, too. Example: *This is Brenna Ann Cassidy. She goes by "B.A."*

6.   Capitalize the names of cities, states, countries, and continents. But do not capitalize articles or prepositions that are part of the name. Example: *United States of America.*

7.   Capitalize the names of bodies of water, geographical features, and the names of roads, buildings, bridges, and monuments.

8.   Capitalize all important words in the title of a book, play, short story, poem, film, article, newspaper, magazine, television series, chapter of a book, or song.

9.   Capitalize the names of schools, clubs or organizations, institutions, political parties, and businesses.

10. Capitalize the main words in names of historic events, periods of time, and documents (e.g., *Bill of Rights*).

11. Capitalize the days of the week, months of the year, and holidays.

12. Capitalize the names of ethnic groups, nationalities, and languages (e.g., *French*), as well as proper adjectives that are formed from the names of ethnic groups and nationalities (e.g., *French bread*).

Punctuation

Punctuation refers to the conventions by which symbols known as punctuation marks are used to separate or link sentences and sentence parts or to convey meanings that cannot be expressed by the words in the sentence. Following are some key examples:

1. *Periods* are used at the ends of declarative and imperative sentences, as well as for abbreviations and for letters or numbers that constitute a list.

2. *Hyphens* are used in certain compound words and numbers and for the division of a word between the end of one line and the beginning of the next.

3. *Colons* are used to introduce lists of items and to separate the hours and minutes in the time of day. Colons are also used to divide a sentence from a clause that extends its meaning.

4. *Semicolons* are used to join clauses that could each function as independent sentences.

5. *Apostrophes* are used to form the possessive case. They are also used in contractions to show where a letter has been removed.

6. *Commas* are used for many purposes. Following are some examples:
   - to separate three or more items in a series
   - to form compound sentences
   - to set off appositives
   - to separate the names of geographic units such as city and state or city and country
   - to separate designations of time such as day and month or month and year
   - to set off nouns of direct address
   - to set off direct quotations

7. *Quotation marks* are used to set off quotations and to indicate the titles of books, stories, essays, films, songs, poems, articles, and chapters.

8. *Italics* are also used for titles and to indicate emphasis.

Conventions and Language Groups

Language varies according to geographic region, ethnic group, social class, and educational level. The language used in U.S. schools is Standard American English (SAE). This formal language is found in textbooks, newspapers, magazines, and news programs. The conventions discussed in this section are conventions of SAE.

There are forms of the English language in addition to SAE. Some variations are used in Appalachia, in urban ghettos, and in the South and Southwest, for example. In each case, the conventions differ somewhat from those of SAE. When instructing students from these areas, teachers should not try to replace their language with SAE. Rather, the goal of instruction is to add SAE to students' language capacities. One method of doing so is the Language Experience Approach.

Language Experience Approach

With the Language Experience Approach, the teacher attempts to facilitate students' language development through the use of experiences, rather than printed material alone. After the class participates in an experience or event, the students, as a group, record what happened (often with the help of the teacher). The teacher writes exactly what the students say—even if they do not use Standard American English. The idea is to enable each student to recognize the following:

- What I say, I can write

- What I can write, I can read

- What others write, I can read

The Language Experience Approach also involves opportunities for the teacher to discuss alternative ways of saying what the students do not say in Standard American English.

Competency 4 : Knowledge of Reading Methods and Assessment

Assessment is essential to instruction. Through the results of assessment, teachers can understand and document the progress of their students and modify instruction accordingly. The focus of Competency 4 is on the assessment of reading and reading-related competencies.

Skill 4.1: Identify Measurement Concepts, Characteristics, and Uses of Norm-Referenced, Criterion-Referenced, and Performance-Based Assessments

Skill 4.2: Identify Oral and Written Methods for Assessing Student Progress

Skill 4.3: Interpret Assessment Data

Skill 4.4: Use individual Student Reading Data to Differentiate Instruction

Skill 4.5: Interpret Student's Formal and Informal Assessment Results to Inform Students and Parents or Guardians

Skill 4.6: Evaluate the Appropriateness of Assessment Instruments and Practices

Skill 4.7: Identify Appropriate Classroom Organizational Formats for Specific Instructional Objectives

Skill 4.8: Identify Instructional Methods for Developing Emergent Literacy

Skill 4.9: Identify Methods for the Diagnosis, Prevention, and Intervention of Common Emergent Literacy Difficulties

Assessment is the systematic process of documenting what a student is able or unable to do. Assessments can be formal or informal based on how information is collected, scored, and recorded. Both formal and informal assessments have a place in the classroom, particularly in the reading class. The effective teacher understands the importance of ongoing assessment as an instructional tool for the classroom and uses both types of assessment measures. However, children should not be labeled or grouped permanently on the basis of one assessment. Any change in the way a student is treated should come about after a consideration of several assessments. If there are groupings, they should be flexible enough to consider individual differences among the students in each group.

Effective teaching includes both formative and summative evaluations.

1. *Formative evaluation* occurs during the process of learning when the teacher and/ or students monitor student progress. The results of formative evaluation are used to modify instruction and/or student approaches to learning.

2. *Summative evaluation* occurs at the end of a specific time or course of study. Usually, a summative evaluation yields a single number or grade that represents a student's performance. Each type of assessment, formal and informal, can be used in a formative or summative way.

Informal Assessment

Assessment need not require the purchase of expensive tests in order to be useful to teachers and students. Almost every book on teaching reading contains its own informal tests. For instance, Clay (1985) developed a simple procedure for sampling the child's reading vocabulary and determining the extent of a child's print-related concepts. Her assessment checks whether children can find the title, show where to start reading a book, and locate the last page or the end of the book. As such, Clay's procedure is an informal way of determining a child's readiness for reading (Davis, 2004).

Many school districts use some sort of inventory or report card to inform parents of the progress that the kindergartner or first grader is making. Although these assessments can be quite helpful, the Southern Regional Education Board's Health and Human Services Commission (SREB, 1994) cautions that assessment should be ongoing and natural. The commission has determined that continual observation of the physical, social, emotional, and cognitive development of students by both parents and teachers is the most meaningful approach to the assessment of young children. To obtain a meaningful, complete view of the development of a young child, the commission endorses the use of portfolios of a child's progress and performance inventories rather than standardized test results. Similarly, the commission indicates that letter or numeric grades are less likely to give a complete picture than narrative reports on the young child.

Teachers can gain much valuable information by simply observing their students at work. Moreover, experienced teachers usually develop through trial and error their own means of assessing the skills of their students. In particular, teachers can develop their own informal reading inventories. The purpose of these assessments is to collect meaningful information about what students can and cannot do in the context of reading.

Running Records

A running record is an oral assessment that provides information about a student's reading level, style, and strategy use. Running records also help determine a student's independent, instructional, and frustrational reading levels. Running records should be taken every three to four weeks to monitor a student's progress.

A running record can be created as follows. As the teacher listens to a student read a page, the teacher uses a copy of the page to mark each word the child mispronounces. The teacher will write the incorrect word over the printed word, draw a line through each word the child skips, and draw an arrow under repeated words. If the student reads 95 percent of the words correctly, the book is said to represent the child's independent reading level. If the student reads 90 to 94 percent of the words correctly, the book is said to be at the child's instructional level; this means the child can perform satisfactorily with help from the teacher. A book in which the student reads 89 percent or fewer words correctly is considered to be at the child's frustration level. In addition to assessing the student's reading skills by means of the running record, the teacher should ask some comprehension questions to be sure that the child understands (comprehends) the passage.

Checklists

One advantage of running records is that they are individualized. This characteristic can be considered a disadvantage, because they require considerable time on the part of the teacher in order to assess each student in the class.

The teacher may make observations during individual or group work by means of a checklist. To do so, the teacher creates in advance a checklist of competencies, skills, or requirements and then uses the list to check off the ones a student or group displays. A teacher wishing to emphasize interviewing skills could devise a checklist that includes personal appearance, mannerisms, confidence, and addressing the questions asked. A teacher who wants to emphasize careful listening might observe a discussion with a checklist that includes paying attention, not interrupting, summarizing the ideas of other members of the group, and asking questions of others.

Advantages of checklists include the potential for capturing behaviors that cannot be accurately measured with a paper-and-pencil test, such as following the correct sequence of steps in an oral presentation, or performing well on all elements of that presentation. One characteristic of a checklist that is both an advantage and a disadvantage is its structure, which provides consistency but inflexibility: those assessed either show or do not show a particular behavior. An open-ended comment section at the end of a checklist can help overcome this disadvantage.

Anecdotal Records

Anecdotal records of student performance are helpful in some instances, such as when attempting to describe the process that a group of students uses to solve a problem. The formative data in this case can be useful during feedback to the group.

One advantage of the anecdotal record is its flexibility: it can include all information that the teacher deems relevant, and it can be as detailed as the teacher would like it to be. Disadvantages include the amount of time necessary to complete the record and, if it is necessary to grade student performance, the difficulty in some cases in assigning a grades.

Portfolios

Portfolios are collections of students' best work. They can be used in any subject area for which the teacher wants students to take more responsibility for planning, carrying out, and organizing their own learning. Like a portfolio created by an artist, a student portfolio provides a succinct picture of the child's achievements over a certain period of time. Portfolios may contain essays or articles that the student has written, audio or video tapes that the student has recorded, multimedia presentations on computer disks that the student has created, and so on. Typically, a portfolio will contain more than one different type of work. Language arts teachers often use portfolios as a means of collecting the best samples of student writing over an entire year, and some teachers pass on the portfolios to the students' teachers for the following year in order to help those teachers with their assessment activities.

Teachers should provide guidelines, or assist students in developing guidelines, for what materials should go in their portfolios, as it would be unrealistic to include every piece of work. Using portfolios requires the students to devise a means of evaluating their own work, or at least to understand how their work is being evaluated. Although a portfolio should not be a scrapbook for collecting handouts or work done by other individuals, it can certainly include work by a group in which the student was a participant.

Some advantages of portfolios are as follows:

- Portfolios present a concrete picture of students' progress over time.

- Portfolios are relatively unaffected by one inferior test grade or assignment.

- Portfolios help develop students' self-assessment skills.

Several disadvantages can also be noted:

- Much time is required to teach students how to develop meaningful portfolios, although the time can be considered well spent if students learn valuable self-assessment skills.

- Teachers must spend much time assessing portfolios once created. However, as students become more proficient at self-assessment, the teacher can spend more time in coaching and advising students throughout the development of their portfolios and less time sifting through them in order to draw conclusions.

- Parents may not understand how the teacher will grade the portfolios. The effective teacher devises a rubric or system that the students and parents understand before work on the portfolios begins.

Other Informal Assessments

Asking a child to retell a story is another type of informal assessment. The ability to retell a story is an informal type of assessment that is useful to the teacher, parent, and—eventually—the child. Informal assessment measures can also include observations, journal entries, written drafts, and conversations.

Through informal observations and through the use of inventories (formal and informal), teachers should determine the learning styles of their students. Student learning styles play an important role in determining classroom structure.

Formal Assessments

Formal assessments include teacher-generated measures, district exams, and standardized tests. In each case, there are specific guidelines for test administration, and the results are typically recorded numerically.

The effective teacher uses a variety of formal assessment techniques, such as the following:

1. *Teacher-generated instruments* are ideally developed at the same time as the planning of goals and outcomes, rather than at the last minute after the completion of the lessons. Carefully planned assessment instruments serve as lesson development guides for the teacher.

2. *Paper-and-pencil tests* are the most common teacher-generated approach for evaluating student progress.

3. *District exams and standardized tests* are common but somewhat less likely to be administered at the initiative of the teacher.

Classroom Tests

The most commonly used type of teacher-generated measure is the classroom test, which is administered to all students in the class and subsequently graded and which provides part of the basis for students' grades in the class.

Constructing effective classroom tests is challenging, but it is as important as any other aspect of teaching. The planning and background work that contribute to effective instruction are incomplete unless evaluation of student performance provides accurate feedback to both the teacher and the student about the learning process.

Good classroom tests are the product of careful planning, creative thinking, hard work, and technical knowledge about the various methods of measuring student knowledge and performance. Classroom tests that accomplish their purpose are the result of the development of a pool of items and then refinement of those items based on feedback and constant revision. It is through this process that a teacher's evaluation of students becomes valid and reliable.

Classroom tests serve as a valuable instructional aid because they help measure student progress as well as teacher effectiveness. Student misunderstandings and difficulties revealed by the tests can help the teacher identify areas of special concern when providing instruction. This information also becomes the basis for the remediation of students and the revision of teaching procedures. Consequently, the construction, administration, and proper scoring of classroom tests are among the most important activities in teaching.

Classroom Test Format.   Classroom tests may be forced-choice, open-ended, or some combination of the two.

- *Forced-choice* questions require students to choose between options provided on the test. Examples include true-false questions and multiple-choice questions.

- *Open-ended questions* require students to generate some sort of content in order to provide an answer. The main example is the essay test.

There are advantages and disadvantages to each type of test.

An advantage of forced-choice tests is that they can be graded objectively, meaning that each student will receive a numerical score that clearly reflects the number of questions they answered correctly. This convenient aspect of forced-choice tests also reflects some of their disadvantages. In particular, test-takers do not get to express their knowledge in their own terms. Some students who perform poorly on such tests might do better when given the opportunity to express themselves. At the same time, some students who perform well on forced-choice tests may perform more poorly when asked to generate answers themselves rather than merely recognize them in, for example, a multiple-choice format.

Advantages of essay questions include the opportunity for students to be creative in their answers, the opportunity for students to explain their responses, and the potential to test for higher-level thinking skills. Disadvantages of essay questions include the time students need to formulate meaningful responses as well as the time teachers need to evaluate the essays. In addition, consistency in evaluating essays can also be difficult, even when a scoring rubric is used.

Criterion-Referenced Tests.   Criterion-referenced tests are used to determine the extent to which each student achieves uniform objectives or criteria. Criterion-referenced tests allow the possibility that all students can score 100 percent because they understand the concepts being tested; in actual practice, scores on these tests vary widely. Teacher-generated tests should be criterion-referenced, because the teacher's goal in developing them is to measure how well students have mastered certain material or skills taught in class. Insofar as teachers have engaged in good instructional practices, and students have mastered the outcomes, scores on criterion-referenced tests will generally be high.

Much may depend on students' performance on criterion-referenced tests, but the tests are not inherently competitive, since there is no limit to the number of students who can score well. Although some commercially developed tests are criterion-referenced, many are norm-referenced.

Norm-Referenced Tests.   The purpose of a norm- referenced test is to compare the performance of a student to some norm or standard. The norm consists of performance by other students who share some characteristic of the student such as age.

Norm-referenced tests are competitive, in the sense that each student's performance will be compared to that of a larger group. Although in theory it is possible for all students in a sixth grade class, for example, to score well on a norm-referenced test, it is not possible for all sixth graders in the country to score well.

When plotted on a graph, norm-referenced tests will resemble a bell curve, with most scores clustering around the center and fewer scores observed at each end (where performance is extremely high or low). Usually the tests are constructed so that the results will resemble the bell curve. In such cases, the midpoint of the distribution is also the numerical average of the test scores. Thus, half the population will score above average and half below average.

Percentile Scores

A percentile score (not to be confused with a percentage) is one way of reporting the results of norm-referenced tests. A percentile score indicates the percentage of the population whose scores fall at or below the student's particular score. For example, an individual whose test score places her at the 81st percentile has scored as well as or better than 81 percent of students of the same age who took the test.

Percentile scores tell us how well students are performing relative to others of the same age and/or background. However, they do not indicate how well the student has mastered content objectives. Raw scores, which indicate how many questions the student answered correctly, can be useful in determining student mastery of content.

Because each student's score on a norm-referenced test will be compared to a broader group of test-takers, teachers must be very careful when selecting norm-referenced tests. Ideally, the test should be one that covers topics that are highly congruent with the school's curriculum.

Reliability and Validity

When choosing a norm- or criterion-referenced test, the teacher must consider both reliability and validity.

- *Reliability* refers to the extent to which a test will yield consistent results. A reliable test is one for which the results for each student would be the same when administered at different times, in different settings, or by different administrators.

- *Validity* refers to the extent to which a test actually measures what it is supposed to measure. A valid test is one for which the test content is closely aligned to the curriculum, and only the test content is measured. If students perform poorly on a math test because the questions are confusing or written at a level they find challenging, the test can be described as having poor validity, because it measures reading ability and not merely mathematical achievement.

A test must be reliable in order to have good validity. If the results of a test vary widely each time a teacher administers the test, then it is impossible to know what the test is measuring. However, reliability does not guarantee good validity. English Language Learners may perform poorly on a particular math test each time they take it, but that does not mean that the test provides a valid assessment of their math skills.

Usually it is not convenient for teachers to evaluate the reliability and validity of the tests they use, although they should be aware of the concepts and do what they can to ensure that tests are strong on these dimensions. Fortunately, commercial test producers gather data on the reliability and validity of their tests and provide the results in test administrators' booklets.

Progress Monitoring

According to the National Center of Progress Monitoring, progress monitoring is a scientifically based practice used to assess students' academic performance and evaluate the effectiveness of instruction. Progress monitoring can be implemented with individual students, with groups of students, or with the entire class, and it can be grounded in either formal or informal assessment.

To implement progress monitoring, each student's current levels of performance are determined and specific goals are identified for learning that will take place over a specific period of time. The student's academic performance is then measured on a regular basis (e.g., weekly or monthly). Progress toward meeting the student's goals is measured by comparing expected versus actual rates of learning over time. Based on these measurements, teaching is adjusted as needed. Because student progress is monitored and instructional techniques are adjusted to meet individual learning needs, progress monitoring can be thought of as a type of formative evaluation.

Performance-Based Assessment

Some states and districts are moving toward performance-based tests, which assess students on how well they perform specific tasks. Rather than simply completing paper-and-pencil tests, performance-based assessment requires students to apply higher-level thinking skills in the completion of a task. For example, a performance-based assessment in biology might require students to read a problem, design and carry out a simple experiment, and then write summaries of their findings. The performance-based assessment in this case would evaluate both the processes students used and the output they produced. A performance-based assessment in English class might ask students to first read a selection of literature and then write a critical analysis. In this case, information about how each student planned and then created the critical analysis would be recorded, along with information about the quality of each analysis.

Advantages of performance-based assessments are as follows:

- Students are allowed a degree of creativity in approaching problems or questions.

- Students are required to use higher-level skills to generate solutions.

- Students address "real life" problems rather than hypothetical scenarios on conventional tests.

Disadvantages to performance-based assessments include the following:

- Considerable time is needed.

- The expense may be high owing to the need for multiple resources.

- Teachers may need training in order to administer the tests.

In spite of the disadvantages, many administrators and teachers consider that performance-based assessments provide a more authentic measure of student achievement than traditional paper-and-pencil tests.

Learning Styles and Assessment

Determining the learning styles of individuals and teaching to those styles transcends cultural boundaries and acknowledges that all people have distinct learning preferences and tendencies. Furthermore, this approach acknowledges that all preferences and tendencies are equally valid and that each style of learning has strengths. At the same time, assessments may need to take into account differences in learning styles.

For example, visual learners flourish when their seat allows them to readily see the teacher, the board, and what is happening in class. They need opportunities to draw pictures, to diagram, to take good notes, to create mind maps, and to use flash cards. Likewise, these students show their best performance on assessments that are presented visually and for which responses can be made through writing or other forms of visual expression.

To take another example, auditory learners flourish in oral language settings, whether lectures, discussion, or the use of audiocassettes as learning aids. Reciting what they have heard (or read) is an important learning strategy for auditory learners, as is finding someone to whom they can explain the information. Thus, these students show their best performance on assessments that are delivered orally and for which they can provide an oral response.

Although it may not be possible or even desirable for a teacher to tailor assessments to each student, teachers should at least be aware that student performance on assessments will vary in part according to the extent of fit between their particular learning style and the format of the assessment.

Diversity and Assessment

The teacher's goal should be to create a range of experiences, activities, and assessments that embrace student diversity. Assessments in particular should rely on materials and questions that are suitable for students with a variety of backgrounds.

Students who are not proficient in speaking English require special consideration. The English language consists of many slang and multidefinitional words that can confuse students, as well as a considerable extent of idiomatic speech. Teachers must keep these considerations in mind when developing the content of tests and other forms of assessment.

Competency 5: Knowledge of Communication

Speaking and listening, as well as reading and writing, allow students to participate in academic and social activities at school and to function in the broader community. The focus of Competency 5 is on students' knowledge of these forms of communication.

Skill 5.1: Demonstrate Knowledge of Penmanship

Penmanship consists of the application of a set of handwriting skills that are partially independent and develop gradually.

The Goal of Penmanship

The overarching goal of penmanship is legibility. Whether writing in manuscript or cursive, this goal is achieved by forming each letter correctly and by appropriately manipulating spacing, size, and alignment.

1. *Spacing* between letters, words, sentences, and lines should meet the following criteria:

   - Letters within a word should be placed side by side.

   - Spacing between words should be greater than between letters.

   - Spacing between sentences should be slightly larger than spacing between words.

   - Spacing between lines should be sufficient for teachers to make written comments, if needed.

   - Excessive spacing should be avoided.

2. *Size* of different letters, and of elements within the same letter, should be consistently similar, with capital letters written larger than those in lower case.

3. *Alignment* of English letters, words, and sentences should be horizontal, from left to right, with a common base.

The Process of Penmanship

As students learn to write, it is important that they develop good habits regarding posture, paper placement, and pencil grip.

1. Good writing posture complies with each of the following requirements:

    - Sit back in the seat with shoulders slightly forward and hips touching back of chair.

    - Position both feet flat on the floor.

    - Face the desk squarely.

    - Rest forearms on the desk with elbows off the desk to allow for free arm movement.

    - Keep the writing arm close to the body with the writing hand below the writing line. Place the free hand on the paper to hold it in place.

2. Good paper position for manuscript writing involves placing the paper straight on the desk with the lower edge of the paper parallel to the lower edge of the desk. For cursive writing, good paper position may involve tilting the writing paper slightly so that the bottom left-hand corner (or right-hand corner for left handed writers) is slanted toward the writer's midpoint. One hand may need to be placed on the paper in either case to hold it in place.

3. Good pencil position reflects the following:

    - Hold pencil loosely between the thumb and the first two fingers.

    - Rest the index finger on the top of the pencil, which will in turn rest upon the middle finger.

    - Allow the ring and small fingers to rest lightly on the desk and curl gently under the index and middle fingers.

    - Hold the pencil about an inch above its point, allowing about a quarter of an inch of the painted portion to remain visible below the index finger.

Skill 5.2: Demonstrate Knowledge of Listening and Speaking Strategies

Listening in order to understand others and speaking in order to make oneself understood to others are both critical to learning and communication. As discussed below, there is not a sharp distinction between listening and speaking skills. The strategies that support one will tend to support the other, and the effective use of one typically requires the effective use of the other.

Listening

Listening is the process of making sense of oral language. It is a process of constructing meaning by attending, anticipating, predicting, focusing, visualizing, making connections, generalizing, and evaluating.

Listening is not a passive process. Effective listeners actively engage what they hear, isolate key points, and make note of anything that seems incomplete, confusing, and/or contradictory. A good listener can identify the general nature, as well as the details, of what the speaker is saying in order to prepare an appropriate response.

Active Listening. Active Listening is the single most useful and important listening skill. Active Listening, as the name suggests, is not the mere acknowledgment that someone else is talking. Rather, during Active Listening, one indicates genuine interest in what the other person is thinking and feeling. Active Listening involves restating or paraphrasing what the other person is saying. This allows one to check whether the other person has been understood, and it allows the other person to verify or correct the listener's understanding. It also allows the speaker to feel understood and thus more confident in expressing him- or herself.

Speaking

Speaking allows students to express themselves, to negotiate relationships, to give definition to their thoughts, and to learn about language, themselves, and their world. Following are some of the most important speaking skills:

1. *Questioning*. Good questions are the key to good communication, as they support both speaking and listening.

2. *Paraphrasing*. The goal of paraphrasing is to restate an idea in your own words while retaining the meaning of the original idea. Although paraphrasing is a speaking skill, it plays a key role in listening (as in the case of Active Listening), and effective listening is required in order to generate accurate paraphrases.

3. *Extemporizing*. Through extemporaneous speech, individuals express their own thoughts and feelings rather than asking about or restating the thoughts and feelings of others. Effective listening is required in order to know when extemporaneous speech is appropriate and to determine the appropriate length and content of what is said. Good extemporaneous speech also requires a mastery of vocabulary, grammar, and diction.

Teachers instill good questioning, paraphrasing, and extemporizing strategies in their students through modeling as well as explicit instruction.

Skill 5.3: Identify Instructional Methods for Developing Listening and Speaking Skills

At least some instructional methods that teachers use should focus on developing their students' listening and speaking skills.

Reading Aloud

Reading aloud every day to students is an important means of teaching listening skills and a powerful way to develop students' vocabulary and language skills. Following are some helpful guidelines for teachers:

- Establish a practice of reading to the class from a variety of fiction and nonfiction books at least once a day.

- Use good quality, age-appropriate books and read at the same times each day, establishing a regular and enjoyable routine.

- Vary the reading routine so that in some cases students read along, perform choral reading, and engage in other participatory activities.

Using Listening and Media Centers

In a listening center, students can use tapes to listen for enjoyment, to listen as they "read along" with the printed text, or to listen to oral texts accompanied by listening guides. Teachers can use a range of commercially prepared tapes as well as those prepared by students, the teacher, or other adults in the school or community. Blank tapes can also be placed at the listening center so students can record themselves reading.

Listening centers give students opportunities to experience a text a number of times. Also, in many cases, they are able to hear stories read by someone other than the teacher. These characteristics help promote their listening skills.

Playing Listening Games

Listening games can help students learn various listening skills and strategies, such as identifying key information or applying critical-thinking skills to what they hear. These games provide practice for listening skills and strategies in fun settings. Following are some games that are commonly used:

- I Spy

- Pass the Whisper (i.e., The Listening Circle)

- Progressive Story (i.e., Add-a-Sentence)

- Simon Says

- *Twenty Questions*

Using Guided Imagery

When students listen to presentations that include visual images, they can be encouraged to form mental pictures that help them remember while listening. This process of creating and updating mental images is a useful listening skill.

LAPS

The acronym LAPS stands for listen, ask, picture, and summarize. LAPS is a simple listening strategy that involves both listening and writing. Before students listen to a speaker, they generate two or three questions and record them. They picture what they hear in response to their questions and quickly sketch that out. They then summarize what they have heard in a paragraph.

SLANT

Another simple listening strategy is referred to by the acronym SLANT, which stands for sit, lean, ask, nod, and track. To use this strategy, students are taught to sit up straight, lean forward slightly, ask questions, nod their heads, and track the teacher. This strategy engages the student in the listening process at a variety of levels.

Listening Guides

Providing students with a framework or guide for listening can help them focus on the listening task and the purpose for listening. These guides can be prepared by the teacher or by the teacher and the students and tailored to the specific purpose for listening.

Partner Retells

For partner retells, students form groups and read a story independently. Each member thinks about the key elements of the story and one member is designated to retell the story to the group. After the storyteller finishes, the listeners go through their books and place a note on any pages or details that the storyteller included in the retell.

Following are some general strategies that teachers can use to promote oral expression:

- Engage students in oral communication activities that reflect a variety of settings: small group, one-to-many, one-to-one, and so on.

- Create oral communication activities designed to achieve specific purposes, such as to inform, persuade and/or solve problems.

- Guide students in oral communication activities that exercise basic competencies needed for everyday life: giving directions, asking for help, requesting clarification, brainstorming, discussing class topics, and so on.

Paraphrasing Activities.   Teachers can ask students to use their own words to restate the main ideas, themes, etc., of various kinds of writing. The teacher can also place a limit on the number of words to be used by students. For example, students can be asked to describe the main character of a story with 20 to 25 words. Students may work on these activities individually or in small groups.

Oral Storytelling

Storytelling often relies on familiar verses, stories, riddles, and jokes with humor and surprise endings. Students can retell these stories aloud, make up different endings to old favorites, or extend the stories with new events. They may also prepare and share a favorite story that is unfamiliar to the class or a personal or family story.

When students tell stories, they can be taught to consider their facial expression, their body language, their intonation of voice, and their strategies for engaging audience interest. They can be encouraged to choose words and literary devices (such as repetition and pauses) to convey feelings and create mood. Explicit instruction, modeling, and guided practice help students create mood as they tell their own and others' stories. They should read or hear stories several times and get a feel for the basic components.

RAP

RAP is an acronym that stands for read, ask, and put. In a RAP, students first read a paragraph silently, thinking about the meanings of the words as they read. After they are finished reading, they ask themselves what are the main ideas and details of the paragraph. They may look back quickly over the paragraph to isolate the ideas and details. Finally, they attempt to put the main idea and details into their own words. They should try to generate at least two details related to the main idea.

Think, Pair, Share

In a Think, Pair, Share activity, students first listen to a presentation, watch a video, or read a text. They work individually to record their ideas (in notes, on a diagram, or in a guide) and then team with a partner or two sets of partners to discuss their ideas. The groups can add to the ideas that they generated individually. "Squares" (i.e., two sets of partners) can share the ideas with the whole class. Another variation is to have students practice retelling the story or sharing the main ideas with a partner.

Promoting Voice

In oral expression, voice refers to the effective use of such elements as diction, tone, syntax, unity, coherence, and audience to create a clear and distinct "personality" as one speaks.

To promote the development of voice, students can be encouraged to pay attention to the basics of oral expression. For example:

- Say it so we can hear it.

- Look at the people you are talking to.

- Say it so that it is exciting.

- Say some parts fast and some slow.

- Stop at the right places.

To illustrate these basic principles, teachers can read one or two paragraphs to their students in a soft monotone, with poor expression, averted gaze, and inappropriate pauses. Students can then be asked whether the presentation was interesting or enjoyable to listen to, and they can brainstorm ideas for improving the quality of the reading. Now the teacher can follow the students' suggestions, and students will see why the principles described earlier are so important for oral expression.

Competency 6: Knowledge of Informational and Media Literacy

A wide array of informational and media resources are available for use as tools of communication in the classroom. As technology advances, the need for students to be technologically savvy is becoming increasingly important. It is important that teachers make information technology resources available to students and both model and provide explicit instruction in their use. Literacy education is no longer limited to reading printed text; students need to also develop reading skills in the context of using various forms of multimedia. The focus of Competency 6 is on students' knowledge of information, in particular media-related information.

Skill 6.1: Demonstrate Knowledge of a Wide Array of Informational and Media Literacy

We live in the so-called "information age." From an educator's perspective, the wealth of information readily available to teachers and students is a mixed blessing. On the one hand, the goals of education are advanced by the quantity of information available as well as the relative ease of access. On the other hand, the sheer volume of information on any topic is overwhelming, and thus a key component of informational literacy is to be able to identify information of greatest relevance to one's needs and to be able to evaluate the sources of the information. Evaluation of sources begins with a distinction between two types: primary and secondary.

Primary Sources

Primary sources consist of first-hand accounts of events, practices, or conditions about which one is seeking information. Generally speaking, these are documents or other records created by witnesses. They may include journalistic accounts, diaries, letters, essays, financial records, memos, websites, blogs, photographs, videos, audio recordings, and so on. The most reliable primary sources are usually considered to be those created closest to the time period in question.

The advantage of primary sources for obtaining information is that they are relatively untouched by others' interpretive or editing activities. This advantage also constitutes a disadvantage, in that primary sources may be difficult to understand without knowing something about the time, place, and event about which information was recorded. Moreover, the reliability of a primary source may not be evident in the source itself. Teachers must help students evaluate reliability and make sense of the context for a particular primary source, as well as help students understand how to do so on their own when a teacher is not immediately available.

Secondary Sources

Secondary sources are interpretations or paraphrases of primary sources. Each secondary source therefore represents someone else's view of the primary source. These sources consist of books, reviews, critical summaries, and, in some cases, they may include journalistic accounts, diaries, and the other materials indicated under Primary Sources above. The key to distinguishing a letter, for example, as a primary or secondary source is whether the letter pertains to the letter-writer's own experience (primary) or the experience of someone else about whom the letter-writer is reporting (secondary).

The advantage of secondary sources is that background information about the time, place, writer, and situation tend to help make these sources understandable to readers. The disadvantage is that the reader experiences the topic second-hand, filtered through the eyes of someone else, rather than directly. Often the preferable approach is to help students access both primary and secondary sources concerning a particular topic.

Multimedia Resources

In the twenty-first century, information comes to students in a variety of forms, including print, video, audio, and multimedia (a combination of the previous). The Center for Media Literacy (2011) defines media literacy as the ability to access, analyze, evaluate, and create media in a variety of forms. Ultimately, the goals of media literacy are essentially the same as those for information learned in a traditional classroom: Students should identify key themes and concepts, make connections between themes, ask questions that elicit additional information, critically evaluate the information, and formulate an opinion or response.

Multimedia presentations are available to students on stand-alone resources, such as CD-ROMs, as well has on the Internet. The Internet is a global information system that facilitates electronic communication and information gathering through both private and public channels. In essence, the Internet is a worldwide system of computer networks through which users of any one computer can, if they have permission, obtain information from any other computer.

Multimedia-related instruction helps students understand and communicate by means of technologies such as the following:

- Websites
- Podcasts
- Streaming video
- Blogs
- PowerPoint presentations
- Digital editing software

Familiarity with these and other forms of multimedia will give students access to the tools that can help them thrive in increasingly multimedia-rich environments. For example, with a teacher's guidance, students can use social networks and other Internet resources to work collaboratively with peers on shared projects and perhaps even to create their own websites to present the results of their work.

Multimedia Literacy

Multimedia literacy involves the following:

- Understanding the differences between different types of multimedia resources, including their purpose, their advantages, and their disadvantages
- Understanding how to obtain information efficiently from different types of multimedia resources
- Understanding how to evaluate information obtained from various forms of multimedia
- Understanding how to use multimedia as a means of personal expression

Evaluating Multimedia Resources. In many but not all respects, the evaluation of multimedia resources involves the same processes as print resources. For example, Florida Diagnostic and Learning Resources (2011) remind educators to ask themselves five questions about an Internet resource:

1. *Who* created the website and what is their expertise?

2. *What* does the creator of the website say about the purpose of the site?

3. *When* was the website created and when, if ever, was it updated?

4.   *Where* does the information on the website come from?

5.   *Why* is the information on the website useful?

Skill 6.2: Demonstrate Knowledge of Systematic and Ethical Processes for Collecting and Presenting Authentic Information

Educators are expected to model professionalism in the gathering and presentation of information. Professionalism in this regard includes working with information in an ethical manner.

Perhaps the first lesson students need to learn is the concept of intellectual property. Teachers should explicitly discuss plagiarism, help students recognize when a source is versus is not plagiarized, and teach the use of citations and other methods for avoiding plagiarism in the use of others' materials.

For example, the Center for Social Media (2011) identifies five principles of acceptable practices for the fair use of copyrighted media materials:

- Employing copyrighted material in media literacy lessons

- Employing copyrighted material in preparing curriculum materials

- Sharing media literacy curriculum materials

- Allowing student use of copyrighted materials in their own academic and creative work

- Developing audiences for student work

To take another example, media etiquette includes adhering to the safe and respectful use of media information, while encouraging students to use an open, critical-thinking approach. Media etiquette has become an increasingly pressing issue owing to the use and abuse of social networks.

Skill 6.3: Identify Current Technology Available for Use in Educational Settings

Computer-related technology available in the classroom can be classified as hardware, software, and Web tools.

Hardware

Personal computers, laptops, notebooks, and so on contain physical parts known as hardware. Technology carts contain essential pieces of hardware enabling technology to happen in the classroom. Each cart contains multi-inputs and outputs for projection of both data (computer) and video sources. A computer switch box allows the use of both a built-in computer and a "guest" laptop. The built-in VCR/DVD player projects both videotape and campus cable playback in the classroom. The amplifier provides sound for both computer and video sources and a built-in monitor displays computer images. Some locations may also contain other types of equipment such as document cameras.

Software

The programs used to direct the operation of a computer are known as *software*. Software is often classified as either application software (programs that do work users are directly interested in) or system software (which includes operating systems and any program that supports application software). Some general kinds of application software include:

- Productivity software, which includes word processors, spreadsheets, and other tools
- Presentation software
- Graphics software for graphic designers
- CAD/CAM software
- Specialized scientific and statistical applications

Choosing Software for Students. Following are several suggestions for choosing the most engaging and productive educational programs:

- Programs should have levels of difficulty that change as your students' skills improve.
- Programs should be fun as well as educational.
- Programs should foster a sense of pride in achievement.
- Programs should encourage students to think and discover things for themselves.
- Programs should be free from bias, stereotypes, and violence.

Web Tools

Web tools are Internet-based communication and collaboration applications designed for use in teaching, learning, research, and other settings. Some examples of Web tools are the following:

- Blogs
- Guestbooks
- Mailing lists
- Message forums
- Photo albums
- Online forums
- Wikis

End-of-Chapter Questions

1. The understanding that words are composed of letters illustrates what?

    (A) Prosody.

    (B) Alphabetic understanding.

    (C) Emergent literacy.

    (D) Phonemic awareness.

2. Structural analysis would enable which of the following?

    (A) Being able to read the word "herded" by dividing it into "herd" and "ed."

    (B) Being able to sound out the word "fish."

    (C) Being able to hear the distinction between the words "bats" and "batch."

    (D) Being able to understand that "feet" is an exception to the rules for pluralization.

3. Double-entry journals, Venn diagrams, and webs are all examples of what?

    (A) Reading strategies.

    (B) Phonics principles.

    (C) Graphic organizers.

    (D) Prosodic cues.

4. Which of the following best illustrates the level of evaluating in Bloom's Revised Taxonomy?

    (A) Identifying a recurrent theme in a story.

    (B) Reciting a brief passage from a story.

    (C) Summarizing an unusual event in a story.

    (D) Explaining an unfamiliar term in a story.

5. Which of the following most accurately summarizes the meaning of the word "plot"?

    (A) The characters and setting of a narrative.

    (B) The theme of a narrative.

    (C) The planning that goes into the creation of a narrative.

    (D) The major events of a narrative.

6. What is the main purpose of expository writing?

   (A) To exhibit their creativity.

   (B) To develop a position on a much-debated topic.

   (C) To be persuasive.

   (D) To present information.

7. What type of question is a multiple-choice question such as this one?

   (A) Criterion-referenced.

   (B) Open-ended.

   (C) Forced-choice.

   (D) Norm-referenced.

Answer Key

1.	(B)		5.	(D)
2.	(A)		6.	(D)
3.	(C)		7.	(C)
4.	(A)			

Social Science

3

Competency 7: Knowledge of Time, Continuity, and Change

Skill 7.1: Identify Historical Events That Are Related by Cause and Effect

Social Science is a set of disciplines that provide knowledge about societies and people. When one teaches social studies in an elementary setting, the teacher takes on various roles, including historian, geographer, political scientist, economist, and, of course, educator. By intertwining these roles, the teacher helps the young students to become good citizens and to make good decisions. The focus of Competency 7 is on history, although other disciplines such as anthropology and economics play a role.

History in the Classroom

History is the study of the past. As historians, teachers relate important information about past happenings, insure that the information is authentic and accurate, and engage students in exploring evidence from various sources. By studying the past, students equip themselves with knowledge and skills that allow them to judge the present and make informed decisions about the future. Making history come alive by investigating historical artifacts will bring relevance and meaning to distant times and places. With recent technological advances and the wealth of information acquired through the Internet, our teachers, as historians, can produce hands-on resources and provide ample opportunities for investigation and exploration.

Cause-Effect Analysis

Knowledge of significant events, ideas, and people from the past is an important part of the social studies curriculum. This knowledge results from careful analysis of cause-effect relationships. For example, the causal forces responsible for each of the following eras can be used to frame the study of American history:

- Colonization and settlement (1585–1763)
- Revolution and the new nation (1754–1815)
- Expansion and reform (1801–1861)
- Civil War and Reconstruction (1850–1877)
- Development of the industrial United States (1870–1900)
- Emergence of modern America (1890–1930)
- Great Depression and World War II (1929–1945)
- Postwar United States (1945–1970)
- Contemporary United States (1968–1999)
- New Millennium (2000–present)

Cause-effect analysis may focus on broad events (e.g., causes of the Civil War) or on specific ones (e.g., causes of victory in one particular Civil War battle). As students learn the narratives of history, they will recognize that particular events and forces are both causes and effects. The Civil War, for example, represents an effect produced by many causes, but it in turn had a dramatic impact on all facets of our nation's development.

When teachers wish to introduce students to historical cause-effect relationships, they create lesson plans that tap into higher levels of critical thinking, such as analysis, synthesis, and evaluation. Tools that support causal analysis include the following:

1. *Timelines* that present events in chronological order.
2. *Charts* that compare and contrast or summarize causal relationships.
3. Graphs that illustrate relationships between variables.

When synthesizing the information they learn, students may create drawings, blueprints, and models. Through evaluative activities, students may produce critical essays and editorials and participate in debates through which they express their points of view on historical topics.

Skill 7.2: Evaluate Examples of Primary Source Documents for Historical Perspective

Evaluating primary source documents is a relatively direct way to analyze and interpret the past. Unlike secondary sources, which are interpretations of historical materials, primary source documents are the materials themselves. These materials include eyewitness accounts, letters, diaries, artifacts, photos, historical sites, and so on. It is through such materials that history can come alive. Although primary source documents may be difficult to understand without background information and commentary from the teacher or some other expert source, these documents can provide students with a unique perspective that may not be attainable through secondary sources.

The U.S. Library of Congress makes available online a wide range of primary source documents, ranging from the Declaration of Independence and the Constitution to recordings and photographs created during the Great Depression. Students can conduct interviews with veterans and examine the diaries, letters, and discharge papers that veterans or members of their families or communities may possess. Visits to local museums, libraries, and courthouses are also good places for students to examine primary source documents.

Skill 7.3: Identify Cultural Contributions and Technological Developments of Africa; the Americas; Asia, Including the Middle East; and Europe

Many countries have made significant cultural and technological contributions to American society, both directly and through those whose families have come to America.

African American Contributions to American Society

African Americans have shaped every aspect of American society. To take just one example, African American inventors have had a substantial impact on the development of technology in the U.S.

Following are some of the more prominent names.

- *Lewis Temple (1800-1854)*, born in Richmond, Virginia, invented a new type of harpoon with a movable head that prevented whales from slipping loose, a common problem with older forms of the harpoon.

- *Granville T. Woods (1856-1910)*, known as the "black Edison," was born in Columbus, Ohio. By the end of his life he had been awarded 150 patents, including an improved steam-boiler furnace, a combination of the telegraph and the telephone, and the Synchronous Multiplex Railway Telegraph, which enabled messages to be sent from moving trains and railway stations.

- *Frederick McKinley Jones (1882-1961)*, born in Cincinnati, Ohio, was awarded more than 60 patents in his life time. Among other things, he invented the first practical refrigeration system for long-haul trucks, a system that was later adapted to other carriers like ships and railway cars.

- *Lewis H. Latimer (1848-1928)*, born in Chelsea, Massachusetts, was a pioneer in the development of the electric light bulb. He was also the only black member of the Edison Pioneers, a group of inventors and scientists who worked with Thomas Edison.

- *Garrett A. Morgan (1875-1963)*, born in Paris, Kentucky, is best remembered for his invention of the gas mask and the three-way traffic signal.

Hispanic and Latino Contributions to American Society

Hispanic and Latino Americans have also contributed to every aspect of American society. One of their many areas of influence is American arts. For example, Placido Domingo and José Carreras are considered giants in opera, and Fernando Bujones and Faustino Diaz are stars of the international ballet scene. Carlos Santana and Gloria Estefan have had enduring success in American pop music.

Among the many prominent actors who could be named are Anthony Quinn, who made over 100 films and won two Oscars. Actor Edward James Olmos received the Los Angeles Drama Critics Award for his performance in the play "Zoot Suit" and an Oscar nomination for best actor in the movie "Stand and Deliver." The movie chronicles the story of Jaime Escalante, who was born in Bolivia. Mr. Escalante may be America's most notable math teacher because he helped transform an East Los Angeles high school from one in which student math test scores were always in the lowest percentile in the country into a national symbol of academic achievement. His dedication and classroom triumphs have continued to inspire students and teachers nationwide.

Other Contributions to American Society

Numerous individuals from Asia and the Middle East, as well as Europe, have made substantial contributions to American society. Teachers in the social sciences can help students learn about the cultural and technological contributions of these individuals.

Skill 7.4: Relate Physical and Human Geographic Factors to Major Historical Events and Movements

Geography and history are inextricably intertwined. One example of their relationship is represented by immigration to the U.S., which has been driven by geographic forces, among others, and which has had a profound impact on the development of the U.S. since the time of Christopher Columbus.

Assimilation

Famines and other natural disasters are among the many forces that spurred a huge influx of immigrants into the U.S. in the nineteenth century. In 1891, the Immigration and Naturalization Service (INS) was created. Its purpose was twofold: to oversee the admission process of applicants, as well as the exclusion and deportation of aliens, and to oversee the naturalization of aliens lawfully residing in the United States. Due to the influx of European immigrants at the turn of the century, an immigration screening station was established at Ellis Island, New York, in 1892, and over the next 30 years more than 30 million immigrants became naturalized citizens.

One consequence of the diversity of immigrants was the creation of the public school system in the late nineteenth and early twentieth centuries. Part of the mandate of public schools was to provide a common language and set of social standards for students from the various cultural backgrounds. The term "melting pot" was used to describe how the immigrants would assimilate into the American culture. A common assumption was that immigrants would let go of their native language, learn English, and conform to the American way of life. In short, creating a homogenous culture was a common value at this time.

Cultural Pluralism

Over time, the assimilationist model described above was gradually replaced by a model that can be described as cultural pluralism. Some of the legal decisions that contributed to cultural pluralism in the twentieth century are as follows:

1. *Brown vs. Board of Education (1954)* laid the groundwork for desegregation.

2. *Pierce vs. Society of Sisters (1925)* established the legitimacy of parochial schools and other private schools.

3. *The Civil Rights Act (1964)* prohibited discrimination on the basis of race, color, or national origin.

4. *The Bilingual Education Act (1968)* provided funding for bilingual programs and acknowledged the importance of language and cultural heritage.

5. *Serrano vs. Priest (1971)* brought about significant changes in the formula used for funding students in low income districts.

6. *Title IX* of the Education Amendments (1972) prohibited discrimination on the basis of sex.

7. *Lau vs. Nichol (1974)* established steps to be taken by a school district if a student was found to have a language deficiency.

8. *The Individual with Disabilities Education Act (1976/1990)* insured that children receive free assessment for disabilities as well as free and appropriate education in the least restrictive environment.

Understanding the various sources of diversity, such as race, ethnicity, language, religion, gender, and socioeconomic status have promoted a pluralistic model where differences among people are valued and appreciated. Rather than a melting pot, the analogy often used now is that of a salad bowl in which all ingredients are mixed but retain distinct flavors that work together to create a healthy society.

Skill 7.5: Identify Significant Historical Leaders and Events That Have Influenced Eastern and Western Civilizations

This section contains a discussion of some of the events and leaders that have influenced eastern and western civilizations down through the nineteenth century.

Prehistorical Period

The Earth is estimated to be approximately 6 billion years old. The earliest known humans, called hominids, lived in Africa 3 to 4 million years ago. Of the several species of hominids that developed, all modern humans descended from just one group, the *Homo sapiens*, who appeared in Africa several hundred thousand years ago.

Historians divide prehistory into three periods.

1. *Paleolithic*. The period from the emergence of the first-known hominids until approximately 10,000 BCE is known as the Paleolithic period, or Old Stone Age. During this period, human beings lived in very small groups of perhaps 10 to 20 nomadic people, constantly moving from place to place. Humans had the ability to make tools and weapons from stone and from the bones of animals they killed. Hunting large game such as mammoths, which were sometimes driven off cliffs in large numbers, was crucial to the survival of early humans, who used the meat, fur, and bones of the animals to survive. Early humans supplemented their diets by foraging for food. They took shelter in caves and other natural formations, and they painted and drew on the walls of caves. Cave paintings discovered in France and northern Spain, created during the Paleolithic period, depict scenes of animals such as lions, owls, and oxen. Around 500,000 years ago, humans began to use fire, which provided light and warmth in shelters and caves, and cooked meat and other foods. Human beings developed means of creating fire and improved techniques of producing tools and weapons.

2. *Mesolithic*. The Mesolithic period, or Middle Stone Age, extending from 10,000 to 7,000 BCE, marks the beginning of a major transformation known as the Neolithic Revolution. During this time, humans domesticated plants and began to shift away from a reliance on hunting large game and foraging. Human beings had previously relied on gathering food where they found it and had moved almost constantly in search of game, wild berries, and other vegetation. During

the Mesolithic age, humans were able to plant and harvest some crops and began to stay in one place for longer periods. Early humans also improved their tool-making techniques and developed various kinds of tools and weapons.

3. *Neolithic.* During the Neolithic period, or New Stone Age, the "agricultural revolution" described above was complete, as humans now engaged in systematic agricultural practices and began domesticating animals. Although humans continued to hunt animals, to supplement their diet with meat, and to use skins and bones to make clothing and weapons, major changes in society occurred as a result of agricultural developments. Humans began to settle in farming villages or towns, the population increased, and communities grew. A more settled way of life led to a more structured social system, a greater level of organization within societies, the development of crafts such as the production of pottery, and an increase in exchanges of goods among groups.

Beginnings of Recorded History

Between 6000 and 3000 BCE, humans invented the plow, developed the wheel, harnessed the wind, discovered how to smelt copper ores, and began to develop accurate solar calendars. Small villages gradually grew into populous cities. Between 4000 and 3000 BCE, writing developed, and the towns and villages settled during the Neolithic period developed more complex patterns of existence. The existence of written records marks the end of the prehistoric period and the beginning of recorded history. The beginning of history in turn coincides with the emergence of the earliest societies that exhibit characteristics enabling them to be considered as civilizations. The first civilizations emerged in Mesopotamia and Egypt.

Mesopotamia

The ancient civilization of Sumer (4000–2000 BCE) included the city of Ur. The Sumerians constructed dikes and reservoirs and established a loose confederation of city-states. They probably invented writing (called cuneiform because of its wedge-shaped letters). After 538 BCE, the peoples of Mesopotamia, whose natural boundaries were insufficient to thwart invaders, were absorbed into other empires and dynasties.

Egypt

Near the end of the Archaic period (5000–2685 BCE), at around 3200 BCE, Menes, or Narmer, probably unified upper and lower Egypt. The capital moved to Memphis during the Third Dynasty (ca. 2650 BCE). The pyramids were built during the Fourth Dynasty (ca. 2613–2494 BCE). After 1085 BCE, in the Post-Empire period, Egypt came under the successive control of the Assyrians, the Persians, Alexander the Great, and finally, in 30 BCE, the Roman Empire. The Egyptians developed papyrus and made many medical advances.

Palestine and the Hebrews

Phoenicians settled along the present-day coast of Lebanon (Sidon, Tyre, Beirut, Byblos) and established colonies at Carthage and in Spain. They spread Mesopotamian culture through their trade networks.

The Hebrews probably moved to Egypt around 1700 BCE and suffered enslavement until about 1500 BCE. The Hebrews fled Egypt under Moses and, around 1200 BCE, returned to Palestine. King David, who reigned circa 1012–972 BCE, defeated the Philistines and established Jerusalem as a capital. The poor and less attractive state of Judah continued until 586 BCE, when the Chaldeans transported the Jews to Chaldea as advisers and slaves, a time known as the Babylonian captivity. The Persians conquered Babylon in 539 BCE and allowed the Jews to return to Palestine.

Greece

During the Archaic period in Greece (800–500 BCE), Greek society organized around the polis, or city-state. Oligarchs controlled most of the polis until the end of the sixth century, when individuals holding absolute power replaced them. By the end of the sixth century, democratic governments in turn replaced many of these tyrants. The fifth century BCE was the high point of Greek civilization and is known as the Classical Age. It opened with the Persian Wars (560–479 BCE), after which Athens organized the Delian League. Pericles (ca. 495–429 BCE) used money from the Delian League to rebuild Athens, including construction of the Parthenon and other buildings on the Acropolis. Athens' political and cultural dominance then led to war with Sparta. At the same time, a revolution in philosophy occurred in classical Athens. The Sophists emphasized the individual and the attainment of excellence through rhetoric, grammar, music, and mathematics. Socrates (ca. 470–399 BCE) criticized the Sophists' emphasis on rhetoric and developed a process of questioning, or dialogues, with his students as a means of obtaining knowledge and making ethical decisions. Like Socrates, Plato (ca. 428–348 BCE) and his student Aristotle (ca. 384–322 BCE) emphasized the importance of ethics in social and political decision-making. Aristotle made enduring contributions to philosophy and natural science and contended that to understand any object it is necessary to examine four factors: its matter, its form, its cause of origin, and its end or purpose.

Rome

The traditional founding date for Rome is 753 BCE. Between 800 and 500 BCE, Greek tribes colonized southern Italy, bringing their alphabet and religious practices to Roman tribes. In the sixth and seventh centuries BCE, the Etruscans expanded southward and conquered Rome. During the time of the early Republic, power was in the hands of the patricians (wealthy landowners). During the 70s and 60s BCE, Pompey (106–48 BCE) and Julius Caesar (100–44 BCE) emerged as the most powerful men. In 60 BCE, Caesar convinced Pompey and Crassus (ca. 115–53 BCE) to form the First Triumvirate. When Crassus died, Caesar and Pompey fought for leadership. In 47 BCE, the Senate proclaimed Caesar dictator and later named him consul for life. Brutus and Cassius believed that Caesar had destroyed the Republic. They formed a conspiracy and, on March 15, 44 BCE (the Ides of March), Brutus and Cassius assassinated Caesar in the Roman forum. Caesar's 18-year-old nephew and adopted son, Octavian, succeeded him. Octavian, who reigned from 27 BCE to 14 CE, gained absolute political control while maintaining the appearance of a republic. When he offered to relinquish his power in 27 BCE, the Senate gave him a vote of confidence and a new title, Augustus. He introduced many reforms, including new coinage, new tax collection, fire and police protection, and land for settlers in the provinces.

The Byzantine Empire

By the first CEntury CE, Christianity had spread throughout the Empire. Around 312 CE, Emperor Constantine converted to Christianity and ordered toleration in the Edict of Milan (ca. 313 CE). In 391 CE, Emperor Theodosius I (reigned 371–395 CE) proclaimed Christianity the Empire's official religion. Emperor Theodosius II (reigned 408–450 CE) divided his Empire between his two sons, one ruling the East and the other ruling the West. After the Vandals sacked Rome in 455 CE, Constantinople became the undisputed leading city of the Byzantine Empire. In 1453 CE, Constantinople fell to the Ottoman Turks.

Islamic Civilization in the Middle Ages

Mohammed was born about 570 CE. In 630 CE, he marched into Mecca. The Sharia (code of law and theology) outlines five pillars of faith for Muslims to observe. The belief that there is one God and that Mohammed is his prophet is the first pillar. Second, the faithful must pray five times a day. Third, the faithful must perform charitable acts. Fourth, they must fast from sunrise to sunset during the holy month of Ramadan. Finally, they must make a *haj*, or pilgrimage, to Mecca. The Koran, which consists of 114 *suras* (verses), contains Mohammed's teachings. The Omayyad caliphs, with their base in Damascus, governed from 661–750 CE. They called themselves Shiites and believed they were Mohammed's true successors. (Most Muslims were Sunnis, from the word *sunna*, meaning "oral traditions about the prophet.") The Abbasid caliphs ruled from 750–1258 CE. They moved the capital to Baghdad and treated Arab and non-Arab Muslims as equals. Genghis (or Chingis) Khan (reigned 1206–1227 CE) and his army invaded the Abbasids. In 1258 CE, they seized Baghdad and murdered the last caliph.

Feudalism in Japan

Feudalism in Japan began with the arrival of mounted nomadic warriors from throughout Asia during the Kofun Era (300–710 CE). Some members of the nomadic groups formed an elite class and became part of the court aristocracy in the capital city of Kyoto, in western Japan. During the Heian Era (794–1185 CE), a hereditary military aristocracy arose in the Japanese provinces; by the late Heian Era, many of these formerly nomadic warriors had established themselves as independent landowners, or as managers of landed estates, or *shoen* owned by Kyoto aristocrats. These aristocrats depended on the warriors to defend their *shoen*, and in response to this need, the warriors organized into small groups called *bushidan*. After victory in the Taira-Minamoto War (1180–1185 CE), Minamoto no Yorimoto forced the emperor to award him the title of *shogun*, which is short for "barbarian-subduing generalissimo." Yorimoto used this power to found the Kamakura Shogunate, a feudal military dictatorship that survived for 148 years. By the fourteenth century CE, the great military governors (*shugo*) had augmented their power enough to become a threat to the Kamakura, and in 1333 CE they led a rebellion that overthrew the shogunate. The Tokugawa shogunate was the final and most unified of the three shogunates. Under the Tokugawa, the *daimyo* were direct vassals of the shoguns and were under strict control. The warriors gradually became scholars and bureaucrats under the *bushido*, or code of chivalry, and the principles of neo-Confucianism. Under the Meji Restoration of 1868, the emperor again received power and the samurai class lost its special privileges.

Chinese and Indian Empires

In the third century BCE, the Indian kingdoms fell under the Mauryan Empire. The grandson of the founder of this empire, named Ashoka, opened a new era in the cultural history of India by embracing the Buddhist religion. The Buddha had disregarded the Vedic gods and the institutions of caste and had preached a relatively simple ethical religion that advocated two levels of aspiration—a monastic life of renunciation of the world and a high, but not too difficult, morality for the layman. Although the two religions of Hinduism and Buddhism flourished together for centuries in a tolerant rivalry, Buddhism virtually disappeared from India by the thirteenth century CE. Chinese civilization originated in the Yellow River Valley, only gradually extending to the southern regions. Three dynasties ruled early China: the Xia or Hsia, the Shang (ca. 1500 to 1122 BCE), and the Zhou (ca. 1122 to 211 BCE). After the Zhou Dynasty fell, China welcomed the teachings of Confucius; warfare between states and philosophical speculation created circumstances ripe for such teachings. Confucius held that the good order of society depends on an ethical ruler who receives advice from scholar-moralists like Confucius himself. In contrast to the Confucians, the Chinese Taoists professed a kind of apparent anarchism; the best kind of government was none at all. The wise man did not concern himself with political affairs but with rather with mystical contemplation of the forces behind the rise and fall of earthly things.

African Kingdoms and Cultures

The Bantu peoples occupied large sections of Africa. Bantu societies lived in tiny chiefdoms, starting in the third millennium BCE, and each group developed its own version of the original Bantu language. The Nok people lived in the area now known as Nigeria. Artifacts indicate that they were peaceful farmers who built small communities consisting of houses of wattle and *daub* (poles and sticks). The Ghanaians lived about 500 miles from what is now Ghana. Their kingdom fell to a Berber group in the late eleventh century CE, and Mali emerged as the next large kingdom in the thirteenth century. The Malians lived in a huge kingdom that lay mostly on the savanna bordering the Sahara Desert. Timbuktu, built in the thirteenth century CE, was a thriving city of culture where traders visited stone houses, shops, libraries, and mosques. The Songhai lived near the Niger River and gained their independence from the Mali in the early 1400s. The major growth of the empire came after 1464 CE, under the leadership of Sunni Ali, who devoted his reign to warfare and expansion of the empire.

Civilizations of the Americas

The great civilizations of early America were agricultural; foremost among these were the Mayan people in Yucatan, Guatemala, and eastern Honduras. Farther north in Mexico, a series of advanced cultures arose that derived much of their substance from the Maya. Peoples like the Zapotecs, Totonacs, Olmecs, and Toltecs evolved a high level of civilization. By 500 BCE, agricultural peoples had begun to use a ceremonial calendar and had built stone pyramids on which they held religious observances. The Aztecs then dominated Mexican culture. A major feature of Aztec society was human sacrifice in repeated propitiation of their chief god. Aztec government was centralized, with an elected king and a large army. Andean civilization was characterized by the evolution of beautifully made pottery, intricate fabrics, and flat-topped mounds, or *huacas*. In the interior of South America, the Inca, who called themselves

"Children of the Sun," controlled an area stretching from Ecuador to central Chile. As sun worshippers, they believed that they were the sun god's vice regents on Earth and more powerful than any other humans. They also believed that every person's place in society was fixed and immutable and that the state and the army were supreme. The Inca reached the apex of their power just before the Spanish conquest. In the present-day southwestern United States and northern Mexico, two varieties of ancient culture are still identifiable. The Anasazi developed adobe architecture, worked the land extensively, had a highly developed system of irrigation, and made cloth and baskets. The Hohokam built separate stone and timber houses around a central plaza.

Medieval Europe

The Frankish Kingdom was the most important medieval Germanic state. Under Clovis I (reigned 481–511 CE), the Franks finished conquering France and the Gauls in 486 CE. Clovis converted to Christianity and founded the Merovingian dynasty. Charles the Great, or Charlemagne (reigned 768–814 CE), founded the Carolingian dynasty. In 800 CE, Pope Leo III named Charlemagne Emperor of the Holy Roman Empire. Through the Treaty of Aix-la-Chapelle (812 CE), the Byzantine emperor recognized Charles's authority in the West, thereby achieving the main purpose of the Holy Roman Empire. Charles's son, Louis the Pious (reigned 814–840 CE), succeeded him. On Louis's death, his three sons vied for control of the Empire. The three eventually signed the Treaty of Verdun in 843 CE. This treaty gave Charles the Western Kingdom (France), Louis the Eastern Kingdom (Germany), and Lothair the Middle Kingdom, a narrow strip of land running from the North Sea to the Mediterranean. During this period, manorialism developed as an economic system in which large estates, granted by the king to nobles, strove for self-sufficiency. The lord and his serfs (also called *villeins*) divided the ownership of the estates. The church was the only institution to survive the Germanic invasions intact. The power of the popes grew during this period. Gregory I (reigned 590–604 CE) was the first member of a monastic order to rise to the papacy. He advanced the ideas of penance and purgatory. He also centralized church administration and was the first pope to rule as the secular head of Rome. Monasteries preserved the few remnants of culture that survived the decline of antiquity. The year 1050 marked the beginning of the High Middle Ages. Europe was poised to emerge from five centuries of decline. Between 1000 and 1350, the population of Europe grew from 38 million to 75 million. New technologies, such as heavy plows, and a slight temperature rise produced a longer growing season and contributed to agricultural productivity.

The Holy Roman Empire

Charlemagne's grandson, Louis the German, became Holy Roman Emperor under the Treaty of Verdun in 843. His descendants governed the empire until 1024, when the Franconian dynasty assumed power, reigning until 1125. Under the leadership of William the Conqueror (reigned 1066–1087), the Normans conquered England in 1066. William stripped the Anglo-Saxon nobility of its privileges and instituted feudalism. He ordered a survey of all property of the realm; the *Domesday Book* (1086) records the findings. William introduced feudalism to England. Feudalism was the decentralized political system of personal ties and obligations that bound vassals to their lords. Serfs were peasants who were bound to the land. They worked on the *demesne*, or lord's property, three or four days a week in return for the right to work their own land. In 1215, the English barons forced King John I to sign the Magna Carta Libertatum, acknowledging their "ancient" privileges. The Magna Carta established the principle of a limited English monarchy. From 710 to 711, the Moors conquered Spain from the Visigoths. Under the Moors, Spain enjoyed a stable, prosperous government. The caliphate of Córdoba became a center of scientific and intellectual activity. The Reconquista (1085–1340) wrested control from the Moors. The fall of Córdoba in 1234 completed the Reconquista, except for the small state of Granada. Most of eastern Europe and Russia was never under Rome's control; Germanic invasions separated the areas from Western influence. In Russia, Vladimir I converted to Orthodox Christianity in 988. He established the basis of Kievian Russia. After 1054, Russia broke into competing principalities. The Mongols (Tartars) invaded in 1221. They completed their conquest in 1245 and cut Russia's contact with the West for almost a century.

The Crusades

The Crusades attempted to liberate the Holy Land from infidels. Seven major crusades occurred between 1096 and 1300. Urban II called Christians to the First Crusade (1096–1099) with the promise of a plenary indulgence (exemption from punishment in purgatory). Younger sons who would not inherit their fathers' lands were also attracted. The Crusades helped to renew interest in the ancient world. However, the Crusaders massacred thousands of Jews and Muslims, and relations between Europe and the Byzantine Empire collapsed.

Scholasticism

Scholasticism represented an effort to reconcile reason and faith and to instruct Christians on how to make sense of the pagan tradition. The most influential proponent of this effort was Thomas Aquinas (ca. 1225–1274), who believed that there were two orders of truth. The lower level, reason, could demonstrate propositions such as the existence of God, but the higher level necessitated that some of God's mysteries, such as the nature of the Trinity, be accepted on faith. Aquinas viewed the universe as a great chain of being, with humans midway on the chain between the material and the spiritual.

The Black Death

Conditions in Europe encouraged the quick spread of disease. Refuse, excrement, and dead animals filled the streets of the cities, which lacked any form of urban sanitation. Living conditions were overcrowded, with families often sleeping in one room or one bed; poor nutrition was rampant; and there was often little personal cleanliness. Merchants helped bring the plague to Asia; carried by fleas on rats, the disease arrived in Europe in 1347. By 1350, the disease had killed 25 percent to 40 percent of the European population.

The Renaissance

The period known as the Renaissance witnessed a surge of interest in antiquity as well as a spirit of humanism and classically inspired innovation. The literature of the period was more secular and wide ranging than that of the Middle Ages. Dante Alighieri (1265–1321) was a Florentine writer whose "Divine Comedy," describing a journey through hell, purgatory, and heaven, shows that reason can take people only so far and that attaining heaven requires God's grace and revelation. Francesco Petrarch (1304–1374) encouraged the study of ancient Rome, collected and preserved works of ancient writers, and produced a large body of work in the classical literary style. The Italian Giovanni Boccaccio (1313–1375) wrote "The Decameron," a collection of short stories intended more to amuse than to edify the reader. Artists also broke with medieval traditions, in both technique and content. Renaissance art sometimes explored religious topics but often dealt with secular themes or portraits of individuals. Oil paints, chiaroscuro, and linear perspectives produced energetic works in both two and three dimensions. Leonardo da Vinci (1452–1519) produced numerous works, including *The Last Supper* and *Mona Lisa*. Raphael Santi (1483–1520), a master of Renaissance grace and style, theory, and technique, deployed wide-ranging skills in his masterpiece *The School of Athens*. Michelangelo Buonarroti (1475–1564) produced enduring works in architecture, sculpture (*David*), and painting (the ceiling of the Sistine Chapel). Michelangelo's work created a bridge to a new, post-Renaissance style known as mannerism. Renaissance scholars were more practical and secular than medieval ones. Manuscript collections enabled scholars to study primary sources and to reject or at least critically evaluate traditions established since classical times. Also, scholars participated in the lives of their cities as active politicians. Leonardo Bruni (1370–1444), a civic humanist, served as chancellor of Florence, where he used his rhetorical skills to rouse the citizens against external enemies. Niccolo Machiavelli (1469–1527) wrote "The Prince," which analyzed politics from the standpoint of expedience rather than morality in the name of maintaining political power.

The Reformation

The Reformation undermined western Europe's religious unity and introduced new ideas about the relationships among God, the individual, and society. Politics greatly influenced the course of the Reformation and led, in most areas, to the subjection of the church to the political rulers. Martin Luther (1483–1546), to his personal distress, could not reconcile the sinfulness of humans with the justice of God. During his studies of the Bible, Luther came to believe that personal efforts—good works such as a Christian life and attention to the sacraments of the church—could not "earn" the sinner salvation but that belief and faith were the only way to obtain grace. By 1515, Luther held that "justification by faith alone" was the road to salvation. On October 31, 1517, Luther nailed 95 theses, or statements, about indulgences (the cancellation of a sin in return for money) to the door of the Wittenberg church and challenged the practice of selling them. At this time he was seeking to reform the church, not divide it. In 1519, Luther presented various criticisms of the church and declared that only the Bible, not religious traditions or papal statements, could determine correct religious practices and beliefs. In 1521, Pope Leo X excommunicated Luther for his beliefs. In 1536, John Calvin (1509–1564), a Frenchman, arrived in Geneva, a Swiss city-state that had adopted an anti-Catholic position. In 1540, Geneva became the center of the Reformation. Calvin's Institutes of the Christian Religion (1536), a strictly logical analysis of Christianity, had a universal appeal. Calvin emphasized the doctrine of predestination, which indicated that God has determined who will obtain salvation before those people are born. Calvin believed that church and state should unite. Calvinism triumphed as the majority religion in Scotland, under the leadership of John Knox (ca. 1514–1572), and in the United Provinces of the Netherlands. Puritans in England and New England also accepted Calvinism.

The Thirty Years' War

Between 1618 and 1648, the European powers fought a series of wars. The reasons for the wars varied; religious, dynastic, commercial, and territorial rivalries all played a part. The battles were fought over most of Europe and ended with the Treaty of Westphalia in 1648. The Thirty Years' War changed the boundaries of most European countries.

The Enlightenment

For the first time in recorded history, the eighteenth century saw the widespread appearance of a secular worldview: the Age of Enlightenment. The philosophical starting point for the Enlightenment was the belief in the autonomy of man's intellect apart from God. The most basic assumption was faith in reason rather than faith in revelation. René Descartes (1596–1650) sought a basis for logic and believed he found it in man's ability to think. "I think; therefore, I am" was his most famous statement. Benedict de Spinoza (1632–1677) developed a rational pantheism in which he equated God and nature. He denied all free will and ended up with an impersonal, mechanical universe. Gottfried Wilhelm Leibniz (1646–1716) worked on symbolic logic and calculus and invented a calculating machine. He, too, had a mechanistic view of the world and life and thought of God as a hypothetical abstraction rather than a persona. John Locke (1632–1704) pioneered the empiricist approach to knowledge, stressing the importance of the environment in human development. Locke thought reason and revelation were complementary and originating from God. With respect to political and economic theory, Locke and Jean-Jacques Rousseau (1712–1778) believed that people were capable of governing themselves, either through a political (Locke) or social (Rousseau) contract forming the basis of society. Most philosophers opposed democracy, preferring a limited monarchy that shared power with the nobility. The assault on mercantilist economic theory was begun by the physiocrats in France, who proposed a laissez-faire (minimal governmental interference) attitude toward land usage that culminated in the theory of economic capitalism associated with Adam Smith (1723–1790) and his notions of free trade, free enterprise, and the law of supply and demand.

The French Revolution

Increased criticism directed toward governmental inefficiency and corruption as well as toward the privileged classes demonstrated the rising expectations of "enlightened" society in France. The remainder of the population (called the Third Estate) consisted of the middle class, urban workers, and the mass of peasants, who bore the entire burden of taxation and the imposition of feudal obligations. The most notorious event of the French Revolution was the so-called Reign of Terror (1793–1794), the government's campaign against its internal enemies and counterrevolutionaries. Louis XVI faced charges of treason, declared guilty, and executed on January 21, 1793. Later the same year, the queen, Marie Antoinette, met the same fate. The middle class controlled the Directory (1795–1799). Members of the Directory believed that through peace they would gain more wealth and establish a society in which money and property would become the only requirements for prestige and power. Rising inflation and mass public dissatisfaction led to the downfall of the Directory.

The Napoleonic Era

On December 25, 1799, a new government and constitution concentrated supreme power in the hands of Napoleon. Napoleon's domestic reforms and policies affected every aspect of society. French-ruled peoples viewed Napoleon as a tyrant who repressed and exploited them for France's glory and advantage. Enlightened reformers believed Napoleon had betrayed the ideals of the Revolution. The downfall of Napoleon resulted from his inability to conquer England, economic distress caused by the Continental System (boycott of British goods), the Peninsular War with Spain, the German War of Liberation, and the invasion of Russia. The actual defeat of Napoleon occurred at the Battle of Waterloo in 1815.

The Industrial Revolution

The term "Industrial Revolution" describes a period of transition when machines began to significantly displace human and animal power in methods of producing and distributing goods and when an agricultural and commercial society became an industrial one. Roots of the Industrial Revolution are evident in the following:

- The Commercial Revolution (1500–1700) that spurred the great economic growth of Europe and brought about the Age of Discovery and Exploration, which in turn helped to solidify the economic doctrines of mercantilism.

- The effects of the Scientific Revolution, which produced the first wave of mechanical inventions and technological advances.

- The increase in population in Europe from 140 million people in 1750 to 266 million people by the mid-nineteenth century (more producers, more consumers).

- The nineteenth century political and social revolutions that began the rise to power of the middle class and that provided leadership for the economic revolution.

A transportation revolution ensued that distributed the productivity of machinery and delivery of raw materials to eager factories. This revolution led to the growth of canal systems, the construction of hard-surfaced "macadam" roads, the commercial use of the steamboat that Robert Fulton (1765–1815) demonstrated, and the railway locomotive that George Stephenson (1781–1848) made commercially successful. The Industrial Revolution created a unique new category of people who depended on their jobs for income and who needed job security. Until 1850, workers as a whole did not share in the general wealth produced by the Industrial Revolution. Conditions improved as the century wore on. Union action combined with general prosperity and a developing social conscience to improve the working conditions, wages, and hours of skilled labor first and unskilled labor later.

Socialism

The Utopian Socialists were the earliest writers to propose an equitable solution to improve the distribution of society's wealth. The name of this group comes from "Utopia" Saint Thomas More's (1478–1535) book on a fictional ideal society. While they endorsed the productive capacity of industrialism, the

Utopian Socialists denounced its mismanagement. Human society was ideally a community rather than a mixture of competing, selfish individuals. All the goods a person needed could be produced in one community. Scientific socialism, or Marxism, was the creation of Karl Marx (1818–1883), a German scholar who, with the help of Friedrich Engels (1820–1895), intended to replace utopian hopes and dreams with a militant blueprint for socialist working-class success. The principal works of this revolutionary school of socialism were *The Communist Manifesto* and *Das Kapital*. Marxism has four key propositions:

1. An economic interpretation of history that asserts that economic factors (main-lycentered on who controls the means of production and distribution) determines all human history.

2. The belief that there has always been a class struggle between the rich and the poor (or the exploiters and the exploited).

3. The theory of surplus value, which holds that the true value of a product is labor; because workers receive a small portion of their just labor price, the difference is surplus value "stolen" from workers by capitalists.

4. The belief that socialism is inevitable because capitalism contains the seeds of its own destruction (overproduction, unemployment, etc.). The rich grow richer and the poor grow poorer until the gap between each class (proletariat and bourgeoisie) becomes so great that the working classes rise up in revolution and overthrow the elite bourgeoisie to install a "dictatorship of the proletariat." The creation of a classless society guided by the principle "from each according to his abilities, to each according to his needs" will be the result of dismantling capitalism.

Skill 7.6: Identify the Causes and Consequences of Exploration, Settlement, and Growth

Beginnings of European Exploration

Europeans were largely unaware of the existence of the American continent, even though a Norse seaman, Leif Eriksson, had sailed within sight of the continent in the eleventh century. Few other explorers ventured nearly as far as America. Before the fifteenth century, Europeans had little desire to explore and were not ready to face the many challenges of a long sea voyage. Just as developments led to changes and conflict in North America and produced an increasing number of distinct cultures and political systems, developments in Europe were about to make possible the great voyages that led to contact between Europe and the Americas. In the fifteenth and sixteenth centuries, technological devices such as the compass and astrolabe freed explorers from some of the constraints that had limited early voyages. Three primary factors—God, gold, and glory—led to increased interest in exploration and eventually to a desire to settle in the newly discovered lands.

Early Challenges

Although Europeans such as Italians participated in overland trade with the East and sailed through the Mediterranean and beyond, it was the Arabs who played the largest part in such trade and who benefited the most economically. Prince Henry the Navigator, ruler of Portugal, sponsored voyages aimed at adding territory and gaining control of trading routes to increase the power and wealth of Portugal. Prince Henry also wanted to spread Christianity and prevent the further expansion of Islam in Africa. Henry the Navigator brought a number of Italian merchant traders to his court at Cape St. Vincent, and subsequently they sailed in Portuguese ships down the western coast of Africa. The initial voyages were extremely difficult owing to the lack of navigational instruments and any kind of maps or charts. Europeans had charted the entire Mediterranean Sea, including harbors and the coastline, but they had no knowledge or maps of the African coast.

The first task of the explorers was to create accurate charts of the African shoreline. The crews on these initial voyages did not encounter horrible monsters or boiling water, which had been rumored to exist in the ocean beyond Cape Bojador, the farthest point Europeans had previously reached. However, the explorers did discover that strong southward winds made it easy to sail out of the Mediterranean but difficult to return. Most people at the time believed that Africa and China were joined by a southern continent, eliminating any possibility of an eastern maritime route to the Indian Ocean. Prince Henry, however, sent ships along the coast of Africa because he believed it was possible to sail east through the Atlantic and reach the Indian Ocean.

Technical Innovations Aiding Exploration

One of the reasons that the explorers sailing from Portugal traveled along the coast was to avoid losing sight of land. By the thirteenth century, explorers were using the compass, borrowed from China, to determine direction; it was more difficult to determine the relative position from the North and South Poles and from landmasses or anything else. In the Northern Hemisphere, a navigator could determine the relative north-south position, or latitude, by calculating the height of the Pole Star from the horizon. South of the equator, one cannot see the Pole Star; until around 1460, captains had no way to determine their position if they sailed too far south.

Although longitude (relative east-west position) remained unknown until the eighteenth century, the introduction of the astrolabe allowed sailors to calculate their latitude south of the equator. Along with navigational aids, improvements in shipbuilding and in weaponry also facilitated exploration. Unlike in the Mediterranean, it was not possible to use ships propelled only by oarsmen in the Atlantic, because the waves there are high and the currents and winds are strong. Europeans had initially used very broad sails on ships that went out into the Atlantic; the ships were heavy and often became stranded by the absence of the favorable tailwinds upon which the ships and sailors depended. The Portuguese borrowed techniques from Arab and European shipbuilding and developed the Caravela Redondo. This ship proved to be more worthy of long voyages because it combined square rigging for speed with lateen sails that were more responsive and easier to handle. Other European states adopted the ship and also the practice of mounting artillery and other weapons on exploration vessels.

Main Elements of European Exploration

As the Portuguese began to trade and explore along the coast of Africa, they brought back slaves, ivory, gold, and knowledge of the African coast. It appeared that the Portuguese might find a route to the Indian Ocean, and it was clear that the voyages sponsored by Prince Henry were benefiting Portugal in many ways. Other European states wanted to increase their territory and wealth and to establish trade routes to the East. Although the desire for control of trade routes and wealth was a primary motive in launching voyages of exploration, it was not the only incentive. Europe in the fifteenth and sixteenth centuries, despite the increase in dissenting views, was still extremely religious. The Catholic Church continued to exert a tremendous influence, and some Christians were motivated to go on voyages of discovery to conduct missionary activities and spread the word of God.

After the beginning of the Reformation, many Lutherans, Calvinists, and other groups who had left the Catholic Church emigrated from Europe in the hopes of settling where they would be free from religious persecution or violent conflicts. Younger sons of families in Europe were able to secure prominent positions in the church; they were often not able to find lucrative opportunities at home, however, because the eldest son usually inherited lands and wealth. The voyages of exploration, therefore, were a means of securing fame and fortune and of obtaining opportunities that would not be available otherwise. Other individuals sponsored or participated in voyages in the hope of gaining wealth or increased opportunities.

Although the motivation of fame and fortune was often secondary to God and glory, many individuals were attracted to exploration by the possibility of adventure and by their desire to explore uncharted territory. These three factors—gold, God, and glory—operated on both individual and state levels; kings and heads of states were as interested as the seamen were in spreading their faith and increasing the wealth and prestige of their states. Portugal was the first European state to establish sugar plantations on an island off the west coast of Africa and to import slaves from Africa to labor there. It was the beginning of the slave trade. The level of trading was initially far less extensive and intense than during the later period of slave trade when Spain and England became involved. In an attempt to maintain control of the slave trade and of the eastern routes to India, the Portuguese appealed to the pope; he ruled in their favor and forbade the Spanish and others to sail south and east in an attempt to reach India or Asia.

Columbus

When Ferdinand and Isabella married and united the two largest provinces in Spain, Castile and Aragon, they not only began the process of uniting all of Spain but also agreed to sponsor Christopher Columbus in his voyage of exploration. Only the heads of states had the necessary resources and could afford the risk involved in sponsoring a major voyage across the oceans of the world, but most monarchs were unwilling to take such a risk. Columbus was an Italian explorer looking for a sponsor and had approached Ferdinand and Isabella after being turned down by the English government. He convinced the Spanish monarchs that a western route to the Indian Ocean existed and that it would be possible to make the voyage. However, Columbus had miscalculated the distance of the voyage from Europe to Asia. His estimate of the circumference of the earth was much less than it should have been for an accurate calculation, and no Europeans were aware of the existence of the American continents. One of the reasons that Ferdinand and Isabella were willing to support Columbus was that the previous agreements prevented all states but Portugal from sailing east to reach India. Therefore, the only chance for Spain to launch an expedition to India and to participate in trade and exploration was in the discovery of a western route to India.

In 1492, Columbus sailed from Spain with 90 men on three ships, the *Niña*, the *Pinta*, and the *Santa María*. After a 10-week voyage, they landed in the Bahamas. On his second trip, Columbus reached Cuba, and then in 1498, during his third trip, he reached the mainland and sailed along the northern coast of South America. Columbus originally thought he had reached India; he referred to the people he encountered in the Bahamas and on his second landing in Cuba as Indians.

There is considerable debate over whether Columbus realized, either during his third voyage or just before his death, that he had landed not in India but on an entirely unknown continent between Europe and Asia. Another question is whether Columbus, who died in obscurity despite his fame for having discovered America, should receive credit for this discovery; earlier explorers had reached the American continent. However, because Columbus's voyages prompted extensive exploration and settlement of the Americas, it is accurate to state that he was responsible for the discovery of the New World by Europeans. Another result of Columbus's voyages was the increased focus of Spain on exploration and conquest. Nevertheless, the New World took its name from the Florentine merchant Amerigo Vespucci–not Columbus. Vespucci took part in several voyages to the New World and wrote a series of descriptions that not only gave Europeans an image of this "New World" but also spread the idea that the discovered lands were not a part of Asia or India. Vespucci, then, popularized the image of the Americas and the idea that the Americas were continents separate from those previously known.

Balboa

It was a Spanish explorer, Vasco Núñez de Balboa, who crossed the Isthmus of Panama and came to another ocean, which separates the American continents from China. The Spanish sponsored another Portuguese sailor, Ferdinand Magellan, who discovered at the southern end of South America a strait that provided access to the ocean west of the Americas. Magellan named this ocean the Pacific because it was much calmer than the strait through which he had sailed to reach it. Later, he reached the Philippines and met his death in a conflict with the natives. Magellan's voyage, nevertheless, was the final stage of the process whereby Europeans completed the first-known circumnavigation of the globe. Although initially the Spanish were eager to find a route around the Americas that would enable them to sail on toward their original goal, the treasures of the Far East, they began to consider the Americas as a possible source of untapped wealth.

Cortez

Eventually the Spanish claimed all the New World except Brazil, which papal decree gave to the Portuguese. The first Spanish settlements were on the islands of the Caribbean Sea. It was not until 1518 that Spain appointed Hernando Cortez as a government official in Cuba; Cortez led a small military expedition against the Aztecs in Mexico. Cortez and his men failed in their first attack on the Aztec capital city, Tenochtitlán, but were ultimately successful. A combination of factors allowed the small force of approximately 600 Spanish soldiers to overcome the extensive Aztec Empire. The Spanish were armed with rifles and bows, which provided an advantage over Aztec fighters armed only with spears. However, weapons and armor were not the main reason that the Spanish were able to overcome the military forces of the natives. The Aztec ruler, Montezuma, allowed a delegation, which included Cortez, into the capital city because the description of the Spanish soldiers in their armor and with feathers in their helmets was similar to the description in Aztec legend of messengers who would be sent by the chief Aztec god, Quetzcoatl. The members of Cortez's expedition exposed the natives to smallpox and other diseases that devastated the native population. Finally, the Spanish expedition was also able to form alliances with other native tribes that the Aztecs had conquered; these tribes were willing to cooperate to defeat the Aztecs and thus break up their empire.

Pizarro

Twenty years after Cortez defeated the Aztecs, another conquistador, Francisco Pizarro, defeated the Incas in Peru. Pizarro's expedition enabled the Spanish to begin to explore and settle South America. Spain funded the conquistadors, or conquerors, who were the first Europeans to explore some areas of the Americas. However, the sole purpose of the conquistadors' explorations was defeating the natives to gain access to gold, silver, and other wealth. Spain established mines in the territory it claimed and produced a tremendous amount of gold and silver. In the 300 years after the Spanish conquest of the Americas in the sixteenth century, those mines produced 10 times more gold and silver than the total produced by all the mines in the rest of the world.

Spanish Interest in the New World

Spain had come to view the New World as more than an obstacle to voyages toward India; over time, Spain began to think that it might be possible to exploit this territory for more than just mining. It was the conquistadors who made it possible for the Spanish to settle the New World, but they were not responsible for forming settlements or for overseeing Spanish colonies in the New World. Instead, Spain sent officials and administrators from Spain to oversee settlements after their initial formation. Spanish settlers came to the New World for various reasons: some came in search of land to settle or buy, others came looking for opportunities that were not available to them in Europe, and priests and missionaries came to spread Christianity to the natives. By the end of the sixteenth century, Spain had established firm control over not only the several islands in the Caribbean, Mexico, and southern North America but also the territory currently within the modern states of Chile, Argentina, and Peru.

Spanish Settlements in the New World

The first permanent settlement established by the Spanish was the predominantly military fort of St. Augustine, located in Florida. In 1598, Don Juan de Onate led a group of 500 settlers north out of Mexico and established a colony in what is now New Mexico. Onate granted *encomiendas* to the most prominent Spaniards who had accompanied him. Under the *encomienda* system, which the Spanish in Mexico and parts of North America established, these distinguished individuals had the right to exact tribute and/or labor from the native population, which continued to live on the land in exchange for the services it provided.

Spanish colonists founded Santa Fe in 1609, and by 1680 about 2,000 Spaniards were living in New Mexico. Most of the colonists raised sheep and cattle on large ranches and lived among approximately 30,000 Pueblo Indians. The Spanish crushed a major revolt that threatened to destroy Santa Fe in 1680. Attempts to prevent the natives—both those who had converted to Catholicism and those who had not—from performing religious rituals that predated the Spaniards' arrival provoked the revolt. The natives drove the Spanish from Santa Fe, but they returned in 1696, crushed the Pueblos, and seized the land. Although the Spanish ultimately quelled the revolt, they began to change their policies toward the natives, who still greatly outnumbered the Spanish settlers. The Spanish continued to try to Christianize and civilize the native population, but they also began to allow the Pueblos to own land. In addition, the Spanish unofficially tolerated native religious rituals, although Catholicism officially condemned all such practices.

By 1700, the Spanish population in New Mexico had increased and reached about 4,000; the native population had decreased to about 13,000 and intermarriage between natives and Spaniards increased. Nevertheless, disease, war, and migration resulted in the steady decline in the Pueblo population. New Mexico had become a prosperous and stable region, but it was still relatively weak and, as the only major Spanish settlement in northern Mexico, was isolated.

Effects of European-American Contact

One cannot underestimate the impact of Europeans on the New World, both before and after the arrival of the English and French. The most immediate effect was the spread of disease, which decimated the native population. In some areas of Mexico, 95 percent of the native population died as a result of contact with Europeans and the subsequent outbreaks of diseases like smallpox. In South America, the native population was devastated not only by disease but also by deliberate policies instituted to control and in some cases eliminate native peoples. Although Europeans passed most diseases to the natives, the natives passed syphilis to the Europeans, who carried it back to Europe. The European and American continents exchanged plants and animals. Europeans brought over animals to the New World, and they took plants like potatoes, corn, and squash back to Europe, where introduction of these crops led to an explosion of the European population. The decimation of the native population and the establishment of large plantations led to a shortage of workers, and Europeans began to transport slaves from Africa to the New World to fill the shortage.

Skill 7.7: Identify Individuals and Events That Have Influenced Economic, Social, and Political Institutions in the United States

English Interest in the New World

In 1497, King Henry VIII of England sponsored a voyage by John Cabot to seek a northwest passage through the New World to the Orient. However, the English made no real attempt to settle in the New World until nearly a century later. By the 1600s, the English became interested in colonizing the New World. Several factors motivated their interest. Many people in England hoped to emigrate overseas because the country's population was increasing, and because the land was being used to raise sheep for wool rather than for growing foodstuffs for survival. The ability to buy land in England was scarce, another primary motivator for emigration.

Some people in England left their homeland because of the religious turmoil that engulfed England after the beginning of the Protestant Reformation. In addition to converts to Lutheranism and Calvinism, a major emigrating group was the Puritans, who called for reforms to "purify" the church. Mercantilism also provided a motive for exploration and for the establishment of colonies. According to mercantile theories, an industrialized nation needed an inexpensive source of raw materials and markets for finished products. Colonies provided a way to obtain raw materials and to guarantee a market for industrial goods.

French and Dutch Settlements

Economic reasons, among others, motivated the French and the Dutch to explore and establish colonies in the New World. In 1609, the year after the first English settlement, the French established a colony in Quebec. Overall, far fewer French settlers traveled to the New World than did English settlers, but the French were able to exercise a tremendous influence through the establishment of strong ties with the natives. The French created trading partnerships and a vast trading network; they often intermarried with the local native population. The Dutch financed an English explorer, Henry Hudson, who claimed for Holland the territory that is now New York. The Dutch settlements along the Hudson, Delaware, and Connecticut rivers developed into the colony of New Netherlands and established a vast trading network that effectively separated the English colonies of Jamestown and Plymouth.

Roanoke

One reason that English settlements began to become more prominent after 1600 was the defeat of the Spanish fleet, the supposedly invincible Armada, by the English in 1588. The changing power balance on the seas encouraged the English to increase their exploration and attempted colonization of the Americas. However, the first few colonies founded by the English in America did not flourish.

Sir Humphrey Gilbert, who had obtained a six-year grant giving him the exclusive rights to settle any unclaimed land in America, was planning to establish a colony in Newfoundland, but a storm sank his ship. Instead, Sir Walter Raleigh received the six-year grant. Raleigh explored the North American coast and named the territory through which he traveled Virginia, in honor of the "Virgin Queen" Elizabeth I of England. In addition, Raleigh convinced his cousin, Sir Grenville, to establish a colony on the island of Roanoke. Roanoke was located off the coast of what later became North Carolina. The first settlers lived there for a year while Sir Grenville returned to England for supplies and additional settlers. However, when Sir Francis Drake arrived in Roanoke nearly a year later and found that Sir Grenville had not yet returned, the colonists left on his ship and abandoned the settlement. In 1587, Raleigh sent another group of colonists to Roanoke, but a war with Spain broke out in 1588 and kept him from returning until 1590. When Raleigh returned to Roanoke, the colonists had vanished. A single word, "Croatan," carved into a tree could have referred to a nearby settlement of natives. This suggested a number of possibilities in regard to the missing settlers; conclusive proof of their fate was never found.

The Jamestown Settlement

In 1606, King James I of England granted to the Virginia Company a charter for exploration and colonization. This charter marked the beginning of ventures sponsored by merchants rather than directly by the Crown. The charter of the Virginia Company had two branches. James I gave one branch to the English city of Plymouth, which had the right to the northern portion of territory on the eastern coast of North America, and he granted the London branch of the company the right to the southern portion.

Considerable difficulties prevented the English from founding and maintaining a permanent settlement in North America. The Plymouth Company failed to establish a lasting settlement. The company itself ran out of money, and the settlers who had gone to the New World gave up and abandoned their established Sagadahoc Colony in Maine. Having decided to colonize the Chesapeake Bay area, the London Company sent three ships with about 104 sailors to that area in 1607. The company's ships sailed up a river, which they named the James in honor of the English king, and they established the fort and permanent settlement of Jamestown. The London Company and the men who settled Jamestown were hoping to find a northwest passage to Asia, gold, and silver, or to be able to find lands capable of producing valuable goods, such as grapes, oranges, or silk. The colony at Jamestown did not allow the settlers to accomplish any of those things, and its location on the river, which became contaminated every spring, led to the outbreak of diseases such as typhoid, dysentery, and malaria. Over half the colonists died the first year, and by the spring of 1609, only one-third of the total number of colonists who had joined the colony were still alive.

The survival of Jamestown initially was largely accomplished through the efforts of Captain John Smith. Smith was a soldier who turned the colony's focus from exploration to obtaining food. Initially, Smith was able to obtain corn from the local Indians led by Powhatan and his 12-year-old daughter Pocahontas. Smith also forced all able men in the colony to work four hours a day in the wheat fields. Attempts by the London Company to send additional settlers and supplies encountered troubles and delays.

Demise of Jamestown

Thomas Gates and some 600 settlers, who left for Jamestown in 1609, ran aground on Bermuda and had to build a new ship. Although some new settlers did arrive in Jamestown, disease continued to shrink the population. When seriously injured Smith had to return to England, his departure deprived the colony of its most effective and resourceful leader. It was not long after Smith left that the colonists provoked a war with Powhatan, who was beginning to tire of the colonists' demands for corn. Powhatan realized that the settlers intended to stay indefinitely and might challenge the Indians for control of the surrounding territory.

Gates finally arrived at Jamestown in June 1610 with only 175 of the original 600 settlers. He found only 60 colonists who had survived the war with the Indians and the harsh winter of 1610, during which they had minimal food and other resources. Gates decided to abandon Jamestown and was sailing down the river with the surviving colonists on board when he encountered the new governor from England, Thomas West, Baron de la Warr. Gates and West returned to Jamestown, imposed martial law, responded to Indian attacks, and survived a five-year war with the Indians. Although the war did not end until 1614, when the colonists were able to negotiate a settlement by holding Pocahontas hostage, the situation in Jamestown began to improve in 1610.

Virginia Settlements

After this time, some of the Jamestown settlers relocated to healthier locations, and in 1613 one of them, John Rolfe, married Pocahontas. In 1614, the settlers planted a mild strain of tobacco, which gave them a crop they could sell for cash. The Crown issued two new charters that allowed Virginia to extend its borders all the way to the Pacific and made the London Company a joint-stock company. Changes in the company led to a new treasurer, Sir Edwin Sandy, who tried to reform Virginia.

Sandy encouraged settlers in Virginia to try to produce grapes and silkworms and to diversify the colony's economy in other ways. Sandy also replaced martial law with English common law. The colonists established a council to make laws, and settlers now had the right to own land. By 1623, about 4,000 additional settlers had arrived in Virginia. Attempts to produce and sell crops other than tobacco, however, failed, and the arrival of large numbers of new colonists provoked renewed conflict with the Indians. A major Indian attack launched in March 1622 killed 347 colonists. Investors in the London Company withdrew their capital and appealed to the king, and a royal commission visited the colony. As a result of this investigation, the king declared the London Company bankrupt and assumed direct control of Virginia in 1624. Virginia became the first royal colony, and the Crown appointed a governor and a council to oversee its administration.

Three trends continued after the Crown assumed control. The first was unrelenting conflict with the Indians. Through war and raids, by 1632 the colonists had killed or driven out most of the Indians in the area immediately around Jamestown. The other two trends were the yearly influx of thousands of new settlers and the high death rate in the colony.

Despite the high mortality rate, the population of the colony began gradually to increase. The expansion of tobacco production led to a demand for labor, and thousands of the young men who came were indentured servants. In exchange for their passage to America and food and shelter during their terms of service, these men were bound to work for their masters for four or five years. After that time, they gained their freedom and often a small payment to help them become established. Most of these men were not able to participate in the running of the colony even after they became free, but some were able to acquire land.

In 1634, the Crown divided Virginia into counties, each with appointed justices and the right to fill all other positions. Under this type of system, individuals from a few wealthy families tended to dominate the government. Most of the counties became Anglican, and the colony continued to elect representatives to its House of Burgesses, an assembly that met with the governor to discuss issues of common law. The king, however, refused to recognize the colony's House of Burgesses. After 1660, the colony became even more dominated by the wealthiest 15 percent of the population, and these individuals and their sons continued to be the only colonists to serve as justices and burgesses. Settlement of the colonies continued, primarily for religious and economic reasons. Conflict between the colonists and the natives was a constant.

Growth of the Slave Trade

The shortage of labor in the southern colonies and a drop in the number of people coming to the colonies as indentured servants forced the colonists to search for other sources of labor. Although the colonists began using African servants and slaves almost immediately after settling in the New World, the slave trade and the slave population in British North America remained small in the first half of the seventeenth century. Toward the end of the seventeenth century, increasing numbers of slaves from Africa became available, and the demand for them in North America further stimulated the growth of the transatlantic slave trade.

By the nineteenth century, millions of Africans had been forcibly taken from their native lands and sold into perpetual slavery. The Europeans sold slaves at forts the slave traders had established on the African coast; the Europeans packed the slaves as closely as possible into the lower regions of ships for the long journey to the Americas. Chained slaves traveled in deplorably unsanitary conditions and received only enough food and water to keep them alive. Many slaves died during this Middle Passage voyage. Plantation owners in the Caribbean, Brazil, or North America bought the slaves to do the work. It was only after 1697 that English colonists began to buy large numbers of slaves. By 1760, the slave population had reached approximately a quarter of a million with most of the slaves concentrated in the southern colonies. Slave labor replaced indentured servitude, and a race-based system of perpetual slavery developed. Colonial assemblies began to pass "slave codes" in the eighteenth century. These codes identified all nonwhites or dark-skinned people as slaves, made their condition permanent, and legalized slavery in British North America.

Salem Witch Trials

During this period of increasing tensions, several communities held witchcraft trials. In Salem, Massachusetts, a group of young girls accused servants from West India and older white members of the community, mostly women, of exercising powers that Satan had given to them. Other towns also experienced turmoil and charged residents with witchcraft. In Salem alone, the juries pronounced 19 people guilty; in 1692 after the execution of all 19 victims, the girls admitted their stories were not true.

The witchcraft trials illustrate the highly religious nature of the New England society, but they also suggest that individuals who did not conform to societal expectations were at risk of serious consequences. Most of the accused were outspoken women who were often critical of their communities, were older, and were either widows or unmarried. Some of these women had acquired property despite the accepted views and limitations regarding women's role in society.

Religion in the Colonies

The religious nature of colonial settlers did not lead to the kind of intolerance or persecution that had plagued Europe since the Reformation. Conflict among various religious groups did break out occasionally, but British North America enjoyed a far greater degree of religious toleration than anywhere else. Among the reasons this toleration existed were that several religious groups had immigrated to North America and that every colony, except Virginia and Maryland, ignored the laws establishing the Church of England as the official faith of the colony. Even among the Puritans, differences in religious opinion led to the establishment of different denominations.

Although there was some religious toleration, Protestants still tended to view Roman Catholics as threatening rivals. In Maryland, Catholics numbered about 3,000, the largest population of all the colonies, and were the victims of persecution. Jews were often victims of persecution; they could not vote or hold office in any of the colonies, and only in Rhode Island could they practice the Jewish religion openly.

In addition to religious toleration, the other main trends at the time were the westward spread of communities, the rise of cities, and a decline in religious piousness. This sense of the weakening of religious authority and faithfulness led to the Great Awakening.

The Great Awakening refers to a period beginning in the 1730s in which several well-known preachers traveled through British North America giving speeches and arguing for the need to revive religious piety and closer relationships with God. The main message of the preachers was that everyone has the potential, regardless of past behavior, to reestablish their relationship with God. This message appealed to many women and younger sons of landowners who stood to inherit very little. The best-known preacher during this period was Jonathan Edwards. Edwards denounced some current beliefs as doctrines of easy salvation. At his church in Northampton, Edwards sermonized about the absolute sovereignty of God, predestination, and salvation by grace alone.

The Great Awakening

The Great Awakening further divided religion in America by creating distinctions among New Light groups (revivalists), Old Light groups (traditionalists), and new groups that incorporated elements of both. The various revivalists, or New Light groups, did not agree on every issue. Some revivalists denounced education and learning from books while others founded schools in the belief that education was a means of furthering religion. While some individuals were stressing a need for renewed spiritual focus, others were beginning to embrace the ideas of the Enlightenment.

The Enlightenment in Colonial America

The Scientific Revolution had demonstrated the existence of natural laws that operated in nature, and enlightened thinkers began to argue that man had the ability to improve his own situation through the use of rational thought and acquired knowledge. Intellectuals of the Enlightenment shifted the focus from God to man, introduced the idea of progress, and argued that people could improve their own situations and make decisions on how to live rather than just having faith in God and waiting for a better life after death and salvation.

Enlightenment thought had a tremendous impact on the North American colonists, who began to establish more schools, encourage the acquisition of knowledge, and become more interested in gaining scientific knowledge. The colleges founded in North America taught the scientific theories held by Copernicus, who argued that planets rotated around the sun not the Earth, and Newton, who introduced the key principles of physics, including gravity. The colonists did not just learn European theories. Benjamin Franklin was among the colonists who began to carry out their own experiments and form their own theories. Franklin experimented with electricity and was able to demonstrate in 1752, by using a kite, that electricity and lightning were the same.

The perspective of the Enlightenment and scientific theories and research in particular also led to inoculations against smallpox. The Puritan theologian Cotton Mather convinced the population of Boston that injections with a small amount of the smallpox virus would build up their resistance to the disease and reduce the likelihood of reinfection. Leading theologians and scientists spread European scientific ideas and developed their own theories and applications using their acquired knowledge.

The Beginnings of the American Revolution

In 1764, George Grenville pushed through Parliament the Sugar Act (the Revenue Act), which aimed at raising revenue by taxing goods imported by Americans. The Stamp Act (1765) imposed a direct tax on the colonists for the first time. By requiring Americans to purchase revenue stamps on everything from newspapers to legal documents, the Stamp Act would have created an impossible drain on hard currency in the colonies.

Americans reacted to these parliamentary acts first with restrained and respectful petitions and pamphlets in which they pointed out that "taxation without representation is tyranny." The colonists began to limit their purchase of imported goods. From there, resistance progressed to stronger protests that eventually became violent. In October 1765, delegates from nine colonies met as the Stamp Act Congress and passed moderate resolutions against the act and asserted that Americans could not be taxed without the consent of their representatives. The colonists now ceased all importation.

In March 1766, Parliament repealed the Stamp Act. At the same time, however, it passed the Declaratory Act, which claimed the power to tax or make laws for the Americans "in all cases whatsoever." In 1766, Parliament passed a program of taxes on items imported into the colonies. The taxes came to be known as the Townsend duties, a name that came from Britain's chancellor of the exchequer, Charles Townsend. American reaction was at first slow, but the sending of troops aroused them to resistance.

Again the colonies halted importation, and soon British merchants were calling on Parliament to repeal the Townsend duties. In March 1770, Parliament repealed all the taxes except that on tea; Parliament wanted to prove that it had the right to tax the colonies if it so desired. When Parliament ended the Tea Act in 1773, a relative peace ensued.

Resumption of Conflict

In desperate financial condition—partially because the Americans were buying smuggled Dutch tea rather than the taxed British product—the British East India Company sought and obtained from Parliament concessions that allowed it to ship tea directly to the colonies rather than only by way of Britain. The result would be that the East India Company tea, even with the tax, would be cheaper than smuggled Dutch tea. The company hoped that the colonists would thus buy the tea, tax and all, save the East India Company, and tacitly accept Parliament's right to tax them. The Americans, however, proved resistant to this approach. Rather than acknowledge Parliament's right to tax, they refused to buy the cheaper tea and resorted to various methods, including tar and feathers, to prevent the collection of the tax on tea. In most ports, Americans did not allow ships carrying the tea to land.

In Boston, however, the pro-British governor Thomas Hutchinson forced a confrontation by ordering Royal Navy vessels to prevent the tea ships from leaving the harbor. After 20 days, this would, by law, result in selling the cargoes at auction and paying the tax. The night before the time was to expire, December 16, 1773, Bostonians thinly disguised as Native Americans boarded the ships and threw the tea into the harbor. This was the Boston Tea Party. The British responded with four acts collectively titled the Coercive Acts (1774), in which they strengthened their control over the colonists. The First Continental Congress (1774) met in response to the acts. The Congress called for strict nonimportation and rigorous preparation of local militia companies.

The War for Independence

British troops went to Massachusetts, which the Crown had officially declared to be in a state of rebellion. General Thomas Gage received orders to arrest the leaders of the resistance or, failing that, to provoke any sort of confrontation that would allow him to turn British military might loose on the Americans. Americans, however, detected the movement of Gage's troops toward Concord, and dispatch riders, like Paul Revere and William Dawes, spread the news throughout the countryside.

In Lexington, about 70 minutemen (trained militiamen who would respond at a moment's notice) awaited the British on the village green. A shot was fired; it is unknown which side fired first. This became "the shot heard 'round the world." The British opened fire and charged, and casualties occurred on both sides. The following month, the Americans tightened the noose around Boston by fortifying Breed's Hill (a spur of Bunker Hill). The British determined to remove them by a frontal attack. Twice thrown back, the British finally succeeded when the Americans ran out of ammunition. There were more than 1,000 British casualties in what turned out to be the bloodiest battle of the war (June 17, 1775), yet the British had gained very little and remained essentially trapped in Boston.

Congress now put George Washington (1732–1799) in charge of the army, called for more troops, and adopted the Olive Branch Petition, which pleaded with King George III to intercede with Parliament to restore peace. However, the king gave his approval to the Prohibitory Act, declaring the colonies in rebellion and no longer under his protection. Preparations began for full-scale war against America.

In 1776, the colonists formed two committees to establish independence and a national government. One committee was created to work out a framework for a national government. The other was created to draft a statement of the reasons for declaring independence. This statement, called the Declaration of Independence, was primarily the work of Thomas Jefferson (1743–1826) of Virginia. It was a restatement of political ideas by then commonplace in America and an explanation of why the former colonists felt justified in separating from Great Britain. Congress formally adopted the Declaration of Independence on July 4, 1776.

The British landed that summer at New York City. General Washington, who had anticipated the move, was waiting for them, but the undertrained, underequipped, and badly outnumbered American army was no match for the British and had to retreat. By December, what was left of Washington's army had made it into Pennsylvania. With his small army melting away as demoralized soldiers deserted, Washington then decided on a bold stroke. On Christmas night, 1776, his army crossed the Delaware River and struck the Hessians at Trenton. Washington's troops easily defeated the Hessians, still groggy from their hard-drinking Christmas party.

A few days later, Washington defeated a British force at Princeton. The Americans regained much of New Jersey from the British and saved the American army from disintegration. Hoping to weaken Britain, France began making covert shipments of arms to the Americans early in the war. These French shipments were vital for the Americans. The American victory at Saratoga convinced the French to join openly in the war against England. Eventually, the Spanish (1779) and the Dutch (1780) joined as well. The final agreement became known as the Treaty of Paris of 1783. Its terms stipulated the following:

1.   The recognition by the major European powers, including Britain, of the United States as an independent nation.

2.   The establishment of America's western boundary at the Mississippi River.

3.   The establishment of America's southern boundary at 31 degrees north latitude (the northern boundary of Florida).

4.   The surrender of Florida to Spain and the retainment of Canada by Britain.

5.   The enablement of Private British creditors to collect any debts owed by United States citizens.

6.   The recommendation of Congress that the states restore confiscated loyalist property.

The Federalist Era

After the adoption of the Articles of Confederation, Congress adopted a new constitution and the Americans elected George Washington as president under the guidelines. George Washington received virtually all the votes of the presidential electors. John Adams (1735–1826) received the next highest number and became the vice president. After a triumphant journey from Mount Vernon, Washington attended his inauguration in New York City, the temporary seat of government.

To oppose the antifederalists, the states ratified 10 amendments—the Bill of Rights—by the end of 1791. The first nine spelled out specific guarantees of personal freedoms, and the Tenth Amendment reserved to the states all powers not specifically withheld or granted to the federal government.

Alexander Hamilton (1757–1804) interpreted the Constitution as having vested extensive powers in the federal government. This "implied powers" stance claimed that the government had all powers that the Constitution had not expressly denied to it. Hamilton's was the "broad" interpretation of the Constitution. By contrast, Thomas Jefferson and James Madison (1751–1836) held the view that the Constitution prohibited any action not specifically permitted in the Constitution. Based on this view of government, adherents of this "strict" interpretation opposed the establishment of Hamilton's national bank. Jeffersonian supporters, primarily under the guidance of James Madison, began to organize political groups in opposition to Hamilton's program. The groups opposing Hamilton's view called themselves Democratic-Republicans or Jeffersonians.

The Federalists, Hamilton's supporters, received their strongest confirmation from the business and financial groups in the commercial centers of the Northeast and from the port cities of the South. The strength of the Democratic-Republicans lay primarily in the rural and frontier areas of the South and West. Federalist candidate John Adams won the election of 1796. The elections in 1798 increased the Federalists' majorities in both houses of Congress that used their "mandate" to enact legislation to stifle foreign influences. For example, the Alien Act raised new hurdles in the path of immigrants trying to obtain citizenship, and the Sedition Act widened the powers of the Adams administration to muzzle its newspaper critics. Democratic-Republicans were convinced that the Alien and Sedition Acts were unconstitutional, but the process of deciding on the constitutionality of federal laws was as yet undefined.

The Jeffersonian Era

Thomas Jefferson and Aaron Burr ran for the presidency on the Democratic-Republican ticket, though not together, against John Adams and Charles Pinckney for the Federalists. Both Jefferson and Burr received the same number of votes in the Electoral College, so the election went to the House of Representatives. After a lengthy deadlock, Alexander Hamilton threw his support to Jefferson. Burr had to accept the vice presidency, the result obviously intended by the electorate.

The adoption and ratification of the Twelfth Amendment in 1804 ensured that a tie vote between candidates of the same party could not again cause the confusion of the Jefferson-Burr affair. Following the constitutional mandate, an 1808 law prevented the importation of slaves. An American delegation purchased the trans-Mississippi territory from Napoleon for $15 million in April 1803 (the Louisiana Purchase), even though they had no authority to buy more than the city of New Orleans.

The War of 1812

Democratic-Republican James Madison won the election of 1808 over Federalist Charles Pinckney, but the Federalists gained seats in both houses of Congress. The Native American tribes of the Northwest and the Mississippi Valley were resentful of the government's policy of pressured removal to the West, and the British authorities in Canada exploited their discontent by encouraging border raids against the American settlements. At the same time, the British interfered with American transatlantic shipping, including impressing sailors and capturing ships. On June 1, 1812, President Madison asked for a declaration of war, and Congress complied. After three years of inconclusive war, the British and Americans signed the Treaty of Ghent (1815). It provided for the acceptance of the status quo that had existed at the beginning of hostilities, and both sides restored their wartime conquests to the other.

The Monroe Doctrine

As Latin American nations began declaring independence, British and American leaders feared that European governments would try to restore the former New World colonies to their erstwhile royal owners. In December 1823, President James Monroe (1758–1831) included in his annual message to Congress a statement that the peoples of the American hemisphere were "henceforth not to be considered as subjects for future colonization by any European powers."

The Marshall Court

Chief Justice John Marshall (1755–1835) delivered the majority opinions in several critical decisions in the formative years of the U.S. Supreme Court. These decisions served to strengthen the power of the federal government (and of the court itself) and restrict the powers of state governments. Following are two key examples:

- *Marbury v. Madison* (1803) established the Supreme Court's power of judicial review over federal legislation.

- In *Gibbons v. Ogden* (1824), a case involving competing steamboat companies, Marshall ruled that commerce includes navigation and that only Congress has the right to regulate commerce among states, thereby voiding state-granted monopolies.

The Missouri Compromise

The Missouri Territory, the first territory organized from the Louisiana Purchase, applied for statehood in 1819. Because the Senate membership was evenly divided between slaveholding and free states at that time, the admission of a new state would give the voting advantage to either the North or the South. As the debate dragged on, the northern territory of Massachusetts applied for admission as the state of Maine. By combining the two admission bills, Maine came in as a free state and Missouri as a slave state. To make the

Missouri Compromise palatable for the House of Representatives, an added provision prohibited slavery in the remainder of the Louisiana Territory north of the southern boundary of Missouri (latitude 36°30¢).

Jacksonian Democracy

Andrew Jackson (1767–1845), the candidate of a faction of the emerging Democratic Party, won the election of 1828. Jackson was popular with the common man. He seemed to be the prototype of the self-made westerner: rough-hewn, violent, vindictive, with few ideas but strong convictions. He ignored his appointed cabinet officers and relied instead on the counsel of his "Kitchen Cabinet," a group of partisan supporters. He exercised his veto power more than any other president before him and, in one of many notable actions, he vetoed the renewal of the national bank.

Jackson supported the removal of all Native American tribes to an area west of the Mississippi River. The Indian Removal Act of 1830 provided for the federal enforcement of that process. One of the results of this policy was the Trail of Tears, the forced march under U.S. Army escort of thousands of Cherokee Indians to the West. One-quarter or more of the Cherokee, mostly women and children, perished on the journey.

The Early Antislavery Movement

In 1831, William Lloyd Garrison started his newspaper, the *Liberator,* and began to advocate total and immediate emancipation. He founded the New England Antislavery Society in 1832 and the American Antislavery Society in 1833. At around the same time, Theodore Weld pursued the same goals but advocated more gradual means. The antislavery movement then split into two wings: Garrison's radical followers and the moderates who favored "moral suasion" and petitions to Congress. In 1840, the Liberty Party, the first national antislavery party, fielded a presidential candidate on the platform of "free soil" (preventing the expansion of slavery into the new western territories).

Manifest Destiny and Westward Expansion

The term "Manifest Destiny" was not coined until 1844, but the belief that the destiny of the American nation consisted of expansion all the way to the Pacific Ocean—and possibly even to Canada and Mexico—was older than that. A common conviction was that Americans should share American liberty and ideals with everyone possible and, if necessary, by force. During the 1830s, American missionaries followed the traders and trappers to the Oregon country and began to publicize the richness and beauty of the land. The result was the Oregon Fever of the 1840s, as thousands of settlers trekked across the Great Plains and the Rocky Mountains to settle the new Shangri-La.

Texas had been a state in the Republic of Mexico since 1822, following the Mexican revolution against Spanish control. The new Mexican government invited immigration from the North by offering land grants to Stephen Austin and other Americans. By 1835, approximately 35,000 "gringos" were homesteading on Texas land. When Mexican officials saw their power base eroding as the foreigners flooded in, they moved to tighten control through restrictions on immigration and through tax increases. The Texans responded in 1836 by proclaiming independence and establishing a new republic. In 1845, after a series of failed attempts at annexation, the United States Congress admitted Texas to the Union.

The Mexican War

Though Mexico broke diplomatic relations with the United States immediately after Texas's admission to the Union, there was still hope of a peaceful settlement. In the fall of 1845, President James K. Polk (1795–1849) sent John Slidell to Mexico City with a proposal for a peaceful settlement, but, like other attempts at negotiation, nothing came of it. Racked by coup and countercoup, the Mexican government refused even to receive Slidell. Polk responded by sending U.S. troops into the disputed territory. On April 5, 1846, Mexican troops attacked an American patrol. When news of the clash reached Washington, Polk sought and received from Congress a declaration of war against Mexico.

At the close of the war, peace was negotiated via the Treaty of Guadalupe Hidalgo on February 2, 1848. Under the terms of the treaty, Mexico ceded to the United States the southwestern territory from Texas to the California coast.

Seeds of the Civil War

The Mexican War had barely started when, on August 8, 1846, a freshman Democratic congressman, David Wilmot of Pennsylvania, introduced his Wilmot Proviso as a proposed amendment to a war appropriations bill. The bill stipulated that "neither slavery nor involuntary servitude shall ever exist" in any territory to be acquired from Mexico. The House passed the proviso, but the Senate did not; Wilmot introduced his provision again amidst increasingly acrimonious debate.

One compromise proposal called for the extension of the 36°30' line of the Missouri Compromise westward through the Mexican cession to the Pacific, with territory north of the line closed to slavery. Another compromise solution was "popular sovereignty," which held that the residents of each territory should decide for themselves whether to allow slavery.

Having more than the requisite population and being in need of better government, California petitioned in September 1849 for admission to the Union as a free state. Southerners were furious. Long outnumbered in the House of Representatives, the South would find itself, should Congress admit California as a free state, similarly outnumbered in the Senate. At this point, the aged Henry Clay proposed a compromise. For the North, Congress would admit California as a free state; the land in dispute between Texas and New Mexico would go to New Mexico; popular sovereignty would decide the issue of slavery in the New Mexico and Utah territories (all of the Mexican cession outside of California); and there would be no slave trade in the District of Columbia. For the South, Congress would enact a tougher Fugitive Slave Law, promise not to abolish slavery in the District of Columbia, and declare that it did not have jurisdiction over the interstate slave trade; the federal government would pay Texas's $10 million pre-annexation debt.

The Kansas-Nebraska Act

All illusion of sectional peace ended abruptly in 1854 when Senator Stephen A. Douglas of Illinois introduced a bill in Congress to organize the area west of Missouri and Iowa as the territories of Kansas and Nebraska on the basis of popular sovereignty. The Kansas-Nebraska Act aroused a storm of outrage in the North, which viewed the repeal of the Missouri Compromise as the breaking of a solemn agreement, hastened the disintegration of the Whig Party, and divided the Democratic Party along North-South lines. Springing to life almost overnight as a result of northern fury at the Kansas-Nebraska Act was the Republican Party. This party included diverse elements whose sole unifying principle was banning slavery from all the nation's territories, confining slavery to the states where it already existed, and preventing the further spread of slavery.

The Dred Scott Decision

In *Dred Scott v. Sanford* (1857), the Supreme Court attempted to settle the slavery question. The case involved a Missouri slave, Dred Scott, whom the abolitionists had encouraged to sue for his freedom on the basis that his owner had taken him to a free state, Illinois, for several years and then to a free territory, Wisconsin. The Court attempted to read the extreme southern position on slavery into the Constitution, ruling not only that Scott had no standing to sue in federal court but also that temporary residence in a free state, even for several years, did not make a slave free. In addition, the Court ruling signified that the Missouri Compromise (already a dead letter by that time) had been unconstitutional all along because Congress did not have the authority to exclude slavery from a territory nor did territorial governments have the right to prohibit slavery.

The Election of 1860

As the 1860 presidential election approached, the Republicans met in Chicago, confident of victory and determined to do nothing to jeopardize their favorable position. Accordingly, they rejected as too radical the front-running candidate, New York Senator William H. Seward, in favor of Illinois's favorite son, Abraham Lincoln (1809–1865). The platform called for federal support of a transcontinental railroad and for the containment of slavery. On election day, the voting went along strictly sectional lines. Although Lincoln led in popular votes, he was short of a majority. He did have, however, the needed majority of Electoral College votes and was elected president.

The Secession

On December 20, 1860, South Carolina, by vote of a special convention, seceded from the Union. By February 1, 1861, six more states (Alabama, Georgia, Florida, Mississippi, Louisiana, and Texas) had followed suit. Representatives of the seceded states met in Montgomery, Alabama, in February 1861 and declared themselves to be the Confederate States of America. They elected former secretary of war and United States senator Jefferson Davis (1808–1889) of Mississippi as president and Alexander Stephens (1812–1883) of Georgia as vice president.

Beginnings of the Civil War

In his inaugural address, Lincoln urged Southerners to reconsider their actions but warned that the Union was perpetual, that states could not secede, and that he would therefore hold the federal forts and installations in the South. Only two remained in federal hands: Fort Pickens, off Pensacola, Florida; and Fort Sumter, in the harbor of Charleston, South Carolina.

From Major Robert Anderson, commander of the small garrison at Fort Sumter, Lincoln soon received word that supplies were running low. Desiring to send in the needed supplies, Lincoln informed the governor of South Carolina of his intentions but promised that no attempt would be made to send arms, ammunition, or reinforcements unless Southerners initiated hostilities. Confederate General P. G. T. Beauregard, acting on orders from President Davis, demanded Anderson's surrender. Anderson said he would surrender if not resupplied. Knowing supplies were on the way, the Confederates opened fire at 4:30 a.m. on April 12, 1861. The next day, the fort surrendered. The day following Sumter's surrender, Lincoln declared an insurrection and called for the states to provide 75,000 volunteers to put it down. In response, Virginia, Tennessee, North Carolina, and Arkansas declared their secession. The remaining slave states—Delaware, Kentucky, Maryland, and Missouri—wavered but stayed with the Union.

The North enjoyed many advantages over the South. It had the majority of wealth and was vastly superior in industry. The North also had an advantage of almost three to one in manpower; over one-third of the South's population was slaves, whom Southerners would not use as soldiers. Unlike the South, the North received large numbers of immigrants during the war. The North retained control of the U.S. Navy; it could command the sea and blockade the South. Finally, the North enjoyed a much superior system of railroads. The South did, however, have some advantages. It was vast in size and difficult to conquer. In addition, its troops would be fighting on their own ground, a fact that would give them the advantage of familiarity with the terrain and the added motivation of defending their homes and families.

The Homestead Act and the Morrill Land Grant Act

In 1862, Congress passed two highly important acts dealing with domestic affairs in the North. The Homestead Act granted 160 acres of government land free of charge to any person who would farm it for at least five years. Many of the settlers of the West used the provisions of this act. The Morrill Land Grant Act offered large amounts of federal land to states that would establish "agricultural and mechanical" colleges. The founding of many of the nation's large state universities was under the provisions of this act.

The Emancipation Proclamation

By mid-1862, Lincoln, under pressure from radical elements of his own party and hoping to create a favorable impression on foreign public opinion, determined to issue the Emancipation Proclamation, which declared free all slaves in areas still in rebellion as of January 1, 1863. At Seward's recommendation,

Lincoln waited to announce the proclamation until the North won some sort of victory. The Battle of Antietam (September 17, 1862) provided this victory.

Northern Victory

In September 1864, word came that General William Sherman (1820–1891) had taken Atlanta. The capture of this vital southern rail and manufacturing center brought an enormous boost to northern morale. Along with other northern victories that summer and fall, it ensured a resounding election victory for Lincoln and the continuation of the war on highly favorable terms for the North.

Confederate General Robert E. Lee (1807–1870) abandoned Richmond on April 3, 1865, and attempted to escape with what was left of his army. Pursued by Ulysses S. Grant (1822–1885), Northern forces cornered Lee's troops and forced his surrender at Appomattox, Virginia, on April 9, 1865. Other Confederate troops still holding out in various parts of the South surrendered over the next few weeks. Lincoln did not live to receive news of the final surrenders. On April 14, 1865, John Wilkes Booth shot Lincoln in the back of the head while the president was watching a play in Ford's Theater in Washington, DC.

Reconstruction

In 1865, Congress created the Freedman's Bureau to provide food, clothing, and education to former slaves and to look after their interests. To restore legal governments in the seceded states, Lincoln developed a policy that made it relatively easy for southern states to enter the collateral process.

Congress passed a Civil Rights Act in 1866, declaring that all citizens born in the United States are, regardless of race, equal citizens under the law. This act became the model of the Fourteenth Amendment to the Constitution.

President Andrew Johnson obeyed the letter but not the spirit of the Reconstruction acts. Congress, angry at his refusal to cooperate, sought in vain for grounds to impeach him. In August 1867, Johnson violated the Tenure of Office Act, which forbade the president from removing from office officials who had been approved by the Senate. This test of the act's constitutionality took place not in the courts but in Congress. The House of Representatives impeached Johnson, and he came within one vote of being removed from office by the Senate.

The Fifteenth Amendment

In 1868, the Republicans nominated Ulysses S. Grant for president. His narrow victory prompted Republican leaders to decide that it would be politically expedient to give the vote to black men, northern as well as southern. The vote was extended only to black *men* because as of 1868 no women were allowed to vote. (Woman suffrage would not come for another half-century.) For this purpose, leaders of the North drew up and submitted to the states the Fifteenth Amendment. Ironically, the idea was so unpopular in the North that it won the necessary three-fourths approval only because Congress required the southern states to ratify it.

Industrialism

In the late nineteenth and early twentieth centuries, captains of industry—such as John D. Rockefeller in oil, J. P. Morgan in banking, Gustavus Swift in meat processing, Andrew Carnegie in steel, and E. H. Harriman in railroads—created major industrial empires. In 1886, Samuel Gompers and Adolph Strasser put together a combination of national craft unions, the American Federation of Labor (AFL), to represent labor's concerns about wages, hours, and safety conditions. Although militant in its use of the strike and in its demand for collective bargaining in labor contracts with large corporations, the AFL did not promote violence or radicalism.

The Spanish-American War

The Cuban revolt against Spain in 1895 threatened American business interests in Cuba. Sensational "yellow" journalism and nationalistic statements from officials such as Assistant Secretary of the Navy Theodore Roosevelt (1858–1919) encouraged popular support for direct American military intervention on behalf of Cuban independence.

On March 27, 1897, President William McKinley (1843–1901) asked Spain to call an armistice, accept American mediation to end the war, and stop using concentration camps in Cuba. Spain refused to comply. On April 21, Congress declared war on Spain with the objective of establishing Cuban independence (Teller Amendment). The first U.S. forces landed in Cuba on June 22, 1898, and by July 17 had defeated the Spanish forces. Spain ceded the Philippines, Puerto Rico, and Guam to the United States in return for a payment of $20 million to Spain for the Philippines.

Progressive Reforms and Social Change

On September 6, 1901, while attending the Pan American Exposition in Buffalo, New York, President McKinley was shot by Leon Czolgosz, an anarchist. The president died on September 14. Theodore Roosevelt, at age 42, became the nation's twenty-fifth president and its youngest president to date.

In accordance with the Antitrust Policy (1902), Roosevelt ordered the Justice Department to prosecute corporations pursuing monopolistic practices. Attorney General P. C. Knox first brought suit against the Northern Securities Company, a railroad holding corporation put together by J. P. Morgan, and then moved against Rockefeller's Standard Oil Company. By the time he left office in 1909, Roosevelt had indictments against 25 monopolies.

Roosevelt engineered the separation of Panama from Colombia and the recognition of Panama as an independent country. The Hay-Bunau-Varilla Treaty of 1903 granted the United States control of the Canal Zone in

Panama for $10 million and an annual fee of $250,000; the control would begin nine years after ratification of the treaty by both parties. Construction of the Panama Canal began in 1904 and was completed in 1914.

In 1905, the African American intellectual and militant W. E. B. DuBois founded the Niagara Movement, which called for federal legislation to protect racial equality and to grant full citizenship rights. Formed in 1909, the National Association for the Advancement of Colored People pressed actively for the rights of the African Americans. A third organization of the time, the radical labor organization called the Industrial Workers of the World (IWW, or Wobblies; 1905–1924), promoted violence and revolution. The IWW organized effective strikes in the textile industry in 1912 and among a few western miners' groups, but it had little appeal to the average American worker. After the Red Scare of 1919, the government worked to smash the IWW and deported many of its immigrant leaders and members.

The nation elected Democratic candidate Woodrow Wilson (1856–1924) as president in 1912. Before the outbreak of World War I in 1914, Wilson, working with cooperative majorities in both houses of Congress, achieved much of the remaining progressive agenda, including lower tariff reform (Underwood-Simmons Act, 1913); the Sixteenth Amendment (graduated income tax, 1913); the Seventeenth Amendment (direct election of senators, 1913); the Federal Reserve banking system (that provided regulation and flexibility to monetary policy, 1913); the Federal Trade Commission (to investigate unfair business practices, 1914); and the Clayton Antitrust Act (improving the old Sherman Act and protecting labor unions and farm cooperatives from prosecution, 1914).

When America entered World War I in 1917, President Wilson maintained that the war would make the world safe for democracy. In an address to Congress on January 8, 1918, he presented his specific peace plan in the form of the Fourteen Points. The first five points called for open rather than secret peace treaties, freedom of the seas, free trade, arms reduction, and a fair adjustment of colonial claims. The next eight points addressed national aspirations of various European peoples and the adjustment of boundaries. The fourteenth point, which he considered the most important and which he had espoused as early as 1916, called for a "general association of nations" to preserve the peace. This point served as the conceptual basis for the United Nations.

Discrimination

Although many Americans had called for immigration restriction since the late nineteenth century, the only major restriction imposed on immigration by 1920 had been the Chinese Exclusion Act of 1882. Labor leaders believed that immigrants depressed wages and impeded unionization. Some progressives believed that they created social problems. In June 1917, Congress, over Wilson's veto, imposed a literacy test for immigrants and excluded many Asian nationalities.

In 1921, Congress passed the Emergency Quota Act. In practice, the law admitted almost as many immigrants as the nation wanted from such nations as Britain, Ireland, and Germany but severely restricted Italians, Greeks, Poles, and eastern European Jews hoping to enter the country. The law became effective in 1922 and reduced the number of immigrants annually to about 40 percent of the 1921 total. Congress then passed the National Origins Act of 1924, which further reduced the number of southern and eastern European immigrants and cut the annual immigration total to 20 percent of the 1921 figure. In 1927, the nation set the annual maximum number of immigrants allowed into the United States at 150,000.

On Thanksgiving Day in 1915, William J. Simmons founded the Knights of the Ku Klux Klan. Its purpose was to intimidate African Americans, who were experiencing an apparent rise in status during World War I. The Klan's methods of repression included cross burnings, tar and featherings, kidnappings, lynchings, and burnings. The Klan was not a political party, but it endorsed and opposed candidates and exerted considerable control over elections and politicians in at least nine states.

Fundamentalist Protestants, under the leadership of William Jennings Bryan, began a campaign in 1921 to prohibit the teaching of evolution in the schools and protect the belief in the literal biblical account of creation. The South especially received the idea well.

The Great Depression

Signs of recession were apparent before the market crash in 1929. The farm economy, which involved almost 25 percent of the population, as well as the coal, railroad, and New England textile industries, had not been prosperous during the 1920s.

After 1927, new construction declined and auto sales began to sag. Many workers lost their jobs before the crash of 1929. Stock prices increased throughout the decade. The boom in prices and volume of sales was especially active after 1925 and was intensive from 1928 to 1929. Careful investors recognized that the overpricing of stocks was occurring and began to sell to take their profits.

During October 1929, prices declined as more people began to sell their stock. "Black Thursday," October 24, 1929, saw the trading of almost 13 million shares; this was a large number for that time, and prices fell precipitously. Investment banks tried to boost the market by buying, but on October 29, "Black Tuesday," the market fell about 40 points, with 16.5 million shares traded.

The effects of the Great Depression were widespread, as many people suffered economic loss.

The Hawley-Smoot Tariff of June 1930 raised duties on both agricultural and manufactured imports. Chartered by Congress in 1932, the Reconstruction Finance Corporation loaned money to railroads, banks, and other financial institutions. It prevented the failure of basic firms, on which many other elements of the economy depended, but many people criticized it as relief for the rich. The Federal Home Loan Bank Act, passed in July 1932, created home loan banks, which made loans to building and loan associations, savings banks, and insurance companies. Its purpose was to help avoid foreclosures on homes.

The First New Deal

Franklin D. Roosevelt (1882–1945), governor of New York, easily defeated Herbert Hoover in the election of 1932. At his inauguration on March 4, 1933, the American economic system seemed to be on the verge of collapse. Roosevelt, assuring the nation that "the only thing we have to fear is fear itself," called for a special session of Congress to convene on March 9 and asked for "broad executive powers to wage war against the emergency." Two days later, he closed all banks for a brief time and forbade the export of gold or the redemption of currency in gold. A special session of Congress, from March 9 to June 16, 1933 ("The Hundred Days"), passed a great body of legislation that has left a lasting mark on the nation. Historians have divided Roosevelt's legislation into the First New Deal (1933–1935) and a new wave of programs beginning in 1935 called the Second New Deal. Following are some of the achievements of the First New Deal:

The *Emergency Banking Relief Act*, passed on March 9, 1933, the first day of the special congressional session, provided additional funds for banks from the Reconstruction Finance Corporation and the Federal Reserve, allowed the Treasury to open sound banks after 10 days and to merge or liquidate unsound ones, and forbade the hoarding or exporting of gold. On March 12, Roosevelt assured the public of the soundness of the banks in the first of many "fireside chats" or radio addresses. People believed him, and most banks were soon open, with deposits outnumbering withdrawals.

The *Banking Act of 1933*, or the *Glass-Steagall Act*, established the Federal Deposit Insurance Corporation to insure individual deposits in commercial banks and to separate commercial banking from the more speculative activity of investment banking. The Federal Emergency Relief Act appropriated $500 million for state and local governments to distribute to aid the poor. The act also established the Federal Emergency Relief Administration under Harry Hopkins (1890–1946).

The *Civilian Conservation Corps* enrolled 250,000 young men aged 18 to 24 from families on relief to go to camps where they worked on flood control, soil conservation, and forest projects under the direction of the War Department.

The *Public Works Administration* distributed $3.3 billion to state and local governments for building projects such as schools, highways, and hospitals.

The *Agricultural Adjustment Act of 1933* created the Agricultural Adjustment Administration. Farmers agreed to reduce production of principal farm commodities and received subsidies in return. Farm prices increased; when owners took land out of cultivation, however, tenants and sharecroppers suffered. The repeal of the law came in January 1936 on the grounds that the processing tax was not constitutional.

The *National Industrial Recovery Act (NIRA)* was the cornerstone of the recovery program. In June 1933, Congress passed this act and created the National Recovery Administration (NRA); the goal was the self-regulation of business and the development of fair prices, wages, hours, and working conditions. Section 7a of the NIRA permitted collective bargaining for workers; laborers would test the federal support for their bargaining in the days to come. The slogan of the NRA was "We do our part." The economy improved but did not recover.

The Second New Deal

Following are some of the accomplishments of the Second New Deal:

The *Works Progress Administration* (WPA) began in May 1935, following the passage of the Emergency Relief Appropriations Act of April 1935. The WPA employed people from the relief rolls for 30 hours of work a week at pay double that of the relief payment but less than private employment.

The *Rural Electrification Administration*, created in May 1935, provided loans and WPA labor to electric cooperatives so they could build lines into rural areas that the private companies did not serve.

The *Social Security Act*, passed in August 1935, established for persons over age 65 a retirement plan to be funded by a tax on wages paid equally by employee and employer. The government paid the first benefits, ranging from $10 to $85 per month in 1942. Another provision of the act forced states to initiate unemployment insurance programs.

Labor Unions

The 1935 passage of the National Labor Relations Act, or the Wagner Act, resulted in a massive growth of union membership but at the expense of bitter conflict within the labor movement. The American Federation of Labor (AFL), formed in 1886, was composed primarily of craft unions. However, some leaders wanted to unionize the mass-production industries, such as automobiles and rubber, with industrial unions. In November 1935, John L. Lewis formed the Committee for Industrial Organization (CIO) to unionize basic industries, presumably within the AFL. President William Green of the AFL ordered the CIO to disband in January 1936. When the rebels refused, the AFL expelled them. The insurgents then reorganized the CIO as the independent Congress of Industrial Organizations. Labor strikes, particularly in the textile mills, marked the end of the 1930s.

American Response to the War in Europe

In August 1939, Roosevelt created the War Resources Board to develop a plan for industrial mobilization in the event of war. The next month, he established the Office of Emergency Management in the White House to centralize mobilization activities.

Roosevelt officially proclaimed the neutrality of the United States on September 5, 1939. The Democratic Congress, in a vote that followed party lines, passed a new Neutrality Act in November. It allowed the cash-and-carry sale of arms and short-term loans to belligerents but forbade American ships to trade with belligerents or Americans to travel on belligerent ships. Roosevelt determined that to aid Britain in every way possible was the best way to avoid war with Germany. In September 1940, he signed an agreement to give Britain 50 American destroyers in return for a 99-year lease on air and naval bases in British territories in Newfoundland, Bermuda, and the Caribbean.

American Entry into World War II

In late July 1941, the United States placed an embargo on the export of aviation gasoline, lubricants, and scrap iron and steel to Japan and granted an additional loan to China. In December, additional articles—iron ore and pig iron, some chemicals, machine tools, and other products—fell under the embargo.

In October 1941, a new military cabinet headed by General Hideki Tojo took control of Japan. The Japanese secretly decided to make a final effort to negotiate and to go to war if there was no solution by November 25. A new round of talks followed in Washington, but neither side would make a substantive change in its position. The Japanese made the final decision on December 1 for an attack on the United States. Specifically, the Japanese planned a major offensive to take the Dutch East Indies, Malaya, and the Philippines and to obtain the oil, metals, and other raw materials they needed. At the same time, they intended to attack Pearl Harbor in Hawaii to destroy the American Pacific fleet to keep it from interfering with their plans.

At 7:55 a.m. on Sunday, December 7, 1941, the first wave of Japanese carrier-based planes attacked the American fleet in Pearl Harbor. A second wave followed at 8:50 am. The United States suffered two battleships sunk, six damaged and out of action, three cruisers and three destroyers sunk or damaged, several lesser vessels destroyed or damaged, and the destruction of all the 150 aircraft on the ground. A total of 2,323 American servicemen were killed and about 1,100 were wounded. The Japanese lost 29 planes, five midget submarines, and one fleet submarine.

On December 8, 1941, Congress declared war on Japan, with one dissenting vote from Representative Jeanette Rankin of Montana. On December 11, Germany and Italy declared war on the United States. Great Britain and the United States then established the Combined Chiefs of Staff, headquartered in Washington, to direct Anglo-American military operations.

On January 1, 1942, representatives of 26 nations met in Washington, D.C., and signed the Declaration of the United Nations, pledged themselves to the principles of the Atlantic Charter, and promised not to make a separate peace with their common enemies.

The End of World War II

The Army Corps of Engineers established the Manhattan Engineering District in August 1942 for the purpose of developing an atomic bomb; the program eventually took the name the Manhattan Project. J.

Robert Oppenheimer directed the design and construction of a transportable atomic bomb at Los Alamos, New Mexico. On July 16, 1945, the Manhattan Project exploded the first atomic bomb at Alamogordo, New Mexico.

The *Enola Gay* dropped an atomic bomb on Hiroshima, Japan, on August 6, 1945. In the short term, the bomb killed about 78,000 persons and injured 100,000 more. Subsequently, there were additional radiation-related casualties. On August 9, the United States dropped a second bomb on Nagasaki, Japan. Japan surrendered on August 14, 1945, and signed the formal surrender on September 2.

The Holocaust

The Holocaust, a systematic ethnic cleansing, began about 1933 and continued to the end of World War II (WWII) in 1945. During this period, Adolph Hitler was the German leader. In addition to Jewish people, the "National Socialist German Worker's Party," or Nazis, also targeted other minority groups such as gypsies, homosexuals, Jehovah's Witnesses, and disabled people. It is estimated that 11 million people were killed during the Holocaust. Six million of these people were Jews. The Nazis killed approximately two-thirds of all Jews living in Europe, and an estimated 1.1 million of these lost lives were children.

The persecution of Jews began on a large scale on April 1, 1933, when the Nazis announced a boycott of all Jewish-run businesses in Germany. In 1935, newly established laws began to exclude Jews from public life. The Nuremberg Laws included a law that stripped German Jews of their citizenship and a law that prohibited marriages between Jews and Germans. These laws set the legal model for more anti-Jewish legislation that the Nazis issued over the next several years. Some of these laws excluded Jews from places like parks, fired them from civil service jobs, made them register their property, and prevented Jewish doctors from working on anyone other than Jewish patients.

In November 1938, the Nazis engaged in terrifying acts against Jews in Austria and Germany in what has been termed "Kristallnacht." This night of violence resulted in the looting and burning of synagogues, breaking the windows of Jewish-owned businesses, and looting of their stores. Many Jews were physically attacked, and approximately 30,000 Jews were arrested and sent to concentration camps that night.

After World War II started in 1939 and the Nazis began occupying surrounding countries, they ordered the Jews to wear an emblem of "The Star of David" on their clothing so that they could be easily recognized and targeted.

Anne Frank

Anne Frank was one of over one million Jewish children wearing "The Star of David" who died in the Holocaust. She was born on June 12, 1929, in Frankfurt, Germany. During the first years of her life, Anne lived with her parents and sister, Margot, in an apartment on the outskirts of Frankfurt. After the Nazis came into power in 1933, the family moved to Amsterdam, in the Netherlands, where Anne's father, Otto Frank, had business connections.

The Netherlands was occupied in May 1940 by the Germans. In July 1942, German authorities and their Dutch collaborators began to assemble Jewish people from throughout the Netherlands at a place called Westerbork, a transit camp near the Dutch town of Assen, in Friesland, not far from the German border. From Westerbork, German officials deported the Jews to the Polish concentration camps in German-occupied Poland.

During the first half of July 1942, Anne and her family went into hiding in a secret attic apartment. For two years, they lived in this apartment behind the office of the family-owned business at 263 Prinsengracht Street, which Anne referred to in her diary as the Secret Annex. Otto Frank and his friends and colleagues, Johannes Kleiman, Victor Kugler, Jan Gies, and Miep Gies, had previously helped to prepare the hiding place and smuggled food and clothing to the Franks at great risk to their own lives. On August 4, 1944, the Gestapo (German Secret State Police) discovered the hiding place after being tipped off by an anonymous Dutch caller. That same day, the Gestapo sent them to Westerbork, and one month later, in September 1944, the SS and police authorities placed the Franks on a train transport from Westerbork to Auschwitz, a concentration camp complex in German-occupied Poland. Because they had been selected for labor due to their youth, Anne and her sister Margot were transferred to the Bergen-Belsen concentration camp near Celle, in northern Germany, in late October 1944. Both sisters died of typhus in March 1945, just a few weeks before British troops liberated Bergen-Belsen on April 15, 1945. Anne's mother, Edith Frank, died in Auschwitz in early January 1945. Only Anne's father, Otto Frank, survived the war. The Soviet forces liberated Otto at Auschwitz on January 27, 1945.

While in hiding, Anne kept a diary in which she recorded her fears, hopes, and experiences. This diary was found in the secret apartment after the family was arrested. The diary was kept for Anne by Miep Gies, one of the people who had helped hide the Franks. It was published after the war in many languages and is used in thousands of middle school and high school curricula in Europe and the Americas. Through this diary, Anne Frank has become a symbol of the children who died in the Holocaust and a source of inspiration to many readers.

American Post-War Foreign Policy

In February 1947, Great Britain notified the United States that it could no longer aid the Greek government in its war against Communist insurgents. The next month, President Truman asked Congress for $400 million in military and economic aid for Greece and Turkey. Truman argued in what is now known as the Truman Doctrine that the United States must support free peoples who were resisting Communist domination.

Secretary of State George C. Marshall proposed in June 1947 that the United States provide economic aid to help rebuild Europe. The following March, Congress passed the European Recovery Program; popularly known as the Marshall Plan, the program provided more than $12 billion in aid.

Spread of Communism

On June 25, 1950, Communist North Korea invaded South Korea. President Truman committed U.S. forces under the United Nations (UN) auspices; General Douglas MacArthur would command the troops. By October, UN forces (mostly American) had driven north of the 38th parallel, which divided North and South Korea. Chinese troops attacked MacArthur's forces on November 26, pushing them south of the 38th parallel, but by spring 1951, UN forces had recovered their offensive. The armistice of June 1953 left Korea divided along virtually the same boundary that had existed before the war.

After several years of nationalist war against French occupation, in July 1954 France, Great Britain, the Soviet Union, and China signed the Geneva Accords, which divided Vietnam along the 17th parallel. The north would be under the leadership of Ho Chi Minh and the South under Emperor Bao Dai. The purpose of the scheduled elections was to unify the country, but Ngo Dinh Diem overthrew Bao Dai and prevented the elections from taking place. The United States supplied economic aid to South Vietnam.

In January 1959, Fidel Castro overthrew the dictator of Cuba. Castro criticized the United States, moved closer to the Soviet Union, and signed a trade agreement with the Soviets in February 1960. The United States prohibited the importation of Cuban sugar in October 1960 and broke off diplomatic relations in January 1961.

Space Exploration

The launching of the Soviet space satellite *Sputnik* on October 4, 1957, created fear that America was falling behind technologically. Although the United States launched *Explorer I* on January 31, 1958, concerns continued unabated. In 1958, Congress established the National Aeronautics and Space Administration, or NASA, to coordinate research and development and passed the National Defense Education Act to provide grants and loans for education. Some of NASA's accomplishments are discussed in Chapter 5.

Civil Rights

Following are some major events in the early years of the Civil Rights Movement:

- President Eisenhower completed the formal integration of the armed forces; desegregated public services in Washington, DC, naval yards and veterans' hospitals; and appointed a civil rights commission.

- In *Brown v. Board of Education of Topeka* (1954), Thurgood Marshall, lawyer for the National Association for the Advancement of Colored People, challenged the doctrine of "separate but equal" (*Plessy v. Ferguson*, 1896). The Supreme Court declared that separate educational facilities were inherently unequal. In 1955, the Court ordered states to integrate "with all deliberate speed."

- On December 11, 1955, in Montgomery, Alabama, Rosa Parks, a 42-year-old African American woman, refused to give up her seat on a city bus to a white man and faced arrest, an act of enduring symbolic importance.

- Under the leadership of the Reverend Martin Luther King Jr. (1929–1968), African Americans of Montgomery organized a bus boycott that lasted for a year and influenced similar actions in other cities.

- In February 1960, a segregated lunch counter in Greensboro, North Carolina, denied four African American students service; the students staged a sit-in. This inspired sit-ins elsewhere in the South and led to the formation of the Student Nonviolent Coordinating Committee, which had a chief aim of ending segregation in public accommodations.

- President Kennedy presented a comprehensive civil rights bill to Congress in 1963. With the bill held up in Congress, 200,000 people marched and demonstrated on its behalf, and Martin Luther King Jr. gave his "I Have a Dream" speech.

The New Frontier

After Democratic Senator John F. Kennedy (1917–1963) won the presidential election of 1960, the Justice Department, under Attorney General Robert F. Kennedy, began to push for civil rights, including desegregation of interstate transportation in the South, integration of schools, and supervision of elections.

America and Cuba

Under President Eisenhower, the Central Intelligence Agency had begun training some 2,000 men to invade Cuba and to overthrow Fidel Castro. On April 19, 1961, this force invaded at the Bay of Pigs; opposing forces pinned them down, demanded their surrender, and captured some 1,200 men.

On October 14, 1962, a U-2 reconnaissance plane brought photographic evidence of the construction of missile sites in Cuba. President Kennedy, on October 22, announced a blockade of Cuba and called on the Soviet premier, Nikita Khrushchev (1894–1971), to dismantle the missile bases and remove all weapons capable of attacking the United States from Cuba. Six days later, Khrushchev backed down and withdrew the missiles. Kennedy lifted the blockade.

Civil Rights and Social Unrest

Following the assassination of John F. Kennedy and the succession of Lyndon B. Johnson to the presidency, the 1964 Civil Rights Act outlawed racial discrimination by employers and unions, created the Equal Employment Opportunity Commission to enforce the law, and eliminated the remaining restrictions on black voting.

In 1965, Martin Luther King Jr. announced a voter registration drive. With help from the federal courts, he dramatized his effort by leading a march from Selma, Alabama, to Montgomery, Alabama, between March 21 and 25. The Voting Rights Act of 1965 authorized the attorney general to appoint officials to register voters.

Seventy percent of African Americans lived in city ghettos at this time. In 1966, New York and Chicago experienced riots, and the following year there were riots in Newark and Detroit. The Kerner Commission, appointed to investigate the riots, concluded that the focus of the riots was a social system that prevented African Americans from getting good jobs and crowded them into ghettos. On April 4, 1968, James Earl Ray assassinated Martin Luther King Jr. in Memphis, Tennessee. Ray was an escaped convict; he pled guilty to the murder and received a sentence of 99 years in prison. Riots in more than 100 cities followed.

Beginnings of the Vietnam War

After the defeat of the French in Vietnam in 1954, the United States sent military advisers to South Vietnam to aid the government of Ngo Dinh Diem. The pro-Communist Vietcong forces gradually grew in strength because Diem failed to follow through on promised reforms and because of support from North Vietnam, the Soviet Union, and China. "Hawks" defended the president's policy and, drawing on the containment theory, said that the nation had the responsibility to resist aggression. The claim was if Vietnam should fall, all Southeast Asia would eventually go. "Doves" argued that the war was a civil war in which the United States should not meddle.

On January 31, 1968, the first day of the Vietnamese new year (Tet), the Vietcong attacked numerous cities and towns, American bases, and even Saigon. Although they suffered large losses, the Vietcong won a psychological victory as American opinion quickly began turning against the war.

The End of the Vietnam War

President Richard M. Nixon (1913–1994) initiated "Vietnamization," the effort to build up South Vietnamese forces while withdrawing American troops. In 1969, Nixon reduced American troop strength by 60,000 but at the same time ordered the bombing of Cambodia, a neutral country. In the summer of 1972, negotiations between the United States and North Vietnam began in Paris. A few days before the 1972 presidential election, Henry Kissinger, the president's national security adviser, announced that "peace was at hand."

Nixon resumed the bombing of North Vietnam in December 1972; he claimed that the North Vietnamese were not bargaining in good faith. In January 1973, the two sides reached a settlement in which the North Vietnamese retained control over large areas of the South and agreed to release American prisoners of war within 60 days. Nearly 60,000 Americans had been killed and 300,000 more wounded, and the war had cost American taxpayers $109 billion. On March 29, 1973, the last American combat troops left South Vietnam. The North Vietnamese forces continued to push back the South Vietnamese, and in April 1975, Saigon fell to the North.

Watergate

What became known as the Watergate crisis began during the 1972 presidential campaign, following which Nixon was reelected. Early on the morning of June 17, a security officer for the Committee for the Reelection of the President, along with four other men, broke into Democratic headquarters at the Watergate apartment complex in Washington, D.C. The authorities caught the men going through files and installing electronic eavesdropping devices. In March 1974, a grand jury indicted some of Nixon's top aides and named Nixon an unindicted coconspirator. Meanwhile, the House Judiciary Committee televised its debate over impeachment. The committee charged the president with obstructing justice, misusing presidential power, and failing to obey the committee's subpoenas. Before the House voted on impeachment impeachment, Nixon announced his resignation on August 8, 1974, to take effect at noon the following day. Gerald Ford (1913–2006) then became president and almost immediately encountered controversy when in September 1974 he offered to pardon Nixon. Nixon accepted the offer although he admitted no wrongdoing and had not yet been charged with any crime.

The Carter Administration

Having won the 1976 presidential election, Jimmy Carter offered amnesty to Americans who had fled the draft and gone to other countries during the Vietnam War. He established the Departments of Energy and Education and placed the civil service on a merit basis. He created a "superfund" for cleanup of chemical waste dumps, established controls over strip mining, and protected 100 million acres of Alaskan wilderness from development.

With respect to foreign policy, Carter negotiated a controversial treaty with Panama, affirmed by the Senate in 1978, that provided for the transfer of ownership of the canal to Panama in 1999 and guaranteed its neutrality. In 1978, Carter negotiated the Camp David Accords between Israel and Egypt. Israel promised to return occupied land in the Sinai to Egypt in exchange for Egyptian recognition, a process completed in 1982. An agreement to negotiate the Palestinian refugee problem proved ineffective.

In 1978, a revolution forced the Shah of Iran to flee the country and replaced him with a religious leader, Ayatollah Ruhollah Khomeini (ca. 1900–1989). Because the United States had supported the Shah with arms and money, the revolutionaries were strongly anti-American, calling the United States the "Great Satan." After Carter allowed the exiled Shah to come to the United States for medical treatment in October 1979, some 400 Iranians broke into the American embassy in Tehran on November 4 and took the occupants captive. They demanded the return of the Shah to Iran for trial, the confiscation of his wealth, and the presentation of his wealth to Iran. Carter rejected these demands; instead, he froze Iranian assets in the United States and established a trade embargo against Iran. After extensive negotiations with Iran, in which Algeria acted as an intermediary, the Iranians freed the American hostages on January 20, 1981.

Attacking Big Government

After election to the presidency in 1980, Ronald Reagan placed priority on cutting taxes. He based his approach on "supply-side" economics, the idea that if government left more money in the hands of the people, they would invest rather than spend the excess on consumer goods. The results would be greater production, more jobs, and greater prosperity, resulting in more income for the government despite lower tax rates. However, from a deficit of $59 billion in 1980, the federal budget deficit increased to $195 billion by 1983. Reagan ended ongoing antitrust suits against IBM and AT&T and fulfilled his promise to reduce government interference with business.

Iran-Contra

In 1985 and 1986, several Reagan officials sold arms to the Iranians in hopes of encouraging them to use their influence in obtaining the release of American hostages being held in Lebanon. Profits from these sales went to the Nicaraguan *contras*—a militant group opposed to the left-leaning elected government—in an attempt to get around congressional restrictions on funding the *contras*. The attorney general appointed a special prosecutor, and Congress held hearings on the affair in May 1987.

Operation Just Cause

Since winning the presidential election in 1988, the Bush administration had been concerned that Panamanian dictator Manuel Noriega was providing an important link in the drug traffic between South America and the United States. After economic sanctions, diplomatic efforts, and an October 1989 coup failed to oust Noriega, Bush ordered 12,000 troops into Panama on December 20 for what became known as Operation Just Cause. On January 3, 1990, Noriega surrendered to the Americans and faced drug-trafficking charges in the United States. Found guilty in 1992, his sentence was 40 years.

Persian Gulf Crisis

On August 2, 1990, Iraq invaded Kuwait, an act that President Bush denounced as "naked aggression." The United States quickly banned most trade with Iraq, froze Iraq's and Kuwait's assets in the United States, and sent aircraft carriers to the Persian Gulf. On August 6, after the UN Security Council condemned the invasion, Bush ordered the deployment of air, sea, and land forces to Saudi Arabia and dubbed the operation Desert Shield.

On February 23, 1991, the allied air assault began. Four days later, Bush announced the liberation of Kuwait and ordered offensive operations to cease. The United Nations established the terms for the cease-fire, which Iraq accepted on April 6.

Health Care

In October 1993, the Clinton administration proposed legislation to reform the health care system, which included universal coverage with a guaranteed benefits package, managed competition through health care alliances that would bargain with insurance companies, and employer mandates to provide health insurance for employees. With most Republicans and small business, insurance, and medical business interests opposed to the legislation, the Democrats dropped their attempt at a compromise package in September 1994.

Presidential Impeachment and Acquittal

President Clinton received criticism for alleged wrongdoing in connection with a real estate development called Whitewater. While governor of Arkansas, Clinton had invested in Whitewater, along with James B. and Susan McDougal, owners of a failed savings and loan institution. After Congress renewed the independent counsel law, a three-judge panel appointed Kenneth W. Starr to the new role of independent prosecutor. The Starr investigation yielded massive findings in late 1998, roughly midway into Clinton's second term, including information on an adulterous affair that Clinton had had with Monica Lewinsky while she was an intern at the White House. It was on charges stemming from this report that the House of Representatives impeached Clinton in December 1998 for perjury and obstruction of justice. The Senate acquitted him of all charges in February 1999.

Continuing Crisis in the Balkans

During President Clinton's second term, continued political unrest abroad and civil war in the Balkans continued to be a major foreign policy challenge. In 1999, the Serbian government attacked ethnic Albanians in Kosovo, a province of Serbia. In response, North Atlantic Treaty Organization (NATO) forces, led by the United States, bombed Serbia. Several weeks of bombing forced Serbian forces to withdraw from Kosovo.

The Election of 2000

The outcome of the 2000 presidential election was unclear for several weeks after the election. Al Gore won the popular vote, but the Electoral College vote was very close, and Florida was pivotal in deciding the election. George W. Bush (1946), son of the former president George H. W. Bush, appeared to win Florida, but by a very small margin. Controversy over how to conduct the recount of the Florida votes led to a series of court challenges, with the matter ultimately decided by the U.S. Supreme Court.

Terrorism

On the morning of September 11, 2001, hijackers deliberately crashed U.S. commercial jetliners into the World Trade Center in New York—toppling its 110-story twin towers—and the Pentagon, just outside Washington, D.C. Thousands died in the deadliest act of terrorism in American history.

Though the person or persons behind the attacks were not immediately known, President Bush cast prime suspicion on the Saudi exile Osama bin Laden, the alleged mastermind of the bombings of two U.S.

embassies in 1998 and of a U.S. naval destroyer in 2000. Bin Laden was captured and killed in a raid, authorized by President Obama, on his Pakistan compound in May 2011. The United States had earlier seen terrorism on its home soil carried out by Islamic militants in the 1993 bombing of the World Trade Center and by a member of the American militia movement in the bombing of the Oklahoma City federal building in 1995. The dispute with Iraq continued, and George W. Bush declared war (a disputed option) with Iraq. The outcome of sending troops to Iraq is undetermined.

Barack Obama

On January 20, 2009, Barack H. Obama became the 44th President of the United States. President Obama was born in Hawaii on August 4, 1961, to a middle-class family; his father was from Kenya and his mother was from Kansas. President Obama was raised by his mother with help from his grandfather, who had served in General Patton's army during World War II, and his grandmother, who was a successful bank employee. As a law student, President Obama was the first African American president of the Harvard Law Review. In the Illinois State Senate, he helped pass the first major ethics reform in 25 years, cut taxes for working families, and expanded health care for children and their parents. As a United States Senator, he helped pass an innovative lobbying reform and to make information about federal spending accessible online. On November 4, 2008, he was elected to the presidency.

Skill 7.8: Identify Immigration and Settlement Patterns That Have Shaped the History of the United States

"The United States is a nation of immigrants" is a frequently quoted remark, although the Europeans who founded the nation came to a country already peopled by those we call Native Americans, and, as discussed in earlier sections, many people who subsequently came to America did not immigrate willingly.

The Earliest Americans

The New World that Columbus and other explorers discovered in the late fifteenth and early sixteenth centuries was neither recently formed nor recently settled. It had actually been settled between 15,000 and 35,000 years before. As in other areas of the world, the native peoples of the "New World" formed communities but did not immediately develop written languages. The lack of any kind of written record makes interpreting the prehistorical past more difficult. Archaeologists and anthropologists working in North and South America have unearthed the remains of these early communities, and it is on this evidence that anthropologists base the earliest theories about the origins, movements, and lifestyles of native peoples. It is known, for example, that by the time Europeans came into contact with the indigenous peoples of the Americas, more than 2,000 distinct cultures and hundreds of distinct languages existed.

Fundamental Immigration Questions

Some of the specific patterns of immigration and governmental response are discussed in earlier sections. Since the recording of the first arrivals in 1820, the United States has accepted 66 million legal immigrants, with 11 percent arriving from Germany and 10 percent from Mexico. However, two centuries of immigration and integration have not yielded consensus on the three major immigration questions:

1. How many immigrants should be permitted?

2. From where should immigrants be permitted?

3. Under what status should immigrants enter the country?

National Immigration Trends

As pointed out by a former director of the U.S. Census Bureau, Kenneth Prewitt, America is the first country in history in which peoples from every part of the world are represented. During the early twenty-first century, it has been calculated that each year the U.S. immigration system recognizes 800,000 to 900,000 foreigners as legal immigrants, admits 35 million nonimmigrant tourist and business visitors, and is aware of another 300,000 to 400,000 unauthorized foreigners who settle in the country. Martin (2002) predicts that these immigration trends are likely to continue at current levels. Recent decades have witnessed contentious debates over the place of immigrants and their children in the educational, welfare, and political systems of the U.S. or, more broadly, whether the immigration system serves U.S. national interests.

Florida Demographics

The population of Florida is characterized by considerable ethnic and racial diversity, as indicated by the 2010 Census. The population of Florida (18,801,310) comprises 6.08 percent of the population of the United States (308,745,538). It has grown 17.6 percent from Census 2000, resulting in two new seats in the U.S. House of Representatives for a total of 27 representatives. Flagler County in particular doubled its population since 2000 and became the fastest-growing county in Florida.

The following chart, derived from U.S. Census categories, illustrates the ethnic and racial diversity of Florida residents and highlights its multiculturalism:

Race	Percentage
White persons of non-Hispanic origin	57.9
Hispanic or Latino origin	22.5
Black	16.0
Asian	2.4
American Indian and Alaska Native	.4
Native Hawaiian or other Pacific Islander	.1
Persons reporting 2 or more races	2.5

According to census data, 25.8 percent of the Florida population speaks a language other than English at home. This statistic underscores the importance of maintaining programs to help the English Language Learner (ELL).

Census data also reveal that 15 percent of Florida's population falls below the poverty line. Children of low-income families face serious obstacles to academic success, including insufficient access to food, unsafe and/or uncomfortable living conditions, and challenges to physical and emotional health. These are challenges to the educational system in Florida that teachers must recognize and deal with.

Skill 7.9: Identify How Various Cultures Contributed to the Unique Social, Cultural, Economic, and Political Features of Florida

During the 1930s, the Works Progress Administration collected folklore from Florida. The collection documented African American, Arabic, Bahamian, British American, Cuban, Greek, Italian, Minorcan, Seminole, and Slavic cultures throughout Florida. The Library of Congress presents these documents as part of the record of the past and a distinctive cultural contribution of Florida.

The many cultural backgrounds of a population that originated from many countries make Florida unique (Florida Smart). Native Americans, descendants of the pioneering settlers, Cubans, Puerto Ricans, Greeks, Asians, African Americans, Caucasians, and dozens of other ethnic groups, old and young, are featured throughout the Florida boundaries. This varied background began with the exploration and settlement of the state.

Early History

About 12,000 years ago, hunters and gatherers reached Florida and settled in areas with a water supply, stones for tools, and firewood. These Floridians created complex cultures. Before the arrival of Europeans, these native peoples developed cultivated agriculture, traded with groups in the southeastern United States, and expanded their social organization. Their temple mounds and villages reflect their complex social organization.

The First European Explorers

The Spanish explorer and adventurer Juan Ponce de León arrived near what is now St. Augustine in 1513. The written record of Florida began with his arrival. He called the land *la Florida*, in honor of the Feast of the Flowers, an Easter celebration in Spain. No evidence exists of other Europeans arriving before him, but it is a possibility. Eight years later Juan Ponce de León, 200 people, 50 horses, and other beasts of burden returned to Florida's southwest coast. With attacks from the natives there, however, the colonization attempt failed. Still, Juan Ponce de León described the area as a suitable place for missionaries, explorers, and treasure seekers.

Hernando de Soto began another treasure-hunting expedition in 1539. His travels through Florida and the southeastern United States took his group to what is now Tallahassee; they camped there for five months. Although de Soto died in 1542 near the Mississippi, some of his expedition reached as far as Mexico.

The First European Settlements

Stories from Ponce de León's and de Soto's parties gradually circulated through Europe and influenced the development of exploration in what is now Florida and other areas. Spain regularly shipped silver, gold, and other products from Cuba, Mexico, Central America, and South America; accounts of these activities also spread rapidly to others interested in exploration. In 1559, Tristán de Luna y Arellano led another group that attempted to settle in Florida. After a series of misfortunes over a two-year period, however, they had to abandon the settlement. The French also arrived in Florida. In 1562, Jean Ribault explored the area near what is now Jacksonville, and in 1564, René Goulaine de Laudonnière established a colony there.

At around this time, Spain began to accelerate its colonization plans. In 1565, Pedro Menéndez de Avilés settled near St. Augustine. This was the first permanent European settlement in what is now America. Pedro Menéndez de Avilés worked to remove all the French and to kill all French settlers except those who were Roman Catholic or noncombatants. Menéndez captured the Spanish Fort Caroline and renamed it San Mateo. Two years later, the Frenchman Dominique de Gourgues captured San Mateo and killed the Spanish there. The Spanish, however, continued to explore, construct forts, and establish Roman Catholic missions among the Floridians. The English also continued to explore. Conflict frequently arose between the Spanish and the English. Sir Francis Drake and his crew burned the Spanish settlement of St. Augustine in 1586.

Spain's power in the southeastern part of the New World was unassailable in the 1600s. The English did establish colonies at that time, but these were primarily in Jamestown, Virginia (1607); Plymouth, Massachusetts (1620); and Georgia (1733). French explorers continued to move down the Mississippi and along the Gulf Coast during that time.

The Eighteenth Century

Feuds between Spain and England—particularly in Florida—continued into the eighteenth century. The Englishman Colonel James Moore, along with the Carolinians and their Creek Indian allies, attacked Spanish Florida in 1702 and destroyed the town of St. Augustine. The fort Castillo de San Marcos was not captured, however. In 1704, the English moved between Tallahassee and St. Augustine and destroyed the Spanish missions they encountered. The French harassed the Spanish on the western side and captured Pensacola in 1719. Then Georgians attacked in 1740, but, like the English, they were unable to take the Castillo de San Marcos at St. Augustine.

In exchange for Havana (which the British had taken from Spain during the Seven Years' War of 1756–1763), the British took control of Florida. Spain evacuated Florida after the exchange, and British surveyors tried to establish relations with the Native Americans—Seminoles of Creek Indian descent—who were moving into the area. To attract other settlers, Britain offered land for settling and help if settlers produced exportable items. The plan lasted only 20 years. Spain captured Pensacola from the British in 1781 and retained it as part of the peace treaty that ended the American Revolution.

American Possession

Other Spanish colonists came pouring into Florida after the British evacuation. Some came because of the favorable terms for obtaining property (i.e., land grants) that the Spanish offered to immigrants; some were escaped slaves trying to find freedom. Spain then ceded Florida to the United States in 1821. Andrew Jackson had already been in Florida battling the Seminoles in 1818, during the First Seminole War. Returning in 1821 to establish a new territorial government, he found a combination of Native Americans, African Americans, and Spaniards. In 1845, Florida became the twenty-seventh state.

Many Southerners now began moving to Florida. A divided state became more unified, with Tallahassee as capital. As the population increased through immigration, the residents began to pressure the federal government to remove the Creeks, the Miccosukees, and the African American refugees, in order to make desirable land more available.

Origins of Reservations

As the federal government began to press Native Americans to leave their homeland, Osceola, a Seminole war leader, refused to relocate his people. While waging the Seminole War of 1835–1842, President Andrew Jackson allocated $20 million and many U.S. soldiers to enforce the movement of the Seminoles to Oklahoma. The war ended, but not as the government had planned. Many Seminoles, private citizens, and soldiers lost their lives. Soldiers captured some of the Seminoles and sent them West under guard, others "volunteered" to go, but some fled into the Everglades and made a life for themselves there. The government eventually established reservations, and forced or encouraged Native Americans to relocate to these areas.

Slavery

By 1840, the population of Florida had reached 54,477; about half of the population consisted of slaves. At this time, the state consisted of three parts: east, middle, and west. The middle area had many plantations, whose owners set the political tone for the state until the time of the Civil War.

Florida residents were concerned about the North's objections to slavery. Most Floridians at the time did not oppose slavery, and Abraham Lincoln did not win the state in the presidential election.

The Civil War and Reconstruction

On January 10, 1861, Florida seceded from the Union. No decisive battles occurred in Florida, but the state provided 15,000 soldiers and many supplies; in addition, 2,000 African Americans and whites from Florida joined the Union army.

The state and the lives of many of its residents changed after the Civil War. Although Tallahassee was the only southern capital east of the Mississippi River to avoid capture during the war, federal troops occupied Tallahassee on May 10, 1865. The ports of Jacksonville and Pensacola subsequently began to thrive. Slaves became free, and plantations did not regain their prewar levels; instead, tenant farmers and sharecroppers—white and African American—began to develop the farming sector.

Beginning in 1868, the federal government began Reconstruction in Florida. Investors in industries brought more people to the state through the increased construction of roads and railroads. Citrus fruit cultivation, sponge harvesting, steamboat tours, and the tourist industry in general flourished. From this time through the beginning of World War I, Florida's offer of free or cheap public land to investors brought diverse cultures into the state. Draining large tracts of land made it more usable, and businessmen such as Henry Flagler and Henry B. Plant built lavish hotels for tourists near their railroad lines. Florida also became the staging area for American troops bound for the war in Cuba during the Spanish-American War, and this too brought many people through the state and permanently changed it.

Early Twentieth Century

By the beginning of the twentieth century, per capita income and population were rising in the Sunshine State. After World War I, increasing numbers of tourists and land developers came into the state, and inflation became a problem. Hurricanes in 1926 and in 1928 helped hasten the bursting of Florida's economic bubble. Money and credit began to dry up, and the "paper" millionaires lost their credibility. By the time the rest of the nation felt the Great Depression, Florida was already accustomed to economic hard times. Adding to Florida's troubles was the invasion of the Mediterranean fruit fly in 1929 that caused citrus production to fall by 60 percent.

The face of Florida's voting population changed after developments such as women winning the right to vote in 1920, the repeal of the poll tax (a tax of a uniform, fixed amount per individual) in 1937, and the U.S. Supreme Court's decision to outlaw a system of all-white primary elections in 1944. In addition, more newcomers entered the state when World War II began. With its mild climate, the state became a major training center for the military, and it continues to attract both U.S. and international citizens as a desirable location for vacations and for retirement.

Postwar Immigration and Migration

With the influx of large numbers of people from places within the United States and from countries within the Western Hemisphere (primarily Cuba and Haiti), Florida has experienced a surge in population in recent years. It is now the fourth most populous state in the nation, and the diverse population has worked to make the Sunshine State a place where all citizens have equal rights under the law.

Many changes have occurred in Florida since the 1950s. Schools and other institutions are integrated. The economy has diversified. Electronics, plastics, construction, real estate, and international banking have recently joined tourism, citrus fruit cultivation, and phosphate production as major elements in

Florida's economy. The state's community colleges, technical colleges, and universities draw large numbers of students to Florida each year, and the tourist industry continues to flourish.

U.S. Space Program

The U.S. Space Program, an integral element of Florida's history since the late 1950s, has generated substantial tourism, media attention, and employment.

The National Aeronautics and Space Administration (NASA) had its beginnings under President Dwight D. Eisenhower in July 1958 with the signing of Public Law 85-568. The Launch Operations Center was established in 1962 on Florida's east coast and was renamed the John F. Kennedy Space Center in 1963 to honor the president who initiated the prospect of exploring the moon.

Cape Canaveral was chosen as the primary site of many space missions, for several reasons. Since the Cape was undeveloped, it became the ideal location for testing missiles without affecting nearby communities. The Florida climate permitted year-round operations and being on the coast allowed launches over water instead of populated areas. As a consequence, Florida has been the hub of numerous missions, from the early days of Project Mercury to the Space Shuttles, the International Space Station, the Hubble Space Telescope, and the Mars Exploration Rovers.

As of August 14, 2011, NASA's Kennedy Space Center established the Ground Processing Directorate (GPD). This organization will focus on future launch processing, overseeing operations for the International Space Station, maintaining a new customer center, and integration of launch complex operations.

Of utmost importance to educators is the Kennedy Educate to Innovate program that connects NASA employees with teachers, students, and the general public. Virtual Lab, one of the associated projects, consists of software that provides virtual access to sophisticated scientific instruments. Students are entertained with hands-on experiences relevant to class material. A variety of virtual tours allows students to be part of teams that work on the space shuttle and other missions. Of deep interest to educators is the Kennedy Launch Academy Simulation System (KLASS). The software and curriculum materials bring a launch countdown into the classroom. Lessons are interactive and inquiry-based.

Competency 8: Knowledge of People, Places, and Environment

As geographers, teachers focus on not only space and place, the physical dimensions of geography, but also the human dimension consisting of the study of people, places, and environments. Students quickly become aware that as a people, we do not live in isolation. We are all interconnected and must therefore concern ourselves with our connections to the environment and to each other. Teachers guide our students to become young geographers through observation, questioning, investigation, and evaluation. The focus of Competency 8 is on geography in these various senses.

Skill 8.1: Identify the Six Essential Elements of Geography, Including the Specific Terms for Each Element

The six essential elements of geography are closely interrelated. According to various scholars, these elements can be described as follows:

1. *Understanding the world in spatial terms.* This element encompasses the characteristics of spatial features and layouts. It enables the student to have a spatial perspective and to be familiar with associated geographic tools used to organize and interpret information about people, places, and environments. These tools include maps, globes, graphs and charts, and databases. Students also develop the ability to construct models depicting Earth-sun relationships, planets, landforms, and other geographic phenomena.

2. *Understanding the world in terms of places and regions.* This element encompasses knowledge of continents, regions, countries, cities, and so on. Both teachers and students must update their knowledge regularly as boundaries and place-names change. In addition, the element of place encompasses knowledge of how places are associated with physical characteristics such as latitude, altitude, climate, landforms, and plants and animals, as well as human characteristics such as language, religion, architecture, music, politics, and ways of life.

3. *Understanding the world in terms of physical systems.* This element encompasses knowledge of the physical features of the world such as mountains, deserts, and oceans, as well as the understanding that that these features are constantly changing as a result of tectonic activity, glaciation process, meteorological events, and human activity. Students learn to identify and understand individual physical features of the environment as well as the functioning of entire ecosystems.

4. *Understanding the world in terms of human systems.* This element encompasses knowledge of human characteristics and groups. Movements of people, materials, and ideas, the evolution of human societies, the establishment of cultural and political institutions, and the development of social and economic interrelationships between groups of humans are among the topics students learn to analyze and discuss.

5. *Understanding the world in terms of environment and society.* This element encompasses knowledge of interactions between humans and their environments and how these ongoing interactions constantly change the nature of society as well as the physical features of the environment such as the quality of the air,

water, and soil and the characteristics of flora and fauna. Students learn how society is shaped by both positive and negative environmental influences and how social practices in turn have beneficial or harmful influences on the environment.

6.   *Understanding the uses of geography.* This element encompasses the understanding of how geography can be used. Students learn that with geographical tools and knowledge one can examine the past, interpret the present, and plan for the future. Students learn that the knowledge obtained through geography influences our understanding of the physical and social worlds and allows us to make informed, useful, and ultimately critical decisions about how to best relate to the physical world and to each other.

Skill 8.2: Interpret Maps and Other Graphic Representations and Identify Tools and Technologies to Acquire, Process, and Report Information from a Spatial Perspective

The study of maps begins with a study of the globe—a model of the Earth with a map on its surface. Regular use of the globe helps provide students with an understanding of the Earth's shape and structure. Some of the features on the globe that students should be able to locate and name include the following:

- The continents

- The United States and major countries

- The Equator

- The North and South Poles

- The Antarctic and Arctic Circles

- Key meridians and parallels

- The International Date Line and time zones

The use of maps requires students to identify four main types of map projections:

- Conic

- Cylindrical

- Interrupted

- Plane

Additional graphics that students use in geography include charts, graphs, and picture maps. Internet resources as well as commercially available software programs provide many geographic tools for students, including interactive maps that allow for deeper exploration of physical geography. The goals for the teacher of geography are to help students understand how to obtain information from these graphic tools and to discuss and analyze their findings. Students will thus need to learn the conventions of each type of graphic representation (e.g., the use of legends on a map or the representation of lines of latitude and longitude on a globe).

Skill 8.3: Interpret Statistics That Show How Places Differ in Their Human and Physical Characteristics

Cultural geography focuses on the relationship between humans and the living and nonliving features of their environments. We know for example that the physical environment in which people reside affects their diet, shelter, clothing, tools, products, religion, and prosperity. Aspects of the physical environment that shape these cultural characteristics include climate, resources, terrain, and location.

Skill 8.4: Identify Ways in Which People Adapt to an Environment Through the Production and Use of Clothing, Food, and Shelter

Humans change their environments to better suit their wants and needs. At the same time, we adapt to our environments in order to survive. These adaptations can be observed in the choice of clothing, foods, and modes of shelter.

Skill 8.5: Identify How Tools and Technology Affect the Environment

Tools and technology are developed to improve people's lives. Along with their benefits, tools and technologies can have negative influences on people as well as the environments. Pollution of the air, water, and soil, which accelerated following the Industrial Revolution, is a critical example of these negative influences.

Skill 8.6: Identify Physical, Cultural, Economic, and Political Reasons for the Movement of People in the World, Nation, or State

When the characteristics of their environments become unpalatable to residents, they may consider relocation. In such cases, people are, so to speak, driven away from their place of residence. In other cases, people may relocate to an area that appears to be highly desirable. In these cases, people are drawn to a new place of residence.

One or more of several kinds of forces are responsible for driving people away from or drawing them to particular areas:

Economic Forces

Economic reasons for relocation are related to the financial conditions and aspirations of residents. Some residents wish to move to more expensive areas, while others wish to move to less expensive ones. In some cases, a change in the financial situation of individuals and individual families is responsible for the relocation, as when a person loses a job and must move to a less expensive area. In other cases, physical or social events are responsible for economic change. Following are some examples:

1. An entire industry in a region begins to flourish or fail (e.g., the demise of the textile industry in nineteenth century New England).

2. Regional or national economic changes impact the financial conditions of individuals in a specific area (e.g., the Great Depression of the 1930s).

3. Discoveries or natural disasters impact the economy of an area (e.g., the discovery of oil in the Gulf of Mexico).

Cultural Forces

Cultural reasons for relocation include a desire to live with people who are more similar to oneself or to find an area with greater diversity (or at least greater tolerance for diversity). The goal of relocation may be essential to a person's cultural identity or simply a matter of finding a more interesting cultural environment. Some of the dimensions of similarity or dissimilarity that motivate people to move for cultural reasons include the following:

- Race

- Ethnicity

- Religion

- Lifestyle

Physical Forces

The purely physical features of an area can influence peoples' interest in relocation. Following are some of the many examples:

1. The climate of an area seems especially desirable or undesirable.

2. A natural disaster (e.g., a hurricane), or the prospect of natural disasters (e.g., forest fires), makes an area undesirable.

3. The physical geography of an area contains especially attractive features (e.g., mountains and lakes) or especially unattractive ones (e.g., insects).

4. The physical location of an area relative to cities or key geographic features seems especially desirable or undesirable.

Political Forces

Political changes, as well as the more enduring qualities of political systems, motivate people to relocate. In some cases, people are legally forced to move, while in others, relocation is simply motivated by the desire for a better life. Following are some examples of political changes that stimulate the movement of peoples:

1. Immigration law changes, such that people must leave an area, or, for the first time, they are permitted to reside in an area.

2. Laws governing freedom of expression, freedom of worship, and other important freedoms become more or less restrictive.

3. The dominant political affiliation of an area shifts in a direction that is considered desirable or undesirable.

4. Political practices in an area begin to strongly encourage or discourage certain kinds of business development.

Skill 8.7: Identify How Transportation and Communication Networks Contribute to the Level of Economic Development in Different Regions

Advances in communication—through the satellite technologies—make it possible for people all over the world to connect with each other, and to learn about each other's situations, in real time. The economic impact of this virtually instantaneous interconnectivity is vast. The food supplier on the West Coast can observe the progress of a hurricane on the East Coast and anticipate changes in consumer needs. Investors in Tokyo and New York can monitor each other's financial markets and make significant decisions rapidly. The joint producers of a new technology who reside in the U.S. and China can collaborate in real time. These are just a few examples of the direct economic impact of new communication technologies on the way people conduct business. At the same time, the communications industry itself is a major economic force. Technologies for communication such as computers and cell phones are among the world's leading industries, and a great deal of revenue is generated through personal and business use of these technologies.

In the same way, developments in transportation technology have had a major and enduring economic impact. In the U.S., the development of railroads and roads, as well as improvements in shipping, significantly altered the economic landscape of the eighteenth and nineteenth centuries. In the twentieth century, the economic effects of automobiles, trucks, and airplanes were also profound.

Development of these transportation technologies facilitates business, as raw materials and products can be moved more quickly and efficiently. The new modes of transportation also allow people to relocate more readily for work-related reasons and have been responsible for numerous mass migrations of people toward areas that offer plentiful opportunities for employment. At the same time, the convenience of modern transportation has supported the development of increasingly profitable tourist industries.

Skill 8.8: Compare and Contrast Major Regions of the World

Following are some examples of the many ways of dividing the world into regions.

1. The equator can be used as the dividing line between the Northern and Southern Hemispheres.

2. A line from pole to pole can be used to divide the Eastern from the Western Hemisphere.

3. Continental land masses can be used to divide the Earth into Africa, Asia, Australia, Europe, North America, and South America. (Some geographers include Antarctica as a separate continent.)

4. Political, cultural, and/or ethnic distinctions can be used to divide the world, as can elements of physical geography such as biomes.

Comparing and contrasting are higher-order thinking skills that teachers encourage among their students. Thinking about dividing the world into major regions is an ideal way to deploy these skills. Students can be presented with an existing system for classifying major regions and can then use their comparing and contrasting skills to understand the similarities within a region as well as the differences across regions. Alternatively, students can be presented with information about the world and encouraged to use their comparing and contrasting skills to create regions based on systematic analysis of similarities and differences. Teachers can provide more or less scaffolding for this kind of activity.

Competency 9: Knowledge of Government and the Citizen

Government is an agency that regulates the activities of people. It is the system that carries out the rules and decisions of the political system and its ruler or rulers. The focus of Competency 9 is on the nature of government and its interrelationship with citizens.

Skill 9.1: Identify the Structure, Functions, and Purposes of Government

Structure of Government

The distribution and separation of powers within the various structures of government is important in understanding governments and comparing different types. Following are some different kinds of governmental structures:

1. *A confederation* is a weak central government that delegates principal authority to smaller units, such as states. The United States had this structure under the Articles of Confederation, before the U.S. Constitution was ratified in 1789.

2. *A federal government* is one in which sovereignty is divided between a central government and a group of states. Contemporary examples of federal systems include the United States, Brazil, and India.

3. *A unitary government* is a centralized authority in which power is concentrated. Contemporary examples include France and Japan.

4. *An authoritarian government* is one in which power resides with one or a few individuals, such that legislative and judicial bodies have little input. Some examples include the People's Republic of China, the former Soviet Union, and Nazi Germany.

5. *A parliamentary government* is one in which the legislative and executive branches are combined, with a prime minister and cabinet selected from within the legislative body. Great Britain exemplifies this form of government.

Structure of American Government

America has a federal system of government; it divides sovereignty between the central government and the states. It also represents a presidential form of government, in that the executive branch is clearly separated from the legislative and judicial branches. Powers are divided across the three branches of government, and a system of checks and balances is in place to prevent any one branch from political dominance.

Functions of Government

The functions of a government include the following:

- Maintaining domestic order
- Protecting its borders
- Enabling a productive economy
- Promoting the well-being of the society and its citizens

Although most or all citizens may agree that this list encompasses the functions of government, not everyone would agree on the details of each function or how it should be implemented. For example, most or all American citizens would agree that the government has at least some responsibility in protecting our borders, but there are ongoing disagreements about the extent of protection needed as well as the methods of protection.

Purposes of Government

Since the time of Plato, there has been substantial debate about the purposes of government. For example, many people believe that the government should play at least some role in the education of citizens, but there is no consensus on the appropriate nature or extent of governmental participation in the educational process, and some would hold that educating citizens is not among the government's fundamental purposes.

Differing ideologies, such as communism, socialism, capitalism, and so on, differ in part through their assumptions about what constitutes the fundamental purposes of government. The points of disagreement are both practical and philosophical and reflect important ethical considerations.

Skill 9.2: Demonstrate Knowledge of the Rights and Responsibilities of a Citizen in the World, Nation, State, and/or Community

Each citizen has both rights and responsibilities. For example, in America some of the legal rights guaranteed to citizens include the following:

- The right to due process
- The right to a fair and speedy trial
- The right to be free from unlawful search and seizure
- The right to avoid self-incrimination

It is essential for students to not only be aware of these and other rights but also to understand where they originate. Students need to know the basis of their rights and responsibilities as citizens, so that they can familiarize themselves with them as needed, and so they can understand and critically evaluate them. Doing so is part of being an active citizen in a democratic society.

Skill 9.3: Identify Major Concepts of the U.S. Constitution and Other Historical Documents

Articles of Confederation

The Articles of Confederation, adopted in 1777, provided for a unicameral Congress, in which each state would have one vote, as had been the case in the Continental Congress. Executive authority under the Articles was to be vested in a committee of 13, with one member from each state. Amending the Articles required the unanimous consent of all the states. Under the Articles of Confederation, the government could declare war, make treaties, determine the number of troops and amount of money each state should contribute to a war effort, settle disputes between states, admit new states to the Union, and borrow money. It could not levy taxes, raise troops, or regulate commerce.

Origins of the U.S. Constitution

As time went on, the inadequacy of the Articles of Confederation became increasingly apparent. In 1787, there was a call for a convention of all the states in Philadelphia for the purpose of revising the

Articles and creating what would eventually be the U.S. Constitution. The assembly unanimously elected George Washington to preside, and the enormous respect that he commanded helped hold the convention together through difficult times.

The 55 delegates who met in Philadelphia in 1787 to draft the Constitution drew on a variety of sources to shape the government that would be outlined in the document. Three British documents in particular were important to the delegates' work: the Magna Carta (1215), the Petition of Right (1628), and the Bill of Rights (1689). These three documents promoted the concept of limited government and were influential in shaping the fundamental principles embodied in the Constitution. The British philosopher John Locke, who wrote about the social contract concept of government and the right of people to alter or abolish a government that did not protect their interests, was another guiding force in the drafting of the Constitution.

Compromise in Establishing the Constitution

One of the most significant principles embodied in the Constitution is the concept of a federal system that divides the powers of government between the states and the national government. The federal government and those of the separate states have powers that may in practice overlap, but in cases where they conflict, the federal government is supreme.

The relationship between the national government and the states is one that reflects a compromise between delegates on how power should be distributed, with some delegates favoring a stronger central government than others.

A specific problem that the delegates faced in determining state participation in national politics involved how to specify the number of state representatives. In some respects, each state should be equal to the others, but in other respects, states with larger populations should have more influence than states with smaller ones. With George Washington presiding over the discussions, the delegates finally adopted a proposal known as the Great Compromise, which provided for a president, two senators per state, and representatives elected to the House according to their states' populations.

Another major crisis in the discussions involved disagreement between the North and the South over slavery. To reach a compromise on this point, the delegates decided that each slave was to count as three-fifths of a person for purposes of apportioning representation and direct taxation on the states. This practice was known as the Three-Fifths Compromise.

Finally, the delegates had to compromise on the nature and power of the presidency. The result was a strong presidency with control over foreign policy and the power to veto congressional legislation. Should the president commit a crime, Congress would have the power of impeachment. Otherwise, the president would serve for a term of four years and was eligible for reelection without limit. As a check to the possible excesses of democracy, an Electoral College elected the president; each state would have the same number of electors as it did senators and representatives combined.

The Content of the U.S. Constitution

The content of the U.S. Constitution consists of a preamble, seven articles, and 27 amendments.

Articles I, II, and III of the U.S. Constitution are concerned with defining and delineating the legislative, executive, and judicial powers. Article IV guarantees citizens of each state the privileges and immunities of the other states and provides protection to the states. Articles V and VII are concerned with amending and ratifying the Constitution, and Article VI concerns federal power. The first 10 amendments to the Constitution are known as the Bill of Rights, and to these have been added 17 additional amendments.

The Bill of Rights

A point of concern among some delegates to the Constitutional Convention was that the emerging document contained no bill of rights. The first Congress met in 1789. On the agenda was the consideration of 12 amendments to the Constitution written by James Madison. The states approved 10 of the 12 amendments on December 15, 1791, and these make up what is known as the Bill of Rights, which can be briefly summarized as follows:

- First Amendment: Guarantees freedom of worship, speech, press, assembly, and petition.

- Second Amendment: Forbids infringement on the right to bear arms.

- Third Amendment: Forbids use of private homes for quartering of troops.

- Fourth Amendment: Forbids unreasonable arrest, search, and seizure.

- Fifth Amendment: Guarantees various legal protections, including due process and provisions that people not testify against themselves.

- Sixth Amendment: Guarantees various legal protections, including access to counsel for those accused of a crime.

- Seventh Amendment: Guarantees a trial by jury in civil cases.

- Eighth Amendment: Forbids excessive penalties, including cruel and unusual punishment.

- Ninth Amendment: Indicates that citizens possess rights over and above those named in the Articles and Bill of Rights.

- Tenth Amendment: Grants to states and citizens those rights not granted to the federal government.

Additional Constitutional Amendments

Making amendments (i.e., additions or revisions) to the Constitution is no small feat. Since 1787, more than 9,000 amendments have been proposed, but only 27 have been approved. Following is a brief summary of those following the Bill of Rights:

- Eleventh Amendment: A citizen of one state may sue a citizen of another state only if that person has the state's permission.

- Twelfth Amendment: Election of the president.

- Thirteenth Amendment: Abolishment of slavery.

- Fourteenth Amendment: Definition and protection of citizens.

- Fifteenth Amendment: Universal male suffrage.

- Sixteenth Amendment: Income tax.

- Seventeenth Amendment: Election of Senators by popular vote.

- Eighteenth Amendment: Prohibition of intoxicating substances.

- Nineteenth Amendment: Women's suffrage.

- Twentieth Amendment: Beginning and ending terms of elected officials.

- Twenty-first Amendment: Repeal of Eighteenth Amendment.

- Twenty-second Amendment: Limitation of presidency to two terms.

- Twenty-third Amendment: District of Columbia given presidential vote.

- Twenty-fourth Amendment: Repeal of poll tax in federal elections.

- Twenty-fifth Amendment: Procedures for unexpected presidential or vice-presidential vacancy.

- Twenty-sixth Amendment: Establishment of 18 as voting age.

- Twenty-seventh Amendment: Limits on change in congressional compensation.

Skill 9.4: Identify How the Legislative, Executive, and Judicial Branches Share Powers and Responsibility

As noted in earlier sections, a key principle of the U.S. Constitution is separation of powers. The national government is divided into three branches—legislative, executive, and judicial—with separate functions, but they are not entirely independent, nor can they operate without constraints imposed by the others. Articles I, II, and III of the main body of the Constitution outline these functions.

The Legislative Branch

Article I of the Constitution deals with the legislative branch. Through this Article, legislative power is vested in a bicameral congress (i.e., one composed of two houses). The expressed or delegated powers of Congress are set forth in Section 8 of the Article and can be divided into several broad categories:

1. Economic powers include the following:

    - Set and collect taxes
    - Borrow money
    - Regulate foreign and interstate commerce
    - Coin money and regulate its value
    - Establish rules concerning bankruptcy

2. Judicial powers include the following:

    - Establish courts inferior to the Supreme Court
    - Provide punishment for counterfeiting
    - Define and punish piracies and felonies committed on the high seas

3. War powers include the following:

    - Declare war
    - Raise and support armies
    - Provide and maintain a navy
    - Provide for organizing, arming, and calling forth the militia

4. Other general peace powers include the following:

    - Establish uniform rules on naturalization
    - Establish post offices and post roads
    - Promote science and the arts by issuing patents and copyrights
    - Exercise jurisdiction over the seat of the federal government (District of Columbia)

The Constitution also grants Congress the power to discipline federal officials through impeachment and removal from office. The House of Representatives has the power to charge officials (impeach), and the Senate has the power to conduct the trials.

Significant also is the Senate's power to confirm presidential appointments (to the cabinet, federal judiciary, and major bureaucracies) and to ratify treaties. Both houses are involved in choosing a president and vice president if there is no majority in the Electoral College. The House of Representatives votes for the president from among the top three electoral candidates, with each state delegation casting one vote. The Senate votes for the vice president. The Senate has exercised this power only twice, in the disputed elections of 1800 and 1824.

The Executive Branch

Article II of the Constitution deals with the powers and duties of the president. The chief executive's constitutional responsibilities include the following:

1. Serve as commander in chief

2. Negotiate treaties (with the approval of two-thirds of the Senate)

3. Appoint ambassadors, judges, and other high officials (with the consent of the Senate)

4. Grant pardons and reprieves for those convicted of federal crimes (except in impeachment cases)

5. Seek counsel of department heads (cabinet secretaries)

6. Recommend legislation

7. Meet with representatives of foreign states

8. See that federal laws are "faithfully executed"

The president's powers with respect to foreign policy are paramount. Civilian control of the military is a fundamental concept embodied in the naming of the president as commander in chief. In essence, the president is the nation's leading general. As such, the president can make battlefield decisions and shape military policy.

The president also has broad powers in domestic policy. The most significant domestic policy tool is the president's budget, which he/she must submit to Congress. Though Congress must approve all spending, the president has a great deal of power in budget negotiations. The president can use considerable resources in persuading Congress to enact legislation, and the president also has opportunities, such as in the "State of the Union" address, to reach out directly to the American people to convince them to support presidential policies.

The Judicial Branch

Article III of the Constitution pertains to the judicial branch. This article provides for the creation and operation of the Supreme Court, as well as those inferior courts (i.e., lower in authority than the Supreme Court) that Congress is authorized to establish.

Skill 9.5: Demonstrate Knowledge of the U.S. Electoral System and the Election Process

To become president, a candidate must meet the following criteria:

- He/she must be a natural-born United States citizen.

- He/she must be a resident of the United States for at least 14 years.

- He/she must be at least 35 years old.

Each political party selects a candidate as its representative in an upcoming election. At the end of the primaries and caucuses, each party holds a national convention and finalizes its selection of its presidential nominee. Each presidential candidate chooses a vice presidential candidate.

The candidates usually begin their campaign tours once they have received the nomination of their parties. In November, U.S. citizens cast their votes, but they are not actually voting directly for the presidential candidate of their choice. Instead, voters cast their votes for electors, who are part of the Electoral College and who are expected to vote for the candidate that their state prefers.

The Electoral College

The 55 delegates who met in Philadelphia in 1787 to draft a constitution established the Electoral College originally as a compromise between presidential election by popular vote and by Congressional election. At first the legislators in some states chose their electors, while in other states voters elected the electors.

In 1796, separate political parties began to operate. At this time each state had the same number of electors as the state had senators and representatives, and each elector voted for two candidates. The person receiving the highest number of votes became the president, and the person receiving the second-highest number of votes became the vice president (as specified in Article II).

The Twelfth Amendment to the U.S. Constitution specifies that the electors must meet in their respective states and cast their votes for president and vice president. The slates of electors pledge to vote for the candidates of the parties that the people select. Each elector must have his/her vote signed and certified. The electors send the votes to the president of the Senate for counting in front of Congress. The person having the majority (two-thirds of the votes cast) is declared president. The House chooses the president from the top three if there is no majority. The Twentieth Amendment dictates the process that must take place if no president has qualified by the third day of January.

The president and vice president are the only two nationally elected officials. (The states elect their senators and representatives on a state-by-state basis.) Both houses of Congress are involved in choosing a president and vice president if no majority is achieved in the Electoral College. The House of Representatives votes for the president from among the top three electoral candidates, with each state delegation casting one vote. The Senate votes for the vice president.

Skill 9.6: Identify the Structures and Functions of U.S. Federal, State, and Local Governments

According to the Constitution, all governmental powers ultimately stem from the people. Local governments generally handle local matters, those issues that affect all state residents are handled by states, and issues that affect all citizens of the country are the responsibility of the federal government. Such a system is a natural outgrowth of the colonial relationship between the Americans and the mother country of England.

Federal Powers

The following powers are reserved for the federal government:

1. Regulate foreign commerce
2. Regulate interstate commerce
3. Mint money
4. Regulate naturalization and immigration
5. Grant copyrights and patents
6. Declare and wage war and declare peace
7. Admit new states
8. Fix standards for weights and measures
9. aise and maintain an army and a navy
10. Govern Washington, D.C.
11. Conduct relations with foreign powers
12. Universalize bankruptcy laws

State Powers

Each state government has the following powers:

1. Conduct and monitor elections
2. Establish voter qualifications within the guidelines established by the Constitution

3. Provide for local governments

4. Ratify proposed amendments to the Constitution

5. Regulate contracts and wills

6. egulate intrastate commerce

7. Provide for education for its citizens

8. Levy direct taxes

Skill 9.7: Identify the Relationships Between Social, Economic, and Political Rights and the Historical Documents That Secure These Rights

The relationships between the rights of citizens and the documents that guarantee those rights can be complicated. In the U.S., for example, citizens' rights are ultimately grounded in the Constitution, but the Constitution does not specify the details of every specific situation in which a person's rights are in question. The Constitution must be interpreted, and there are disagreements about interpretation. Moreover, some of the rights of citizens, although not in conflict with the guidelines of the Constitution, have been established through social or legal practice and are only locally normative. For this reason, people who move to a new city may experience differences in some of their specific rights.

Skill 9.8: Demonstrate Knowledge of the Processes of the U.S. Legal System

The contemporary judicial branch consists of thousands of courts and is, in essence, a dual system, with each state having its own judicial structure functioning simultaneously with a complete set of federal courts.

The Supreme Court

The most significant piece of legislation with reference to establishing a federal court network was the Judiciary Act of 1789. That law organized the Supreme Court and set up the 13 federal district courts and 3 circuit (appeal) courts.

The Supreme Court today is made up of one chief justice and eight associate justices. The president, with the approval of the Senate, appoints the justices for life. The justices often come from the ranks of the federal judiciary. In recent years, the public has examined the appointment of Supreme Court justices with intense scrutiny and, in some cases, heated political controversy has accompanied the choices for appointment.

Judicial Principles and the Constitution

Understanding the role of law in a democratic society results from knowledge of the nature of civil, criminal, and constitutional law and how the organization of the judicial system serves to interpret and apply such laws. Essential judicial principles include comprehension of rights, such as the right of due process, the right to a fair and speedy trial, and the right to a hearing before a jury of one's peers. Additional judicial principles include an understanding of the protections granted in the Constitution, which include protection from self-incrimination and unlawful searches and seizures.

The U.S. Constitution makes two references to trials by jury (Article III and the Sixth Amendment). The accused seems to benefit by the provision because a jury consists of 12 persons; the accused cannot be convicted unless all 12 agree that the defendant is guilty. There is mention of a speedy trial to prevent incarceration indefinitely unless the jury finds the accused guilty and the person receives such a sentence. The public trial statement ensures that the defendant receives just treatment. In 1968, the Supreme Court ruled that jury trials in criminal courts extended to the state courts as well as the federal courts. The Sixth Amendment uses the phrase "compulsory process for obtaining witnesses." This means that it is compulsory for witnesses for the defendant to appear in court, although there is some flexibility in the nature of the appearance.

Women on the Supreme Court

In its 220-year history, only four women justices have served on the Supreme Court: Sandra Day O'Connor (1981-2005); Ruth Bader Ginsburg (1993-present); Sonia Sotomayor (2009-present), and former U.S. Solicitor General Elena Kagan (2010-present). The latter two, nominated by President Barack Obama, each earned a distinct footnote in history. Confirmed by the U.S. Senate on August 6, 2009, Sotomayor became the first Hispanic on the Supreme Court. When Kagan was confirmed on August 5, 2010, the Supreme Court became one-third female for the first time in its history.

Sandra Day O'Connor was nominated by President Reagan in 1981 and was regarded as a conservative. She served for 24 years on the Supreme Court until resigning in 2005 in order to care for her ailing husband. The second female justice, Ruth Bader Ginsburg, was nominated by President Clinton in 1993 and is viewed as liberal. O'Connor and Ginsburg served together until O'Connor's retirement in 2005. Ginsburg remained as the lone female justice on the Supreme Court until Sonia Sotomayor was nominated by President Obama and took the bench in the fall of 2009. Sotomayor brought more federal judicial experience to the Supreme Court than any other justice in the past century. Finally, Elena Kagan was nominated to the Supreme Court by President Obama and confirmed by the U.S. Senate in 2010.

Skill 9.9: Identify the Roles of the United States in International Relations

The United States does not exist in isolation. Understanding global interdependence begins with recognition that world regions include economic, political, historical, ecological, linguistic, and cultural regions. This understanding includes knowledge of military alliances such as NATO, of economic alliances and cartels, and of the effects of each on political and economic policies within regions. The effects of these various alliances pertain to food production, human rights, use of natural resources, prejudice, poverty, trade, and so on. For political, economic, and military reasons, the United States emerged as a world leader in the twentieth century. The U.S. is deeply involved in international relations and sustains a variety of interdependent relationships with other nations. Some of these relationships are considered more positive than others.

Competency 10: Knowledge of Production, Distribution, and Consumption

Economics is a broad field of study. As economists, teachers insure that their students obtain basic knowledge of production, distribution, and consumption. Students learn how resources have a powerful impact on political functioning and individual decision-making as the importance of interconnectedness is emphasized and global awareness is explored. By introducing students to basic economic concepts such as scarcity, opportunity, cost, and capital, the teacher as economist helps students think locally, nationally, and internationally. The focus of Competency 10 is on knowledge of some of the most fundamental economic concepts.

Skill 10.1: Identify Ways That Limited Resources Affect the Choices Made by Government and Individuals

A basic understanding in economics is that wants are unlimited while resources are limited. When resources are limited, the impact is observed in prices (the amounts of money needed to buy goods, services, or resources). Individuals and institutions must, therefore, make choices when making purchases. These seemingly local decisions may affect other people and even other nations.

A true sense of global interdependence results from an understanding of the relationship between local decisions and global issues. For example, individual or community actions regarding waste disposal or recycling can affect the availability of resources worldwide. A country's fuel standards can affect air pollution, oil supplies, and gas prices. The government can provide the legal structure and support needed to maintain competition, redistribute income, reallocate resources, and promote stability.

Combining resources may result in entrepreneurship. As a human resource that also takes advantage of economic resources to create a product, entrepreneurship is characterized by nonroutine decisions, innovation, and the willingness to take risks.

Skill 10.2: Compare and Contrast the Characteristics of Different Economic Institutions

Following are the main economic institutions of the United States:

1. *Banks* serve the general public. They are owned by small groups of investors who expect a certain return on their investments. Only the investors have voting privileges; customers do not have voting rights, cannot be elected board members, and do not participate in governing the institution. The Federal Deposit Insurance Corporation (FDIC) insures the banks. Typically, banks do not share information, ideas, or resources.

2. *Credit unions* are owned by members. Each person who deposits money is a member, not a customer. Surplus earnings go to the members in higher dividends, low-cost or free services, and lower loan rates. The National Credit Union Share Insurance Fund insures credit unions. All credit unions share ideas, information, and resources.

3. *The Federal Reserve System* is the central banking system of the United States. It has a central board of governors in Washington, D.C. There are 12 Federal Reserve Bank districts in major cities throughout the nation. The district banks issue bank notes, lend money to member banks, maintain reserves, supervise member banks, and help set the national monetary policy. Alan Greenspan served as the chairman of the board of governors for 18 years. Upon Greenspan's retirement on January 31, 2005, Ben Bernanke succeeded him.

4. *The stock market* is an abstract concept. It is the mechanism that enables the trading of company stocks. It is different from the stock exchange, which is a corporation in the business of bringing together stock buyers and sellers.

Skill 10.3: Identify the Role of Markets from Production Through Distribution to Consumption

Market Economies

A market is the interaction between potential buyers and sellers of goods and services. Money is the usual medium of exchange. Market economies have no central authority, and custom plays a very small role. Every consumer makes buying decisions based on his or her own needs, desires, and income. In short, individual self-interest rules.

In a market economy, every producer decides personally what goods or services to produce, what price to charge, what resources to employ, and what production methods to use. Profits motivate the producers. There is vigorous competition in a market economy. Supply and demand may affect the availability of resources needed for production, distribution, and consumption. After production, the producer ideally distributes the product to the places where consumers need/want the product—and have the money to pay for the goods or services. In the United States, there is a large and active government sector, but greater emphasis emanates from the market economy.

Types of Economies

Following are the major types of economies in the world today:

1. *Command economies* rely on a central authority to make decisions. The central authority may be a dictator or a democratically constituted government. For example, the Russian economy relies mainly on the government to direct economic activity; there is a small market sector as well.

2. *Traditional economies* rely mainly on custom to determine production and distribution practices. While not static, traditional economies are slow to change and are not well equipped to propel a society into sustained growth. Many of the poorer countries of the developing world have traditional economies.

3. *Mixed economies* contain elements of each of the two previously defined systems. All real-world economies are mixed economies, but the proportions of the mixture can vary greatly.

4. *Capitalist economies* produce resources owned by individuals.

5. *Socialist economies* produce resources owned collectively by society. In other words, resources are under the control of the government.

Efficiency occurs when a society produces the types and quantities of goods and services that most satisfy its people. Failure to do so wastes resources. Technical efficiency occurs when a society produces the greatest types and quantities of goods and services from its resources. Again, failure to do so wastes resources. Equity occurs when the distribution of goods and services conforms to a society's notions of "fairness." These goals often determine the type of economic system that a country has.

Skill 10.4: Identify Factors to Consider When Making Consumer Decisions

Adam Smith (1723–1790) was a Scottish economist whose work helped inaugurate the modern era of economic analysis. Published in 1776, "The Wealth of Nations" is Smith's analysis of a market economy.

Smith believed that a market economy was a superior form of organization from the standpoint of both economic progress and human liberty. Smith acknowledged that self-interest was a dominant motivating force in a market economy; this self-interest, he said, was ultimately consistent with the public interest. An "invisible hand" guided market participants to act in ways that promoted the public interest. Profits may be the main concern of firms, but only firms that satisfy consumer demand and offer suitable prices earn profits.

Supply and Demand

Goods and services refer to things that satisfy human needs or desires. Goods are tangible items, such as food, cars, and clothing; services are intangible items, such as education and health care. A market is the interaction between potential buyers and sellers of goods and services. Money is usually the medium of exchange. The supply of a good is the quantity of that good that producers offer at a certain price. The collection of all such points for every price is the supply curve. Demand for a good is the quantity of a good that consumers are willing and able to purchase at a certain price. The demand curve is the combination of quantity and price, at all price levels.

Skill 10.5: Identify the Economic Interdependence Among Nations

Economic interdependence among nations is studied primarily from the perspective of macroeconomics. Macroeconomics is the study of entire economies, including national and international economies. Some of the topics considered include trade, economic growth, and unemployment.

Microeconomics, in contrast, focuses on problems specific to a household, firm, or industry, rather than national or global issues. Microeconomics gives particular emphasis to how these smaller units make decisions as well as the consequences of those decisions.

Skill 10.6: Identify Human, Natural, and Capital Resources and How These Resources Are Used in the Production of Goods and Services

There are three main types of resources:

1. *Economic resources* include the labor, capital, productive agents, and entrepreneurial ability used in the production of goods and services.

2. *Human resources* include the physical and mental talents and efforts of people that are necessary to produce goods and services.

3. Natural resources include the materials that are available in a natural state and have economic value, such as water, timber, and mineral deposits.

Traditionally, the term "capital" referred to profit. Currently, it refers to how much real, usable money is in the possession of a person, group, or company.

Competency 11: Knowledge of Instruction and Assessment In the Social Sciences

The focus of Competency 11 is on appropriate resources and strategies for social science instruction and assessment.

Skill 11.1: Identify Appropriate Resources for Teaching Social Science Concepts

The ability to understand and apply skills and procedures related to the study of social sciences involves knowledge of the use of systematic inquiry. Inquiry is essential for use in examining individual social sciences topics as well as integrated social sciences. Inquiry requires the ability to acquire information from a variety of sources and to organize and interpret the acquired information. The process of inquiry begins with designing and conducting investigations that lead to the identification and analysis of social sciences issues.

Systematic social science inquiry relies on numerous resources. Among the most commonly used resources are the following:

- Textbooks

- Monographs

- Articles

- Films

- Encyclopedias

- Almanacs

- Atlases

- Government documents

- Artifacts

- Oral histories

These sources of information may be available on the Internet, on digital media such as CD-ROMs and DVDs, or in print.

Effective Use of Resources

Following are some of the hallmarks of effective use of resources in social science instruction:

- Use of a variety of educational resources (including people and technology) to enhance both individual and group learning

- Familiarity with the school library, the local public library, education service center resources, and the library of any college or university in the area

- Use of a variety of resources in the classroom that relate to instructional objectives

- Previewing resources available from librarians or elsewhere before use in the classroom

Textbooks

The most common print material used for instructional purposes is the textbook, which teachers on the campus usually select from a list of books approved by the state. Some of the advantages of textbooks are as follows:

- Convenience

- Wide breadth of coverage

- Alignment with state-mandated curriculum and assessments

The disadvantages of textbook use include the following:

- Increasing costs

- Slow adoption process (and thus risk of obsolescence)

- Divergence in some cases from curriculum

Another limitation of textbooks is their tendency to provide sketchy or minimal information, partly because publishers must include such a broad range of topics. An ineffective teacher may use the "chapter a week" approach with a textbook. This method gives no consideration to the importance of information in each chapter or its relevance to the overall district curriculum. Merely covering the material does not promote critical thinking on the part of the teacher or the student. Students tend to believe the textbook is something they must endure and not necessarily employ as a tool for learning.

The effective teacher focuses sections from the textbook that are relevant to the learning goals and, in some cases, may omit the rest. The teacher may supplement the textbook by using an abundance of other resources. For example, local, state, and national newspapers and magazines are important sources of up-to-date information not available in textbooks. Some newspapers and magazines have special programs to help teachers use their products in the classroom as sources of information and for reading and writing opportunities. Local newspapers may even be willing to send specialists to work with students or act as special resource persons.

Visual Materials

The most widely available visual tools in classrooms are the chalkboard and the overhead projector. In both cases, several principles govern effective use:

- Text should be large and clear.

- Presentations should be free of clutter.

- Old information should be removed before adding new information.

- Graphics strategies should be used to highlight key information.

- Advance planning should be used.

- Information should be explained and discussed, not merely presented.

Posters and are also helpful visual materials. They can complement lessons, but they should not clutter the walls so that they become a distraction, and they should be removed when no longer useful. Teachers may wish to display them on a rotating basis.

Some of the best graphic aids are those that individustudents or student groups develop. While learning about subject area concepts, students become familiar with the design and presentation of information. Students can take pictures of their products to put in a portfolio or scrapbook.

Films, Discs, and Interactive Video

Films and video clips are appealing to students because they are engaging and familiar. They are useful educational tools owing in part to their appeal and in part to the fact that teachers can stop them periodically for discussion. Students will comprehend and remember the material in a film or video clip better if the teacher introduces the film or clip appropriately and stops it frequently to discuss it with the students. This method also helps keep students' attention focused and assists them in learning note-taking skills.

CDs and DVDs provide sturdy, condensed systems of storage for pictures and sound. These discs can store many separate frames of still images and several hours of music or motion pictures. These media share the same advantages as films and video clips. Moreover, with a CD or DVD one can pause and evaluate each frame separately and quickly.

A CD or video program can become interactive with a computer link. The teacher can then access individual images, sequence images, and integration information from an interactive system. A social studies teacher with a collection of pictures of the world's art treasures can choose which pictures to use, order the images, and design custom-made lessons for repeated use or for easy revision. The teacher can develop numerous lessons from one CD or videotape. More comprehensive interactive programs use the computer to present information, access a disc to illustrate main points, and ask for responses from the student.

A multimedia production can include images, text, and sound from a videodisc, CD-ROM, graphics software, word processing software, and a sound-effects program. Teachers can develop classroom presentations, but students can also develop learning units as part of a research or inquiry project. The cost of a multimedia system is relatively high, but if students can use it, they will have an excellent opportunity to develop high-level thought processes, collaborative work habits, research skills, content knowledge, and topical understanding.

Human Resources

Parents and other members of the community can serve as experts from whom students can learn about any subject: economics from bankers, history from veterans, music from a specific period from local musicians or collectors, community history from local historians or librarians, business from owners of companies, and so on. Effective teachers ensure that any invited guest understands the purpose of the visit and the goals or objectives of the presentation. Preparation can make the class period more focused and meaningful.

Community members can also interact with students in the context of a field trip. Field trips are excellent sources of information, especially about careers, the local community, and topics of contemporary interest. One field trip can yield assignments in a variety of subjects. Teachers can collaborate with each other to produce thematic assignments for the field trip or to coordinate the students' assignments.

Instructional Strategies

There are many useful instructional strategies for the social studies classroom. Together these strategies convey content in a clear and engaging way, and prepare students to be citizens in a democratic society. Some examples are as follows:

1. Provide opportunities to gain knowledge through primary sources as well as concept development and attainment.

2. Enhance skills through discovery learning, questioning, and inquiry learning.

3. Develop democratic dispositions through the fostering of multiple perspectives, the establishment of a democratic classroom, and efforts toward community building.

Strategies that should be used in the social studies classroom are as follows:

1. Primary sources should be examined and discussed with guidance from the teacher.

2. Concept development should be promoted by helping students analyze characteristics, group similar characteristics, and then identify the concept.

3. Discovery learning should be implemented by helping students seek information through research, analysis, and interpretation in the context of problem-solving activities.

4. Good questioning should be promoted to help students stay engaged, to learn, and to exercise critical-thinking skills.

5. Inquiry learning should be implemented so that students participate in topic selection as well as the process of acquiring information, thereby enhancing motivation and learning.

6. The development of multiple perspectives should be fostered, so that students from all backgrounds are respected and understood and so that students themselves can understand and respect others.

7. A democratic classroom should be established, so that students understand the importance of participating in creating and maintaining the rules and so they are consequently more likely to respect and follow the rules.

8. Community building should be fostered, so that students develop a sense of belonging and safety and can both support and disagree with each other.

By implementing these strategies throughout the social studies curriculum, students develop their knowledge base, their critical-thinking skills, and their appreciation of diversity.

Skill 11.2: Identify Appropriate Assessment Methods in Teaching Social Science Concepts

The basic goals of assessment are to enhance teachers' knowledge of learners and their needs, to monitor students' progress toward goals and outcomes, and to modify instruction whenever needed.

Extensive discussion of assessment can be found under Competency 4 in the chapter on Language Arts and Reading. Although specific methods for the assessment of literacy skills, such as running records, are not suitable for social studies classes, the general principles, concepts, and strategies of assessment are the same. In addition, authentic assessments such as projects are particularly important in social studies. Projects allow students to integrate and apply what they have learned and to exercise self-assessment skills as they evaluate their progress at each step of the project.

End-of-Chapter Questions

1. The era when machines began to displace human and animal power in the production and distribution of goods is known as the...?

   (A) Classical age.

   (B) Industrial Revolution.

   (C) Roman Empire.

   (D) Renaissance.

2. The National Aeronautics and Space Administration (NASA) had its beginning under which president?

   (A) J. F. Kennedy.

   (B) Lyndon Johnson.

   (C) Dwight D. Eisenhower.

   (D) Richard Nixon.

3. In which country did Anne Frank live and write her story, later known as *The Diary of Anne Frank*?

   (A) Italy.

   (B) England.

   (C) Netherlands.

   (D) Germany.

4. The organizations and processes that contribute to the decision-making process of a country comprise the...

   (A) Economic system.

   (B) Social system.

   (C) Educational system.

   (D) Political system.

5. When a president serves as commander in chief, he/she is fulfilling the duties or obligations bestowed uponhim/her through the...?

   (A) Executive Branch.

   (B) Congressional Branch.

   (C) Legislative Branch.

   (D) Judicial Branch.

6.   Who was the first woman to serve on the Supreme Court?

(A)   Sandra Day O'Connor.

(B)   Elena Kagan.

(C)   Sonia Sotomayor.

(D)   Ruth Bader Ginsburg.

7.   Which of the following terms best describes the study of economic issues specific to a household, firm, or industry?

(A)   Macroeconomics.

(B)   Microeconomics.

(C)   Global interdependence.

(D)   Economic theory.

Answer Key

1.	(B)		5.	(A)
2.	(C)		6.	(A)
3.	(C)		7.	(B)
4.	(D)			

Music, Visual Arts, Physical Education, and Health

Competency 12: Knowledge of Skills and Techniques in Music and Visual Arts

The focus of Competency 12 is on those skills and techniques in music and visual arts that teachers should be able to convey to their students.

Skill 12.1: Identify Appropriate Varieties of Music

When selecting vocal literature (music for singing), the teacher must consider the *age* of the students and their vocal abilities. Children's vocal ranges vary from one child to the next. However, one study showed that 67 percent of first-grade children had a vocal range of one octave (8 notes); 64 percent were able to sing as high as C_5 (C_4 is middle C on a piano), and 90 percent could sing as low as C_4. In sixth grade, 98 percent of the singers had a vocal range of an octave or more; 52 percent could vocalize two octaves or more. The voice ranges of girls and boys remain about the same until the boys' voices begin to change—usually during middle school.

The materials used for a quality music program in any grade should reflect various musical periods and styles, cultural and ethnic diversity, and a gender balance. The goal of a quality music program is to make students aware that music is both a part of and a reflection of many cultures and many ethnic groups. The teacher should provide students with opportunities to sing, play instruments, and listen to music of many cultural and ethnic groups.

Skill 12.2: Identify Developmentally Appropriate Singing Techniques

The voices of singing children should sound as if they are "floating out" rather than forced. To help students achieve the preferred sound, the teacher might ask students to imagine trying to support a feather fluttering a few inches from their mouths.

Three dimensions of singing technique that are particularly important beginning at an early age are posture, breath, and tone.

Posture

Posture is an important part of good singing. Children should stand or sit erect, not slouch, as they sing. An excellent way to attain the desired straight spine is to have the students stand. Standing helps to allow for sufficient movement of breath.

Breath

Inhaling the breath should mimic directing it to the area just below the rib cage; as the child takes in a breath, the wall of the abdomen should move out. The expansion that is necessary for the inhalation should not come from raising the shoulders or from puffing up the chest; instead, the inhalation should result from the diaphragm moving toward the waistline. Because the flow of air should be steady, the child's mouth should remain open. The child should not try to manipulate the voice box; the idea is not to sing *with* the larynx but to sing *through* the larynx (Hoffer 1982). Whether standing or sitting, children should make sure that both feet are flat on the floor. When standing, children should be certain that their hands are down at their sides or clasped loosely in front; children should not clasp their hands tightly in the back or place their hands in their pockets.

Tone

The tone (also called *timbre*) is the musical sound or quality of the voice. For instance, one might say that someone sings with a "nasal tone," a "thin tone," a "raspy tone," or a "full tone."

The voice of the average child is similar to the voice of the adult in terms of range but not quality. The teacher should not encourage children to imitate the heavier and fuller quality of the mature adult voice. Children can sing high, but, as with adults, tension results when the pitch is too high.

The average voice range is from around middle C to F (fifth line) on the piano—about 13 notes; the range between D and E-flat (a little more than an octave) is, however, far more comfortable. For the beginner, a very comfortable range is from E-flat (first line) to B-flat or C (about 6 notes).

Skill 12.3: Identify Correct Performance Techniques for Rhythmic and Melodic Classroom Instruments

Music is the arrangement of sounds for voice and musical instruments and, like dance, requires training and practice. Making music is a natural part of the human experience. Mothers sing to their babies. Children beat sticks together, make drums, and sing during play. Adults whistle or sing along with tunes on the radio. Sound and music naturally attract people, and music is an important part of culture, religious practice, and personal experience for all people. Some people become professional musicians, while others do nothing more than whistle, sing, or play instruments for their own enjoyment or that of friends and family.

Students should have the opportunity to experience as many ways to make music as possible. The acquisition of basic skills in singing and playing instruments allows people to grow in their ability to express themselves through music. As students develop skills, they are also exposed to basic musical concepts such as melody, harmony, rhythm, pitch, and tone. With experience, students come to make decisions about what is acceptable or not acceptable within a given cultural or historical context and thereby develop their own aesthetic awareness.

The child does not usually begin the study of orchestral instruments until the fourth or fifth grade. At that point, a music teacher—not the classroom teacher—gives instruction in orchestral instruments. The instruments that the classroom teacher normally teaches include the rhythmic instruments (e.g., triangle, tambourine, blocks, and sticks); melodic instruments (e.g., melody bells and simple flutes); and harmonic instruments (e.g., chording instruments, like the autoharp). However, if the teacher decides on the instruments the class will use, who will use them, and when, music instruction becomes a teacher-directed activity that can stifle the children's creativity. Often what is preferable to a teacher-directed approach is allowing the students to make decisions about what and when to play. For example, the teacher might write out a piece of music on a large sheet of paper and allow the students to draw pictures indicating where they should play their instruments.

Another student-directed approach is to have students first listen to a piece of music and then allow them to decide on the instruments they want to play and when it seems right to play them. This more creative approach is appropriate for young children who cannot read music and forms music readers who want to produce their own performance techniques. Upper-grade students can even try making their own instruments.

Rhythmic Instruments

After students have a chance to move with music in the manner that the music suggests, and after they have experienced singing games and action songs, they may be ready to try rhythmic instruments, which are primarily intended for rhythmic rather than melodic purposes. The students will need opportunities to experiment with triangles, tambourines, sticks, blocks, and so on. Students might try striking the tambourine with the hand to create one sound and with the knee to create another, for instance.

Melodic Instruments

Melodic instruments produce individual notes differing in pitch, at least. These instruments are helpful to use as the children are learning to read music. For example, melodic bells are instruments that the child strikes with a mallet or rings by hand. In classroom settings, each child typically has only one bell. Some of the bells may be color-coded, allowing the students to "read" music according to the colors that are displayed. Another type of melodic instrument is the simple flute. This category is represented by trade names such as Flutophone, Song Flute, and Tonette. Teachers usually include these simple flutes with music instruction at about the fifth grade. For most of these flutes, the right thumb supports the flute, and the fingers of the right hand are used to play the notes. The use of the fingers to create the sounds varies from one instrument to the other.

Harmonic Instruments

Harmonic instruments generate combinations of notes and chords. For example, the wooden base of an autoharp (which is approximately rectangular in shape) has wire strings stretched across it, along with wooden bars attached at right angles. When the child presses the bars and strums the wires, the instrument produces chords. Students can experiment with harmony using the autoharp. They will find that sometimes a variety of chords "sounds right," but that at other times only one choice works.

Skill 12.4: Read and Interpret Simple, Traditional, and Nontraditional Music Notation

Music notation is a way of writing music. Teaching students to use, read, and interpret music notation can heighten their enjoyment of music. Among the many musical characteristics conveyed by notation, three dimensions of particular importance to early learners are rhythm, melody, and harmony.

1. *Rhythm* consists of the contrast among the various lengths of musical tones. For instance, in the first six notes of *The Star-Spangled Banner,* the rhythm is short, short, medium, medium, medium, long. To indicate the lengths of the tones, musical notation is used to describe various types of notes and rests (see figure below).

Notes	Values	Rest
o	Whole Note 4 Beats	▬
♩	Half Note 2 Beats	▬
♩	Quarter Note 1 Beat	𝄽
♪	Eighth Note ½ a Beat	𝄾
♪	Sixteenth Note ¼ of a Beat	𝄿

Figure 4.1: Types of Notes and Rests

2. *Melody* consists of a succession of notes that differ in pitch. In the opening of *The Star-Spangled Banner,* for example, the downward-moving melody of the first three notes is reversed in the next three. To indicate pitch, musical notation is used to describe various notes.

3. *Harmony* is the "vertical" quality when groups of notes are played in close succession or when more than one note is played at the same time. Melody and harmony are usually conveyed by means of the same notation.

Simple Music Notation

Students can begin learning to read music by means of simple music notation. For example, students might try listening to a simple melody and making dashes on the board or on their papers to indicate the length the notes are held. As they sing "Three Blind Mice," for instance, they would mark dashes of similar length for the words/notes "three" and "blind" and a longer dash for "mice."

Traditional Music Notation

With traditional music notation, the students use the lines and spaces on the conventional staff. They observe, for instance, that the staff contains four spaces and five lines (see figure below). They might also notice the strange looking symbol at the beginning of the staff. This is called a clef. The clef indicates the notes and pitches on the staff. The most common clef symbols are for the treble clef and the bass clef. Students might also notice that the appearance of the notes indicates the length, and the placement of the notes on the staff corresponds to the various tones.

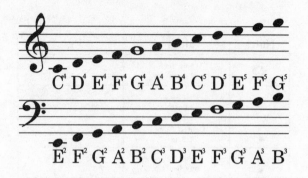

Figure 4.2: Treble and Bass Clefs with Notation

Nontraditional Music Notation

Students in the upper grades may encounter nontraditional music notation in their books. In the South, for example, many of the hymnals use a nontraditional type of music notation called shape notes (see figure below). Instead of the elliptical note head used in traditional notation, the heads of the shape notes are represented by various shapes to show the position of the notes on the major scale. Another form of nontraditional music notation is Braille notation.

Figure 4.3: Shape Notes

Skill 12.5: Select Safe and Developmentally Appropriate Media, Techniques, and Tools to Create Both Two-Dimensional and Three-Dimensional Works of Art

The art room is the scene for many activities. Following are some recommendations from the South Carolina Visual and Performing Arts Curriculum Framework Writing Team (1993) for effective instruction and safety:

1. There should be one art room for every 400 to 500 elementary school students.

2. The art room should contain least 55 square feet of workspace per student— excluding storage and teacher workspace—to ensure safety. If there is a kiln room, at least 45 square feet of space is essential for that room, and venting is necessary.

3. The art room should allow for individual as well as small-group and large-group seating arrangements.

4.   The art room should contain areas for the teacher to lecture and display students' work, space for learning centers, and areas for drawing and painting, printmaking, creating computer graphics, working with ceramics, modeling, assembling crafts, and sculpting.

5.   Ideally, the art room will be near the service entrance to facilitate deliveries.

6.   Both natural and artificial lighting should be available in the art room.

7.   Locked storage is necessary for hazardous materials in the art room.

8.   Proper ventilation is essential, especially in the kiln room and in areas of the art room devoted to printmaking, ceramics, and spraying.

9.   Sinks and surfaces in the art room must have durable, cleanable finishes.

Skill 12.6: Identify Appropriate Uses of Art Materials and Tools for Developing Basic Processes and Motor Skills

Art materials for the elementary art program include scissors, wet and dry brushes, fabrics, different types and weights of paper, simple digital cameras, computers, clay, glue, Styrofoam, crayons, beads, and much more.

Grade-Appropriate Activities

Art activities at each grade are intended to support both large and small motor development as children become familiar with new techniques.

1.   Throughout the lower elementary grades, students should engage in drawing, painting, designing, constructing, crafts, sculpting, weaving, finger painting, and Styrofoam carving.

2.   In the middle elementary grades, students should continue to work with drawing, painting, designing, constructing, crafts, and sculpting and can start new techniques like sponge painting, graphics, digital animation, and environmental design.

3.   In the upper elementary grades, students continue with the earlier activities and add jewelry making and intaglio (printmaking).

Competency 13: Knowledge of Creation and Communication in Music and Visual Arts

One of the purposes of fostering creativity in the arts is to provide students with a means of self-expression and communication with others. The focus of Competency 13 is on knowledge of how to create and communicate by means of self-expression in music and the visual arts.

Skill 13.1: Identify the Elements of Music and Ways They Are Used in Expression

Music consists of several elements:

- Rhythm, or the contrast among the various lengths of musical sounds.

- Melody, or the succession of sounds.

- Form, or the underlying structure or patterns of a song.

- Timbre, or the quality of musical sounds.

- Texture, or the context in which simultaneous sounds occur.

- Dynamics, or the volume of musical sounds.

These elements work together to create a musical expression of texts, ideas, emotions, settings, times, and places.

Skill 13.2: Demonstrate Knowledge of Strategies to Develop Creative Responses Through Music to Ideas Drawn from Text, Speech, Movement, and Visual Images

Music uses the elements described in the previous section to evoke thoughts, memories, and feelings. To help develop creative responses to music, teachers can introduce students to various genres of music and ask them to describe what the songs make them think of, recall, or feel. Their expression could be verbal and/or nonverbal, in that they could present a description, tell a story, improvise a pantomime, or dance to the music. Students could create their own melodies and/or rhythms in response to what they have heard. And students could choose existing music to accompany stories, plays, images, or dance.

Skill 13.3: Demonstrate Knowledge of Strategies to Develop Creative Responses Through Art to Ideas Drawn from Text, Music, Speech, Movement, and Visual Images

To respond creatively through art to text, music, and other forms of expression, students need to be able to deploy a variety of techniques and media. Ideally, even the child in the earliest grades engages in various modes of visual expression. Teachers can model creative responses through art, allow students to explore on their own, and provide explicit instruction in certain techniques. Students should be encouraged in their work in order to build confidence.

Skill 13.4: Identify the Elements of Art and Principles of Design and Ways They Are Used in Expressing Text, Ideas, Meanings, and Emotions

The ideas, meanings, and emotions conveyed through art are varied and numerous. To be able to respond to these elements, as well as to express them, students must be familiar with and be able to manipulate both the elements of art and the basic principles of design. Following are some of these elements and principles.

1. *Lines* consist of discrete marks with shape and direction or the edges created where two shapes meet.

2. *Colors* consist of visible hues and can be divided into the following categories:
    - Primary colors (red, yellow, blue)
    - Secondary colors (green, orange, violet)
    - Tertiary colors (those that fall between primary and secondary colors)
    - Compound colors (those containing a mixture of the three primary colors)

3. *Shapes* are the self-contained, more-or-less clearly defined areas of things.

4. *Textures* are the surface qualities of shapes. Some dimensions of texture are as follows:
    - Smooth
    - Rough
    - Soft
    - Hard
    - Patterned
    - Plain
    - Glossy
    - Dull

5. *Balance* is how the elements of art are arranged to create stability or proportion.

6. *Movement* is how the elements of art are combined to produce the appearance of action.

7. *Form* is the synthesis of all elements of a work of art.

Competency 14: Knowledge of Cultural and Historical Connections in Music and Visual Arts

Skill 14.1: Identify Characteristics of Style in Musical Selections

Often, after listening to a piece of music, a person can determine the specific artist by putting several clues together, as in a detective story. To help students reach this level of discernment, the teacher should expose them to diverse styles (i.e., basic musical languages) and genres (i.e., artistic categories).

Dividing music into categories is difficult because styles are constantly emerging and many songs reflect multiple genres. Following are some of the most widely recognized genres:

- Classical
- Gospel
- Jazz
- Latin American
- Blues
- Rhythm and Blues
- Rock
- Country
- Pop
- Contemporary African
- Electronic
- Electronic Dance
- Melodic
- Hip Hop
- Rap
- Punk
- Reggae
- Dub

Skill 14.2: Demonstrate Knowledge of How Music Reflects Particular Cultures, Historical Periods, and Places

Throughout history, music has come from a community or ethnic group feeling the need to express celebration, commemoration, or sorrow. Music is also often linked to storytelling or poetry. By having students listen to music from countries such as China, Japan, Germany, Australia, or Africa when they are studying the cultures, the teacher enriches students' learning experience and makes it more memorable for them.

Cultural Differences in Music

Particularly engaging for students is having the opportunity to view live or videotaped performances of the music and dance of other cultures. Performers often dress in traditional costume with traditional instruments that may be very different from modern instruments. Seeing the costumes and the movements that accompany the performance is an important part of understanding the culture.

In music, the system of tonal scales is often unique to a culture. For example, the Chinese have traditionally relied on the pentatonic scale of five notes, while Western musicians have primarily used a scale of seven notes (and with the first note repeated to create an octave). Indian musical pieces include the *raga* (meaning "mood" or "color"), which is based on melodic patterns of five to seven tones. Indian compositions feature repetitive patterns and use scales whose octaves have 22 intervals.

Merely experiencing a piece of music and recognizing, for example, differences in tonal scale are not sufficient for an appreciation of the cultural meaning of the music. Students must be able to understand the music in its historical context. They must be able to appreciate why the music reflects that context, and to be able to compare and contrast music across different contexts. For example, Joseph Haydn, Wolfgang Amadeus Mozart, and William Billings were composers of the late-eighteenth to early-nineteenth centuries. These composers used simple melodies in their works. However, Haydn and Mozart wrote many large works, such as operas and symphonies, and Billings wrote short choral pieces. Students must be aware of these facts and then consider why more highly developed forms were preferred in the "Old World," while basic psalms and songs were more common in the American colonies. The depth of the ensuing discussion would depend on the level of the students.

Ancient Music

In the ancient world, Egyptian, Sumerian, and Hebrew cultures used song and such instruments as lyres, harps, drums, flutes, cymbals, and trumpets. The ancient Greeks accompanied the recitation of poetry with the stringed lyre. The *aulos*, or double-piped oboe (an instrument used in the worship of Dionysus), often accompanied Athenian drama, and in between recited passages the audience often heard choral songs.

Christian Era

During the late sixth century, Pope Gregory the Great often codified and arranged the *plainsong*, or unaccompanied religious chant, using early forms of music notation. This is the origin of the Gregorian chant.

By the twelfth and thirteenth centuries, the important form of polyphony, which is the basis of the distinctive art music of the West, enabled supportive melodies to be added to the main chant. The Italian Benedictine monk Guido d'Arezzo invented the basic form of music notation, representing pitch through the use of a staff. The later Middle Ages saw the composition of both religious and secular polyphonic music. Melodies and rhythms became more diversified.

Renaissance Period

During the Renaissance, with the resolution of many technical problems, the spirit of humanism and rationalism pervaded polyphonic music, and music became a mark of culture. Emphasis on secular music, dance, and instrumental music ensembles increased, as did emphasis on complex combinations of voices and instruments.

Baroque Period

Baroque music of the seventeenth and early eighteenth centuries employed a greater complexity of melodies and forms, the beginnings of harmony, the use of instrumental ensembles, and great drama and emotion. The new dramatic forms became popular entertainment. Other innovative forms included the oratorio, the cantata, the sonata, the suite, the concerto, and the fugue. Composers of some of the great works of baroque music include Johann Pachelbel, Antonio Vivaldi, Henry Purcell, George Frederic Handel (*The Messiah*), and Johann Sebastian Bach.

Classical Period

In the latter half of the eighteenth century, the music of the classical period was distinguished by clarity of form, logical thematic development, and adherence to sonata form. The sonata form was a style consisting of the exposition of a musical theme, the subsequent elaboration of the theme, and the resolution of harmonies and theme in a final recapitulation.

The greatest composers of the classical period were Ludwig van Beethoven, Franz Joseph Haydn, and Wolfgang Amadeus Mozart. Mozart's structurally exquisite works approach perfection of form while adding inventive melodic diversity. Mozart wrote 41 symphonies and 22 operas, including innovative works like *The Marriage of Figaro* and *The Magic Flute*.

Romantic Period

Beethoven, a German composer, ushered in the romantic school of symphonic music. His symphonies and piano sonatas, concertos, and string quartets explode with dramatic passion, expressive melodies and harmonies, and complex thematic development. His most famous works are the so-called Fifth and Ninth symphonies and the *Moonlight* sonata. Much of the romantic music that followed was less formal and more expressive, often associated with grandiose concepts and literary themes and more complex instrumentation. Art songs, piano concertos and sonatas, and symphonic poems (which try to paint a musical picture or tell a story) became important forms for romantic composers. These composers include Frédéric Chopin (who mainly created piano music, including *nocturnes*), Franz Liszt (known for the *Mephisto Waltz*), Richard Strauss (known for the orchestral piece *Don Juan*, and the operas *Salome* and *Elektra*), and Felix Mendelssohn (known for his symphonies and incidental music to *A Midsummer Night's Dream*).

Nineteenth Century Developments

Other important symphonic composers of the nineteenth century were Robert Schumann, Johannes Brahms, Pyotr Ilich Tchaikovsky, and Gustav Mahler. Throughout the century, musical development continued in the direction of a greater richness of harmony, a more varied use of musical instruments and orchestral color, and increased employment of *chromaticism* (the use of tones not related to the key of the composition).

Nineteenth-century music was increasingly influenced by folk melodies, music of a nationalistic vein, and popular songs—often linked to composers who were outstanding melodists and harmonic innovators. Composers who wrote in these styles include Giacomo Rossini (e.g., *The Barber of Seville* and *William Tell*), Georges Bizet (e.g., *Carmen*), Giuseppe Verdi (e.g., *Aida* and *La Traviata*), Giacomo Puccini (e.g., *La Bohème* and *Tosca*), Modest Mussorgsky (e.g., *A Night on Bald Mountain*), and Nicholas Rimsky-Korsakov (e.g., *Scheherazade*).

Mussorgsky's and Wagner's idiomatic and chromatic harmonies greatly influenced the French "impressionist" composers Claude Debussy (*Prelude to the Afternoon of a Faun*) and Maurice Ravel (*Mother Goose* Suite and *Bolero*). Debussy, Mussorgsky, and Wagner for the most part eschewed the traditional larger forms and wrote dramatic sonatas and tone poems (one-movement orchestral pieces based on poems, novels, or other nonmusical sources). These composers used oriental tonalities and rhapsodic forms freely. One of the great innovators in opera, Richard Wagner, sought to create a new form of musical drama, using continuous music and relentless, swirling harmonies to underlie massive spectacle and recitative or sung dialogue.

Twentieth Century

The concert music of the twentieth century increasingly sought to enlarge the boundaries of rhythm, form, and harmony.

At the outset of the century, musical compositions began to diverge more from traditional structures and melodies, shifting toward intellectual experiments, abstraction, and highly personal modes of expression. In this respect the development of music paralleled that of the visual arts. For example, during the years before World War I, Igor Stravinsky broke up traditional rhythms and introduced radical harmonies in works like *Firebird* Suite, in somewhat the same way that Pablo Picasso and the cubists rearranged the space of the traditional canvas and its representations of objects. Stravinsky sought to use the new rhythms and harmonies in structurally clear and less orchestrally dense pieces than those of the traditional canon.

Ethnic and popular influences continued to exert an important pull in the creation of twentieth-century music. Folk music was a major element in the works of the English composers and often in the music of Stravinsky and the Soviet Union's Sergei Prokofiev. Ragtime, blues, jazz, and other popular music provided material for some of the most innovative and exciting twentieth century compositions, including Stravinsky's *Ragtime for Eleven Instruments*, George Gershwin's *Rhapsody in Blue* and *Porgy and Bess*, and many pieces by Leonard Bernstein. Composers after World War II continued to experiment with tape-recorded sound and, eventually, digital editing.

Skill 14.3: Identify Characteristics of Style in Works of Art

A style is an artist's manner of expression. When a group of artists during a specific period (usually a few months, years, or decades) reflects a common style, reference is made to a school or movement in art. Art movements can be discerned in all forms of art.

With respect to Western architecture, eight historical periods can be identified, with various styles and movements within each. Although some periods have only one or two styles, the twentieth century reflects more than thirty unique styles. Some of the best-known styles throughout history are summarized in the following table:

Historical Periods in Art	
Time Period	**Examples**
Prehistoric (30,000 BCE-2500 BCE)	Cave painting, fertility goddesses, megalithic figures
Ancient (3500 BCE-500 CE)	Development of differing styles by various civilizations (e.g., Mesopotamian warrior art and stone relief narration; Egyptian focus on afterlife; Greek/Hellenistic focus on balance and perfection of form; Roman realism and development of the arch; Byzantine mosaics and maze-like design)
Medieval/Middle Ages (500-1400)	Gothic architecture with ribbed vaulting, pointed roofs, flying buttresses; panel painting (painting, often with oils, on a thin board)

(continued)

Historical Periods in Art *(continued)*	
Time Period	**Examples**
Renaissance (1400-1550)	Early Renaissance focused on religious themes, later Renaissance emphasized classicism (recapturing the beauty of Greek and Roman art) and realism
Baroque (1550-1750)	Emphasis on splendor of God; art as a motivator and weapon for religious wars
Romanticism (1780-1850)	Emphasis on imagination and individuality; gracefulness and lightness
Realism (1848-1900)	Focus on rustic painting, working class and peasant themes, situations, dilemmas
Impressionism (1865-1885)	Attention to effects of natural light; visible brushstrokes and other signs of spontaneity
Twentieth Century (1900-2000)	Harsh colors and flat surfaces (fauvism); effects of emotion distorting form (expressionism); simultaneous representation of multiplicity of object's features (cubism); abstract representation (abstract expressionism); lifelike representation photos (photorealism); blending of art and consumerism (pop art); striking visual effects (op art); marking, scratching, spray painting of surfaces (graffiti)

Skill 14.4: Demonstrate Knowledge of How Visual Arts Reflect Particular Cultures, Historical Periods, and Places

As with musical history, the history of the visual arts can be divided into historical periods, such as the following:

Prehistorical Era

Some of the oldest known examples of art, dating from 30,000 to 20,000 BCE, are the "Venuses"—small stylized stone carvings of women found in modern France, Italy, and Austria—that may be been symbols of fertility. Paleolithic peoples in Europe painted animal pictures on the cave walls at Lascaux and Altamira from about 15,000 to 13,000 BCE. The artists of the ancient civilizations of Sumer, Babylon, and Assyria skillfully carved even the hardest rocks, such as granite and basalt, into narratives of battles and historical records. Egyptian statues—like their architectural monuments, the pyramids—were often of colossal size to exalt further the power of the society's leaders and gods.

Ancient Greece and Rome

The art of ancient Greece has its roots in the Minoan civilization on the island of Crete, which flourished from about 2500 to 1400 BCE. The palace at Knossos contains distinctive wall paintings that suggest a people who were fond of games, leisure, and the beauty of the sea. The mainland Greeks of the classical period, about 1,000 years later, were fascinated by physical beauty as well. The Greeks recreated their Olympian gods in idealized and gracefully proportioned sculptures, architecture, and paintings.

During the Hellenistic period, the populace increasingly appreciated these various objects of art for their beauty alone. The Romans borrowed heavily from the artistic developments of the Greeks in the process of creating their own civilization. The culture of Rome excelled in engineering and building, skills intended to organize a vast empire and provide an aesthetic environment for private and public use. The Romans built temples, roads, bathing complexes, civic buildings, palaces, and aqueducts. One of the greatest of their artistic and engineering accomplishments was the massive-domed temple of all the gods, the Pantheon, which is today one of the most perfectly preserved of all buildings from the classical period.

Early Christian Era

The early Christian era borrowed the basilica form of Roman architecture for its churches, as is particularly evident in the extant churches in the town of Ravenna in northeastern Italy. The seventh-century church of San Vitale echoes the mosaic mastery of the Byzantine Empire in Constantinople (which flourished as a center of civilization for a thousand years after the decline of Rome). Its grandiose apse mosaic depicts Emperor Justinian and Empress Theodora.

Romanesque Style

The Romanesque style of art and architecture was preeminent from about 800 to 1200. By then many local styles, including the decorative arts of the Byzantine Empire, the Near East, and the German and Celtic tribes, were contributing to European culture. Common features of Romanesque churches are round arches, vaulted ceilings, and heavy walls that are ornately decorated. The decorations consist primarily of symbols and symbolic figures in Christianity, as realism had become less important than the underlying theological message.

Gothic Style

Gothic art flourished in Europe for 300 years. The cathedrals reflecting this style combine efforts at structural improvement with stylistic features that convey a relentless verticality, a reach toward heaven, and the unbridled adoration of God. Soaring and airy, the construction of the Gothic cathedrals employed such elements as flying buttresses and pointed arches and vaults; a profusion of sculptures and stained-glass windows that were, for the worshippers, visual encyclopedias of Christian teachings and stories.

The Early Renaissance

When the painter Giotto began to compose his figures into groups and depict expressive human gestures, he laid the cornerstone of the Italian Renaissance. The fifteenth century witnessed the invigoration of art, architecture, literature, and music. Renaissance artists revived classical styles and values and developed new forms, guided by a belief in the importance of the human experience on Earth. Great sculptors approached true human characterization and realism. Lorenzo Ghiberti created the bronze doors of the Florence Baptistry (early fifteenth century), and Donatello produced *Gattamelata*, the first equestrian statue since the Roman era. Architecture, in the hands of Filippo Brunelleschi and Leon Battista Alberti, revived elements of Greek architecture. Like the painters of the period, Renaissance architects took a scientific, ordered approach and emphasized perspective and the calculated composition of figures in space.

The Renaissance artists sought to produce works of perfect beauty and engaged in a constant search for knowledge, most often portraying religious subjects and wealthy patrons. The stylistic innovations of such fifteenth-century painters as Masaccio, Paolo Uccello, Fra Angelico, Piero della Francesca, Andrea Mantegna, and Sandro Botticelli formed the basis of the High Renaissance of the next century.

The High Renaissance

During the High Renaissance, art became more emotional and dramatic, the use of color and movement increased in vigor, and references to classical iconography and the pleasures of an idyllic golden age abounded. Typical examples of this emotional, dramatic art are Michelangelo's magnificent Sistine Chapel frescoes and his powerful sculptures of David and Moses, Leonardo's *Mona Lisa*, Raphael's *School of Athens* fresco, and the increasingly dramatic and colorful works of the Venetian and northern Italian masters Titian, Correggio, Giorgione, and Bellini.

The northern European Renaissance also emphasized also a renewed interest in the material world. Works by Albrecht Dürer, Lucas Cranach, Matthias Grünewald, and Albrecht Altdorfer, for example, typify an emphasis on the symbolism of minutely observed details and accurate realism based on observation of reality rather than prescribed principles.

Baroque Style

Presaged by the works of the Venetian artist Tintoretto (e.g., *The Last Supper*) and El Greco in Spain (e.g., *View of Toledo* and *The Immaculate Conception*), the baroque period of the seventeenth century produced artists who added heightened drama to Renaissance forms. Caravaggio (e.g., *The Calling of Saint Matthew* and *The Conversion of Saint Paul*), the Italian sculptor Gianlorenzo Bernini (e.g., *Saint Teresa in Ecstasy*), and the Flemish masters Peter Paul Rubens (*Marie de Medici Lands at Marseilles*) and Jacob Jordaens all portrayed figures in constant motion, with draperies of agitated angle and effects of lighting and shadow that amplified emotional impact and mystery.

In this dramatic spirit followed such painters of court life and middle-class figures as Velazquez, Rembrandt, Anthony Van Dyck, and Frans Hals. Rembrandt used expressive brushwork and mysterious light contrasts to enliven genre painting and portraiture, particularly of groups. His influence has remained potent as modern viewers continue to resonate to the universal truths in his canvases, as well as areas of the canvases that glow with a mysterious inner light often unrelated to realistic effects (e.g., *The Night Watch*).

Rococo Style

The Rococo style characterizes the art of the early eighteenth century. Painters like Jean-Antoine Watteau (e.g., *Embarkation for Cythera*), Giambattista Tiepolo (e.g., *Wurzberg Residenz* frescoes), François Boucher, and Jean-Honore Fragonard, often using walls or ceilings as their canvases, turned the agitated drama of the baroque style into light, pastel-toned, swirling compositions that seem placed in an idyllic land of a golden age.

Genre Art

In the seventeenth and eighteenth centuries, European artists responded to both middle-class life and everyday objects with the creation of realistic genre paintings. Some of the more prominent realists were Jan Vermeer, Adriaen van Ostade, and Jean-Baptiste Chardin. Jean-Baptiste Greuze in France and William Hogarth in England endowed their everyday subjects with a wealth of narrative detail that aimed to impart a specific moral message. Such narrative art combined in the nineteenth century with political events and romantic literature to produce works in a variety of styles with political points of view or stories to tell.

Neoclassicism

Jacques-Louis David used a severe neoclassical sculptural style in his paintings to revive classical art and ennoble images of the French Revolution and Napoleon's empire (e.g., *The Death of Marat, The Oath of the Horatii,* and *Napoleon in His Study*). The neoclassical sculpture of Jean-Antoine Houdon, Antonio Canova, Bertel Thorvaldsen, and Horatio Greenough revived the aloof severity and perfection of ancient forms—a style also reflected in Thomas Jefferson's architectural designs for his Monticello home and the University of Virginia.

Romantic Art

The Spanish painter Francisco de Goya commented powerfully on the atrocities of war in his painting *May 3, 1808*. In France, Eugene Delacroix (e.g., *The Death of Sardanapalus, Liberty Leading the People*) and Theodore Gericault (e.g., *The Raft of the Medusa*) imbued subjects from literature, the Bible, exotic lands, and current events with dramatic and heroic intensity. Romantic art is characterized by emphasis on the grandeur and transcendence of nature, as well as on emotional reactions to inner dreams and metaphysical truths. These characteristics are evident in the work of such mystical artists as William Blake, Henry Fuselli, John Martin, and Thomas Cole. Caspar David Friedrich in Germany and the English Pre-Raphaelites (William Holman Hunt, John Everett Millais, Dante Gabriel Rossetti, Ford Madox Brown, Arthur Hughes, and others) accurately re-created the natural world in brilliantly colored landscapes. These works are minutely detailed and imbued with a romantic spirit of poetic yearning and literary references.

Realism

In the first half of the nineteenth century, landscape painting in England reached a zenith with the works of John Constable and Joseph Mallord William Turner. Turner's landscapes form a bridge between the spirit of romanticism and the expressionistic brushwork and realism of the Barbizon School in France, whose chief painters were Charles Daubigny and Jean-Baptiste-Camille Corot. Beginning with the Barbizon School, the French painters of the nineteenth century concentrated increasingly on the journalistic-like depiction of everyday life and the natural environment in a free, painterly style.

The realist pioneers were Gustave Courbet (e.g., *The Stone Breakers* and *A Burial at Ormans*), Jean-Francois Millet (e.g., *The Sower* and *The Angelus*), and Honoré Daumier (e.g., *The Third-Class Carriage*). Renowned as a political caricaturist, Daumier made the lithograph his chief medium and paved the way for the stylistic and subject innovations of the impressionists. Realists rejected traditional means of composing pictures, academic methods of figure modeling and color relations, and accurate and exact rendering of people and objects. Their preference was for an art that emphasized quickly observed and sketched moments from life, the relation of shapes and forms and colors, the effects of light, and the act of painting itself.

Impressionism

Beginning with Edouard Manet (e.g., *Le Déjeuner sur l'Herbe* and *Olympia*) in the 1860s, French artists continually blurred the boundaries of realism and abstraction; the landscapes and everyday-life paintings of impressionist artists like Claude Monet, Camille Pissarro, Auguste Renoir, Alfred Sisley, Edgar Degas, and Mary Cassatt gave way to the more experimental arrangements of form and color of the great postimpressionists: Paul Gauguin, Vincent van Gogh, Georges Seurat, and Henri de Toulouse-Lautrec. In the area of sculpture, Auguste Rodin produced powerful figures with the freedom of impressionist style.

Japanese art, including the flattened space, distinctive shapes, and strong colors of Japanese woodblock prints, influenced the development of impressionism. Manet, Degas , Toulouse-Lautrec, the Nabis (Edouard Vuillard, Pierre Bonnard, and Maurice Denis) and others used paintings, pastels, and lithography to break down the boundaries between representational art and abstraction. The new, freer form of art, centered on the personality of the artist, celebrated personal style and the manipulation of form and color, and evolved in a number of directions in the late nineteenth and early twentieth centuries.

The Emergence of Abstract Art and Architecture

Around the turn of the century, some artists looked inward to explore mystical, symbolic, and psychological truths. These artists included symbolists, expressionists, and exponents of art nouveau like Odilon Redon, Jan Toorop, Edvard Munch (e.g., *The Scream*), James Ensor (e.g., *The Entry of Christ into Brussels*), Gustav Klimt (e.g., *The Kiss*), Ernst Kirchner, and Max Pechstein. Other artists, including Paul Cézanne, Henri Matisse, Pablo Picasso, Georges Braque, and Juan Gris, pursued formal innovations. During his cubist period, Picasso, Georges Braque, and others seemed to call for the total destruction of realistic depiction; Picasso's use of African and Oceanic tribal art and his emphasis on deconstructing objects and then reconstructing them led to similar experiments by Fernand Leger, the dadaist Marcel Duchamp, the sculptors Alexander Archipenko and Jacques Lipchitz, and the Italian futurist Umberto Boccioni (e.g., *Unique Forms of Continuity in Space*).

The more emotional, expressionistic, and color-oriented paintings of Wassily Kandinsky, Roger Delauney, and Paul Klee approached pure abstraction with little or no relation to the outside world. More cerebral arrangements of abstract geometrical shapes and colors were the mark of Kasimir Malevich, Piet Mondrian, and the Bauhaus School of Design in Germany, whose stripped-down, simplified, and usually geometrically oriented aesthetics influenced architecture, industrial and commercial design, sculpture, and the graphic arts for half a century.

Important sculptors during this period who created evocative shapes that were nearly or completely abstract include Constantin Brancusi, Henry Moore, Hans Arp, and Alberto Giacometti. Alexander Calder created floating assemblies called mobiles, and Louise Nevelson made constructions and wall sculptures from scraps of everyday objects.

Architecture displays the most obvious effect of the move toward abstraction, from the simplified, sleek structures of Le Corbusier and Walter Gropius to the boxlike glass skyscrapers of Philip Johnson. The pioneering giant of twentieth-century architecture was the American Frank Lloyd Wright, whose rejection of eclectic decorative styles of the previous century's architecture and use of new engineering techniques paralleled the German Bauhaus aesthetic. From the early 1900s, Wright's buildings (e.g., the Robie House, Fallingwater, and Tokyo's Imperial Hotel) exhibited a personal and bold originality based on a philosophy of "organic architecture," or the belief that natural surroundings, purpose, and building materials should dictate the form of a structure.

Surrealism

Inspired by the psychoanalytic writings of Sigmund Freud and Carl Jung, artists made the subconscious and the metaphysical important elements in their work. The influence of psychology is especially evident in the work of the surrealist artists Salvador Dali (e.g., *The Persistence of Memory*), Giorgio de Chirico, Max Ernst, René Magritte, Joan Miro, and Yves Tanguy.

Abstract Expressionism

Obsession with the self and abstract representation also led to abstract expressionism, the major American art movement after World War II. The chief proponents of this style were Clifford Still, Jackson Pollock, Franz Kline, Willem de Kooning, and Robert Motherwell. Other Americans extended this movement into the area of color-field painting, a cooler, more reserved formalism of simple shapes and experimental color relationships. Artists representative of this movement include Mark Rothko, Barnett Newman, Joseph Albers, and Ad Reinhardt.

Other Trends

Other important trends in American art in the twentieth century can be thought of as both reflections of and reactions to a democratic, consumer society. For example, the muralists and social realists created art that seemed to celebrate a simpler time. Their subjects were engaging and readily accessible to the average person. John Sloan, George Bellows, Edward Hopper, Thomas Hart Benton, Grant Wood, and John Stuart Curry were among those who celebrated the American scene in paintings, frequently in murals for public buildings, and through widely available fine prints. The great Mexican muralists, who usually concentrated on political themes—Diego Rivera, José Clemente Orozco, and David Siqueiros—brought their work to the public both in Mexico and in the United States. At the same time as their peers were distancing themselves from contemporary culture, the icons of American popular culture found their way onto canvases by Andy Warhol, Robert Indiana, Larry Rivers, Jasper Johns, Roy Lichtenstein, and Robert Rauschenberg. These artists represent the pop art school, one of many that developed around the middle of the twentieth century.

Competency 15: Knowledge of Aesthetic And Critical Analysis of Music and Visual Arts

Music and art are engaging subjects through which students can learn aesthetic principles and continue to develop their critical-thinking skills. The focus of Competency 15 is on aesthetic and critical analysis in these areas.

Skill 15.1: Identify Strategies for Developing Students' Analytical Skills to Evaluate Musical Performance

Although students can experience music and find it satisfying, challenging, or beautiful without prior knowledge of a piece, knowing something about its formal qualities and cultural meaning can enrich the experience. To share their thoughts and feelings about music, students must learn how to express themselves with musical terminology. As students become more able to think about, discuss, and critically evaluate music, they gain a deeper understanding of music and can better express their responses to it.

There are many ways to develop students' musical evaluation skills. A common experience is a crucial starting point. After students listen attentively to several pieces of music, the teacher might ask them to describe how each piece made them feel. Then, the teacher might ask them to explain why each piece of music made them feel the way they indicated. Young students will likely describe simple, straightforward, emotional responses to music (e.g., "It made me feel happy!"). Older students can explore why the music affected their feelings, both through discussion of musical concepts (e.g., "It made me feel sad because it was in a minor key.") as well as nonmusical associations (e.g., "It made me feel happy because it sounded like a circus, and I like to go to the circus.").

At first, children will need scaffolding in the form of modeling and simple questions. Following are some examples of questions that foster musical evaluation skills:

- Is this song fast or slow? Is it loud or quiet? Is it easy to tap your foot to?

- Does this song sound happy or sad?

- Would this song be good to march to on the playground? (Why or why not?)

- Which instruments can you hear in this song?

- Why do you think this song is fast (or slow)?

- Do you like this song? (Why or why not)?

Skill 15.2: Identify Strategies for Developing Students' Analytical Skills to Evaluate Works of Art

As with music, art can be appreciated without formal knowledge, but what we can learn about the elements of art and its cultural context can enhance the meaning. Here again, asking children how they feel about particular works of art is a good starting point for developing their evaluative skills. In addition, as students become more experienced with looking at and judging art works, they can be encouraged to consider the following questions:

1. What could be the purpose of this work of art?

2. Does the work achieve its purpose?

3. Has the artist created something unique, or could anyone have created this work?

4. Do the elements of the work, such as the style, fit the purpose?

5. Is the work memorable and interesting?

6. What does this work make you feel?

Viewing many types of art, examining the works of many artists, and experimenting with various media themselves help students develop analytical and evaluative skills. Learning the vocabulary associated with art and art criticism is an important prerequisite as they learn to formulate and express their opinions.

Competency 16: Knowledge of Appropriate Assessment Strategies in Music and Visual Arts

Assessment is critical to all areas of instruction. The focus of Competency 16 is on assessment in music and the visual arts in particular.

Skill 16.1: Identify a Variety of Developmentally Appropriate Strategies and Materials to Assess Skills, Techniques, Creativity, and Communication in Music

The overall goals of music education include the following:

- encouraging responsiveness to music

- increasing involvement in music

- aiding in music discrimination

- promoting understanding of music and music structure

- increasing listening awareness

- developing sensitivity to the expressive qualities of music

The following table describes the elements of an elementary and middle school music curriculum.

Appropriate assessment in music will be closely aligned to the information in the table on the following pages.

Elementary and Middle School Music Curriculum

Grades	Strategies	Materials	Skills	Techniques	Creativity	Communication
K-2	a. Provide exposure to a wide variety of sounds: recorded music, sheet music, live performances. b. Experiment with ways to change sounds. c. Use simple instruments in the classroom.	a. Simple instruments. b. Compact discs (CDs), tapes, records. c. Live programs.	a. Classify sounds as high and low; use body to show high and low. b. Play simple rhythm instruments.	a. Play simple rhythm instruments. b. Sing, especially rote songs. c. Move in time with the music.	a. Walk, run, jump to music. b. Create simple songs.	a. Create symbols to notate sounds of music. b. Use musical terms and concepts to express thoughts about music.
3-5	a. Provide experiences with music of many periods and cultures. b. Experiment with ways to change sounds.	a. Simple instruments. b. CDs, tapes, records. c. Attend programs and study written programs.	a. Sing rounds. b. Sing two-part songs by rote. c. Conduct simple songs. d. Move to music.	a. Play music. b. Dance to music. c. Conduct duple and triple meter.	a. Encourage students to express themselves through music. b. Encourage students to create sounds. c. Encourage students to improvise.	a. Sing and play instruments from written notation. b. Create own notation system. c. Hear, read, and learn about careers in music. d. Notate a simple phrase. e. Create a simple phrase.

(continued)

Elementary and Middle School Music Curriculum *(continued)*

Grades	Strategies	Materials	Skills	Techniques	Creativity	Communication
	c. Use simple instruments in the classroom. d. Move to music.		e. Distinguish between classical and popular music.			f. Practice basic etiquette for performing and as audience. g. Read music notation. h. Express ideas about origin, culture, etc., of music listened to in class.
6–8	a. Provide occasions to listen to music of many cultures and many periods. b. Encourage students to respond to music and create their own music. c. Provide opportunities for students to communicate with notation. d. Use a range of instruments and types of music.	a. Simple instruments. b. CDs, tapes, records. c. Programs. d. Autoharp and/or guitar.	a. Sing rounds. b. Sing three-part songs by rote. c. Conduct simple songs. d. Move to music. e. Identify major and minor scales. f. Dance.	a. Play simple accompaniment on autoharp, guitar, etc. b. Read some music. c. Use correct terminology d. Perform dance steps.	a. Create some simple songs. b. Create an accompaniment. c. Create a dance.	a. Write notation for original song. b. Write own idea of notation for song heard. c. Read notation.

Skill 16.2: Identify a Variety of Developmentally Appropriate Strategies and Materials to Assess Skills, Techniques, Creativity, and Communication in Art

The overall goals of art education include:

- developing aesthetic perception

- providing opportunities to examine many art forms

- providing opportunities to reflect on and discuss observations and reactions

- providing opportunities to develop students' own art abilities

- providing opportunities to identify symbols and characteristics of art, objects of art, and natural art forms

- increasing awareness of tactile art

- fostering the ability to select and enjoy arts

- promoting the ability to analyze and enjoy art based on informed judgments

The tables on the following pages summarize an elementary and middle school art curriculum:

Elementary and Middle School Art Curriculum

Grades	Strategies	Materials	Skills	Techniques	Creativity	Communication
K-2	a. Provide a wide variety of art: natural and human-made forms. b. Experiment with art materials. c. Provide opportunities to view art in the classroom, the art room, and elsewhere.	a. Art materials to use in the art room and classroom. b. Art forms from nature and humans, slides, art shows, visiting guests, trips, the computer, etc.	a. Use terms like line, color, value, shape, balance, texture, repetition, rhythm, and shape. b. Respond to art. c. Describe feelings and ideas while viewing art. d. Use various art materials to produce art in the art room and classroom. e. Use a program from an art exhibit. f. Practice acceptable behavior at an art exhibit or as a member of an audience.	a. Try various art media and produce art forms. b. Behave as a responsible member of an audience. c. Use an art program to locate exhibits at an art show.	a. Experiment with various art supplies. b. Create simple art projects. c. Respond to art in an individual way.	a. Create feelings, ideas, and impressions through art products. b. Use art terms and concepts to express thoughts about art.

(continued)

Elementary and Middle School Art Curriculum (continued)

Grades	Strategies	Materials	Skills	Techniques	Creativity	Communication
3-5	a. Experience art of many periods and many cultures through art exhibits, computer, slides, speakers, etc. b. Experiment with ways to produce art using many media.	a. Actual art materials to use in the classroom and art room. b. Actual art forms from speakers and teacher. c. Slides, computer programs, etc. d. Attend programs and study written programs.	a. Continue to use terms like line, color, value, shape, balance, texture, repetition, rhythm, and shape. b. Continue to respond to art. c. Become more adept at describing feelings and ideas while producing and viewing art. d. Continue to use various art materials to produce art in the art room and classroom. e. Use a program from an art exhibit. f. Practice acceptable behavior at an art exhibit or as a member of an audience. g. Distinguish between classical and popular art.	a. Try various art media and produce art forms. b. Behave as a responsible member of an audience. c. Use an art program to locate exhibits at an art show. viewing art. d. Describe feelings about own art and the art of others.	a. Encourage to express self through art. b. Encourage to create art. c. Encourage to improvise. d. Encourage to respond to art.	a. Create art using various materials to express self. b. Create original art. c. Hear, read, and learn about careers in art. d. Practice basic etiquette for showing own art and as a member of an audience. e. Read art programs. f. Express ideas about origin, culture, etc., of art.

Elementary and Middle School Art Curriculum *(continued)*

Grades	Strategies	Materials	Skills	Techniques	Creativity	Communication
6-8	a. Provide occasions to view art of many cultures and many periods through exhibits, slides, books, computer searches, speakers, etc. b. Encourage students to respond to art and create own art. c. Give chances to communicate orally and in written form. d. Use a range of types of art.	a. Many art media, including weaving, film, crafts, etc. b. CDs, Internet searches, slides, books. c. Programs for art shows. d. Exhibits and guest speakers.	a. Use art to express self. b. Use many different art media to produce many art forms. c. Identify major artists, media, and periods.	a. Produce simple art products. b. Demonstrate understanding of terms when others use them. c. Use correct terminology. d. Read about art.	a. Create some simple art. b. Explain the art and the feelings it produces.	a. Realize that art can be a career. b. Produce an original art piece for display. c. Express a feeling for an event by producing art. d. Analyze art. e. Talk about ways that art can be used as a career.

Appropriate assessment in art will be aligned with the information in this table. For example, older students should be able to describe a work of art using terms like *line, color, value, shape, balance, texture, repetition, rhythm,* and *shape.* Students should be able to discuss some of the major periods in the history of the visual arts. It is important that students be able to confront a work and judge its aesthetic merits, regardless of their ability to recognize it from memory. Analytical questions a teacher might ask include the following:

- What do you think is the purpose of the work?

- To what culture does it belong, and to what geographical region and period? How does it reflect that cultural/geographic context?

- What style does the work represent?

Competency 17: Knowledge of Personal Health and Wellness

Health and wellness depend on a set of attitudes and behaviors that students should begin learning at an early age. The focus of Competency 17 is on knowledge of personal health and wellness.

Skill 17.1: Demonstrate Knowledge of the Interrelatedness of Physical Activity, Fitness, and Health

The axiom "Use it or lose it" certainly holds for the human body. Our bodies thrive on physical activity, which is any bodily movement produced by skeletal muscles and resulting in energy expenditure. Unfortunately, Americans tend to be relatively inactive. U.S. physical activity statistics indicate that 25 percent of adult Americans have not participated in any leisure-time physical activities in the past month. A Centers for Disease Control and Prevention survey found that only 3.8 percent of elementary schools, 7.9 percent of middle schools, and 2.1 percent of high schools provide daily P.E.

The Importance of Physical Fitness

Physical fitness enables a person to meet the physical demands of work and leisure without strain. It is a multi-component trait reflective of the ability to perform physical activity. A person with a high level of physical fitness is also at lower risk of developing chronic disease.

Lack of activity contributes to many health problems, including poor muscle tone, poor circulation, shortness of breath, obesity, coronary artery disease, hypertension, Type 2 diabetes, osteoporosis, and certain types of cancer. Overall, mortality rates from all causes are lower in physically active people than in sedentary people. In addition, physical activity can help people manage mild-to-moderate depression, control anxiety, and reduce stress.

By increasing physical activity, a person may improve heart function and circulation, respiratory function, and overall strength and endurance. All of these changes lead to improved vigor and vitality. Exercise also lowers the risk of heart disease by strengthening the heart muscle, lowering pulse and blood pressure, and lowering the concentration of fat in both the body and the blood. Exercise can also improve appearance, increase range of motion, and lessen the risk of back and other skeletal problems.

Each person should engage in regular physical activity and reduce sedentary activities to promote health, psychological well-being, and a healthy body weight. On most days of the week, children should engage in at least 60 minutes of physical activity. However, proper hydration is important during physical activity. Two steps that help prevent dehydration during prolonged physical activity or when it is hot are consuming fluid regularly during the activity and drinking several glasses of water or other fluid after the physical activity is completed.

Skill 17.2: Demonstrate Basic Knowledge of Nutrition and Its Role in Promoting Health

Along with exercise, knowledge of and participation in a healthy lifestyle are vital to good health and longevity. The elements of good nutrition, the role of vitamins, elimination of risk factors, and strategies to control weight are all part of a healthy lifestyle.

Food Choices

In 2011, the U. S. Department of Agriculture (USDA) replaced the Food Pyramid with a new food-group symbol to help consumers think about food choices by building a healthy plate (see figure below). Half of the plate should be fruits and vegetables. Vegetables should be varied and include those that are dark green, red and orange, starchy, and so on, as well as beans and peas. About one-quarter of the plate should be grains and half of these should be whole grains. Proteins (eggs, fish, meat, nuts, beans and peas) should be lean. Dairy products should be fat-free or low-fat.

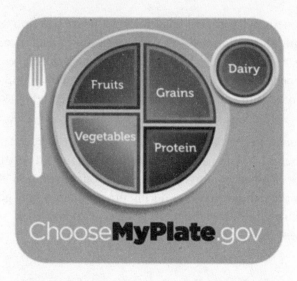

Figure 4.4: New Food-Group Symbol

Source: U.S. Department of Agriculture, *www.ChooseMyPlate.gov*

Fats

There is a link between high-fat diets and many types of cancer. Diets high in saturated fats cause the body to produce too much low-density lipoprotein (LDL), which is one type of cholesterol. (The other type of cholesterol is high-density lipoprotein, or HDL.) Some cholesterol is essential to brain function and to the production of certain hormones, but too much LDL cholesterol encourages the buildup of plaque in the arteries. LDL cholesterol can be controlled through proper diet, and HDL cholesterol levels can be raised by exercise. Triglycerides are other types of fat in the blood that are important to monitor; triglycerides seem to be inversely proportional to HDLs, meaning that as one increases, the other decreases.

Unsaturated vegetable fats are preferable to saturated fats. Unsaturated fats appear to offset the rise in blood pressure that accompanies too much saturated fat and may lower cholesterol and help with weight loss. Unsaturated fats are present in vegetable products. Although milk products contain saturated fat, the calcium they contain is vital to health. For this reason, weight-loss diets still recommend dairy products as long as they are low-fat or skim (e.g., low-fat yogurt or cheese; skim or reduced-fat milk).

Vitamins and Minerals

Vitamins and minerals are essential to proper body function. They support normal growth and development, boost the immune system, and help cells and organs do their jobs.

Vitamins are organic substances made by plants or animals. They are either fat soluble or water soluble. Fat-soluble vitamins—A, D, E, and K—dissolve in fat and can be stored in the body. Too much of the fat-soluble vitamins can cause dangerous side effects. Water-soluble vitamins—C and the B-complex vitamins (such as vitamins B6, B12, niacin, riboflavin, and folate)—must dissolve in water before they can be absorbed in the body. Because of this, your body cannot store water-soluble vitamins and will thus need a daily supply. Excess water-soluble vitamins are excreted through urine or sweat.

Minerals are inorganic. They come from soil or water and are absorbed by plants or eaten by animals. The body needs large quantities of some minerals, such as calcium. Other minerals (e.g., iron and zinc) are called trace minerals because the body only needs very small amounts.

The following chart identifies key vitamins and minerals, their purposes, and sources.

Key Vitamins and Minerals		
Vitamin/Mineral	**Purpose**	**Sources**
Vitamin A	Promotes vision and skin health; boosts immunity, contributes to cell growth and repair	Milk, eggs, liver, cereals, dark orange or green vegetables (such as carrots, sweet potatoes, pumpkin, spinach, broccoli), and orange fruits (such as cantaloupe, apricots, peaches, papayas, mangos)
Vitamin D	Absorption of calcium and phosphorus; promotes bone, teeth, and nail growth	Sun, fish and fish oils, such as cod, mackerel, salmon, tuna; often added to milk products
Vitamin E	Protects cells from damage; contributes to red blood cell health	Vegetable oils, nuts, green leafy vegetables, whole grains
Vitamin B1 (also called thiamin)	Helps convert carbohydrates into energy; promotes heart, muscle, and nervous system function	Fortified breads, cereals, and pasta; meat and fish; dried beans, soy foods, and peas; whole grains
Vitamin B2 (also called riboflavin)	Converts carbohydrates into energy; contributes to red blood cell production and vision health	Proteins (such as meat, eggs, peas and lentils, nuts), dairy products, green leafy vegetables, broccoli, asparagus, fortified cereals

(continued)

Key Vitamins and Minerals *(continued)*		
Vitamin/Mineral	**Purpose**	**Sources**
Vitamin B3 (also called niacin)	Helps convert food into energy; contributes to skin health and nerve function	Red meat, poultry, fish, fortified hot and cold cereals, peanuts and peanut products
Vitamin B9 (also called folate or folic acid)	Contributes red blood cell and DNA production	Liver, dried beans and peas, green leafy vegetables, asparagus, orange juice; fortified bread, rice, and cereal
Vitamin B12	Promotes red blood cell production and nerve cell function	fish, red meat, poultry, milk, cheese, eggs; added to some breakfast cereals
Vitamin C (also called ascorbic acid)	Contributes to tissue, bone, teeth and blood vessel health; helps body absorb iron and calcium, aids in wound healing, contributes to brain function	Red berries, kiwi, bell peppers, tomatoes, broccoli, spinach; guava, grapefruit, orange juice
Sodium	Helps maintain blood pressure and balances acids and bases; involved in nerve transmission and muscle contraction	Salt and anything with salt (e.g., processed foods, cured meats, canned vegetables, salty snacks, condiments)
Potassium	Contributes to muscle and nervous system function; aids in maintaining the balance of water in blood and body tissues	Broccoli, potatoes (with skins), green leafy vegetables, citrus fruits, bananas, dried fruits, peas, lima beans
Zinc	Aids in normal growth, immunity, wound healing	Red meat, poultry, seafood, nuts, dried beans, soy foods, milk and other dairy products, whole grains, fortified cereals
Iron	Helps red blood cells carry oxygen	Red meat, pork, fish and shellfish, poultry, lentils, beans and soy foods, green leafy vegetables, raisins, fortified grain products

Key Vitamins and Minerals (continued)		
Vitamin/Mineral	**Purpose**	**Sources**
Calcium	Builds bones and teeth	Dairy products, broccoli, dark green leafy vegetables, soy foods, fortified juice
Phosphorus	Helps form bones and teeth; contributes to cell function	Dairy products, meat, fish
Magnesium	Contributes to muscle and nerve function; maintenance of heart rhythm; bone health; energy and protein production	Whole grain products, nuts and seeds, green leafy vegetables, potatoes, beans, avocados, bananas, milk, chocolate

Skill 17.3: Identify the Processes of Decision Making and Goal Setting in Promoting Individual Health and Wellness

The teaching of physical education helps instill a willingness to exercise and encourages students to make good decisions about their health. To that end, it is important to understand the benefits of participating in a lifelong program of exercise and physical fitness and of avoiding the risks of choosing an unhealthy lifestyle.

Fortunately, it is easy to justify the need to exercise and maintain a consistently high level of health and fitness. The benefits of a consistent program of diet and exercise include improved cardiac output, maximum oxygen intake, and enhancement of the blood's ability to carry oxygen.

Another aspect of physical education concerns awareness and avoidance of lifestyle risks, such as overeating and obesity, smoking, drug use and abuse, unprotected sex, and stress. Although education is the key to minimizing the presence of these risk factors, peer pressure and the lack of parental control often diminish the effectiveness of education.

Weight

Statistics show that Americans get fatter every year. According to the Get America Fit Foundation, obesity is the second-leading cause of preventable death in the United States. The Centers for Disease Control and Prevention report that 1 in 3 American adults is obese, as is almost 1 in 5 children under the age of 19.

What does it mean to be overweight or obese? Both are determined by body-mass index (BMI), which relates weight to height and is used to calculate body fat. For example, an adult with a height of 5'9" should have a BMI of 18.5-24.9 with a weight between 125 and 168. A BMI of 25-29.9 (weight of 169-202) is defined as overweight. A BMI of 30 or more (weight of 203 or more) is defined as obese. Being overweight or obese increases the risk of health conditions and diseases that include breast cancer, heart disease, Type II diabetes, sleep apnea, gall bladder disease, osteoarthritis, colon cancer, high blood pressure, and stroke. Although information about healthy lifestyles is easily found on the Internet or in various media (TV, magazines, newspapers), the classroom is often the only place a student gets reliable information about diet.

Conversely, being underweight (a BMI of less than 18.5) presents problems as well. Our society often places too much emphasis on being thin and losing weight. Women are especially prone to measuring their self-worth by the numbers they read on the bathroom scale. Ideal weight and a good body fat ratio are the goals when losing weight.

Weight Loss

To lose weight, calories burned must exceed calories consumed. No matter what kind of diet is tried, that principle applies. Although commercials and other sources promise quick and easy results, the truth is that there are no shortcuts to weight loss and good health. Crash diets, which bring about rapid weight loss, are not only unhealthy but also ineffective in the long run because if calorie intake is restricted too much, the body goes into starvation mode and operates by burning fewer calories. Slower weight loss is more permanent.

Exercise combined with caloric reduction is the best method for long-term weight loss. Just a 250-calorie-drop per day combined with a 250-calorie-burn can result in a loss of one pound a week. Aerobic exercise (activity that increases the body's demand for oxygen, resulting in a temporary increase in rate of respiration and heart rate) is the key to successful weight loss. Exercise speeds up metabolism and causes the body to burn calories. Timing of exercise can also improve the benefits. Exercising before meals speeds up metabolism and helps suppress appetite. Losing weight and maintaining a healthy weight is not easy, however. Through education, people will be better able to make the lifestyle choices that result in maintenance of a healthy weight and life.

Skill 17.4: Demonstrate Knowledge of Common Health Problems and Risk Behaviors Associated with Them

The health of students and their families depends not only on individual and family decisions about diet and exercise but also on various social factors. For example, advertising often encourages children to make unhealthy decisions.

Students as young as kindergarten and first grade can learn how to recognize advertisements (e.g., for candy or sugar-laden cereal) that might lead them to unhealthy behavior. By third or fourth grade, children should be able to demonstrate that they are able to make health-related decisions regarding advertisements in various media. Teachers can encourage students in the following health-related behaviors:

- Avoid alcohol, tobacco, stimulants, and narcotics.

- Get plenty of sleep and exercise.

- Eat a well-balanced diet.

- Receive the proper immunizations.

- Avoid sharing toothbrushes, combs, hats, beverages, and food with others.

In addition, any study of the physical environment—in science, social studies, or other subjects—should relate to health whenever possible. Examples include:

- The effects of pollution on health

- Occupation-related diseases

- The different health-care options available to people in different parts of the world and in different economic circumstances

- Differentiation between communicable and noncommunicable diseases

- The importance of washing one's hands frequently

Older children should be able to explain the transmission and prevention of communicable diseases, and all children should learn which diseases can and cannot be transmitted through casual contact.

Competency 18: Knowledge of Physical, Social, and Emotional Growth and Development

Health and wellness are promoted by knowledge of how one grows and changes, both physically and mentally. The focus of Competency 18 is on fostering student knowledge of physical, social, and emotional growth and development.

Skill 18.1: Identify the Principles of Sequential Progression of Motor-Skill Development

Physical changes play a significant role in the development of children as they gradually gain control of the movements and functions of their bodies. As they develop physically, their motor skills become refined, enabling them to engage in increasingly complex physical lessons and activities. For teachers to be able to identify patterns of physical development, they must create educational activities that are developmentally appropriate for their students' physical abilities.

Ages 3-4

Children between the ages of 3 and 4 have mastered standing and walking. At this stage, children are developing gross motor skills involving the large muscles of the arms and legs, including the ability to hop on one foot and balance, climb stairs without support, kick a ball, throw overhand, catch a ball that has bounced, move forward and backward, and ride a tricycle. Children between the ages of 3 and 4 are also developing fine motor skills involving the smaller hand muscles, such as using scissors, drawing simple shapes, and copying shapes like capital letters.

Ages 4-5

By age 4 or 5, when most children enter school, they are developing the gross motor ability to do somersaults, swing, climb, and skip. These skills require increasing coordination. In addition, children at this age can begin to dress themselves using zippers, buttons, and possibly tying shoes. They can eat independently using utensils. Children at this age are increasingly capable of copying shapes, including letters and numbers. They can cut and paste and draw a person with a head, body, arms, and legs. These fine motor skills develop quickly.

Ages 6 and up

By age 6, children can bounce a ball, skate, ride a bike, skip with both feet, and dress themselves independently. As the student develops year by year, the physical skills, both fine and gross motor, become increasingly complex and involve more muscles and more coordination. By age 9, children can complete a model kit, learn to sew, and cook simple recipes. By age 10, children can catch fly balls and participate in all elements of a softball game. Recognizing the basic milestones that most children will achieve by a certain age will assist teachers in making decisions about academic lessons and tasks. In addition, teachers may be able to identify children who may not be reaching their developmental milestones with the rest of the class.

In sum, the physical ability of students to engage school activities gradually increases as they develop. Teachers must adjust and adapt classroom and playground activities to be developmentally appropriate for the specific skill levels of students. To this end, it is important for teachers to be able to identify the physical development patterns of their students.

Skill 18.2: Demonstrate Knowledge of Human Growth and Development and Its Relationship to Physical, Social, and Emotional Well-Being

A teacher need not be an expert in anatomy and physiology to see the physical changes that accompany student growth and increasing maturity. Although the preschool child has trouble grasping pencils and crayons in a manner that facilitates handwriting, most children at this age can grasp crayons sufficiently to make marks on papers and thus enjoy the creative excitement of art.

Physiological changes play a significant role in the development of children as they gain increasing control of bodily movements and functions and refine their motor skills. Children's ability to engage classroom and playground activities increases as they develop. Teachers must adjust and adapt classroom and playground activities to be developmentally appropriate for students' various skill levels.

A theoretical approach to understanding human development is offered by Erik Erikson (1963), who described the stages of psychosocial development. For each of eight stages, he identified a developmental challenge and explained it in terms of two polar outcomes. This guide discusses only the stages describing school-age individuals (see table below).

Erikson's Stages of Psychological Development During the School Years.		
Ages	**Stage**	**Focus**
Preschool	Initiative vs. Guilt	Independence and control over environment
Elementary School Age	Industry vs. Inferiority	Social and academic competence
Adolescence	Identity vs. Role Confusion	Sense of self and personal identity
Young Adulthood	Intimacy vs. Isolation	Relationships with others

Initiative vs. Guilt

According to Erikson, preschoolers and primary grade students must be able to function in the outside world independent of parents. When children are able to do this, they achieve a sense of initiative. When children are not able to move away from total parental attachment and control, they experience a sense of guilt. Thus, this first stage of psychosocial development is the stage of initiative versus guilt. The child's first venture away from home and into the world of school has considerable significance in light of Erikson's theory. It is imperative that teachers assist students in their first experiences on their own, away from parental control.

Industry vs. Inferiority

Erikson's next stage of development involves a tension between industry and inferiority. For example, if a child who enters school (thus achieving initiative) acquires the skills necessary for success in school (including academic skills like reading, writing, and computation, as well as social skills like playing with others, communicating, and forming friendships), the child achieves a sense of industry. Failure to achieve these skills leads to a sense of inferiority.

Identity vs. Role Confusion

Around the time students enter middle school, they begin the developmental task of achieving identity. According to Erikson, the struggle to achieve identity is one of the most important developmental tasks and can create serious psychosocial problems for adolescents. For example, even the individual who has successfully achieved all the important developmental milestones (such as initiative and industry) will be in a state of flux. Everything about oneself and one's peers is changing—physically, emotionally, and psychologically. For adolescent middle school students, this is often a time of experimentation with different sports, interests, clothing styles, and attitudes as they try to answer the questions, "Who am I?" Erikson theorized that once adolescents find out what they believe in—what their goals, ideas, and values are—they can attain identity achievement. Failure to discover these things leads to identity diffusion.

Intimacy vs. Isolation

By the time many students reach high school, they are entering a stage of young adulthood. Erikson described this as a psychosocial stage characterized by the polarities of intimacy and isolation. Individuals at this stage of development begin to think about forming lasting friendships, even marital unions. Erikson argued that many psychosocial problems experienced by young adults have their origin in the individual's failure to achieve identity during the preceding stage; the young men and women who do not know who they really are cannot achieve true intimacy.

For the classroom teacher, knowledge of psychosocial stages of human development can result in greater effectiveness. For example, the effective teacher realizes the importance of helping students to achieve the skills necessary to accomplish crucial developmental tasks. According to Erikson's theory, teachers of elementary school learners would do well to focus on teaching academic and social skills and to help students gain proficiency in skills that will enable learners to be productive members of society. By understanding the key principles of human development in its multiple dimensions, effective teachers provide students with both age-appropriate and developmentally-appropriate instruction. The best instruction addresses all the needs of students—physical, emotional, social, and cognitive.

Skill 18.3: Identify Major Factors Associated with Social and Emotional Health

Many major factors are necessary for building social and emotional health. For teachers, having a basic understanding of the principles of human development in its many dimensions—physical, mental, emotional, and social—is critically important. In addition, teachers must view human development as a dynamic and interactive process.

A dynamic approach to understanding human development is one that recognizes that human beings do not develop in a vacuum. People exist in environments that are friendly or unfriendly, supportive or unsupportive, and each environment tends to provoke certain reactions from people. Moreover, human development is not driven solely by the environment. People also act in certain ways to shape and form their environments.

A constant interaction or interplay occurs between people and their environments. Thus, effective teachers must be sensitive to and knowledgeable of both personal characteristics of students (internal factors) and characteristics of their environments. Students' internal factors are not limited to the general characteristics that humans share as they grow and mature. These factors also include personality characteristics, self-concept and sense of self-esteem, self-discipline and self-control, the ability to cope with stress, and one's general outlook on life.

Communication Skills

Communication with others is important to both social and academic development. James Cummins makes a useful distinction between the kinds of language used in each area:

1. Social language includes basic interpersonal communication skills. It is context-embedded and supported by the use of illustrations, immediately present objects and events, demonstrations, and so forth.

2. Academic language also includes basic communication skills, but it is more abstract and decontextualized.

Both forms of language are critical to social and emotional health.

Self-Esteem and Self-Efficacy

Self-esteem refers to one's belief in one's own self-worth. A related concept is self-efficacy, which refers to one's confidence in how well one can manage specific kinds of tasks. The two concepts are not identical. One can have a very positive self-esteem and yet still recognize that one is not good at math, or driving, or being persuasive. At the same time, one can have very low self-esteem while still recognizing that one is gifted in particular areas. Positive self-esteem and self-efficacy are both important to social and emotional health.

Ideas about self-esteem and self-efficacy begin to form during the preschool years. As a result, it is critical for teachers to help all children feel that they are worthwhile human beings, with specific strengths, and that each child regardless of strengths has some control over his or her ability to succeed in school.

Locus of Control

Locus of control refers to what people believe to be the sources of their own behavior, in particular their successes and failures. There are two types of locus:

1. *External.* People with an external locus of control believe that their behavior is strongly affected by external forces such as luck and the actions of other people.

2. *Internal.* People with an internal locus of control believe that forces within themselves or under their own control strongly affect their behavior.

For example, consider a group of students who has done well on a test and whose teacher asks, "Why did you do so well on that test?" Students with an external locus of control might reply, "I just got lucky," or "I have a great teacher." Students with an internal locus of control might say "I studied hard," or "I'm very smart." Thus, although students may have similar experiences, the ways they explain those experiences reflect differences in each student's locus of control.

Teachers should notice that what is most desirable is not an internal or an external locus of control per se, but rather that students are accurate about the sources of their own academic successes and failures. For example, a student with an external locus of control who believes he did poorly on a test because the teacher did not explain the material well may need to be encouraged to understand that the key factor underlying his performance was lack of effort. A student with an internal locus of control who believes he did poorly on a test because he is not very smart may need to be encouraged to understand that he or she does have skills that can be fostered through additional effort.

Generally, some degree of internal locus of control is healthy, because students with this locus will recognize that they have at least some control over situations. However, a student with an internal locus of control also needs to be able to see when external factors play a role in performance. The student who is distracted by classmates and misunderstands an assignment should recognize that simply trying harder would not have guaranteed better performance on the assignment. Rather, a different approach to dealing with external forces (i.e., distracting peers) is what was needed.

Internal Voices

Social and emotional health is also affected by what students believe about themselves and their resulting self-talk or internal voices. Internal voices are ongoing messages, either positive or negative, that we send to ourselves. People with a generally positive outlook on life experience positive internal voices ("You're okay," "People like you," "Things will be all right," and so on), while those with a generally negative outlook on life experience negative messages ("You're not okay," "You're too fat, skinny, ugly, stupid," and so on).

Psychologists indicate that internal voices develop at an early age. Two tools that can help students "reprogram" their beliefs about themselves and their inner voices are affirmations and visualizations (Ellis, 2010).

1. *Affirmations* are statements describing what students want. Affirmations must be personal, positive, and written in the present tense. What makes affirmations effective are details. For example, instead of saying, "I am stupid," the teacher can encourage students to say, "I am capable. I do well in school because I am organized, I study daily, I get all my work completed on time, and I take my schoolwork seriously." Students should repeat these affirmations until they say them with total conviction.

2. *Visualizations* are images students can create whereby they see themselves the way they want to be. For example, students wanting to improve their test-taking skills would imagine what successful test-taking looks like, sounds like, and feels like. For example, a student might visualize herself confidently preparing for a test, walking into the classroom with confidence, examining the test calmly, taking the test without stress, and seeing a good grade on the returned test. Once students identify the images, they should rehearse those images in their minds.

Conflict Resolution and Violence Prevention

Violence prevention strategies at school range from adding social skills training to the curriculum to installing metal detectors at the entrances to buildings. Educational experts recommend that schools teach all students procedures in conflict resolution and anger management, in addition to explaining the school's and classroom's rules, expectations, and disciplinary policies.

The federal Gun-Free Schools Act of 1994 mandates that every state pass zero-tolerance laws on weapons at school or face the loss of federal funds. Every state has complied with this law and requires school districts to expel students for at least a year if they bring weapons to school.

The U.S. Department of Education and the Department of Justice (1998) produced a joint report recommending actions to promote school safety. Following are some key recommendations:

1. Open discussion of safety issues is essential. Schools should instruct students about the dangers of firearms, the proper strategies for addressing negative feelings, and effective and nonviolent ways to settle conflicts.

2. Students must realize that they are responsible for their own actions, choices, and decisions.

3. Students should be treated with equal respect.

4. Students should be given opportunities to share their concerns in safe, nonthreatening settings.

Stress Management

Stress is a physiological effect that results from exposure to a threat. The threat may be actual or perceived; in either case, exposure to the threat over time causes physiological changes that ultimately begin to damage body and brain.

Following are some of the causes of stress:

1. *Environmental factors* such as noise, air pollution, and crowding

2. *Physiological factors* such as sickness and physical injuries

3. *Psychological factors* such as self-deprecating thoughts and negative self-image

4. *Life events* such as moving, divorce, or a new baby

In addition to the normal stressors that students typically experience in school (e.g., interpersonal conflict, tests, family expectations, extracurricular competitions), some students may be dealing with economic hardship, substance abuse in the family, and even emotional, physical, or sexual abuse. Thus, students need to learn appropriate ways of coping with stress.

The first step in coping with stress is to recognize the role that stress plays in our lives. A teacher might lead a class through a brainstorming activity to help the students become aware of the various sources of stress that affect them. Next, the teacher could identify positive ways of coping with stress, including the following:

- Improving internal voice

- Physical exercise

- Proper nutrition

- Adequate sleep

- Appropriate time-management strategies

- Good study habits

- Relaxation exercises

- Talking to a trusted friend or family member

- Seeking help at school

Students who are under stress may experience a wide range of emotions. They may be sad, depressed, frustrated, or afraid. Their emotional state in turn plays a significant role in classroom performance and achievement. Thus, effective teachers seek to create a classroom environment supportive of students' emotional needs. These teachers have appropriate compassion for the emotional conflicts facing students, as well as an awareness of the sources of stress in classroom settings. These teachers also know how to reduce stress in the classroom by maintaining a nonthreatening environment, by making expectations clear, and by giving students chances to improve.

Skill 18.4: Identify Problems Associated with Physical, Social, and Emotional Health

If a student continually misbehaves or exhibits disturbing behavior, the effective teacher tries to determine if any external influences are at play, and the school may request additional intervention from the teacher and/or family. Teachers should also be concerned about the physical, social, and emotional health of their students. For instance, nervousness caused by a test or a school play audition may cause a student to speak out of turn or appear skittish. The loss of a loved one may cause a student to become depressed. Such behaviors are normal reactions to stress. However, teachers must pay attention to these situations and observe both the severity of the reaction and whether it occurs for an extended period.

Teachers must observe the frequency, duration, and intensity of any misconduct or atypical behaviors they observe and attempt to determine the causes. The role of the teacher in such situations is to help determine if the student is acting out as a reaction to a particular issue or if there is a deeper emotional problem. The teacher should record any atypical behaviors, such as lying, stealing, fighting, or withdrawal, and should attempt to determine the motivation behind the behavior. Is the child lying to avoid a reprimand? Is the student stealing in order to hide feelings of insecurity? Does the student become withdrawn during a particular subject or at random moments during the school day? These are some of the many questions the teacher may need to consider.

Support Beyond the Classroom

Some students may require referrals to other school personnel and various forms of therapy to treat the emotional disturbances that cause their problem behaviors. Evaluation and therapy may determine the causes for such behaviors. The teacher and appropriate school personnel may need to be in constant discussion with the student's parents and to establish an open dialogue with the student's family to facilitate the student's treatment. Together, the parents and teacher may acquire important and unique insights into the student's situation.

School professionals are a valuable resource for advice, assistance, and support when treating students' emotional disturbances. Guidance counselors, school psychiatrists, and other specialists can aid in the counseling of these students and make recommendations for the parents and teacher. With the student's family, these professionals may develop or recommend a particular program or therapy for treatment.

Classroom Management

When working with a class of students with emotional disorders, the management of the classroom must be flexible to aid in the students' development. While the goal of any management system is to prevent misbehavior, the teacher must be prepared to provide an area or opportunity for the students to regain control should difficult episodes occur.

Teachers should also be aware that drug therapy is a widely prevalent form of treatment. Prescribed by medical doctors, the drug treatments that are available can help students gain independence from their disorders. However, these drugs treat the symptoms rather than the cause of the disorder and can have severe side effects. The classroom teacher and the school nurse must help to monitor the impact as well as the side effects of any drug treatments.

Problem Behavior Patterns

Among the problem behavior patterns that teachers should be aware of are those that can be classified under the headings of neurotic disorders, psychotic disorders, and autism.

Neurotic disorders, or neuroses, manifest in various emotional and physical signs. Depression can be revealed in a lack of interest in activities, constant crying, sleep disturbances, and/or talk of suicide. Anxiety or obsessive thoughts may be revealed through a disruption in eating or sleeping patterns, headaches, nausea and stomach pain, or diarrhea. The teacher needs to consider these neuroses as a cause for serious concern and further inquiry.

Psychotic disorders, such as schizophrenia, are serious psychological disorders. These disorders are relatively rare in young children and difficult to diagnose. For example, schizophrenia is responsible for an individual exhibiting a sharp break from the reality of his or her surroundings. Some schizophrenics may appear confused and have difficulty expressing themselves, resulting in unusual speech patterns or muteness. Others may seem overly paranoid or withdrawn, and in the extreme case visual or auditory hallucinations may occur. Schizophrenics, who are more likely to be boys than girls, may exhibit facial expressions that are either markedly absent of emotion or reflective of emotion that does not fit the situation.

Autism is a serious emotional disorder that appears in early childhood. Characteristics include social withdrawal, repetitive movement, interest in objects and patterns, and delayed or absent language and communication skills. Symptoms of autism may appear in children between four and eighteen months of age. Autistic children will usually distance themselves from others and appear unable to experience empathy. They tend to avoid physical contact as well as eye contact. In addition, they often cannot distinguish or appreciate humor. While autistic children range widely in intelligence, some children may have unusually well-developed skills in just one area, such as music or math. Treatment for autistic children tends to involve some combination of therapy, drugs, or, in the extreme case, residential living.

Substance Abuse and the Law

Teachers should be aware of suspicious behaviors that might indicate substance abuse. Such abuse affects physical, social, and emotional health. Florida state law requires that school personnel report suspicions of use, possession, or sale of any controlled substance, model glue, or alcoholic beverage to the appropriate school authorities.

The Social Environment of School

Schools, regardless of grade level, are fundamentally social environments. Students form social relationships with adults, with peers who are their own age, and with students in different age and developmental groups.

In the context of school, teachers can encourage a positive social environment through their interactions with students. For example, teachers can provide icebreakers during the first week of class to get to know students and help students acquaint or reacquaint themselves with each other. Icebreakers are especially helpful for new students as well as for those who are less outgoing. Information sheets can be used to gather information about student behaviors, interests, preferences, or concerns (e.g., What do you like to read? What is your favorite TV program or movie? What accomplishment are you most proud of? What is your biggest concern about this class? What grade do you hope to get in this class? How many students do you know in this class? Do you play a sport or musical instrument? Which one? What do you do to prepare for tests?).

Cooperative and collaborative groups of different sizes and compositions provide opportunities for students to improve social skills and work together. Group activities should be preceded by instruction on how to work with others. For example, the teacher could address goal-setting, time management, conflict resolution, communication skills, and other aspects of project management as appropriate for the age of the students and complexity of the assignment. Finally, teachers should provide both contingent feedback and noncontingent attention:

1.   *Contingent feedback* should be given when a student has learned a new skill, when a behavior requires effort, or when the behavior is one that the student is proud of. Such feedback should be accurate, specific, and descriptive. For example, the teacher might say, "You showed improvement in grammar and creativity of word choice from your first draft to your final paper" instead of "Good work on your paper."

2.   *Noncontingent attention* consists of interactions with a student that are not based on behavior or work. For example, if a teacher knows a student participated in a competition or event, the teacher could comment on the event (e.g.," I know you are on the basketball team and won the game last weekend. What's the secret to

the team's success?") Or, the teacher could ask about something the student provided on an information sheet (e.g., "I remember that you said you like to design websites. Did you see the school competition for website ideas?")

In summary, teachers should be concerned about the physical, social, and emotional health of their students. When problems arise, teachers can turn to appropriate school personnel and the administration for further support.

Skill 18.5: Identify Factors Related to Responsible Sexual Behavior

Teachers should make note of children who show premature interest in sex acts. Pre-pubertal children who act in a sexual manner have often learned this behavior by example, and they are possible victims of sexual abuse. For example, young children who masturbate in the classroom or attempt to foist sexual behavior on their classmates are neither sexually developed nor mature enough to understand the consequences of their actions.

A sudden show of promiscuity may follow molestation. Kissing, usually considered a positive interaction between parent and child, constitutes abuse if done in a sexual manner. Even leering in a sexual way constitutes abuse. Parents are not the only ones to sexually abuse children; other family members, including siblings or grandparents, or even family friends or other teachers may be the perpetrators of abuse.

Reporting Suspicions of Abuse

A teacher may want to comfort a child who admits to being sexually abused. However, the teacher must be careful not to interview the child but rather to wait for the trained professional to interact with the child.

A state-licensed teacher must report any suspicion of child abuse or neglect. Such reports are required of anyone, but educators have a particular responsibility to speak up when abuse is suspected. Failure to report suspected abuse can result in a fine, criminal charges, or revocation of teacher certification; moreover, it is not only illegal but might adversely affect the child's life. A teacher has the right to have his or her report kept confidential but including the teacher's name could save time and effort if more information needs to be gathered.

The difficult challenge of deciding whether the suspected child abuse or neglect is real is the responsibility of the counselor, not the teacher. If it is deemed necessary, the counselor initiates an investigation immediately. If there is no immediate threat to the child, an investigatory team begins to collect further evidence within 24 hours.

After making a report, the teacher should realize that the child may feel that his or her private life has been exposed. While accepting the child's feeling of betrayal, the teacher can explain that the report was necessary and that the child will be protected against reprisals for having told someone about the abuse. Sometimes the child benefits from just knowing that others do care about his or her well-being.

After the filing of the report, the teacher should avoid the person suspected of the abuse or neglect. Should the teacher experience harassment or persecution from this person, the teacher should go to the police. If the report turns into a legal issue, the teacher should retain an attorney. Although legal protection should be available for the teacher, legal matters can take unusual directions, and a teacher may need legal advice to avoid future problems.

Every teacher should know that the phenomenon of sexual abuse influences ordinary classroom interactions. The teacher should ask for permission before patting a student on the back or otherwise making appropriate physical contact with the student. The student has the right to decide whether he or she wants the teacher's touch, and the teacher must acknowledge that decision.

Competency 19: Knowledge of Community Health and Safety Issues

Healthy behavior depends in part on knowledge of health and safety. Competency 19 focuses on important community health and safety information that students need to know.

Skill 19.1: Identify Factors Contributing to Substance Use and Abuse and Identify Signs, Symptoms, Effects, and Prevention Strategies

Drug and alcohol problems can affect anyone, regardless of age, sex, race, marital status, place of residence, income level, or lifestyle. However, there are certain identifiable risk factors for substance abuse.

Risk for Substance Abuse

Risk factors are characteristics that occur statistically more often among those who develop alcohol and drug problems than among those who do not. Having one or more risk factors does not mean that the individual will necessarily develop a substance abuse problem but simply that the likelihood of doing so is greater than chance or greater than it is for other people.

The risk factors for substance abuse can be divided into three categories: personal, family, and community. Following are some of the known examples of each.

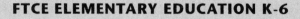
Personal factors:

- Aggressiveness
- Aggressiveness combined with shyness
- Decreased social inhibition
- Inability to express feelings appropriately
- Hypersensitivity
- Inability to cope with stress
- Problems with relationships
- Low self-esteem
- Tendency to overreact

The presence of physical disabilities, physical or mental health problems, or learning disabilities can add to the student's vulnerability to substance abuse, as can being at risk for academic failure.

Family factors:

- One or more parent with a history of substance abuse problems
- One or more socially isolated parent
- One or more mentally ill parent
- High levels of family stress, instability, conflict, and/or violence Parental absenteeism due to separation, divorce, or death
- Parental abuse or neglect of children

Community factors:

- Neighborhoods with high rates of substance abuse
- Neighborhoods with inadequate housing
- Economically depressed neighborhoods
- High-crime-rate neighborhoods

Again, the various risk factors only indicate increased potential for substance abuse. Some children who are exposed to very adverse conditions grow up to be healthy, productive adults free from substance abuse problems. Even so, if teachers are aware of the risk factors, they will be better prepared to identify children who are vulnerable to substance abuse and to take whatever measures they can to prevent that outcome.

Fetal Alcohol Syndrome

Teachers must sometimes contend with the results of parental substance abuse. This problem can take many forms, including developmental delays that are attributable to prenatal drug abuse. A prominent example is that mothers who drink alcohol heavily during pregnancy may give birth to infants with fetal alcohol syndrome (FAS). Children with FAS exhibit a distinct pattern of facial abnormalities, growth retardation, and central nervous system dysfunction. Their central nervous system damage manifests in poor motor skills, hand-eye coordination problems, and complex behavioral and learning problems, including difficulties with memory, attention, and judgment. The National Organization on Fetal Alcohol Syndrome provides extensive information about children with FAS and effective strategies for working with these students.

Identifying Signs and Symptoms of Substance Use and Abuse

Every educator should be aware of those behaviors that indicate a tendency toward the use of drugs and/or alcohol or that indicate that students are under the influence. Moreover, to protect other students and to secure assistance for the abuser, teachers must be able to make immediate referrals when there is an indication that a student is using drugs and/or alcohol.

It can be difficult to tell if someone is using illegal drugs or alcohol because people who do so make considerable effort to hide their behavior. However, certain warning signs may point to substance use or abuse:

- Excessive lying

- Avoiding longtime friends

- Giving up activities that once brought pleasure and positive feedback

- Getting into legal trouble

- Taking unusual risks

- Reporting feelings of fatigue, hopelessness, depression, and/or suicidality

- Missing classes or performing poorly, particularly when past performance was superior

Other suspicious behaviors include avoiding eye contact, slurred speech, complaints of nausea or dizziness, difficulty staying awake, and difficulty participating in class activities. These behaviors in themselves do not indicate a substance abuse problem, but, in combination and when displayed consistently over time, they are strong indicators. Teachers should record their observations and keep written reports of behavioral changes they witness. Moreover, they should report any suspicions to the appropriate school authorities.

Prevention of Substance Abuse

Education constitutes the backbone of substance abuse prevention. By providing accurate information to students concerning substance abuse, teachers diminish the likelihood that students will begin or continue to use substances illegally. In addition, schools should adopt zero-tolerance policies for alcohol and drugs and sponsor prevention programs, including those that teach responsible decision-making, mentoring, mediation, and other activities aimed at changing unsafe, harmful, or destructive behaviors.

The prevention of substance abuse is fostered not only by discussions of substance use and abuse but also by implementing positive strategies for emotional and social development. The knowledge, skills, and attitudes that help children become productive citizens also help them resist temptation and peer pressure, make wise choices, protect their own health, and consider the impact of their behavior on others. Thus, the following strategies may help benefit substance abuse prevention efforts if combined with prevention efforts more specifically tailored to substance use and abuse:

- Require children to be helpful to classmates and provide opportunities to do so.
- Help children develop assertiveness skills and ask for help when needed.
- Help children elicit positive responses from others in the classroom.
- Enable a sense of community in the classroom through cooperation and collaboration,
- Encourage children to form bonds with school and community.
- Provide students with consistently caring responses and messages.

Treatment of Substance Abuse

In addition to school resources, students with substance abuse problems can find help through a number of community resources, including community drug hotlines, community treatment centers, emergency health care clinics, local health departments, Alcoholics Anonymous, Narcotics Anonymous, Al-Anon, Ala-teen, and hospitals.

Florida State Law Concerning Substance Use and Abuse in Schools

Florida state law requires that school personnel report to the principal or principal's designee "any suspected unlawful use, possession, or sale by a student of any controlled substance, any alcoholic beverage, or model glue." The law further states that school personnel "are exempt from civil liability when reporting in good faith to the proper school authority such suspected unlawful use, possession or sale by a student. Only a principal or the principal's designee is authorized to contact a parent or legal guardian of a student regarding this situation." (Florida Statute, Chapter 232.277, Item 1).

Skill 19.2: Demonstrate Knowledge of Resources from Home, School, and Community That Provide Valid Health Information, Products, and Services

Teachers can readily find helpful resources for teaching students about the dangers of substance abuse and for promoting prevention by contacting the following agencies or organizations, or searching their websites for updated statistics, reports, and educational materials:

- American Council for Drug Education 50 Jay Street , Brooklyn, NY 11201 (646)505-2061 www.acde.org/

- National Center on Addiction and Substance Abuse at Columbia University 633 Third Avenue, 19th Floor New York, NY 10017-6706 (212) 841-5200 www.casacolumbia.org/

- Substance Abuse and Mental Health Services Administration (SAMHSA) 1 Choke Cherry Road, Rockville, MD 20857 www.samhsa.gov/

- National Institute on Drug Abuse (NIDA) 6001 Executive Boulevard, Room 5213, Bethesda, MD 20892-9561 301-443-1124 www.nida.nih.gov/nidahome.html

Prevention education promotes healthy and constructive lifestyles that discourage drug abuse and foster the development of drug-free lifestyles.

Skill 19.3: Identify Appropriate Violence Prevention Strategies in the Home, School, and Community

School-Level Risk Factors for Violence

Events such as the shootings in Columbine, Colorado, in 1999 serve as reminders that teachers must be vigilant about the possibility of violence among students, even if the extent of violence is relatively minor. Following are some of the common school-level risk factors for violent behavior in the home, school, or community:

- Overcrowding
- Poor use of school space
- Lack of disciplinary procedures
- Inconsistent discipline
- Student alienation
- Multicultural insensitivity
- Lack of support for at-risk students
- Troubled neighborhood

Individual-Level Risk Factors for Violence

Teachers must also be aware that some risk factors are associated particularly with individual students. Following are some key examples:

- Prior instances of violence toward family and/or peers
- History of aggressive or disruptive classroom behavior
- High levels of violence in the home and/or neighborhood
- History of parental rejection, inconsistent discipline, and lack of supervision
- Access to firearms
- Involvement in substance use
- Living caregivers with history of substance abuse
- Associations with antisocial and/or violent peer group
- Poor school achievement and attendance and/or numerous suspensions
- Poor social skills and peer relations
- Poor impulse and emotional control

Warning Signs of Imminent Violence

Although the presence of risk factors does not guarantee that a student will be violent and, indeed, there is no way to predict that violence *will* occur, teachers should be aware of the warning signs:

- Irrational beliefs and ideas, including externalization of blame
- Verbal, behavioral, or written threats or intimidation
- Fascination with weaponry and/or acts of violence
- Expressions of a plan to hurt oneself or others
- Fear reaction on the part of family and/or peers
- Drastic change in belief systems and/or stress levels
- Displays of unwarranted anger
- Inability to handle criticism
- Intoxication
- Expressions of hopelessness, heightened anxiety, or sense of victimization
- Violence toward inanimate objects
- Stealing or sabotaging projects or equipment
- Lack of concern for the safety of others

Effective teachers must be alert to the presence of these warning signs, while at the same time acknowledging that the signs can easily be misinterpreted and misunderstood. Warning signs should be used to get help for children, not to stereotype, exclude, punish, or isolate them. Teachers must also remember that referrals based on early warning signals must be kept confidential and that, except for cases of suspected child abuse or neglect, referrals to outside agencies must have parental consent.

When teachers observe the warning signs noted above, they must remain aware that violence is a genuine possibility. According to the Southeastern Regional Vision for Education, if a violent outburst does occur, teachers should take certain actions as part of the school response team. These include the following:

- Provide accurate information to students.

- Lead class discussions to give everyone the opportunity to express personal feelings, ideas, and concerns.

- Dispel rumors by truthfully answering questions.

- Model appropriate responses of care and concern.

- Give permission for a range of emotions.

- Identify students who need counseling.

- Provide activities to reduce trauma and express emotions through artwork, music, and writing.

School Safety

Effective school-wide disciplinary policies include a code of conduct, specific rules, and consequences that can accommodate student differences on a case-by-case basis when necessary. School policies need to include antiharassment and antiviolence policies and due process rights. These policies should reflect the cultural values and educational goals of the community. Finally, schools must have zero tolerance for illegal possession of weapons, drugs, or alcohol.

In its publication *Creating Safe and Drug-Free Schools: An Action Guide*, the U.S. Department of Education suggests ways that schools can ensure safety and combat drug use. Among the recommendations in this guide are the following:

- Establish a team of educators, students, parents, law enforcement, juvenile justice officials, and community leaders to develop a plan for a safe and drug-free school.

- Ensure that students are engaged in schoolwork that is challenging, informative, and rewarding.

- Establish, publish, publicize, and enforce policies that clearly define acceptable and unacceptable behavior with zero tolerance for weapons, violence, gangs, and use or sale of alcohol and drugs.

- Take immediate action on all reports of drug use or sales, threats, bullying, gang activity, or victimization.

- Create an environment that encourages parents and other adults to visit the school and participate in activities.

- Encourage staff to treat students and each other with respect.

- Involve youth in policy and program development.

- Offer programs that teach peaceful, nonviolent conflict-management methods to students, their families, and school staff.

- Work with the media to increase public awareness of safety issues.

Skill 19.4: Identify Appropriate Safety and Injury Prevention Strategies in the Home, School, and Community

A feeling of safety at home, at school, and in the community is vital for healthy development, according to Abraham Maslow. Maslow's hierarchy of human needs (1943) is applicable to many fields, including education. The hierarchy is summarized in the figure below.

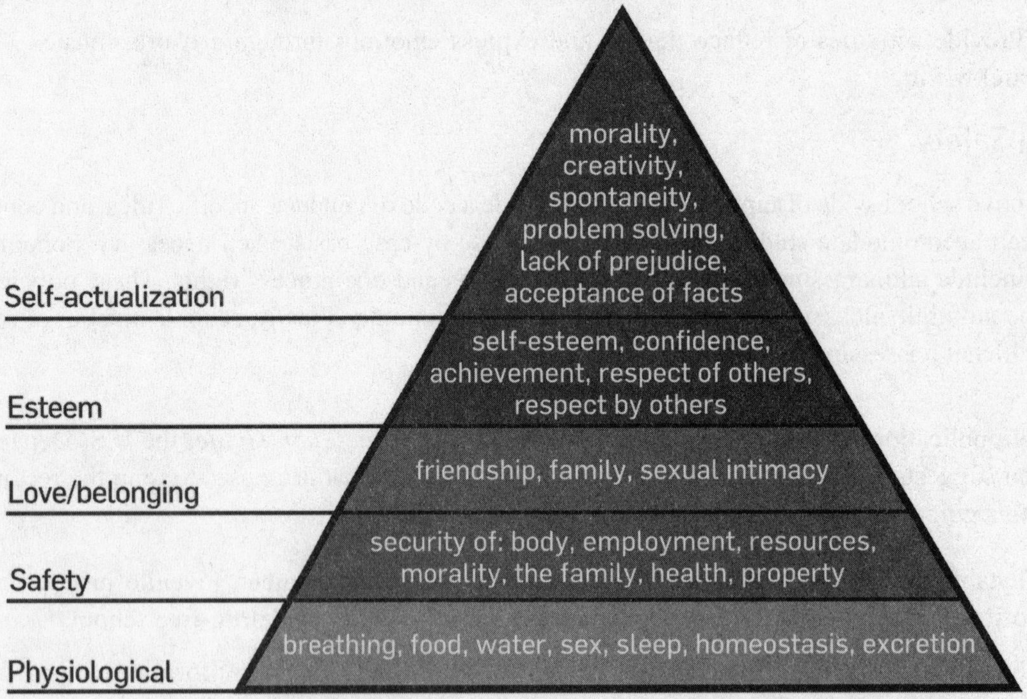

Self-actualization
morality, creativity, spontaneity, problem solving, lack of prejudice, acceptance of facts

Esteem
self-esteem, confidence, achievement, respect of others, respect by others

Love/belonging
friendship, family, sexual intimacy

Safety
security of: body, employment, resources, morality, the family, health, property

Physiological
breathing, food, water, sex, sleep, homeostasis, excretion

Figure 4.5: Maslow's Hierarchy of Needs

In this hierarchy, lower level needs (physiological and safety) must be satisfied before individuals can focus adequately on higher levels. In educational terms, the satisfaction of physiological needs at level 1 (to have hunger and thirst satisfied, to be adequately warm or cool, and so forth) and safety needs at level 2 (freedom from fears of physical or emotional injury) is necessary before students can perform school tasks. As a result, many schools provide nutritious meals (free breakfast and lunch) for students in an effort to meet the physiological needs. Schools install heating and cooling in school buildings so that learning can occur in comfort. Schools also must ensure that students feel safe and secure, as discussed earlier.

The third level of need, according to Maslow's theory, is the need for affiliation or the need for belonging and acceptance by others. Children must feel accepted by their families, their peers, and their communities. Acceptance is not a matter of the physical environment but rather the social environment. Students need the opportunity to develop social relationships and to establish friendships among their peers. Satisfaction of these needs, and lower ones, allows students to develop self-esteem and maximize potential (Levels 4 and 5).

First Aid

First aid is the immediate, temporary care of an injured or ill person. Occasionally, during physical education classes or during the school hours, injuries and illnesses occur. A basic knowledge of first aid is thus important for physical education teachers and other faculty. Since a teacher should not attempt first aid if procedures are unclear, a first aid course is essential.

The following table lists common injuries, symptoms, and a brief description of first aid treatments:

Common Injuries, Symptoms, and Treatments		
Injury	**Description And Symptoms**	**First Aid Treatment**
Fracture	Break in a bone that can be simple (a break in the bone), multiple (many breaks in the bone), or compound (a break in the bone and the skin).	Immobilize, use ice to control swelling, and seek medical aid. In the case of a compound fracture, stop the bleeding.
Traumatic Shock	Severe compression of circulation caused by injury or illness. Symptoms include cool clammy skin and a rapid, weak pulse.	Minimize heat loss and elevate legs without disturbing rest of the body. Seek medical help.
Sprain	Injury to a joint caused by the joint being moved too far or away from its range of motion. Both ligaments and tendons can be injured. Ligaments join bone to bone, and tendons join muscle to bone.	Rest, ice, compression, and elevation (RICE).

(continued)

Common Injuries, Symptoms, and Treatments *(continued)*		
Injury	**Description And Symptoms**	**First Aid Treatment**
Strain	Muscle injury caused by overwork	Use ice to lessen the swelling. Applying some heat after icing can be beneficial, although opinion on the value of heat varies.
Dislocation	Joint injury; bone ends out of place at the joint; holding ligaments severely stretched and torn.	Immobilize and seek medical help. Some people advocate "popping" the dislocation back into place, but this can be risky for both the injured person and for the person giving the first aid (liability).
Heat Exhaustion	Cold and clammy skin, nausea, dizziness, and paleness; not as severe as heat stroke.	Increase water intake, replace salt, and get out of the heat.
Heat Stroke	High fever, dry skin, and possible unconsciousness	Attempt to cool off gradually, get into the shade, and seek medical attention immediately.
Heart Attack	Shortness of breath, pain in the left arm, pain in the chest, nausea, and sweating	Elevate head and chest, give cardio-pulmonary resuscitation, if indicated, and seek medical assistance.
Seizures	Violent muscle contractions, muscle rigidity, and possible loss of consciousness	Clear the area around the victim to avoid injury during the seizure. Do not place anything in the victim's mouth; seek medical help after the seizure.

Recognizing Abuse and Neglect

Despite all the media attention given to child abuse and neglect, some teachers still believe that it cannot happen to one of their students. They may think, "This is a nice neighborhood," or "Most of these students have both a mother and a father living at home." However, abuse and neglect occur in intact families from every socioeconomic stratum.

Abused children may be hyperactive, unruly, and/or belligerent. They may flinch when they feel threatened. They may seem withdrawn. There is no single behavior or set of behaviors that definitively indicates abuse. The same can be said for neglected children, although they are more likely to appear unsociable and withdrawn.

One of the noticeable signs of abuse is welts or bruises caused by being hit. Marks from the hand, fist, or belt are usually recognizable. Marks in geometric shapes—from eating utensils, paddles, and so on—can also signify child abuse.

Although there may be an explanation for the marks other than abuse, teachers should make note of their observations, and be especially vigilant for reoccurring marks, changes in attitude or behavior, and other signs of a serious problem. The teacher should make note of the size, shape, and location of any welts or bruises.

Teachers must also make note of children who discuss or act out sexual themes. Young children who behave in a sexual manner may simply be acting out something they saw on television, but it also possible that the child's behavior reflects sexual abuse.

Competency 20: Knowledge of Subject Content and Appropriate Curriculum Design

Along with pedagogy, which concerns effective teaching skills and strategies, teachers must teach content. The focus of Competency 20 is on the teacher's knowledge of content in particular subject areas and the application of that knowledge to curriculum design.

Skill 20.1: Distinguish Between Developmentally Appropriate and In-appropriate Instructional Practices That Consider the Interaction of Cognitive, Affective, and Psychomotor Domains

There are three domains or areas of learning (Bloom, 1956):

1. *The psychomotor domain* concerns physical activities and skills. For example, playing basketball demands skills such as dribbling, passing, and shooting.

2. *The affective domain* concerns attitudes and feelings. For example, along with being fun, playing basketball can promote a positive attitude toward oneself, as well as a sense of teamwork and camaraderie.

3. *The cognitive domain* concerns thinking and the expression of thoughts in language. For example, playing basketball requires knowledge of the rules, the ability to understand and implement plays requested by the coach, and the capacity to make quick decisions during a game.

As the basketball example illustrates, most activities provide an opportunity for learning in each of the three domains. As long as instructional activities are developmentally appropriate, learning can progress in each area.

Skill 20.2: Identify Various Factors to Consider When Planning Physical Activities

When planning physical activities, the teacher should do the following:

- Create and sustain a safe and supportive learning environment.
- Evaluate the appropriateness of the physical environment to facilitate student learning and promote safety.
- Prepare to establish smooth, efficient, and well-paced routines.
- Prepare to involve students in the process of establishing rules and standards for behavior.
- Identify emergency procedures for student and campus safety.

While there are certain physical aspects of the classroom that are permanent, others can be modified to support instructional needs or enhance safety. For example, most classrooms have movable desks, which allow for varied seating arrangements and for opening up areas of the classroom for group activities. When rearranging desks and implementing activities, the teacher should ensure that students do not fall over or bump against desks and other furniture. The teacher can do so by careful arrangement of desks as well as reviewing the safety rules with the class.

Skill 20.3: Analyzing the Influence of Culture, Media, Technology, and Other Factors When Planning Health and Wellness Instruction

Health and wellness instruction has natural connections to children's lives beyond the classroom. Some of these connections are initiated by the teacher. For example, the teacher may introduce students to games and dances from other cultures as a way of broadening children's perspectives and teaching them about diversity. In other cases, it is the outside world that makes its way into the classroom in the form of health-related beliefs and practices that children bring to school. Children are exposed to a variety of messages from the media and/or parents, not all of will be consistent with what the teacher hopes to convey in class. When teachers discuss healthy and unhealthy food choices, for example, they must anticipate the possibility that at least some of their students had "junk food" for breakfast or dinner the previous evening and that they think junk food is just fine.

End-of-Chapter Questions

1. What is the general purpose of musical notation?

    (A) To provide a means of visually representing music.

    (B) To allow listeners to compare and contrast pieces.

    (C) To facilitate understanding of cultural differences in music.

    (D) To support critical analysis of musical style.

2. Which of the following are the secondary colors?

    (A) Red, yellow, blue.

    (B) Brown, violet, yellow.

    (C) Green, orange, violet.

    (D) Green, blue, brown.

3. The music of which of the following periods reflected clarity of form, logical thematic development, and adherence to sonata form?

    (A) Christian Era.

    (B) Classical.

    (C) Romantic.

    (D) 20th century.

4. In which of the following periods did Romanesque art and architecture flourish?

    (A) 400-800.

    (B) 800-1200.

    (C) 1200-1600.

    (D) 1600-2000.

5. Too much saturated fat in the diet can lead to which of the following?

    (A) Too much LDL.

    (B) Too much HDL.

    (C) Low cholesterol.

    (D) Low blood pressure.

6. Which of the following is among the main functions of calcium?

(A) Helping red blood cells carry oxygen.

(B) Conversion of carbohydrates to energy.

(C) Contributing to lymph production.

(D) Building bones and teeth.

7. What kind of receptor transmits information about pain?

(A) Interoceptors.

(B) Proprioceptors.

(C) Medioreceptors.

(D) Exteroreceptors.

Answer Key

1.	(A)	5.	(A)
2.	(C)	6.	(D)
3.	(B)	7.	(D)
4.	(B)		

Science and Technology

Competency 21: Knowledge of the Nature of Matter

One of the building blocks of scientific knowledge is an understanding of matter. Competency 21 focuses on fundamental descriptive concepts concerning the nature of matter.

Skill 21.1: Identify the Fundamental Physical Properties of Matter

Mass and Volume

Matter is anything with mass and volume. Mass is the amount of matter in an object; while volume is the amount of space an object occupies. Water can be considered matter because it takes up space (i.e., it has volume), whereas light is not matter because it does not take up space.

Weight

Weight, although often confused with mass, is a measure of the force of gravity on an object. A spring scale can determine weight. An electronic scale may display an object's mass in grams, but it is dependent on gravity for its operation, and it is only accurate when an expert has adjusted the electronics for the local gravitational force. Although an object appears "weightless" as it floats inside the space shuttle, it is not; gravitational forces from both the Earth and the sun keep it in orbit and affect the object.

Gravity

The force of gravity is proportional to the product of the masses of the two objects under consideration divided by the square of the distance between them. For example, Earth, being larger and more massive than Mars, has proportionally higher gravitational forces.

Density, Buoyancy, Viscosity

Density is the ratio of mass to volume. An intrinsic property, density depends on the type of matter but not the amount of matter. Thus, the density of a 5-ton cube of pure copper is the same as that of a small copper penny. (However, the modern penny consists of a thin shell of copper over a zinc plug, and so the density of the coin may be significantly lower than that of the older, pure copper coin.)

Density is related to buoyancy. Objects sink in liquids or gases if they are denser than the material that surrounds them. Archimedes's principle, also related to density, states that an object is buoyed up by a force equal to the mass of the material the object displaces. Thus, a canoe floats in water because the volume of the submerged portion of the canoe is equal to the volume of the water that is displaced.

Density is not the same as viscosity, a measure of thickness or ability to flow. The strength of intermolecular forces between molecules determines, for example, that molasses will be slow in January or that hydrogen bromide is a gas in any season.

Skill 21.2: Compare Physical and Chemical Changes

Matter can change in one of two ways, chemically or physically.

1. *A physical change* (e.g., melting, bending, cracking) affects the size, form, or appearance of a material. Physical changes do not alter the molecular structure of a material. For example, water that is frozen to form ice or boiled to form steam changes in form but is still water.

2. *A chemical change* does alter the molecular structure of matter. Examples of chemical changes are burning, rusting, and digestion. Under the right conditions, compounds can break apart, combine, or recombine to form new compounds; each of these processes is called a chemical reaction.

Skill 21.3: Compare the Characteristics of Elements, Compounds, and Mixtures

Classifications of matter include elements, compounds, mixtures, and solutions.

1. *An element* (e.g., iron, carbon, copper) consists of only one type of atom. A symbol of one or two letters, such as Fe (iron) or C (carbon), represents an element.

2. *A compound* is matter that comprises atoms chemically combined in definite weight proportions. An example of a compound is water, which is oxygen and hydrogen combined in the ratio of two hydrogen molecules to one oxygen molecule (H_2O).

3. *A mixture* is made up of one or more types of molecules, not chemically combined and without any definite weight proportions. For example, milk is a mixture of water and butterfat particles. Mixtures can be separated by either physical or chemical means. An example of physical means would be straining the butterfat from milk to make skim milk.

4. *A solution* is a homogeneous mixture—that is, mixtures with evenly distributed substances. An example of a solution is seawater. Separating the salt from seawater requires the process of evaporation.

Skill 21.4: Compare the Physical Properties of Solids, Liquids, and Gases

The three main states of matter are solids, liquids, and gases.

• *A solid* has a definite volume and a definite shape (e.g., ice).

• *A liquid* has a definite volume but has no definite shape (e.g., water).

• *A gas* has no definite volume or shape (e.g., water vapor or steam).

Skill 21.5: Compare the Properties of Liquids During Phase Change Through Heating and Cooling

When matter changes from one state to another (e.g., solid to liquid), a phase change is said to occur. For example, liquids undergo phase changes as a result of heating and cooling. Water becomes a solid when frozen and then a liquid when it melts. If water is heated sufficiently, it evaporates and becomes vapor. Cooling then results in condensation and a phase change back to the liquid state.

Skill 21.6: Demonstrate Knowledge That All Matter Is Composed of Parts Too Small to be Seen

Atoms are the basic chemical building blocks of matter (see figure below). Atoms are composed of three types of subatomic particles: protons, neutrons, and electrons, which have mass and charge. Protons and neutrons reside in the nucleus, or solid center, of an atom. Electrons, the lightest subatomic particles known, orbit the outer portion of an atom.

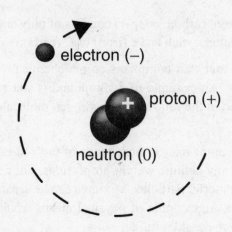

Figure 5.1: Basic structure of an atom

Under most conditions, atoms are indivisible. However, during atomic reactions atoms may split or combine to form new atoms. Atomic reactions occur deep inside the sun, in nuclear power reactors, in nuclear bombs, and in radioactive decay.

An atom is the smallest particle of an element that retains the characteristics of that element. Atoms of the same element have the same number of protons in their nuclei. Each element has an atomic number, which is equal to the number of protons in an atom of that element. The periodic table is an arrangement of all the elements in order according to their atomic number. The periodic table is a reference tool and summarizes the atomic structure, mass, and reactive tendencies of elements; the periodic table groups elements vertically according to their chemical properties. Two or more atoms may combine to form molecules.

COMPETENCY 22: Knowledge of Forces, Motion, and Energy

An understanding of the physical world depends not only on knowledge of matter but also on knowledge of the fundamental abstract constructs of force, motion, and energy and their manifestations in more specific constructs. Competency 22 focuses on knowledge of forces, motion, and energy.

Skill 22.1: Apply Knowledge of Temperature, Heat, and Heat Transfer

The term "heat" refers to the energy of moving molecules. Transfer of heat is thus a form of energy transfer.

Temperature is not a reflection of heat but rather of the speed that the molecules in a material are moving. The faster the molecules are moving, the hotter the temperature becomes.

A thermometer measures temperature. There are several types of thermometers, but the most common ones are glass tubes containing mercury or a liquid, such as colored alcohol. Thermometers usually use the Fahrenheit scale or the Celsius scale.

Skill 22.2: Identify the Types and Characteristics of Contact Forces and At-a-Distance Forces

A force can be thought of simplistically as a push or a pull. There are two main types of force: contact and at-a-distance. Contact force, as the name suggests, involves contact between objects, as in the example of mechanical force exerted by a machine on an object. At-a-distance force acts between objects that are not in contact. Following are three examples of at-a-distance force:

1. *Gravitational force.* Gravitational force is the attraction or pull that every body in the universe exerts on every other body.

2. *Electrostatic force.* Two negatively charged materials will repel, or move away from, each other. Two positively charged materials will also repel each other. However, a positively-charged material and a negatively-charged material will attract each other. These phenomena together illustrate the law of electrostatic repulsion.

3. *Magnetic force.* Magnets are materials that pick up or attract other materials made of iron, steel, cobalt, or nickel; such materials are defined as magnetic materials. Some magnets, known as lodestones, are naturally occurring, while others are created by people.

Magnetic Forces

Magnetic forces make magnets attract or repel each other. The regions in magnets that create magnetic forces are magnetic poles, and the poles are where magnetic force is strongest. All magnets have a north and a south pole. The following phenomena can be observed:

- The north pole of one magnet will repel the north pole of another magnet

- The south pole of one magnet will repel the south pole of another magnet

- The north pole of one magnet will attract the south pole of another magnet

A magnetic field is the area that the magnetic force affects. A magnetic field surrounds both poles of a magnet; an electric current can create a magnetic field. Electromagnets create large magnetic fields with electric current. Similarly, moving a wire through a magnetic field produces a current.

The Earth has a magnetic field. Compasses are magnets that align themselves with the Earth's magnetic field, allowing users to identify direction.

Skill 22.3: Apply Knowledge of Light and Optics to Practical Applications

Light is a form of energy. The sun and other bodies radiate or give out light (i.e., radiant energy). Light is in the form of waves and is one of a group of waves—the electromagnetic waves. Among the other kinds of electromagnetic waves are X-rays, radio waves, and ultraviolet rays.

Properties of Light

Light has several important physical properties:

1. Light rays travel at 186,000 miles each second. That is considerably faster than the speed of sound (about 1,100 feet per second). Therefore, we see a bolt of lightning before we hear the clap of thunder.

2. Light can pass through some materials but other materials stop its passage. Most light rays pass through transparent materials such as air, water, and clear glass. Only some of the light passes through a translucent substance (e.g., frosted glass). It is not possible to see through opaque materials, like a brick wall, because none of the light passes through.

3. Light can change direction, but it always travels in a straight line. When a light ray strikes a mirror, for instance, the light changes direction and is reflected but continues traveling in a straight line.

Refraction

Light passes through a transparent material, like water, at a slant or angle. The bending of light rays is called refraction. For example, if you try to use your hands to catch a fish that appears in the clear water of a stream, you find that the fish is not where it appears to be. The refracted light gives a distorted view.

Lenses

A lens is a piece of transparent material, like glass, that is curved. When light passes through the curved lens, the light undergoes refraction. There are two types of lenses, as illustrated in the figure below.

- *A convex lens* is thicker in the middle. It acts as a magnifying glass and can help a farsighted person's ability to focus on a near object. A convex lens bends the light inward before it enters the eyes; the rays come together and form sharper, clearer images on the retina. Projectors use a convex lens to change a small photograph into a larger picture on the screen.

- *A concave lens* is thinner in the middle. The concave lens spreads the light rays before they enter the eyes, and the rays merge farther back in the eye to form a clear image on the retina. Concave lenses can help a nearsighted person to see better at a distance.

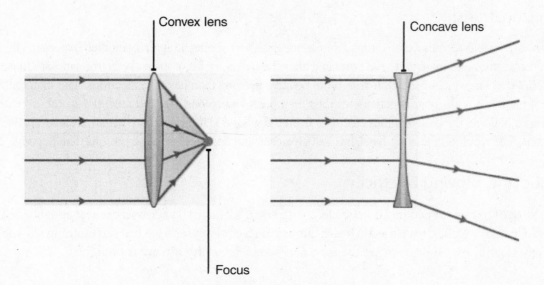

Figure 5.2: Concave and convex lens

A prism is a transparent geometric solid that diffuses (or breaks apart) a white light ray into parts. The white light is really a mixture of seven colored lights: red, orange, yellow, green, blue, indigo, and violet. Diffusion—the breaking of the white light into a rainbow—reverses when the rainbow of colors passes through another prism; the second result is white light.

Skill 22.4: Apply Knowledge of Electrical Currents, Circuits, Conductors, Insulators, and Static Electricity to Real-World Situations

Atoms make up all things. As noted earlier, each atom contains electrons with negative charges, protons with positive charges, and neutrons with neither negative nor positive charges. Usually, the atom has the same number of electrons and protons; in such cases it will be electrically neutral. The charges of the protons and electrons cancel each other, so the atom has no net charge. If an atom has more electrons than protons, the atom has a negative charge. If an atom has fewer electrons than protons, the atom has a positive charge. A material stays charged only as long as electrons do not have a way to enter or leave the material.

Insulators and Conductors

Materials can be classified as insulators or conductors depending on whether they allow electrons to flow through them.

- *Insulators* are materials that hold their electrons very tightly, such that electrons do not move through them very well. Examples of insulators are glass, cloth, dry air, and plastic.

- *Conductors* are materials that permit loosely held electrons to flow through them. Examples of conductors include metals such as copper.

Electron Transfer

It is possible to remove electrons from a material by rubbing it against another material. The electrons then move from one material to the other and alter the balance of protons and electrons in both materials. The material that loses electrons is left with more positive protons than negative electrons. The material that gains electrons is left with more negative electrons than positive protons. For instance, if you rub a piece of wool against a balloon, the balloon gains electrons from the wool and thus has more negative electrons than positive protons. The wool, on the other hand, has lost electrons and has more positive protons than negative electrons.

Static and Moving Electricity

Most of us have experienced static electricity when we have slid across a car seat and touched the door handle in cool weather, have tried to brush our hair on a cool day, or have had our clothing stick to us when the day is cold. We might even see the sparks of static electricity if there is no light.

Friction can produce static (i.e., nonmoving) electricity. For instance when two different materials—particularly nonmetals—rub together, they can attract lightweight objects because these materials have become electrically charged. By contrast, moving electricity is current electricity such as the electricity that powers your home.

Laws of Electrostatic Attraction and Repulsion

The law of electrostatic attraction states that materials with opposite charges attract each other. When a negatively charged balloon is brought near a wall, the balloon will stick to the wall because they have opposite charges (see figure below).

The law of electrostatic repulsion states that materials with the same charges repel each other.

For example, a balloon that does not have a negative charge will fall to the ground instead of sticking to the wall.

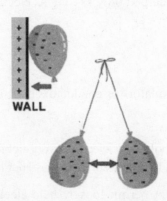

WALL

Figure 5.3: Illustration of Laws of Electrostatic Attraction and Repulsion Currents

As noted earlier, electrons can flow through conductors. The flow of electrons produces an electric current. Copper, for example, is a good conductor of electricity, and thus electric wires are often made of copper to allow the current to flow easily. These wires may be covered with rubber, an insulator, to help prevent electric shock if someone touches them.

Circuits

Circuits are paths through which electric current flows. A circuit can comprise one or more complete paths made up of connections of electrical elements through which the current passes.

Circuits can be in series or parallel.

- *Series circuits* are made of a single path through which all current must flow. If any part of a series circuit breaks, the circuit is "opened," and the flow of the current must stop. Some sets of Christmas tree lights are designed in series. If one bulb in the string of lights burns out, none of the lights in the string will work; the current is disrupted for the entire string.

- *Parallel circuits* provide more than one path for current to flow. When one pathway opens so that current cannot flow in it, the current continues to move through the other paths. Wired homes use parallel circuits so that burned-out light bulbs and turned-off television sets do not disrupt electricity used in other parts of the house.

Skill 22.5: Distinguish Between Different Types of Energy and Their Characteristics As They Apply to Real-World Situations

Energy takes on many different forms. Throughout this chapter, different forms are discussed, including the following:

- Light energy (Competency 22, Skills 22.3 and 22.7)
- Electrical energy (Competency 22, Skill 22.4)
- Heat Energy (Competency 22, Skill 22.1)
- Chemical Energy (Competency 21, Skill 21.2)
- Mechanical Energy (Competency 21, Skill 21.2)
- Solar Energy (Competency 22, Skill 22.5)
- Electromagnetic Energy (Competency 22, Skill 22.7)

Sound is an additional form of energy that students need to be familiar with.

Sound Energy

Sound results when an object vibrates rapidly. Plucking, stroking, blowing, or hitting cause vibrations. When an object vibrates, the vibrations travel as waves in all directions. The waves stop when the vibration stops.

When a guitar string vibrates, it rapidly moves back and forth. The string pushes against the air molecules in front of it; it presses the air molecules in front of it together. The compacted molecules create a space called compression. The space behind the strings is a rarefaction. A rarefaction and a compression compose a complete vibration.

When vibrations, or sound waves, reach the ear, the auditory nerve carries the result to the brain. This creates a sensation of sound. Most of us hear the sounds after they travel through the air, which is a gas. The speed is about 1,100 feet per second. When the air is warm, the molecules move faster, and the vibrations will reach our ears sooner. Vibrations travel better through liquids because the molecules are closer together. They travel even better through solids. Vibrations do not travel well in a vacuum that lacks molecules.

Characteristics of Sounds

Sound can differ in pitch, intensity, and quality.

1. *Pitch* is the highness or lowness of a sound. The faster an object vibrates, the higher the frequency and the sound it makes. Slower vibrations result in lower frequencies and sounds (see figure below).

2. *Intensity* is the loudness or softness of a sound. Stronger vibrations produce louder sounds.

3. *Quality* is what distinguishes a sound from sounds that are otherwise the same in pitch, duration, and intensity. When an object vibrates, it can vibrate as a whole or in parts; the resulting sound is the quality. For example, it is possible to differentiate between a voice and a musical instrument expressing the same note because of the quality of the sounds.

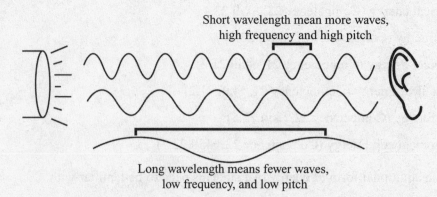

Short wavelength mean more waves, high frequency and high pitch

Long wavelength means fewer waves, low frequency, and low pitch

Figure 5.4: Sound Waves

Skill 22.6: Apply Knowledge of the Ability of Energy to Cause Motion or Create Change

Work

Scientists conceptualize energy as the ability to do work. One way to define work is to say that it occurs when an effort or a resistance moves through a distance. The effort is the force exerted on a machine, and the object that the machine lifts or moves is the resistance.

Another way to define work is to say that it occurs when applied force (push or pull) to an object results in movement of the object. The formula for work is: Work = Force × Distance.

According to this formula, the greater the force applied, or the longer the distance traveled, the greater the work done.

EXAMPLES OF SIMPLE MACHINES		
Simple Machine	**Defintion**	**Example**
Lever	A rigid bar resting on a pivot (fulcrum) which lets the user exert a small force at a large distance to move a load.	
Ramp (inclined plane)	Use of a plane to allow a user to push to move objects upward with relatively small amounts of applied force compared with direct lifting.	
Wedge	A variation of an inclined plane in which a weak force is applied to the larger end of the plane to move it through an object.	

(continued)

245

	EXAMPLES OF SIMPLE MACHINES *(continued)*	
Simple Machine	**Defintion**	**Example**
Screw	A variation of an inclined plane in which the inclined plane is wrapped around a cylinder. Power is applied to the head of the screw which compresses into a fixed object.	
Pulley	Use of a wheel and rope to make lifting easier by changing the direction of the lifting force.	
Wheel and Axle	Use of two circular objects of differing size in which force applied to the larger object (wheel) is turned by the smaller one (axle)	THE WHEEL AND AXLE IS A WHEEL CONNECTED TO A RIGID POLE.

Skill 22.7: Demonstrate Knowledge That Electrical Energy Can Be Transformed into Heat, Light, Mechanical, and Sound Energy

Energy transformation from one type to another is possible. Electrical energy, for example, can be transformed into heat, light, sound, or mechanical energy. However, energy is never created or destroyed in any transformation.

The relationship between some of the different forms of energy is illustrated by a consideration of electromagnetic waves. Just as all matter consists of the same fundamental parts (protons, neutron, electrons, etc.), many forms of radiation consist of these waves that travel at 186,000 miles per second (see figure below).

Visible Light

Visible light represents only one-tenth of the length of the electromagnetic spectrum. Radio, television, radar, visible light, X-rays, cosmic rays, and gamma rays are some of the effects of the electromagnetic spectrum. The wavelengths vary from 2 miles (radio wave) to 1 millionth of 1 millionth of an inch (gamma ray). X-rays have a shorter wavelength and a higher frequency compared with ultraviolet rays. X-rays can pass through nonmetals, are useful in taking pictures of the human body, and can help to inspect fruit for frostbite damage.

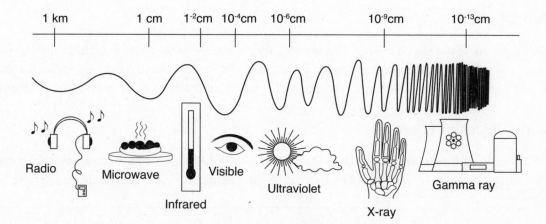

Figure 5.5: The Electromagnetic Spectrum

In light, different wavelengths produce different visible colors. Thus, the colors of the rainbow appear in the order of the lengths of the waves: red, orange, yellow, green, blue, indigo, and violet, which can be remembered by the acronym ROY G. BIV. The deepest red visible to the eye has a 1/30,000-inch wavelength; at the other end of the spectrum, the deepest violet has a 1/60,000-inch wavelength.

Invisible Light

Just as some sound waves (i.e., those that are ultrasonic) are inaudible to the human ear, some waves of light are invisible to the human eye. Beyond the deepest violet wave with its 1/60,000-inch spectrum is the ultraviolet wave, which is shorter than violet waves. Ultraviolet waves from the sun are important to human health because they stimulate the production of vitamin D. Ultraviolet radiation is responsible for the sun tanning—or burning—of human skin.

At the other end of the color spectrum, just beyond the deepest red, is another wave that is invisible to the eye: the infrared wave. Infrared waves are the radiant waves that warm the Earth. Sunlight and all warm bodies radiate infrared light. Long in wavelength and low in frequency, infrared waves are useful in photography in the dark, in fingerprint detection, and in medicine.

Skill 22.8: Demonstrate Knowledge of Potential and Kinetic Energy

There are two main types of energy: kinetic and potential.

Kinetic Energy

Kinetic energy is the energy of a moving object. The formula for kinetic energy is: $KE = \frac{1}{2}mv^2$. In this formula, m is the mass of an object and v is its velocity. Thus, the greater the mass, the greater the kinetic energy. And, the greater the velocity, the greater the kinetic energy.

Potential Energy

Potential energy is stored energy. The formula for potential energy is $PE = mgh$. In this formula, m is mass, g is the gravitational force constant, and h is the height. In the case of a hanging icicle, the greater the mass, the greater the potential energy. And, the higher it is from the ground, the greater the potential energy.

Specific Types of Energy

All energy is kinetic or potential. Within these two broad types, there are many specific types of energy, including thermal, mechanical, electrical, light, chemical, sound, and nuclear (see table below).

Some Types of Energy			
Type	**Definition**	**Examples**	**Potential or Kinetic**
THERMAL (HEAT)	Energy caused by or related to heat created by increased kinetic movement in molecules which is transferred by conduction, convection, or radiation	Sun (solar energy); stove burner; fire	Kinetic
MECHANICAL	Energy of objects based on position (potential energy) or motion (kinetic energy)	Movement of the physical body; simple machines	Kinetic or Potential

(continued)

Some Types of Energy (continued)			
Type	Definition	Examples	Potential or Kinetic
ELECTRICAL	Energy produced by moving electrons	Electrical current; lightning	Kinetic
RADIANT	Energy produced by electro-magnetic waves	Visible light and colors, X-rays, gamma rays; ultra-violet; radio waves and microwaves	Kinetic
CHEMICAL	Energy resulting from the bonds of atoms and mol-ecules	Coal; oil; natural gas; batteries; food; wood	Potential
NUCLEAR	Energy that results when the nucleus of an atom splits in two (fission) or when the nu-clei of atoms become fused together (fusion)	Uranium	Potential

Skill 22.9: Demonstrate Knowledge That Motion of All Matter Can Be Changed by Forces Observed, Described, and Measured

By definition the movement of an object will be affected by forces acting upon it. For example, under ordinary circumstances gravity constantly acts on objects. Gravity causes objects to fall when unsupported and to accelerate during their fall. Gravity also contributes to friction, which can slow the lateral movement of an object across a surface. These changes can be observed, described, and even measured in the science classroom given suitable conditions.

Skill 22.10: Differentiate Between Balanced and Unbalanced Forces and How They Affect Objects

The forces acting on an object at a particular moment can be described as balanced or unbalanced.

- Balanced forces result in no motion or motion at a constant speed.

- Unbalanced forces result in an acceleration or deceleration.

Competency 23: Knowledge of Earth and Space

Through geology, meteorology, and astronomy, students learn about physical structures and mechanisms that exist beneath, on, and above the earth. The focus of Competency 23 is on knowledge about the physical features of Earth and space.

Skill 23.1: Identify Characteristics of Geologic Formations, the Mechanisms by Which They Were Formed, and Their Relationship to the Movement of Tectonic Plates

Geology is the study of the structure and composition of the Earth. Although most of the physical features of the Earth appear stable to us, they are in fact constantly changing.

Composition of the Earth

The three layers that compose the Earth are the core, mantle, and crust.

1. The core, which is about 7,000 kilometers in diameter, is made up of solid iron and nickel.

2. The mantle is the semi-molten layer between the crust and the core. It is about 3,000 kilometers thick.

3. The crust is the solid outermost layer, composed of bedrock overlaid with mineral and/or organic sediment (soil) and ranging from 5 to 40 kilometers thick.

Plate Tectonics

At times, large sections of the Earth's crust move and create faults, earthquakes, volcanoes, and mountains. These moving sections of the Earth are plates, and the study of their movements is plate tectonics. Plate tectonics revolutionized the way geologists think about the Earth. According to the theory, large lithospheric plates form the surface of the Earth. The size and position of these plates change over time. The edges of the plates, where they move against each other, are sites of intense geologic activity, such as earthquakes, volcanoes, and mountain building.

Continental Drift and Seafloor Spreading

Plate tectonics reflects the convergence of two earlier ideas: continental drift and seafloor spreading.

- *Continental drift* is the movement of continents over the Earth's surface and their change in position relative to each other.

- *Seafloor spreading* is the creation of new oceanic crust at mid-ocean ridges and movement of the crust away from the mid-ocean ridges.

The main evidence for continental drift and plate tectonics is as follows:

1. The shapes of many continents look like pieces of a jigsaw puzzle. For example, the east coasts of North America and South America and the west coasts of Africa and Europe appear to fit together.

2. Many fossil comparisons along the edges of continents that look like they fit together suggest species similarities that would only make sense if the two continents were joined at some point in the past.

3. Seismic, volcanic, and geothermal activity occurs more frequently along plate boundaries than in sites far from boundaries.

4. There are ridges, such as the Mid-Atlantic Ridge; these occur where plates are separating because of lava welling up from between the plates as they pull apart. Likewise, there are mountain ranges forming where plates are pushing against each other (e.g., the Himalayas, which are still growing).

Earthquakes and Volcanoes

Faults are cracks in the crust that result from the movements of plates. Faults play a role in the occurrence of earthquakes and volcanoes.

Earthquakes occur when plates slide past one another quickly. (Volcanoes may also cause earthquakes.) A seismograph is used to measure earthquakes, and the severity of each quake is defined by means of the Richter Scale.

Volcanoes form when two plates separate enough to let magma reach the crust. Magma is molten rock beneath the Earth's crust. Lava is molten rock on the Earth's surface. A volcano shoots out magma, which eventually hardens into lava, and releases ash. Sometimes the erupting volcano forms rivers of lava. Volcanoes occur all over the Earth—for example, Submarine locations in the Pacific Ocean, on the Hawaiian Islands, and along the southeastern border of Asia. The composition of volcanoes is fiery igneous rock, ash, and many layers of dirt and mud that have hardened from previous eruptions. Volcanic activity causes the crust of the Earth to buckle upward and form mountains.

Skill 23.2: Identify the Characteristics of Soil and the Process of Soil Formation

Soil is a mixture of water, air, minerals, and organic materials. Although the content of soil varies in different locations and is constantly changing, there are three main components of soil that give it its texture: sand, silt, and clay.

- Sand is the largest particle in soil, and it does not hold many nutrients.

- Silt particles are smaller than sand but larger than clay. Silt feels smooth and powdery when dry; when set, it feels smooth and not sticky.

- Clay is the smallest of particle. It is smooth when dry and sticky when wet. Clay holds nutrients well, and it holds more water than other materials, thereby resulting in less runoff.

Skill 23.3: Identify the Major Groups and Properties of Rocks and Minerals, Examples of Each, and the Processes of Their Formation

Rocks are naturally occurring solids found on or below the Earth's surface. One or more minerals, which are pure substances made of just one element or chemical compound, compose the rocks.

Types of Rocks

There are three groups of rocks, which are classified according to their method of formation:

1. *Igneous rocks* are fire rocks; their place of formation can be either under or above ground. Sometimes melted rock, called magma, becomes trapped in small pockets deep within the Earth. As these pockets of magma slowly cool underground, the magma becomes igneous rock. When volcanoes erupt and the magma rises above the Earth's surface, it is called lava. Igneous rocks are the result of the lava cooling aboveground. Examples include granite and obsidian.

2. *Sedimentary rocks* are the result of wind or water breaking down or wearing little pieces of earth; often the bits of earth settle to the bottom of rivers, lakes, and oceans. Over thousands or even millions of years, layer after layer of eroded

earth, silt, or deposited rock fragments, by compaction at high pressures and/ or cementation, forms rock. This formed sedimentary rock includes shale and limestone.

3.   *Metamorphic rocks* are those that have "morphed," or changed into other kinds of rocks. Igneous or sedimentary rocks heated under tons of pressure change into metamorphic rocks. Geologists examining metamorphic rock samples have found that some of the grains in the rocks are flattened. Marble and slate are two examples of metamorphic rocks.

Weathering of Rocks

Weathering is the breaking down of rock into small pieces. Acid rain, freezing, wind abrasion, glacier scouring, and running water weather rock. Erosion transports rock or sediment to new areas. Agents of erosion include wind, running water, and glaciers.

Skill 23.4: Identify Ways in Which Land and Water Interact

A number of natural and artificial structures allow for distinctive interactions between water, land, and/or air. Following are some important examples.

Aquifers

An aquifer is an underground layer of water-bearing, permeable (porous) rock. The water or other matter in the rock may pass gradually through porous stone or a bed of sand down to another level; this filtering process is called percolation. When the matter percolates to another level, it may carry with it materials and minerals it has leached from the area above. Leaching is the extracting of a substance from a solid by dissolving it in a liquid.

Reservoirs

A reservoir is a container for storing something, like water. On the Earth, a reservoir is an artificial lake that natural acts, such as flooding, may create or that people may construct to collect and store water for public use. When beavers build a dam, the land behind the dam becomes a reservoir; the halting of the water flow, the collection of rainfall, and flooding may increase the depth of the water.

Sinkholes

Sinkholes occur in nature in low areas, but some sinkholes are the result of human activity. For example, in underground mines, the upper level may collapse into the cavity underneath. Viewed from above, the collapsed earth looks like a huge hole. Sinkholes can also form when drainage pipes collapse under the ground or even under a roadway.

Runoff

Precipitation falls on the land, flows overland as runoff, and runs into creeks, rivers, and eventually the ocean. Rivers also gain and lose water to the ground, but most of the water in rivers seems to come from runoff from the land surface. Human activities can affect runoff. For example, parking lots, shopping centers, buildings, roads, and other kinds of construction reduce the infiltration of water into the ground, producing more runoff. An increase in runoff can also result from the removal of vegetation, grading, and the construction of drainage networks. Flooding frequently occurs in urban areas because of the increased runoff resulting from human actions.

Air Masses

An air mass is a huge body of air that may cover a large portion of the Earth's surface and may be high and wide. The temperature and the humidity are relatively constant throughout the air mass. The weather that can result from an air mass depends mostly on the humidity and the temperature of that air mass.

Fronts

An air mass forms when the largely undisturbed atmosphere over one part of the Earth's surface picks up the temperature and humidity of that part of the Earth. The condition of an air mass may change when the mass moves from one place to another. When two air masses meet, the boundary between them is called a front. Most stormy weather occurs at these fronts.

Wind

Differences in pressure govern air movement, or wind, in the atmosphere. In general, high pressure and low moisture content characterize air masses at the poles. Air masses near the equator usually have low pressure and high moisture content. (Heating decreases the density of air at the equator and increases it at the poles.) Therefore, wind tends to flow from high to low pressure regions. The rotation of the Earth also plays a role in air movement. In addition, belts of high-speed winds called jet streams in the upper troposphere (the lowest layer of the Earth's atmosphere) also affect air movement.

Jet Streams

A jet stream is like a narrow current flowing around the Earth. The two jet streams in the Northern Hemisphere are near the pole and near the middle latitudes; similar ones are apparent below the equator.

Clouds

Clouds are visible masses of water droplets, ice crystals, and/or other materials suspended in the atmosphere. The three main types of clouds are stratus, cumulus, and cirrus. Each type has a different appearance and can help predict the weather, as indicated in the table below:

Types of Clouds and their Association with Weather			
Type	**Appearance**		**Weather**
Stratus	Flat	Light	Stable weather
		Dark	Rain expected soon
Cumulus	Fluffy	Solid, light	Good weather
Cirrus	Thin	Wispy	Changes in weather expected
Cumulonimbus (also called Nimbus)	Tall and thick	Dark	Heavy rain, perhaps a thunderstorm

Storms

Students are most familiar with the three main types of storms: hurricanes, tornadoes, and thunderstorms.

1. *Hurricanes* are cyclones (or intense lows) that form over the oceans in the tropics—usually between June and November. The large amounts of heat energy created during these months cause ocean waters to evaporate and to form warm moist air. When cooler air pushes on the warm air, a violent storm with much rain often results.

A hurricane has no front, but it does have an "eye," which is a calm area. The winds in a hurricane move swiftly, but the hurricane itself moves slowly. The waves that a hurricane produces usually cause much damage. Hurricanes in the western Pacific Ocean are called typhoons. In the Indian Ocean, they are cyclones; in Australia, they are willy-willies; and in the Philippines they are baguios.

2. *Tornadoes* are violent, small, short-lived storms. They occur almost exclusively in the United States. The tornado cloud is very thick, black, and funnel-shaped and can travel quickly. A deafening roar accompanies the tornado. If the tornado passes over a body of water, it becomes a waterspout.

3. *Thunderstorms* are meteorological events that include lightning, heavy rain, gusts of wind, thunder, and sometimes hail. Cumulonimbus clouds are often a predictor of strong thunderstorms. A thunderstorm rarely lasts more than 2 hours, but it is possible for a region to experience more than one thunderstorm a day. There are two main types of thunderstorms:

• A frontal thunderstorm forms when a cold front pushes warm air ahead of it.

• An air-mass thunderstorm (also called summer thunderstorm) forms within an air mass, usually on hot summer afternoons.

Water Cycle

The hydrologic cycle, or water cycle, is a series of movements of water above, on, and below the surface of the Earth. The water cycle consists of four stages: evaporation, condensation, precipitation, and collection, as summarized in the figure below:

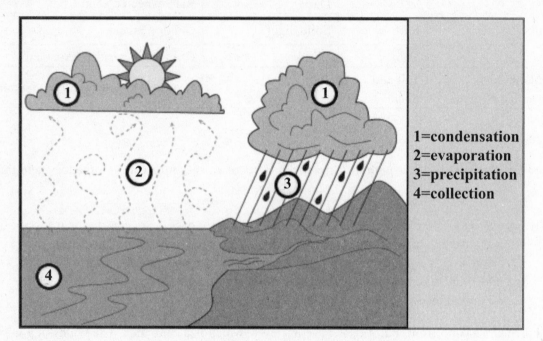

1=condensation
2=evaporation
3=precipitation
4=collection

Figure 5.6: Illustration of Water Cycle

- Evaporation occurs when the sun heats up water and turns it into water vapor or steam; this water vapor leaves the river, lake, or ocean and goes into the air.

- Condensation occurs when the water vapor in the air resulting from evaporation gets colder and changes back into liquid and forms clouds.

- Precipitation occurs when so much water has condensed that the air cannot hold it anymore; the clouds get heavy and water falls back to the Earth in the form of rain, hail, sleet, or snow.

- Collection occurs after precipitation, when the moisture that has fallen is soaked up by oceans, lakes, rivers, or soil.

Water covers about 70 percent of the Earth's surface. As that water slowly evaporates, the atmosphere holds some of the vapor. It is the water vapor in the Earth's atmosphere that causes precipitation. Some of the main types include rain, snow, hail, dew, and fog.

Rain

Heat energy warms the air and increases water evaporation; warm air expands and rises above cooler surrounding air. When the rising air cools and water vapor condenses, clouds form, and the result is usually precipitation. If the surrounding air is above 32° Fahrenheit, the precipitation is likely to be in the form of rain.

Snow

Snow comes from cooled droplets of water that the clouds or the upper air holds. Snow consists of crystals of water. Crystals formed in the low clouds are usually large and branching; those formed in the high clouds are small and compact.

Hail

The white, rolling cloud that often appears at the beginning of a thunderstorm is typically where hail forms. The air in the cloud is whirling parallel to the Earth. A raindrop caught in the cloud and carried up high in the atmosphere turns to snow. When it comes down, water might coat it again. Then it might rise again and freeze. The longer the hailstone travels, the larger it gets, the more violent the whirl of air becomes, and the larger the hailstone is before it hits the Earth. Hail is a part of a thunderstorm, and it usually occurs in the summer.

Dew

Warm air holds moisture. In the summer, the warm, moist air may cool when it comes in contact with the ground. This cooling on the ground, the grass, and items near the ground may result in the collection of drops of moisture, or dew.

Fog

Fog is a large mass of water vapor that has condensed to fine particles. These fine drops often attach to particles in the air—like dust—just as drops near the Earth attach to grass, rocks, and other objects to form dew. Fog is often found at or just above the Earth's surface.

Skill 23.5: Differentiate Between Radiation, Conduction, and Convection, the Three Mechanisms by Which Heat Is Transferred Through Earth's System

There are three mechanisms of heat transfer.

1.   *Radiation* is the transfer of energy through space. Electromagnetic waves such as those in sunlight transfer energy by means of radiation. When the waves reach an object, they transfer their energy.

2.   *Conduction* is the transfer of energy across objects that are in contact with each other. Conduction may also occur within an object. Conduction can involve solids, liquids, or gases. It is the result of a difference in temperature between objects or regions of objects.

3.   *Convection* is the transfer of energy expressed as movement of molecules within liquids and gases. As liquids or gases are heated or cooled, the movement of the molecules changes. Convection plays in important role in oceanic processes and in weather conditions.

Skill 23.6: Identify the Components of Earth's Solar System and Compare Their Individual Characteristics

The solar system consists of the sun and its orbiting planets. The sun, composed of hydrogen, has a mass 750 times that of all the planets combined.

The names of the planets in order from the sun are Mercury, Venus, Earth, Mars, Jupiter, Saturn, Uranus, and Neptune. (Pluto was recently removed from the list of planets.) The innermost planets of Mercury, Venus, Earth, and Mars are primarily composed of metallic materials, while the outermost planets of Jupiter, Saturn, Uranus, and Neptune are largely made up of hydrogen, helium, and ices of ammonia and methane. Jupiter—a giant, half-formed sun composed largely of hydrogen gas—is an exception among the planets.

The planets can be compared and contrasted in terms of various physical characteristics. For example, Mercury is the smallest planet and Jupiter is the largest. Saturn has distinctive rings while Jupiter has a giant red spot. Some of the planets (e.g., Earth, Mars, Jupiter) have satellite moons while others do not. And some planets, like the Earth and Venus, have significant atmospheres, while others do not.

Skill 23.7: Demonstrate Knowledge of Earth's Place in Our Changing Universe

Early Years of Space Exploration

During and after World War II, scientists began to develop rockets and to make great advances in our understanding of the physical universe. They sent rockets—often containing instruments and cameras—into space for extended periods. The nations involved in space exploration, primarily the United States and Russia, were motivated by numerous goals:

- To learn more about space

- To observe Earth from a broader perspective

- To develop weather satellite stations

- To establish sky laboratories

- To prepare for the possibility of space-based warfare

In the process of establishing and accomplishing these goals, the two nations learned the importance of cooperation in order to achieve success.

The "Space Race"

The launching of the Soviet space satellite Sputnik on October 4, 1957, created fear that America was falling behind technologically. Sputnik was the first satellite to travel through space in orbit around Earth. Although the United States launched Explorer I on January 31, 1958, concern about Soviet space exploration continued to stimulate development of the U.S. space program.

In 1958, Congress established the National Aeronautics and Space Administration (NASA) to coordinate space research and development. In another important action, Congress passed the National Defense Education Act to provide grants and loans for space-related education. The explosion of Pioneer 0 and the failures of Pioneer 1 and Pioneer 3 to reach escape velocity heightened concerns about the progress of the American space program, although in 1959 Pioneer 4 did reach solar orbit.

Quest for the Moon

In 1964, the United States launched Ranger 7 in order to obtain pictures from the moon, but the first spacecraft to actually reach the moon without crashing into it was the USSR's Luna 9, which arrived in January 1966 and transmitted pictures from the surface. The following April, the U.S. successfully landed Surveyor 1 on the lunar surface, and four months later, America's Lunar Orbiter 1 orbited the moon, photographed the far side, and landed on command.

In 1968, Frank Borman, James A. Lovell Jr., and William Anders made 10 orbits of the moon, thereby becoming the first people to fly around the moon and return. Their success was followed by explorations of Mars (Mariner 6 and Mariner 7) and manned lunar orbits. On July 20, 1969, two men (Neil A. Armstrong and Edwin E. Aldrin Jr.), left the Apollo 11, which had launched from the Kennedy Space Center four days earlier, to walk on the moon and gather samples.

Apollo 12 was another successful manned lunar landing for the United States in November 1969. In April of the following year, an explosion destroyed the power and the propulsion systems of the command service module of the Apollo 13. James A. Lovell Jr., Fred W. Haise Jr., and John L. Swigert Jr. used the lunar module as a lifeboat and safely returned to Earth. Other successful manned lunar landings for the United States followed in early 1971 (Apollo 14), the summer of 1971 (Apollo 15), and April 1972 (Apollo 16). It was the USSR, however, that landed the first spacecraft on another planet, with the Venera 7 reaching Venus on December 15, 1970. Japan, the USSR, and the United States continued to send space craft on flybys and orbits of the planets and even explored comets and the sun.

Other Achievements

Among the many missions sponsored by the U.S., one of the most important began on May 26, 1973, when America established Skylab, its first space station, and manned it for 171 days. Another major achievement was IMAGE. Established in 2000, IMAGE is the first weather satellite to study the global response to changes in the solar wind by Earth's magnetosphere. In January 2006, the return capsule from the rendezvous with comet P/Wild 2 returned to Earth with samples from the comet. From 1981 through 2011, NASA's Space Transportation System (commonly known as the Space Shuttle) constituted the only reusable vehicle that made multiple flights into orbit. The Space Shuttle launched satellites, contributed to the development of the International Space Station, and performed other service missions as well.

Skill 23.8: Demonstrate Knowledge of the Phases of the Moon and the Moon's Effect on Earth

The moon is a satellite that orbits the Earth at the rate of one revolution every 29½ days.

Although it is the second brightest heavenly body, the moon does not give off its own light. Rather, it reflects the sun's light. The amount of lighted moon we see on Earth changes over time. When the moon is becoming brighter, it is waxing. When the moon is growing less bright, it is waning. These changes in the amount of the lighted surface that is visible from the Earth are referred to as the phases of the moon (see figure below).

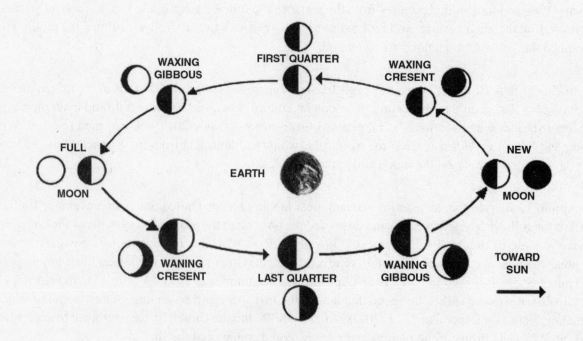

Figure 5.7: Phases of the Moon

1. *The new moon* occurs when the moon is between Earth and the sun, so that the dark side of the moon is turned toward Earth, and the moon is difficult to see.

2. *The crescent moon* occurs as the moon revolves around Earth (west to east), and a little more of the lighter side is visible. The part of the moon that is visible is crescent-shaped.

3. *The half moon* occurs about a week after the crescent moon, when about one-half of the moon is visible.

4. *The gibbous moon* occurs a few days after the half moon, when almost all the moon is visible.

5. *The full moon* occurs when the Earth is between the sun and the moon.

When Earth blocks sunlight from reaching the moon, it creates a shadow on the moon's surface, known as a lunar eclipse. If the moon blocks sunlight from hitting Earth, a solar eclipse is created.

The moon exerts a gravitational pull on Earth. This pull causes tides, or periodic changes in the ocean depths.

Skill 23.9: Identify Earth's Tilt and Orbital Pattern and How They Determine the Seasons

Earth revolves around the sun. The axis of Earth is tilted at a 23½-degree angle, and the axis always points toward the North Star (Polaris). It is the tilt and revolution about the sun that is primarily responsible for the seasons rather than the distance from the sun. In fact, the Northern Hemisphere is closer to the sun in the winter, not in the summer.

The Northern Hemisphere experiences summer when the Northern Hemisphere tilts toward the sun. Summer begins in the Northern Hemisphere on June 21st, when the rays of the sun shine directly on the area. The rays of the sun are stronger and cover a smaller part of this surface of Earth in the summer. In the summer, therefore, the Northern Hemisphere has hot surface temperatures and, because of the tilt of Earth, more hours of sunlight than darkness. This means that the longer direct rays of the sun last longer in the summer.

When the Northern Hemisphere tilts away from the sun, winter occurs in the area. Winter begins in the Northern Hemisphere on December 22. During this season, the days are shorter, fewer direct rays from the sun reach the Northern Hemisphere, and the hours of night are longer than in the summer.

When it is summer in the Northern Hemisphere, it is winter in the Southern Hemisphere, and when it is winter in the Northern Hemisphere, it is summer in the Southern Hemisphere. In the fall and spring, Earth is not tilted toward or away from the sun very much. The days and nights have an almost equal number of hours at this time. The Northern Hemisphere has equal days and nights at the vernal equinox (March 21) and at the autumnal equinox (September 23).

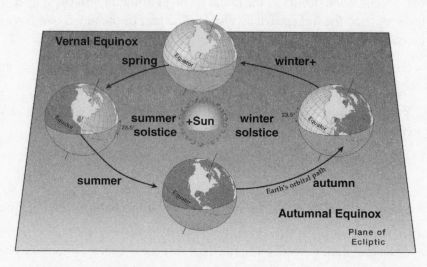

Figure 5.8: Relationship Between Tilt and Seasons

Skill 23.10: Analyze Various Conservation Methods and Their Effectiveness in Relation to Renewable and Nonrenewable Natural Resources

Conservation is the practice of using natural areas with little or no disruption to their ecosystems. Conservation also includes activities intended to protect or restore natural areas.

Conservation implies interdependence among people and their environments. Effective conservation practices recognize a distinction between renewable and nonrenewable resources.

- *Renewable resources* are those that can endure indefinitely if carefully managed. Examples include soil, vegetation, animals, and fresh water.

- *Nonrenewable resources* are those that will be depleted if used, regardless of how carefully managed. These include coal, oil, and metals.

A major component of conservation is educating people on the importance of managing nonrenewable natural resources. Laws that oversee the mining and drilling of natural resources, as well as laws governing the use of these resources, are examples of efforts to conserve nonrenewable resources.

Skill 23.11: Identify the Sun as a Star and Its Effect on Earth

The sun is an enormous star comprising more than 99 percent of the mass of the solar system. Life on Earth would not be possible without its radiant energy. Most plants require sunlight to create self-sustaining energy through photosynthesis, and the existence of animals is largely dependent on the presence of plant life. In addition, both plant and animal life depend on the temperatures sustained by the sun. Other essential processes, such as the hydrologic cycle, rely on the sun's thermal energy as well.

Competency 24: Knowledge of Life Science

The biological sciences and related fields are responsible for our understanding of physiology, genetics, evolution, and ecology. The focus of Competency 24 is on knowledge of these facets of life science.

Skill 24.1: Compare and Contrast Living and Nonliving Things

Although life can be a difficult concept to define, a number of activities, taken together, distinguish living from nonliving things. The following table lists the activities that are distinctive to living things:

Properties of Living Things	
Activity	**Description**
Energy Intake	Procuring energy by eating, absorption, or photosynthesis
Respiration	Exchanging of gases
Excretion	Eliminating wastes
Growth	Increasing in size over part or all of a life span
Repair	Repairing or regenerating damaged tissue
Movement	Moving part or all of body
Response	Reacting to events or things in the environment
Secretion	Producing and distributing chemicals that aid survival
Reproduction	Making new living things similar to the parent

Skill 24.2: Distinguish Between Infectious Agents and Their Effects on the Human Body

Pathogens

There are two broad categories of pathogens, or microorganisms, that cause disease:

- *Primary pathogens* generally cause disease when someone is exposed to them.

- *Opportunistic pathogens* cause disease when someone's defenses are impaired. People are often exposed to these pathogens without any resulting disease.

Both primary and opportunistic pathogens can be classified into different types depending on the nature of the microorganism.

Bacteria

Bacteria are single-celled living organisms. They can reproduce by themselves by means of duplication. They do not need a host for survival.

Bacteria are responsible for a wide variety of diseases, including infectious diseases such as tuberculosis, tetanus, and salmonella. Good hygiene, effective sanitation, a healthy lifestyle, and caution in contact with ill persons are the main approaches to the prevention of these diseases. Once a person has contracted such a disease, antibiotics are the main form of medical intervention.

Viruses

Viruses are small agents that require a living host for survival. Viruses live and multiply within the cells of their hosts.

Like bacteria, viruses are responsible for a wide variety of infectious diseases, including colds, flu, and AIDS. Prevention of these diseases consists of a healthy lifestyle (to maintain immune system functioning), avoiding contact with infected individuals, and, in some cases, vaccines. Once contracted, viral diseases are not responsive to antibiotics. Medical interventions focus on alleviating symptoms and helping the body fight the virus.

Skill 24.3: Differentiate Structures and Functions of Plant and Animal Cells

Plant cells and animal cells, though generally similar, have distinct differences owing to unique plant structures such as cell walls and chloroplasts. The following figure illustrates the structures of animal and plant cells.

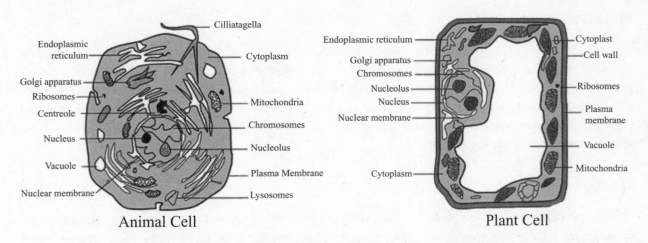

Figure 5.9: Parts and Structures of Animal Cell (left) and Plant Cell (right)

Skill 24.4: Identify the Major Steps of Plants' Physiological Processes of Photosynthesis, Transpiration, Reproduction, and Respiration

Plant cells are responsible for numerous chemical processes related to metabolism, the conversion of food into life-sustaining energy. The following table lists several processes related to plant metabolism and the organelles involved.

Processes Related to Metabolism in Plants		
Process	**Organelle**	**Activity**
Diffusion	Cell membrane	Nourishment, respiration, excretion
Osmosis	Cell membrane	Nourishment, excretion
Phagocytosis	Cell membrane	Nourishment
Photosynthesis	Chloroplasts	Nourishment
Respiration (aerobic)	Mitochondrion	Provides energy
Fermentation	Mitochondrion	Provides energy

Diffusion

Cells need to acquire materials in order to gain energy and grow. Cell membranes only allow certain small molecules to freely pass. The flow of chemicals from areas of high concentration to areas of low concentration is called diffusion.

Osmosis is diffusion of water across a semi-permeable membrane. The cell membrane may engulf and store particles too large to pass through the cell membranes in vacuoles until digestion can occur. This engulfing process is called phagocytosis.

Photosynthesis

All cells need energy to survive. Photosynthesis allows the energy in sunlight to be converted to chemical energy and become biologically available. Photosynthesis occurs in the chloroplasts of a plant's green cells. Chlorophyll, the pigment found in chloroplasts, catalyzes (i.e., causes or accelerates) the photosynthetic reaction that turns carbon dioxide and water into glucose (sugar) and oxygen. Sunlight and chlorophyll are necessary for the reaction to occur. Chlorophyll, because it is a catalyst, is still available after the reaction for subsequent use.

Transpiration

The process by which moisture is carried the from roots of a plant to the small pores on the underside of the leaves is called transpiration. Temperature, relative humidity, wind and air movement, soil moisture, and the type of plant will all impact plant transpiration.

Respiration

The term respiration has two distinct meanings:

- As a life activity, respiration is the exchange of gases in living things.

- As a metabolic process, respiration is the release of energy from sugars for sustaining life.

All living things obtain energy from the digestion of glucose. Metabolic respiration may occur with oxygen (aerobic) or without oxygen (anaerobic respiration), but the term respiration most commonly refers to the aerobic variety, which occurs in most plant and animal cells.

Fermentation

Fermentation refers to the anaerobic respiration occurring in yeast cells and other cells in the absence of oxygen. Fermentation by yeast produces the alcohol in alcoholic beverages and the gases that make yeast breads rise and have a light texture.

Reproduction

Reproduction is a process whereby living organisms or their cells produce offspring. In plants, inherited characteristics and environmental conditions may impose growth limitations on individual plants, and reproduction may be either asexual or sexual.

1. *Asexual plant propagation*, also known as vegetative reproduction, is the method by which plants reproduce without the union of cells or nuclei of cells. The product of asexual plant propagation is genetically identical to the parent. Asexual propagation takes place either by fragmentation or by special asexual structures. An example of fragmentation is the growth of new plants from cuttings.

2.   *Sexual plant propagation* almost always involves seeds produced by two individual plants: male and female. Seed germination begins when a sufficient amount of water is absorbed by the seed, precipitating biochemical changes that initiate cell division.

Skill 24.5: Demonstrate Knowledge of How Plants Respond to Stimuli

Plant cells are composed of smaller structures called organelles, which are surrounded by a fluid known as cytoplasm. The following table lists the functions of several organelles.

Organelle	Function
Cell membrane	Controls movement of materials into and out of cells
Cell wall	Gives rigid structure to cells
Chloroplast	Contains chlorophyll, which enables green plants to make their own food
Cytoplasm	Comprises the cytosol and organelles but not the nucleus (a jellylike substance within a cell)
Mitochondrion	Liberates energy from glucose in cells for use in cellular activities
Nucleus	Directs cell activities and holds DNA, the genetic material
Ribosome	Makes proteins from amino acids
Vacuole	Stores materials in a cell

Skill 24.6: Identify the Structures and Functions of Organs and Systems of Both Animals and Humans

Not all cells are alike. Cells that perform different functions differ in size and shape.

- A group of the same kind of cells is a tissue.

- A mass of the same kind of tissue that contributes to a common function is an organ. Examples of animal organs are the brain, stomach, heart, liver, and kidneys.

- A group of organs that work together to accomplish a special activity is a system.

The complex organism of the human body is made up of several organ systems.

Skeletal System

Bones, cartilage, and ligaments compose the skeletal system.

1. The human skeleton consists of more than 200 bones. The area where two or more bones come together is a joint.

2. Cartilage often covers bone surfaces at the joints and reduces friction there.

3. Ligaments are connective tissues that link bones to joints. Contractions of the skeletal muscles, to which the bones are attached by tendons, bring about movements.

Muscular System

The muscular system controls movement of the skeleton and movement within certain organs. There are three types of muscle:

- Striated, which control voluntary movement

- Smooth, which control involuntary movement

- Cardiac

Skeletal muscles work in pairs. The alternating contractions of muscles within a pair cause movement in joints.

Nervous System

The nervous system controls all bodily functions. Among the many divisions of the nervous system is the distinction between somatic and autonomic.

- The somatic system enables voluntary control over skeletal muscle.

- The autonomic system exerts involuntary control over cardiac and glandular functions.

Nerve impulses arising in the brain, carried by cranial or spinal cord nerves connecting to skeletal muscles, cause voluntary movement. Involuntary movement occurs in direct response to outside stimulus. Involuntary responses are reflexes. Various nerve terminals, which are receptors, constantly send impulses to the central nervous system. There are three types of receptors:

- *Exteroceptors*, including receptors for pain, temperature, and touch

- *Interoceptors*, including receptors for internal events

- *Proprioceptors*, including receptors for movement, position, and tension

Each receptor routes nerve impulses to specialized areas of the brain for processing.

Digestive and Excretory Systems

The digestive system receives and processes food in life-sustaining fashion. The digestive system includes the following:

- Mouth

- Esophagus

- Stomach

- Large intestine

- Small intestine

The excretory system eliminates wastes from the body. Excretory organs include the following:

- Lungs (excrete gaseous waste)

- Kidneys (filter blood and excrete wastes)

- Large intestine (absorbs water and transports waste)

- Bladder (holds liquid wastes until excretion)

- Rectum (holds solid wastes until excretion)

- Skin (excretes wastes through perspiration)

Skill 24.7: Demonstrate Knowledge of Animals' Physiological Processes

Physiology is the study of biological functions from the cellular level all the way up to the level of the organism. Following are some examples of physiological processes.

Circulation

The circulatory system includes the heart, blood vessels, lymph vessels, blood, and lymph.

The heart is a muscular four-chambered pump. The upper chambers are the atria and the lower chambers are the ventricles. During circulation, the heart pumps blood through the right chambers of the heart and through the lungs, where it acquires oxygen. From there the blood is pumped back into the left chambers of the heart. Next, it is pumped into the main artery, the aorta, which branches into increasingly smaller arteries. Beyond that, blood passes through tiny, thin-walled structures called capillaries. In the capillaries, the blood gives up oxygen and nutrients to tissues and absorbs a metabolic waste product containing carbon dioxide. Finally, blood completes the circuit by passing through small veins, joining to form increasingly larger vessels until it reaches the largest veins that return it to the right side of the heart.

Respiration

The expansion and contraction of the lungs produce the essential process of respiration in humans. In the lungs, oxygen enters tiny capillaries, where it combines with hemoglobin in the red blood cells. The capillaries then help carry the red blood cells to the tissues. At the same time, carbon dioxide passes through capillaries into the air contained within the lungs. Inhaling draws air that is higher in oxygen and lower in carbon dioxide into the lungs; exhaling forces air from the lungs that is high in carbon dioxide and low in oxygen. Some animals make use of gills and other means of respiration.

Digestion

Digestion begins when mastication, or chewing, breaks down the food physically and mixes it with saliva. Next, the stomach chemically breaks down food by means of gastric and intestinal juices. Thereafter, the mixture of food and secretions makes its way down the alimentary canal by peristalsis, the rhythmic contractions of the smooth muscle of the gastrointestinal system. The small intestine absorbs nutrients from food, and the large intestine absorbs water from solid food waste. The excretory system then eliminates wastes from the body.

Reproduction

Reproduction is the process whereby organisms or cells produce offspring. In almost all animals, reproduction occurs during or after the period of maximum growth.

Reproduction in animals is either asexual or sexual.

1. *Asexual reproduction* occurs primarily in single-celled organisms. Through the process of fission, the parent organism splits into two or more offspring, thereby losing its original identity. In some instances, cell division results in the production of buds that arise from the body of the parent and then later separate to develop into a new organism identical to the parent

2. *Sexual reproduction* results from the fertilization of ovum or ova by sperm. The primary means of sexual reproduction are insemination (copulation between male and female) and cross-fertilization (the depositing of ova and sperm in water, most commonly by fish).

Skill 24.8: Demonstrate Knowledge of Cell Theory As the Fundamental Organizing Principle of Life on Earth

A cell is the basic structural unit of living things and the smallest unit that can, by itself, be considered living.

Skill 24.9: Demonstrate Knowledge of Heredity, Evolution, and Natural Selection

Heredity is the passing of traits from parent to offspring by means of reproduction. Inherited traits are attributable to heredity, while acquired traits are learned or otherwise attained through experience.

Evolution refers to changes in species over time. Some evolutionary changes are very small and only affect a single feature (e.g., the size of a bird's beak). Other changes are more extensive and are seen in changes to many features, as well as the overall shape and size of the organism.

According to Darwin's theory of evolution, natural selection is a central mechanism in evolutionary change. Through natural selection, characteristics that are favorable to the survival of individual species members tend to emerge over time, while unfavorable characteristics get weeded out.

The role of natural selection in evolution can be summarized as follows:

1. Members of a species vary in physical characteristics. Some of this variability is due to heredity and some is due to experience. For example, among a particular species of heron, some of the birds will have longer beaks than others.

2. Some characteristics are more conducive to the survival of an individual than others. For example, longer beaks may make it easier for a particular species of heron to catch fish. When fish are scarce, those birds with longer beaks are more likely to survive.

3. Individuals who are more likely to survive are also more likely to pass their genes along to the next generation. Thus, assuming that fish continue to be scarce, birds with longer beaks will be more likely to have offspring, and their offspring will tend to have longer beaks. The offspring in turn will be more likely to survive and have long-beaked babies. Meanwhile, birds with shorter beaks will continue to die out. In this way, the average size of the beaks of this particular species will increase over time.

Skill 24.10: Demonstrate Knowledge of the Interdependence of Living Things with Each Other and with the Environment

Ecosystems

An ecosystem consists of all the living and nonliving things in a given environment as well as their interactions and interdependencies. Cooperative, competitive, and conflictual relationships exist among the organisms in an ecosystem. As a result of their interactions and the influence of natural forces, ecosystems are constantly evolving.

The energy pyramid for an ecosystem illustrates relationships between organisms and identifies those organisms most dependent on others in the system. For example, higher-order organisms such as vertebrates cannot survive for long without the other organisms (e.g., plants) beneath them in the energy pyramid.

Ecology

Ecology is the study of the relationship between living things and their environment.

A population is a group of similar organisms, like a herd of deer. A community is a group of populations that interact with one another. A pond community, for example, consists of all the plants and animals in the pond. An ecosystem is a group of populations that shares a common pool of resources and a common physical or geographical area.

Each population lives in a particular area and serves a special role in the community. This combination of defined role and shared living area illustrates the concept of niche. The niche of a pond snail, for example, is to decompose materials in ponds. The niche of a field mouse is to eat seeds in fields. When two populations try to fill the same niche, competition occurs. If one population replaces another in a niche, succession occurs. Succession is the orderly and predictable change of communities as a result of population replacement in niches.

There are many forms of interdependence, ranging from those that impact the microscopic constituents of the air to those that form the basis of human society. Following are just a few of the many possible examples.

Carbon Dioxide–Oxygen Cycle

The amount of oxygen and carbon dioxide in the air remains the same as a result of the carbon dioxide–oxygen cycle. To make food, green plants take in carbon dioxide from the air. The waste product that plants give off in the process is oxygen. When animals breathe in oxygen to digest their food, they give off carbon dioxide as a waste product.

Nitrogen Cycle

The amount of nitrogen in the air remains constant as a result of the nitrogen cycle. Nitrogen-fixing bacteria live in the soil and in the roots of legumes (e.g., beans, peas, and clover). Bacteria change the nitrogen in the air into a form of nitrogen. After animals eat plants, they give off waste materials that contain nitrogen. Bacteria in the soil act on the animals' waste materials as well as on dead plants and animals, breaking down these materials and making the remaining nitrogen available. Some of these bacteria, called nitrifying bacteria, return the nitrogen to the soil for plants to use. Others, called denitrifying bacteria, change some of the nitrogen in the materials to free nitrogen, which returns to the air and continues the nitrogen cycle.

Air Pollution

Any material added to an ecosystem that disrupts its normal functioning is pollution. Among the many forms of pollution is air pollution resulting from industrial emissions as well as vehicular exhaust. Continuous exposure to air pollution can cause lung diseases or aggravate existing health conditions.

When weather conditions prevent the distribution of polluting materials, air pollution can become increasingly severe. For example, when cold air is near the ground beneath a layer of warm air (i.e., a temperature inversion), the polluting materials will tend to remain concentrated in one area.

Acid Rain

Acid rain, a relatively recent phenomenon, is a form of precipitation that contains high levels of sulfuric or nitric acid. Acid rain occurs when sulfur dioxide and nitrogen oxide combine with moisture. Acid rain can pollute drinking water, damage plant and animal life, and even erode monuments and buildings. Among the primary causes of acid rain are forest fires, volcanic eruptions, and the burning of certain fuels, including the gas used to power automobiles.

Competency 25: Knowledge of the Nature of Science

Students must not only learn the specific content of science but also its methods, tools, assumptions, and terminology. The focus of Competency 25 is on knowledge of the fundamental nature of science.

Skill 25.1: Demonstrate Knowledge of Basic Science Processes

Scientific Method

The scientific method is not a recipe that one applies mechanically. Rather, it describes in a formal way the somewhat less clearly organized steps that scientists take in order to achieve an understanding of some phenomenon.

The steps that make up the scientific method can be summarized as follows:

- Observation of a phenomenon
- Formulation of hypotheses and predictions
- Testing of predictions
- Deriving conclusions

The scientific method is most readily applied to situations in which the experimenter can control variables, eliminate or account for all extraneous factors, and perform repeated independent tests that change only one variable at a time.

Both students and scientists must be able to communicate their observations, interpretations, questions, and other results of using the scientific method. Their communication can be either written or oral and may be accompanied by graphs, diagrams, charts maps, concrete models, and so on.

Skill 25.2: Apply Knowledge of Scientific Inquiry to Learning Science Concepts

In conducting a study, the scientist or student is generally attempting to test a hypothesis. A hypothesis is an educated guess that is subject to testing and verification. The outcome of a well-designed study answers questions suggested by the hypothesis in a clear and unambiguous way.

In planning and conducting a study, the scientist or student must do the following:

- Identify relevant variables

- Identify necessary equipment for measuring and recording the variables

- Eliminate or suppress any other factors that could influence the measured variables

- Decide on a means of analyzing the data obtained

- Summarize and interpret the findings

Testable Questions

A scientific study must be based on a testable question. An example of a testable question might be, "Does a five-pound steel sphere fall to earth more quickly than a three-pound steel sphere?" This is a testable question because variables are identified and clearly defined. An example of a question that is not testable would be: "Are private schools better than public schools?" This question is not testable because the variables are not clearly defined (e.g., it is not clear what "better" means).

Skill 25.3: Identify the Appropriate Laboratory Equipment for Specific Activities

Scientific research relies on a variety of tools and instruments, including telescopes, microscopes, graduated cylinders, scales, voltmeters, ammeters, meter sticks, and micrometers.

The proper use of measuring devices includes recognition of their limitations in accuracy and precision. Precision concerns the number of places that can be reliably read from any measurement device. For example, a meter stick generally reflects three-place precision, the first two places being determined by scale markings and the third place determined by the estimated position between scale markings.

Scientific process skills, including the proper and accurate use of laboratory equipment, are an important component of science education. Instruction is necessary to guide the effective use of each tool or instrument. As students develop their measurements, they move from simple observations and teacher-directed activities to using tools and instruments to find answers to questions that they develop themselves.

Skill 25.4: Identify State Safety Procedures for Teaching Science, Including the Care of Living Organisms and the Accepted Procedures for the Safe Preparation, Use, Storage, and Disposal of Chemicals and Other Materials

Following are Florida's current rules and regulations on safety procedures for teaching science. It is important for teachers to keep informed about any changes.

Handling Living Organisms Safely

- Live vertebrates are not appropriate for elementary students, except for observation.

- Students should not touch or handle reptiles, as the animals may carry Salmonella bacteria.

- Some plants may be toxic.

- Students and teachers should wash hands after handling plants and animals.

- Both students and teachers should use gloves when handling animals that might bite or scratch.

- Children should not bring pets to class. If the students do bring animals, only the owner should handle the animal.

- The teacher and students should treat animals with care and respect.

- The teacher should remember that animal hair, scales, and waste can cause allergies.

- Plant and animal specimens from ponds, ditches, canals, and other bodies of water may contain microorganisms that cause disease. Suppliers can provide cultures that are safer.

- Set aquariums on stable furniture away from traffic.

- Be sure electrical accessories are plugged into a GFI (ground-fault interrupter) outlet.

- Ensure that thermostats and heating elements are working correctly.

Safe Preparation, Use, Storage, and Disposal of Chemicals and Other Materials

- Teachers and students must wear eye-protective devices when using hazardous materials in activities such as treating materials with heat, tempering a metal, working with caustic or explosive materials, and working with hot liquids or solids.

- School boards should give out or sell plano glasses to students, visitors, and teachers.

- Fire extinguishers must be available to classrooms.

- Fire blankets must be available in each classroom where a fire hazard exists.

- Fire alarms, detector systems, lighting, and electrical outlets should be in operating condition, even in storage rooms.

- The teachers should make sure that the outlets are grounded.

- Outlets within two feet (six feet for new constructions) of water supplies must have a ground fault circuit interrupt protection device.

- All buildings must have ground fault circuit interrupt protected outlets.

- The teacher should make sure that there are no stapled, spliced, or taped extension cords.

- The teacher should make sure that there are no extension cords running through or over doors, windows, or walls.

- Extension cords must be in only continuous lengths.

- Adapters must be UL-approved.

- Adapters must have over-current protection with a total rating of no more than 15 amperes.

- Every classroom with electrical receptacles at student workstations should have an emergency, unobstructed shut-off switch within 15 feet of the teacher's workstation.

Additional rules are specified for classrooms containing hazardous materials, a situation that does not typically occur in the elementary classroom.

Monitoring Guide for Chemical Storage

- Secured chemical storage areas with lock and key and limited student access are necessary.

- There must be clearly posted signs prohibiting student access.

- Chemical storage areas must be well lighted to avoid mix-ups.

- The floor space must not be cluttered.

- The area must be inventoried at least once a year. The chemical labels and the inventory list must have the name, supplier, date of purchase of mix, the concentration, and the amount available.

- Chemicals must be purged at least once a year.

- Chemical storage must use recognized storage patterns and chemicals should be in compatible groups—not in alphabetical order.

- There must be materials to dilute and absorb a large-volume (one-gallon) chemical spill.

- Certain chemicals that present a potential for explosion are not permitted in science classrooms or storage areas. These chemicals include benzoylperoxide, phosphorus, carbon disulfide, ethyl ether, isopropyl ether, picric acid, perchloric acid, potassium chlorate, and potassium metal.

- Some chemicals present a danger as a human carcinogen and are not allowed in science classrooms or chemical storage areas. These include arsenic compounds, benzene, chloroform, nickel powder, asbestos, acrylonitrile, benzidine, chromium compound, ortho-toluidine, cadmium compounds, andethylene oxide.

Additional resources for safety in science can be obtained from the Council of State Science Supervisors (*www.csss-science.org/safety.shtml*).

Skill 25.5: Demonstrate Knowledge of Basic Scientific Vocabulary

An understanding of science includes mastery of basic scientific vocabulary, including the terms used throughout this chapter.

Competency 26: Knowledge of the Relationship of Science And Technology

The focus of Competency 26 is on the many points of connection between science and technology.

Skill 26.1: Identify the Interrelationship of Science and Technology

Technology is, loosely, the application of science for the benefit of humanity. Although few would debate the benefits of the wheel and axle, the electric light, or the polio vaccine, the benefits of science and technology become more complicated to evaluate when considering gene splicing for genetically modified foods, the use of nuclear energy to replace fossil fuels, or reproductive technologies that may allow parents to choose the sex of the babies. Science can tell us how to do something, not whether we should.

Scientific literacy helps students participate in the decision-making process of our society as well-informed and contributing members. Real-world decisions have social, political, and economic dimensions, and scientific information is often used to both support and refute those decisions.

Skill 26.2: Identify the Tools and Techniques of Science and Technology Used for Data Collection and Problem Solving

The science teacher should incorporate the effective use of technology to plan, organize, deliver, and evaluate instruction for all students.

Although many technological tools are available to assist in observation, collection of data, analysis, and presentation of scientific findings, none of these tools replaces the investigator whose research must be guided by meaningful questions and interpretation and whose judgment in the selection of tools and techniques is essential. Following are some decisions the investigator must make:

- Determine the type of scientific investigation that best addresses a given question or hypothesis.

- Select the tools and techniques that are most suitable for conducting the research.

- Choose the best approach for staying current on guidelines for appropriate use of tools and techniques, including safety practices.

- Decide how to apply concepts and skills of relevance to data collection, organization, analysis, interpretation, and communication.

Skill 26.3: Identify Ways in Which Technology Can Be Used by Students to Represent Understanding of Science Concepts

Following are some examples of how students can use technology to represent and communicate science concepts:

1. Graphics or paint programs allow students to produce freehand drawings of cells viewed under a microscope, plants or animals observed outdoors, meteorological events, or other phenomena.

2. Concept mapping templates or concept map programs allow students to organize and represent complex ideas and details, such as the hydrologic cycle, the functioning of the circulatory system, or natural selection.

3. Spreadsheets allow students to manipulate quantitative data and to create tables and figures to represent relationships between variables such as forces and changes in motion.

4. Simulation programs allow students to observe, represent, and manipulate processes such as respiration and energy transfer.

Competency 27: Knowledge of Instruction and Assessment

The focus of Competency 27 is on appropriate instructional and assessment practices in science.

Skill 27.1: Identify a Variety of Appropriate Instructional Strategies for Teaching Specific Topics

Skill 27.2: Select Manipulatives, Physical Models, and Other Classroom Teaching Tools for Teaching Specific Topics

Skill 27.3: Identify a Variety of Methods for Assessing Scientific Knowledge, Including Analyzing Student Thinking Processes to Determine Strengths and Weaknesses

Deductive and Inductive Teaching

Teaching methods can be described as either deductive or inductive.

- *Deductive teaching* is direct instruction in which the teacher provides information and examples and allows students to practice applying the information.

- *Inductive teaching* encourages students to study, conduct research, collect and analyze data, and then develop generalizations and rules based on their observations and findings. During inductive lessons, the teacher first introduces a hypothesis or concept. Then, on the basis of inferences from the data they gather, the students develop generalizations.

Inquiry Teaching

Inquiry or discovery lessons are inductive in nature. An inquiry lesson starts with a thought-provoking question for which students are interested in finding an explanation. After posing the question, the teacher guides students in brainstorming a list of what they already know about the topic and then categorizing the information. Students use these categories as topics for group or individual research. The lesson typically ends with students presenting their research to the class (a form of deductive learning).

A teacher who uses inquiry strategies takes the role of a facilitator who plans outcomes and provides resources for students as they work. In their role as inquirers, students must take responsibility for their own learning by planning, carrying out, and then presenting their research and projects.

Some advantages of inquiry lessons include the following:

- Promotion of higher-level thinking

- Greater student interest and motivation

- Greater retention

Disadvantages to inquiry lessons can also be noted:

- Additional preparation by the teacher

- Additional resources

- Additional time for students to conduct research

Mastery Lectures

The mastery lecture is a deductive method whereby the teacher presents information to students. New teachers are especially attuned to lecturing because that is the usual mode of instruction in college classes. An advantage of the mastery lecture is that teachers can present large amounts of information in an efficient manner. To be most effective, mastery lectures should be short, usually no more than 10 or 15 minutes, with opportunities for students to ask questions.

Supplemental Strategies

Teachers should supplement lectures with an array of visual materials, as well as models and manipulatives. Teachers should also be careful to instruct younger students on how to take notes while listening to a speaker.

Field activities like visiting nature centers or other outdoor facilities or museums can bring valuable enrichment to the science curriculum in all disciplines. However, the teacher must assume responsibility for planning and implementing activities that not only increase students' learning but also maintain their health and safety.

Computer Technology

Computer-assisted instruction in the form of software and online applications can be used in ways that maximize instructional time. While drill and practice programs provide practice for basic facts or skills, tutorials also include explanations and information.

Science Fair

The science fair project is a common tool for both instruction and assessment in science. Many formal and informal sources can be consulted for suggested science fair topics but not all the topics are experiments. For younger students, the focus should be on models and demonstrations—for example, a model of the solar system, a volcano, or a clay cross-section of an egg. Older students are more suited to conducting true experiments that focus on testing a hypothesis and controlling all experimental variables but the one of interest.

End-of-Chapter Questions

1. What is the density of an object?

   (A) A measure of its buoyancy.

   (B) Its weight under ideal conditions.

   (C) Its average viscosity.

   (D) The ratio of its mass and volume.

2. What does the electromagnetic spectrum consist of?

   (A) Many kinds of waves, including visible and nonvisible light.

   (B) Only visible and nonvisible light.

   (C) Only visible light.

   (D) Only nonvisible light.

3. What is plate tectonics?

   (A) The study of volcanoes and their formation.

   (B) The study of the Earth's plates and their movements.

   (C) The study of soil conservation techniques.

   (D) The study of processes at the Earth's core.

4. An underground layer of water-bearing permeable rock is called what?

   (A) Runoff.

   (B) Sinkhole.

   (C) Aquifer.

   (D) Reservoir.

5. What term is used to describe a moon that is mostly visible at night?

   (A) New.

   (B) Crescent.

   (C) Gibbous.

   (D) Full.

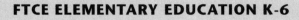
6. Which country was the first to launch a satellite that orbited the Earth?

   (A) U.S.

   (B) France.

   (C) Germany.

   (D) U.S.S.R.

7. Which of the following scenarios most clearly reflects the presence of an opportunistic pathogen?

   (A) A person is exposed to a rare virus for the first time and immediately becomes ill when the virus infects him.

   (B) A virus spreads from person to person in a community until everyone, regardless of age or prior health status, becomes ill.

   (C) A person is infected by a virus the second time he is exposed to it because the virus did not actually enter his body at the time of first exposure.

   (D) A person who has been exposed to a particular virus for many years does not become ill until he has a very stressful year and his immune system functioning declines.

Answer Key

1.	(D)	5.	(C)
2.	(A)	6.	(D)
3.	(B)	7.	(D)
4.	(C)		

Mathematics

Competency 28: Knowledge of Number Sense, Concepts, and Operations

The focus of Competency 28 is on what students need to know about numbers, numerical concepts, and the basic mathematical operations.

Skill 28.1: Associate Multiple Representations of Numbers Using Word Names, Standard Numerals, and Pictorial Models for Real Numbers

Numbers are the basic building blocks of mathematics. Numbers can be shown or represented in different ways, including those listed in the following table:

Some Ways to Represent Numbers	
Type of Representation	**Examples**
Word Names	five, forty-eight, three hundred, five thousand
Standard Numerals	5, 48, 300, 5000

(continued)

Some Ways to Represent Numbers *(continued)*	
Type of Representation	**Examples**
Pictorial Models for Quantities	
Pictorial Models for Relationships	

Although one number might seem like any other, there are conceptual differences among them. Some of the basic types of numbers are summarized in the following table:

Kinds of Numbers	**Definition**	**Examples**
Counting numbers	Numbers that start with 1 and continue	1, 2, 3, 4, 5, and so on
Whole Numbers	Counting numbers and zero	0, 1, 2, 3, 4, 5, and so on
Integers	Whole numbers preceded by either a + (positive) or − (negative) sign. Integers without signs are assumed to be positive.	−5, 2, +21, −350, 0, +111
Common Fractions	Numbers in the form a/b where a and b are whole numbers. The top number—the dividend—is called the numerator. The bottom number—the divisor—is called the denominator. Zero (0) can never be the denominator because division by 0 is undefined.	½, ¾, $^{11}/_{100}$
Decimals	Fractions written in powers of 10 (10, 100, 1000, and so on). A relationship exists between the number of digits following the period and the power it represents. 1 digit after the period represents a power of 10; 2 digits after the period represent a power of 100; 3 represent a power of 1000.	0.25 ($^{25}/_{100}$ which can be reduced to ¼), .1 ($^{1}/_{10}$), .02 ($^{2}/_{100}$ which can be reduced to $^{1}/_{50}$)

Mathematical Operations

The ways in which numbers can be manipulated or used are called operations. There are four basic mathematical operations:

1. *Addition* can be defined as the calculation of the sum of two or more numbers.

2. *Subtraction* can be defined as the deduction of one number from the other.

3. *Multiplication* can be defined as adding a number to itself a specified number of times.

4. *Division* can be defined as subtracting one number from another a specified number of times.

Skill 28.2: Compare the Relative Size of Integers, Fractions, Decimals, Numbers Expressed as Percents, Numbers with Exponents, and/or Numbers in Scientific Notation

Integers

Integers consist of all whole numbers and their opposites.

Integers are preceded by either a positive (+) or negative (−) sign. An integer presented without any sign is assumed to be positive.

On a number line, integers to the left of zero are negative and integers to the right of zero are positive, as can be seen in the figure below.

Fractions

Following are some principles and other observations concerning fractions:

*   All integers can be written as fractions, but not all fractions can be written as integers.

*   For example, the number 4 can be expressed as $^4/_1$. However, the fraction ¼ cannot be expressed as an integer.

*   Common fractions take the form a/b, where a and b are whole numbers, and b ≠ 0.

- There are more fractions than whole numbers because between every integer is a fraction. Between the fraction and the whole number is another fraction; between the fraction and the other fraction is another fraction, and so on. For example, ¼ is between 0 and ½. $\frac{1}{8}$ is between 0 and ¼. $\frac{1}{16}$ is between 0 and $\frac{1}{8}$.

- Negative and positive fractions are not integers (unless they are equivalent to whole numbers or their negative counterparts).

Decimals

Following are some principles and other observations concerning decimals:

- Decimal numbers are fractions written in special notation. For instance, 0.25 is the same as the fraction ¼. Thus, all decimal numbers are actually fractions.

- When expressed as decimals, some fractions terminate and some do not. For instance, 0.315 is a terminating decimal; however, 0.0575757. . . is a repeating (nonterminating) decimal.

- Because a decimal is the same as a fraction, there are more decimals than integers, just as there are more fractions than integers.

- A percentage is a special decimal. It is a fraction or ratio with 100 understood as the denominator. For instance, 0.87 equals a percentage of 87.

Conversion

Fractions, decimal numbers, and percents are different ways of representing values. Any one of these forms can be converted to any one of the others. For example, the fraction ¼ can be converted to either the decimal .25 or the percentage 25%. Conversions can be done by hand or by using a calculator. The following table summarizes some of the approaches that can be taken when carrying out conversions:

Some Types of Conversions			
Task	**Process**	**Example**	**Notes**
Convert fraction to a decimal	Divide numerator by denominator	¼ becomes 0.25 when 1 is divided by 4 $$\begin{array}{r} .25 \\ 4\overline{)1.00} \\ -.80 \\ \hline .20 \\ -.20 \\ \hline 0 \end{array}$$	If the fraction includes a whole number, as in $2^3/_5$, the whole number is not a part of the division. The decimal number may terminate or repeat. Converting a simple fraction to a decimal number never results in an irrational number.

(continued)

Some Types of Conversions *(continued)*			
Task	**Process**	**Example**	**Notes**
Convert nonrepeating (terminating) decimal to fraction in lowest terms	Write decimal as a fraction with the denominator a power of 10 and then reduce to lowest terms	0.125 can be written as $^{125}/_{1000}$, which reduces to $^{1}/_{8}$.	
Convert decimal to percent	Shift decimal point 2 places to the right and add percent symbol (%)	.145 = 14.5%	If the number preceding the percent symbol is a whole number, there is no need to show the decimal point
Convert percent to decimal	Shift decimal point 2 places to the left and drop the percent symbol (%)	68.8% = .688	
Convert percent to a fraction	Write percent (without percent symbol) over 100 and reduce to lowest terms	25% = $^{25}/_{100}$ = ¼	

Exponents

Exponential notation is a way to simplify the representation of repeated multiplication. For example, $2 \times 2 \times 2$ in exponential notation is 2^3 and is equal to 8. (Note that 2^3 does not mean 2×3.) In this example, the 2 is called the base. The 3 is called the exponent or power. Thus a base of 2 with an exponent of 3 is read 2 to the 3rd power or 2 to the power of 3.

An exponent of 1 is equivalent to the base number. For example 3^1 is equivalent to 3, 5^1 is equivalent to 5 and 9^1 is equivalent to 9. An exponent of 0 for any number is equivalent to 1. However, 0^0 is not defined.

Scientific Notation

Scientific notation is a special form of exponential notation most useful for very large or very small real numbers in which a number (n) is represented as falling between 1 and 10 and multiplied by a power of 10. In large numbers, the exponent is positive and shows the number of places to the left. For example, 1,000,000,000 can be rewritten as $1. \times 10^9$. The exponent of 9 shows the decimal has moved 9 places to the left to form a number between 1 and 10. In small numbers (e.g., less than 1), the exponent is negative and shows the number of places to the right. For example, 0.0001 can be rewritten as $1. \times 10^{-4}$. The exponent of $^{-4}$ shows the decimal has moved 4 places to the right. An exponent of 0 is equivalent to the original number. For example, 3.0×10^0 is 3 because the exponent of ^{0} shows the decimal hasn't been moved in either direction. Some additional examples are shown in the following table:

Examples of Scientific Notation	
Number	**Scientific notation**
1956	1.956×10^3
0.0036	3.6×10^3
59600000	5.96×10^7

Skill 28.3: Apply Ratios, Proportions, and Percents in Real-World Situations

Ratio notation is another way to represent fractions. For example, $^3/_5$ can be expressed as "the ratio of 3 to 5." The use of ratio notation emphasizes the relationship of one number to another. To show ratios, the numbers are depicted with a colon between them; thus, 4:5 is the same ratio as 4 to 5 and $^4/_5$. The relationship between two ratios is one of equality; that is, they are equivalent ratios. An equation of two equivalent ratios is one of proportion.

The table below illustrates some examples of conversions across fractions, decimals, percents, and ratios:

Examples of Specific Conversions			
Fraction	**Decimal**	**Percent**	**Ratio**
$^{17}/_{20}$	.85	85%	17 to 20 or 17:20
½	.5	50%	1 to 2 or 1:2
$^{99}/_{100}$	.99	99%	99 to 100 or 99:100

Skill 28.4: Represent Numbers in a Variety of Equivalent Forms, Including Whole Numbers, Integers, Fractions, Decimals, Percents, Scientific Notation, and Exponents

Numbers may be represented in many ways, as shown in the following chart:

Representations of Numbers	
Form	**Representation**
Blocks	0 2
Whole number	2
Integer	+2 or 2
Fraction	$^2/_1$
Decimal	2.0
Percent	200%
Exponential Notation	2^1
Scientific Notation	2×10^0

Skill 28.5: Perform Operations on Rational Numbers Using Multiple Representations and Algorithms and Understand the Relationships Between These Operations

Addition

Addition is an operation (or procedure) in which two or more numbers are combined to form a new total called the sum ($a + b = c$). Adding two whole numbers always results in a whole number.

Subtraction

Subtraction is the inverse of addition. In subtraction, one number or amount is "taken away" or removed from another with the resulting number called the difference ($a - b = c$). Given two whole numbers, subtracting the smaller number from the larger one results in a whole number (e.g., $6 - 2 = 4$). However, subtraction of whole numbers does not result in a whole number if the larger whole number is subtracted from the smaller one (e.g., $2 - 6 = -4$).

Multiplication

Multiplication is a process of repeated addition ($a \times b = c$) in which a number (a) is added b times to form a new number called the product. Thus, 3 x 4 is really $3 + 3 + 3 + 3$ or 200×3 is the same as

200 + 200 + 200. Any number (a) multiplied by 1 results in the original number (a). For example, $10 \times 1 = 10$, $257 \times 1 = 257$. Any number (a) multiplied by 0 results in 0. For example, $10 \times 0 = 0$, $257 \times 0 = 0$.

Division

Division is the operation of determining how many times one quantity is contained in another ($^a/_b = c$). Thus, division is repeated subtraction. For example, $^{12}/_3$ is really asking how many 3s are in 12 ($12 - 3 = 9$; $9 - 3 = 6$; $6 - 3 = 3$; $3 - 3 = 0$). Thus, the 3 was subtracted 4 times. Division has the same inverse relationship to multiplication that subtraction has to addition. What multiplication does, division undoes.

Skill 28.6: Select the Appropriate Operation(s) to Solve Word Problems Involving Ratios, Proportions, and Percents and the Addition, Subtraction, Multiplication, and Division of Rational Numbers

Many people dislike word problems; however, word problems are often, in essence, real-life problems. Few people are asked to multiply 35 by 16 in isolation. However, you many need to estimate the total cost of a product assuming 35 monthly payments of $16 per month, or how many books are needed if you have 16 classes of 35 students each, and so on.

General Strategies for Solving Word Problems

There are two general strategies for solving word problems:

1. Put the problem in context and think about the logic of it and the reasonableness of particular strategies and answers. For example, if you have to determine the total cost of 35 monthly payments of $16 per month, you might realize that addition ($35 + 16 = 51$) doesn't seem to fit because 1 payment would be $16, 2 payments would be $16 + $16 = $32, 3 payments would be $16 + $16 + $16 = $48, and so on. If just 3 payments are $48, 16 payments would be much greater than that, so addition is not a logical process. Similarly, subtraction and division will result in a smaller amount. The mathematical operation needed is clearly multiplication.

2. Translate words and phrases into numbers and operations. Look for "key" words in solving problems, as these words provide clues as to which operation to use. The following table provides a list of common key words for each operation as well as examples of their use in word problems.

Mathematical Operations in Word Problems		
Operation	**Key Words**	**Examples**
Addition	Increased by	The class size of 25 was increased by 5. How many students are in the class? 25 + 5 =
	More than	Mr. Smith has 5 more students in his class that Ms. Jones. Ms. Jones has 25 students in her class. How many students does Mr. Smith have? 25 + 5 =
	Combined	If one math exercise has 25 problems and a second exercise has 5 problems, what is the combined number of problems in both exercises? 25 + 5 =
	Together	If one math exercise has 25 problems and a second exercise has 5 problems, how many problems are together in both exercises? 25 + 5 =
	Total of	If one math exercise has 25 problems and a second exercise has 5 problems, what is the total number of problems in both exercises? 25 + 5 =
	Sum	If one math exercise has 25 problems and a second exercise has 5 problems, what is the sum of the problems in both exercises? 25 + 5 =
	Added to	Mr. Smith assigned one math exercise of 25 problems added to a second exercise of 5 problems. How many problems are to be solved? 25 + 5 =
Subtraction	Decreased by	Mr. Smith's class was decreased by 5. Mr. Smith had 25 students last year. How many does he have now? 25 − 5 =
	Minus	How much is 25 minus 5? 25 − 5 =
	Less	What is 25 students less 5 students? 25 − 5 =
	Difference of	There is a difference of 5 students between Mr. Smith's class this year and his class last year. His class last year had 25 students. How many are in his class this year? 25 − 5 =

(continued)

Mathematical Operations in Word Problems *(continued)*		
Operation	**Key Words**	**Examples**
Subtraction (continued)	Difference between	The difference between the number of students in Mr. Smith's class last year (25 students) and the number in his class this year is 5. How many students are in his class this year?
	Less than	Mr. .Smith's class this year is 5 less than his class last year. Last year he had 25 students. How many does he now have? $25 - 5 =$
	Fewer than	Mr. Smith has 5 fewer students than he had last year. Last year he had 25 students. How many students are in his class this year? $25 - 5 =$
	Reduced by	Mr. Smith's class of 25 was reduced by 5. How many students are in the class now? $25 - 5 =$
Multiplication	Times	The length of a classroom is two times the width of the classroom. The width is 20 feet. What is the length? $2 \times 20 =$
	Multiplied by	The length of the classroom is 2 multiplied by the width. The width is 20. What is the length? $2 \times 20 =$
	Product of	The product of a classroom's width (20 feet) and 2 equals its length. What is the length? $2 \times 20 =$
	Increased by a factor of	The width of a classroom was increased by a factor of 2 to determine the length of the classroom. What is the length of the classroom? $2 \times 20 =$
Division	How many to each	Mr. Smith has 25 students in his class. If he has 5 groups of students, how many students are in each group? $^{25}/_5 =$
	How many groups	Mr. Smith has 25 students in his class. If he wants to put exactly 5 students in each group, how many groups will he have? $^{25}/_5 =$
	Share	The 25 students in Mr. Smith's class shared 5 computers. How many students share one computer? $^{25}/_5 =$
	Separate	Mr. Smith separated the 25 students in his class into 5 rooms. How many students were in each room? $^{25}/_5 =$

Mathematical Operations in Word Problems *(continued)*		
Operation	**Key Words**	**Examples**
Division (continued)	Equal groups	Mr. Smith has 25 students in his class. If he wants to divide students into equal groups, how many groups will he have? $^{25}/_5 =$
	Divide	What is the quotient of 25 divided by 5?
	Quotient/Per	Mr. Smith has 25 students in his class. He assigned 5 students per computer. How many computers does he have?

To illustrate what it means to think about the logic of a problem and the reasonableness of various possible strategies and answers, consider the following problem:

Center Town Middle School has an enrollment of 640 students. One day, 28 students were absent. What percent of the total number of students were absent?

(A) 28% (C) 4%

(B) 1% (D) 25%

Even if someone forgot how to compute percents, some possible answers could be rejected instantly. For example, 28% could not be the answer, because 28 students would be 28% of 100 students, not 640. Likewise, 1% could not be the answer, because 28 students would be 1% of 2800 students.

Solving Ratio Problems

Most modern math programs introduce the concept of ratio and use ratio to solve various problems. For example:

Pencils are 2 for 25 cents. How many pencils can Teresa buy for 50 cents?

The phrase "Two pencils for 25 cents" suggests the fixed constant of $^2/_{25}$, or:

$$\frac{2\,(\text{pencils})}{25\,(\text{cents})}$$

With a fixed ratio, it should be possible to figure out how many pencils Teresa can buy for 50 cents by setting up an equivalent ratio:

$$\frac{x\,(\text{number of pencils})}{50\,(\text{cents})}$$

The relationship between the two ratios is one of equality; that is, they are equivalent ratios. An equation of two equivalent ratios is one of proportion. There are several ways to solve the equivalent ratios problem with the pencils. An efficient way to do it is to use cross multiplication:

$$\frac{x}{50} \quad \frac{2}{25}$$

To perform cross multiplication, multiply the numerator of one side by the denominator of the other side, and vice versa. The two resulting terms should be equal. Thus $25x = 100$. Now, solving for x requires dividing 100 by 25 to get 4. Thus, Teresa can buy 4 pencils for 50 cents.

Another way to approach the preceding problem is to set up a chart, from which the answer can be inferred:

Pencils	Cost
2	25 cents
x	50 cents

Specific Strategies for Solving Word Problems

The following strategies can help in solving word problems. These strategies can be used separately or, in some cases, in combination. Some yield solutions while others merely rule out options or provide assistance with generating solutions.

1. *Guessing and checking* involve making one's best guess and then checking the answer to see whether it is right. Ideally the initial guess is a reasonable one, perhaps developed after one or more of the response options has been ruled out. Even if the guess does not immediately provide the solution, it may help to get students closer to it so that they have some guidance as they continue to work on the problem.

To illustrate the guess and check strategy, consider the following problem:

Three persons' ages add up to 72, and each person is one year older than the last person. What are their ages?

Because the three ages must add up to 72, it is reasonable to take one-third of 72 (24) as the starting point. Although 24 + 24 + 24 gives a sum of 72, the solution does not match one of the requirements of the problem ("each person is one year older than the last person"). Students might then guess that the ages are 24, 25, and 26. Checking that guess by addition would reveal that the sum of 75 is too high. Then, by lowering the guess to 23, 24, and 25, which indeed add up to 72, the solution would be obtained.

2. *Making a sketch* can be helpful because some problems become clearer when visualized. For example:

Mr. Rosenberg plans to put a 4-foot-wide concrete sidewalk around his backyard pool. The pool is rectangular, with dimensions 12 ft. by 24 ft. The cost of the concrete is $1.28 per square foot. How much concrete is required for the job?

Students with exceptional visualization abilities may not need a sketch. For others, a sketch like the one shown below may be helpful in solving this problem:

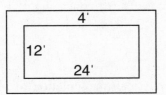

3. *Making a chart* can be helpful if the data in a problem are associated with a particular category or categories. For example:

How many hours will a car traveling at 75 miles per hour take to catch up to a car traveling 55 miles per hour if the slower car starts one hour before the faster car?

A chart with 3 rows (hour, slower car distance, faster car distance) organizes the data in a useful way, even though it does not provide a specific solution. As the chart below indicates, the distance of the faster car is greater than the distance of the slower car in hour 4, so the faster car caught up with the slower car in hour 3.

Hour	1	2	3	4
Slower Car	55	110	165	220
Faster Car	0	75	150	225

A chart also can be used to organize information by leaving a blank space for information that is not known. For example:

A book has 185 pages in it. John is on page 133. How many more pages does he still need to read?

Pages Already Read	Pages Still to Read	Total Number of Pages
133	??	185

4. *Making a list* can help organize information and provide or hint at the solution. For example:

How many different outcomes are there if you roll two regular six-sided dice?

To solve this problem, one could create a list consisting of 1−1, 1−2, 1−3, 1−4, 1−5, 1−6, 2−2, 2−3, 2−4, 2−5, 2−6, 3−3, 3−4, 3−5, 3−6, 4−4, 4−5, 4−6, 5−5, 5−6, 6−6, and then sum up the outcomes.

5. *Acting* can be helpful if physical manipulation of self, with or without props, contributes to finding the solution. For example, here is a class problem that could be solved in this manner:

If five strangers meet and everyone shakes everyone else's hand once, how many total handshakes will there be?

6. *Looking for patterns* is helpful for certain kinds of problems.

For example: *Nevin's weekly savings account balances for the past 15 weeks are as follows: $125, $135, $145, $120, $130, $140, $115, $125, $135, $110, $120, $130, $105, $110, $115. What might Nevin's balance be next week?*

7. Writing an open mathstatement, also known as "translating" a problem into mathematics, is useful when solving for variables. For example:

Tina earned grades of 77%, 86%, 90%, and 83% on her first four weekly science quizzes. Assuming all grades are equally weighted, what score will she need on the fifth week's quiz to have an average (i.e., mean) score of 88%?

Using the available information, students could set up and solve the following equation to answer the question:

$$\frac{(77+86+90+83+x)}{5}=88$$

8.   *Working backward* from the solution can be helpful. For example:

If you add 12 to some number and then multiply the sum by 4, you will get 60. What is the number?

One way to solve this problem is to start with the solution, 60. The problem states that the 60 resulted from multiplying some unknown sum by 4. When 15 is multiplied by 4, the result is 60. The sum in question must therefore be 15. With this information, one can now find the solution to the problem.

Skill 28.7: Use Estimation in Problem-Solving Situations

Estimation is a useful tool in predicting and then checking possible answers to a problem.

Estimation is typically carried out by simplifying the problem, and one of the main approaches to simplification is to substitute round numbers for those that are given. For example, to find the product of 23 and 184 when no calculator or pencil and paper are handy, one could estimate the answer by considering the exact value of 20×200. To take another example, consider again this problem discussed earlier:

Center Town Middle School has an enrollment of 640 students. One day, 28 students were absent. What percent of the total number of students were absent?

(A)   28%   (C)   4%

(B)   1%   (D)   25%

Many approaches could be taken to round the numbers for the sake of estimation. For example, one could note that since 25 is 10% of 250, 25 must therefore be 5% of 500. In the same way, since 28 is 10% of 280, 28 must therefore be 5% of 560. The problem asks, in essence, what percent of the 640 students is represented by 28 students. Since 640 is greater than 560, the answer must be some percentage less than 5%.

As this example illustrates, estimation does not provide specific solutions but rather approximate solutions and guidance in ruling out options. As applied to this example, estimation tells us that only options

B or C could be correct. We must then apply additional problem solving strategies to distinguish between the two remaining options. (For example, since 28 is 1% of 280, we can tell by a process of elimination that C is the correct answer.)

Skill 28.8: Apply Number Theory Concepts

Factors

For any number x, factors are those numbers that can be multiplied together to yield x. For example, the whole-number factors of 12 are 1, 2, 3, 4, 6, and 12 (because the number 12 results from multiplying 1 and 12, or 2 and 6, or 3 and 4).

Primes and Composites

A number with only two whole-number factors—1 and the number itself—is a prime number. The smallest seven primes are 2, 3, 5, 7, 11, 13, and 17.

Most whole numbers are composite numbers, which means that they are composed of more than two whole-number factors. The number 1 is neither prime nor composite, because it has only one whole-number factor. Likewise, it does not make sense to consider 0 as either prime or composite.

Multiples

The multiples of any whole number are the results of multiplying that whole number by the counting numbers (1, 2, 3, 4, and so on). The multiples of 7 are 7, 14, 21, 28, and so on. Every whole number has an infinite number of multiples.

Number Properties

Key properties of whole numbers and related concepts are summarized in the table below:

Key Numerical Properties				
Property	**Meaning**	**Notation**	**Example**	**Notes**
Multiplicative identity property of 1	Any number multiplied by 1 remains the same	$a \times 1 = a$	$45 \times 1 = 45$	
Property of reciprocals	Any number (except 0) multiplied by its reciprocal (1 divided by that number) equals 1.	$a \times {}^1/_a = 1$	$45 \times {}^1/_{45} = 1$	Division by 0 has no meaning.
Additive identity property of 0	Adding 0 (the additive identity) to any number will not change the number.	$a + 0 = a$	$45 + 0 = 45$	
Commutative property for addition and multiplication	The order of adding addends or multiplying factors does not determine the sum or product.	$a + b = b + a$ $a \times b = b \times a$	$45 + 5 =$ $5 + 45$ $45 \times 5 =$ 5×45	Division and subtraction are not commutative.
Associative property for addition and multiplication	Associating, or grouping, three or more addends or factors in a different way does not change the sum or product.	$a + (b + c) =$ $(a + b) + c$ $a \times (b \times c)$ $= (a \times b) \times c$	$(3 + 7) + 5 =$ $3 + (7 + 5)$ $3 \times (7 \times 5)$ $= (3 \times 7) \times 5$	Division and subtraction are not associative.
Distributive property of multiplication over addition	A number multiplied by the sum of two other numbers can be distributed to both numbers, multiplied by each separately, with the products added.	$a(b + c) =$ $(a \times b) +$ $(a \times c)$	$6 \times (40 + 7) =$ $(6 \times 40) +$ (6×7)	The product of a number and a sum can be expressed as a sum of two products

Number Sequences

Most children start school with some knowledge of number sequences. For example, most children are aware of the positive integer sequence, in that they can count from 1 to 10. In school, children learn about other sets of numbers, such as the set of whole numbers (which includes zero), negative integers, and fractions. Teachers may use a number line, a temperature thermometer, a countdown, or other strategies to introduce these sequences.

Divisibility

The rules of divisibility are as follows:

- Division by zero is not possible.
- Only whole numbers ending in 0, 2, 4, 6, and 8 are divisible by 2.
- Only whole numbers whose digits add up to a number divisible by 3 are divisible by 3.
- A number is divisible by 4 if the number named by the last two digits are divisible by 4.
- A number is divisible by 5 if the ones place has a 5 or zero.
- A number is divisible by 6 if it is divisible by both 2 and 3. For example, 6666 has digits that add to 24, which is divisible by 3; it ends in 6 so it is divisible by 2. Because it is divisible by both 2 and 3, it is also divisible by 6.
- A number is divisible by 8 if the number named by the last three digits are divisible by 8. For example, 99816 has 816 as its last digits; 800 can be divided evenly by 8, and 16 is divisible by 8. The number 8 is, therefore, a factor of 99816.
- A number is divisible by 9 if the sum of the digits is divisible by 9. The number 245 has digits that add to 11; 11 is not evenly divisible by 9, so 9 is not a divisor of 245. The number 333 has digits that add to the number 9; because 9 divides evenly into 9, 333 is divisible by 9.
- A number that has a 0 in the ones place is divisible by 10.

Skill 28.9: Apply the Order of Operations

Some mathematical expressions indicate several operations. Simplifying these expressions requires that a universally consistent order be followed when performing these operations. The order of steps can be summarized as follows:

1. *Parentheses.* Terms inside parentheses or brackets should be calculated first.
2. *Exponents.* Exponents and roots should be calculated next.

3. *Multiplication and Division.* The operations of multiplication and division should be performed next. These operations should be carried out from left to right as the terms appear.

4. *Addition and Subtraction.* The operations of addition and subtraction should be performed last. These operations should also be carried out from left to right as the terms appear

This ordering of steps can be remembered by the acronym PEMDAS (which stands for parentheses, exponents, multiplication, division, addition, subtraction), or the mnemonic phrase "Please Excuse My Dear Aunt Sally."

For example, solving the expression $3 + 7 \times 4 - 2$ requires multiplying 7 by 4 before doing the addition and subtraction to obtain the result of 29.

To take a more elaborate example, $36 \div (2 \times 3^2) - 2$ would be solved in the following way:

$$36 \div (2 \times 3^2) - 2 =$$
$$36 \div (2 \times 9) - 2 =$$
$$36 \div (18) - 2 =$$
$$2 - 2 = 0$$

The rules for performing operations on integers, fractions, decimals, and negative numbers are generally the same. However, two rules on multiplication when at least one negative number is involved must be remembered:

1. Two positives or two negatives yield a positive. For example, $-6 \times -4 = 24$.

2. "Mixing" a positive and a negative gives a negative. For example, $-5 \times 3 = -15$.

Competency 29: Knowledge of Geometry and Measurement

The focus of Competency 29 is on geometry as the branch of math concerned with the measurement and manipulation of spatial entities, properties, and relationships such as points, lines, angles, surfaces, polygons, and solids.

Skill 29.1: Analyze Properties of Two-Dimensional Shapes

Perimeter

Perimeter is a two-dimensional measurement of the distance around a figure. Perimeter is expressed in linear units (e.g., inches, feet, meters). The following table provides formulas used to calculate the perimeters of rectangles, squares, and triangles:

Perimeter Calculations		
Figure	**Formula**	**Example**
Rectangle	$P = 2l + 2w$ where l = length and w = width	5m 10m $$P = 2(5m) + 2(10m)$$ $$P = 10m + 20m$$ $$P = 30m$$
Square	$P = 4s$ where s = measure of the side length	5m $$P = 4(5m)$$ $$P = 20m$$
Triangle	$P = s_1 + s_2 + s_3$ in which s is the measure of each side of the triangle	3m 5m 4m $$P = 3m + 4m + 5m$$ $$P = 12m$$

Area

Area is a measurement of the two-dimensional interior space of a figure. The measurement of area is expressed in square units (e.g., square inches, square feet, square meters). The following table illustrates the formulas used to measure the areas of rectangles, squares, and triangles:

Simple Area Calculations		
Figure	**Formula**	**Example**
Rectangle	A = l × w where l = length and w = width	5m [rectangle] 10m A = 5m × 10m A = 50m^2
Square	A = s^2 where s is the measure of the side length	5m [square] A = 5^2 A = 25m^2
Triangle	A = ½ bh where b is the base of the triangle and h is its height. The height of the triangle is determined by drawing a perpendicular line from one vertex to the opposite side. The opposite side forms the base (see below). [triangle labeled a, c, h, b]	11 cm [triangle] 7.5 cm, 7 cm, 11 cm A = ½ (11 cm x 7 cm) A = ½ (77cm^2) A = 38.5 cm^2

Circumference and Area of Circles

Just as perimeter is the distance around the edge of a square, rectangle, or triangle, so the circumference is the distance around the rim of a circle.

The circumference of a circle is related to its radius and diameter (see figure below). Often, information about radius or diameter will be used to calculate circumference. The radius (r) of a circle is the distance from the center of the circle to the edge of the circle. The diameter (d) of a circle is a line segment that passes through the center of the circle, the end points of which lie on the circle. The measure of the diameter of a circle is twice the measure of the radius; thus, d = 2r. The number "pi," symbolized as "π" and equal to approximately 3.1416, is often used in computations involving circles.

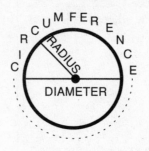

Some Parts of a Circle

The following table provides the formulas for finding a circle's circumference and area.

Circumference and Area of Circles		
Property	**Formula**	**Example**
Circumference	C = π × d (diameter) or C = 2 × π × r (radius)	d = 8 cm C = π × 8 cm C = 3.14 × 8 cm C = 25.12
Area	A = π × r^2 or A = π × (½ d)^2	r = 3 in A = π × 3in^2 A = π × 9in A = 3.14 × 9in A = 28.26

Skill 29.2: Apply Geometric Properties and Relationships to Solve Problems Using Appropriate Strategies and Formulas

Students must learn to apply their knowledge of geometric properties and relationships to problem-solving exercises in which they make use of the formulas described above. For example, consider the following problem:

Sophie's Carpet Store charges $9 per square foot for the type of carpeting Tony would like in his bedroom (padding and labor included). How much would Tony pay to carpet his 9-by-12-foot room?

One way to find the solution is apply the formula for calculating the area of a rectangle. The size of Tony's room is 108 square feet. Thus, the total cost will be $108 \times \$9$, or $972.

Often, what is most challenging to students about problems such as this is not the application of mathematical operations (in this case, multiplication) but rather in understanding what aspect of geometry and which formula to apply in representing the problem. This example can be thought of as an area problem in which the solution relies on use of the formula for calculating the area of a rectangle. Students need practice not only in applying formulas but also in recognizing when each formula should be applied.

As concepts, formulas, and problems become more complex, students must learn to be careful about keeping track of the various details. For example, consider the following problem:

When Maria leaves her house to visit her favorite Aunt, she rides her bicycle south for 3 miles, then she turns east and rides for another 4 miles. If she could ride in a straight line from her Aunt's house back to her own house, how far would she travel?

In order to solve this problem, the following is necessary:

1.   Students must be able to visualize or draw the route that Maria takes. In order to do so, they must be able to appropriately represent two of the cardinal directions (south and east).

2.   Students must be able to visualize or draw the route from Maria's house to her Aunt's house, followed by a straight line back to her own house. They must recognize that what they have drawn or visualize forms a right triangle.

3.   Students must recall the Pythagorean Theorem, which states that for a right triangle, the sum of the squares of the sides equals the square of the hypotenuse.

4.   Students must apply the Pythagorean formula correctly, as follows:

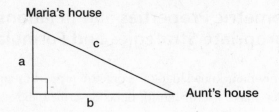

Maria's house
c
a
Aunt's house
b

a = distance that Maria travels south

b = distance that Maria travels east

c = straight line from the Aunt's house back to Maria's house

$$a^2 + b^2 = c^2$$
$$3^2 + 4^2 = ?$$
$$9 + 16 = 25$$
$$c^2 = 25$$
$$c = 5 \text{ miles}$$

Skill 29.3: Apply the Geometric Concepts of Symmetry, Congruency, Similarity, and Transformations

Congruency

Two figures that have the same shape and size are called congruent. For example, the two triangles below are congruent because they differ only in orientation.

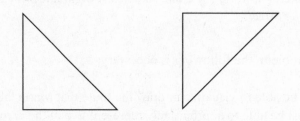

Symmetry

Symmetry occurs when an object can be divided into two congruent, mirror-image figures. Squares have four lines of symmetry, and nonsquare rectangles have two. Circles have an infinite number of lines of symmetry.

Similarity

Geometric figures are similar if they have exactly the same shape, even if they are not the same size. In the figure below, triangles A and B are similar:

Transformations

Scaling is a linear transformation that enlarges or reduces an object. If the scale factor is the same in all directions, then this uniform scaling results in a transformed object that is geometrically similar to the original object. An example would be triangles A and B in the previous figure. If scaling has a separate scale factor for each axis direction, the result is a change in shape, and the transformed object is no longer geometrically similar to the original object.

Transformations encompass a variety of different geometric operations, including rotations, reflections, and translations. Students should have hands-on experiences with transformations such as flips, turns, slides, and scaling. For example, the teacher might ask students to select a shape that is a parallelogram. Then the teacher might ask the students to do the following:

1. Describe the original position and size of the parallelogram. Students can use labeled sketches if necessary.

2. Rotate, translate, and reflect the parallelogram several times. Students should list the steps they followed.

3. Challenge a classmate to return the parallelogram to its original position.

4. Determine if the classmate used a reversal of the original steps or a different set of steps.

Skill 29.4: Identify and Locate Ordered Pairs in a Rectangular Coordinate System

The coordinate plane is useful for graphing relationships between pairs of numbers. The coordinate plane is divided into four quadrants by an x-axis (horizontal) and a y-axis (vertical). The upper-right quadrant is quadrant I, and the others (moving counterclockwise from quadrant I) are quadrants II, III, and IV. Ordered pairs indicate the locations of points on the plane. For instance, the ordered pair $(-3,4)$ describes a point that is three units left from the center of the plane (the origin) and four units up, as shown in the following diagram:

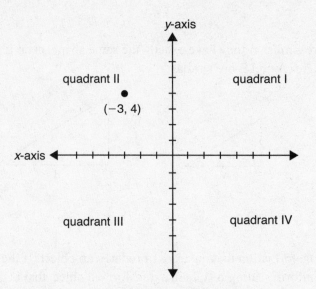

Figure 6.1: Coordinate System and Point

Ordered pairs can be displayed in a chart and graphed on the coordinate plane. For example, the chart on the left side below provides information for four ordered pairs. The graph on the right side below shows the ordered pairs on the coordinate plane. Both the chart and the graph suggest a linear relationship between *x* and *y*: as one increases, so the other increases as well.

Ordered Pairs in Chart (Left) and Graph (Right)

Ordered Pairs in Chart (Left) and Graph (Right)	
x	*y*
3	5
4	6
5	7
6	8

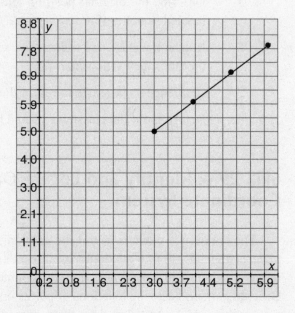

Skill 29.5: Analyze Properties of Three-Dimensional Shapes

The outer surface of a three-dimensional figure is composed of edges and faces. The interior contains vertices, or corners.

Volume is a measure of the interior space of a three-dimensional figure. A rectangular solid is a rectilinear (i.e., right-angled) figure that has length, width, and height. A cube is a rectangular solid for which the length, width, and height are exactly the same.

The table below shows how volume is calculated for rectangular solids and for cubes.

Volume of Rectangular Solids		
Figure	**Formula**	**Example**
w l h	$V = l \times w \times h$	l = 4 w = 2 h = 2 $V = l \times w \times h$ $V = 4 \times 2 \times 2$ $V = 16$
Figure	**Formula**	**Example**
e e e e	$V = e^3$	e = 3 e = 3 e = 3 e = 3 $V = 3^3$ $V = 27$

Skill 29.6: Compose and Decompose Two-Dimensional and Three-Dimensional Geometric Shapes

With an understanding of two- and three-dimensional shapes, students should be able to analyze their constituent parts as well as identify and compose different types of shapes. Examples of important parts and shapes include lines, angles, and polygons.

Points and Lines

A fundamental concept of geometry is the point. A point is a specific location, taking up no space, having no area, and frequently represented by a dot.

A line is a one-dimensional entity that connects two points. Through any two points, there will be exactly one straight line.

Following are some concepts used in describing lines:

1. *Intersecting lines* have a point in common.

2. *Perpendicular lines* contain the sides of a right angle.

3. *Parallel lines* do not intersect.

Angles

An angle is commonly thought of as two "arrows" joined at their bases; the point at which they join is called the vertex. The angle below may be specified as angle ABC or angle CBA. It can also be written as ∠ ABC or ∠ CBA. Note that the vertex is always the center letter.

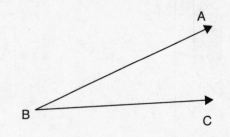

Two angles are adjacent if they share a common vertex, they share only one side, and one angle does not lie in the interior of the other. For example, the following adjacent angles are angle ABC and angle CBD.

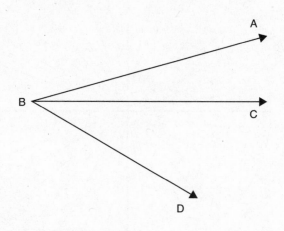

Angles are usually measured in degrees (°) ranging from 0 to 180. As illustrated in the figure below, an angle measuring less than 90° is called acute. An angle with a measure of 90° is a right angle. An angle measuring more than 90° and less than 180° is called obtuse. An angle of 180° is called a straight angle.

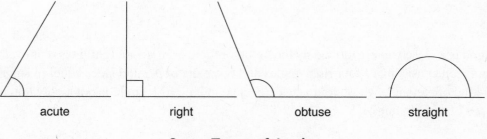

Some Types of Angles

A circle has a measure of 360° (see figure below). The angle formed by a half circle is 180°, or a straight angle.

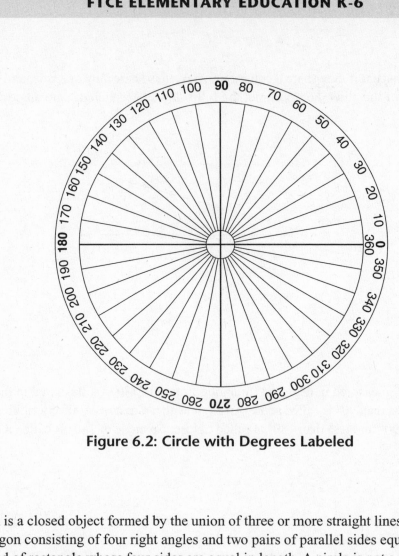

Figure 6.2: Circle with Degrees Labeled

Polygons

A polygon is a closed object formed by the union of three or more straight lines. For example, a rectangle is a polygon consisting of four right angles and two pairs of parallel sides equal in length. A square is a special kind of rectangle whose four sides are equal in length. A circle is not a polygon, because it is not composed of straight lines.

Skill 29.7: Determine How a Change in Length, Width, Height, or Radius Affects Perimeter, Circumference, Area, Surface Area, or Volume

To understand properties such as perimeter, circumference, area, surface area, and volume, students must be able to do the following:

- Recognize the formula used to calculate each property

- Identify the terms of each formula

- Apply each formula appropriately to word problems

- Understand how changes in object dimensions result in changes to these properties

To illustrate the latter, recall that the formula for the circumference of a circle is $\pi \times d$, or $2\pi r$ and that the formula for the area of a circle is πr^2. Students should recognize from these formulas that as the radius of a circle increases, the circumference and the area will increase as well. However, the rate of increase will not be the same. As the radius of a circle increases in size, the area will tend to increase at a faster rate than the circumference.

Skill 29.8: Within a Given System (i.e., Metric or Customary), Solve Real-World Problems Involving Measurement with Both Direct and Indirect Measures and Make Conversions to a Larger or Smaller Unit

Customary System

American students are most familiar with the customary system:

- Customary units of length include inches, feet, yards, and miles.

- Customary units of weight include ounces, pounds, and tons.

- Customary units of volume include teaspoons, tablespoons, cups, pints, quarts, and gallons.

Metric System

The metric system of measurement relies on base-10 place values. Some of the common metric prefixes are listed in the table below:

Metric Prefixes		
Prefix	**Meaning**	**Abbreviation**
Kilo-	Thousand (1,000)	k
Deci-	Tenth (0.1)	d
Centi-	Hundredth (0.01)	c
Milli-	Thousandth (0.001)	m

The basic units of measurement in the metric system are given in the table below:

Metric Units		
Type	**Basic Unit**	**Abbreviation**
Linear (size or distance)	Meter	m
Mass (Weight)	Gram	g
Capacity (Volume)	Liter	L or l

Information from the previous two tables can be combined to create metric units. For example, a kilometer would be one thousand meters, while a kiloliter would be one thousand liters. A centimeter would be one hundredth of a meter, while a centigram would be one hundredth of a gram. The following table shows each of these units and their values:

Metric Conversions		
Linear	**Weight**	**Volume**
1 kilometer (km) = 1,000 m	1 kilogram (kg) = 1,000 g	1 liter (l) = 1,000 milliliters (ml)
1 meter (m) = 1.0 m	1 gram (g) = 1.0 g	1 deciliter (dl) = 100 ml; 10 cl
1 decimeter (dm) = 0.1 m 1 centimeter (cm) = 0.01 m	1 milligram (mg) = 0.001 g	1 centiliter (cl) = 10 ml
1 millimeter (mm) = 0.001 m		

Conversions

Following are some commonly used customary-to-metric ratios. (Values are approximate.)

- 1 inch = 2.54 centimeters
- 1 yard = 0.91 meter
- 1 mile = 1.61 kilometers
- 1 ounce = 28.35 grams
- 1 pound = 0.45 kilograms
- 1 quart = 0.94 liter

One can determine the metric-to-customary conversions by taking the reciprocals of each of the factors noted above. For instance, one finds that 1 kilometer is equal to about 0.62 milesby dividing 1 by 1.61.

Skill 29.9: Solve Real-World Problems Involving Estimates and Exact Measurements

All measurements are limited by the devices and procedures used to take the measurements. For example, if a pie is divided into three pieces, a calculator might report that each piece consists of 0.33333333 of the pie. This measurement is limited in two ways. First, it underestimates the size of each piece, because the "3" should repeat infinitely, but this calculator only reports 8 decimal places. Second, even if the calculator were accurate, tiny crumbs will undoubtedly remain in the pan after dividing the pie, so that the actual size of the pieces could not match the values yielded by the calculator.

In spite of these considerations, scientists—as well as eaters of pie—take measurements and attempt to be as accurate as possible. In solving real-world problems, we recognize that a degree of inaccuracy is always present, and we make decisions about the extent of accuracy that is desirable. In some cases, estimation is necessary. Students learn to use rounding in order to work with multiples of 10, for example, or to round numbers to two decimal places. In other cases, estimates require simplification of the real-world problem that students are attempting to solve. For example, in calculating the total length of a trip that involves three cities, students may draw a triangle and calculate perimeter. Students understand that no matter what mode of transportation is used, the actual movement between cities would not involve perfectly straight lines. They recognize that drawing lines between the cities and calculating the perimeter of the triangle merely provides an estimate of the distance. With information about actual flight distance or road mileage, students can compare their estimates to the exact measurements and engage the concept of measurement error.

Skill 29.10: Select Appropriate Measurement Units to Solve Problems

Following are some questions that students must address when solving problems:

1.   Should customary or metric system measurements be used?

2.   Does the problem involve dimensions of length, size, weight, volume, or temperature?

3.   Which dimensions must be used to generate a solution?

4.   In which dimension will the solution be expressed?

With respect to a particular problem, students should be able to answer each of these questions by means of a careful reading of the problem. The kinds of information available to answer each question are as follows:

1.   Information about properties will be included in the problem in either customary or metric terms. If a combination of terms is used, students will need to perform conversions so that the problem can be restated using one system. If no system

is used (e.g., one cube is described as having twice the volume of another cube), then students will not need to choose between systems.

2. Terms such as "length" or "volume" may be used in the problem. If these terms are not used, students will need to make decisions as to which dimensions are indicated by the details of the problem. Students may need to look for clues, such as whether a particular object is two-dimensional or three-dimensional. A drawing of a beach ball, for example, would be two-dimensional, while the actual ball would be three-dimensional.

3. As students choose the formula or formulas that are suitable for addressing the problem, they will recognize which dimensions are versus which dimensions are not important in generating a solution.

4. An important part of reading the problem is understanding what the solution would look like. Often, this is the first step, and it may be challenging.

Skill 29.11: Visualize Three-Dimensional Objects from Two-Dimensional Representations of Objects and Vice Versa

Development of geometrical competence depends in part on the ability to visualize three-dimensional objects based on drawings and other two-dimensional representations. The concept of the volume of a sphere will not make sense, for example, unless the student examining a picture of the sphere in a textbook can imagine the actual object.

Competency 30: Knowledge of Algebra

The simple algebra that students learn introduces the representation of variables in order to express quantities and relationships. Students learn to use symbols (typically letters) in place of numbers and to manipulate these symbols in order to solve problems. The focus of Competency 30 is on elementary algebraic knowledge.

Skill 30.1: Extend and Generalize Patterns or Functional Relationships

Algebraic equations are used to represent quantities, variables, patterns, and functional relationships. For example, if s represents the number of students in a school and t represents the number of teachers, the total number of students and teachers in the school is $s + t$. If the school has 10 times as many students as teachers, an algebraic expression equating the number of students and teachers in the school is $s = 10t$.

In this example, there are two variables: the number of students and the number of teaches. In an algebraic equation, if the values of all the variables but one are known, then the value of the unknown variable can be calculated. For example, if we know that a school has 10 times as many students as teachers, and that the school has 43 teachers, we can calculate that there are 430 students. In algebraic terms:

$$s = 10t$$
$$t = 43$$
$$s = 10(43)$$
$$s = 430$$

Skill 30.2: Interpret, Compare, and Translate Multiple Representations of Patterns and Relationships by Using Tables, Graphs, Equations, Expressions, and Verbal Descriptions

The representation of information by means of equations, graphs, tables, and so on often serves the purpose of simplifying what would otherwise be overabundant and/or confusing information.

Equations

Equations express quantities, patterns, and relationships in numerical terms, with letters often used in place of unknown quantities. Equations are essential both in representing problems and in solving them. For example, consider the following problem:

John is 3 inches less than twice as tall as his little sister Lakeisha, while his cousin Mary is only 6 inches taller than Lakeisha. Lakeisha is 34 inches tall. How much taller is John than Mary?

This first sentence of this statement could be simplified by means of the following equations:

$$J = 2L - 3$$
$$M = L + 6$$

With these formulas, the correct answer can now be obtained by substituting 34 for L in each equation, and then comparing the results for J and M.

Graphs

Graphs and tables are visual aids that help simplify, organize, and concretely summarize information. The main types that students first encounter are line graphs, bar graphs, and pie charts.

1. *A line graph* shows quantitative trends for one or more items along some continuous dimension such as time. The lines are composed of connected points

displayed on the graph through each period of the dimension (e.g., years, days, seconds). For example, the line graph below depicts numbers of teachers and pupil/teacher ratios from 1960 to 2008

Numbers of Teachers and Pupil/Teacher Ratios from 1960 through 2008

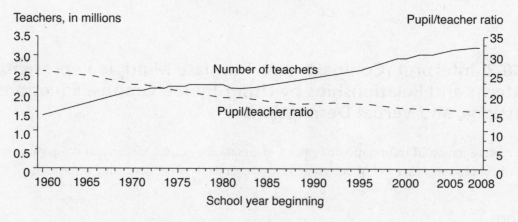

Source: National Center for Education Statistics, *Digest of Education Statistics 2010*

To read a line graph, one must examine the title, heading, or captions to identify the general group of items being compared, the labels of headings for each item, and the units used to measure the items.

Line graphs are useful for illustrating changes or points of change of interest. For example, in the previous graph you might want to see how many teachers there were when you were in school and what the pupil/teacher ratios were during that time period.

2.   *A bar graph* is used for comparing and contrasting categorical values. Although the units in which the items are measured must be equal, units can be of any size and start at any value. For example, the following bar graph shows unemployment rates of persons 25 years old and over, by highest level of educational attainment: 2009

Unemployment Rates by Highest Level of Educational Attainment
25 years old and over

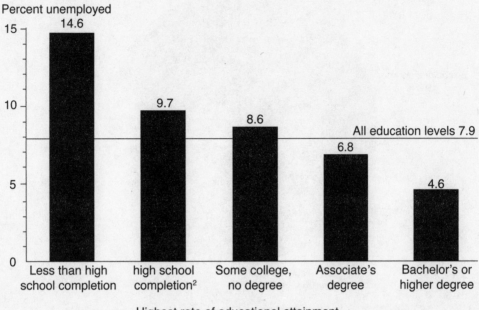

Percent unemployed

Source: National Center for Education Statistics, *Digest of Education Statistics 2010*.

To read a bar graph, examine the title, labels, and units for the graph. Then, begin at the base of a bar and trace the bar to its full length to determine quantity. For example, the bar graph above shows that individuals with more education are more likely to be employed.

3.   *A pie chart* shows the division of a whole unit into parts. An entire pie represents 100 percent of a given quantity. Each "slice" of the pie represents some proportion or percentage of the whole. In the following pie chart, individuals 25 years and older are divided by level of education attained.

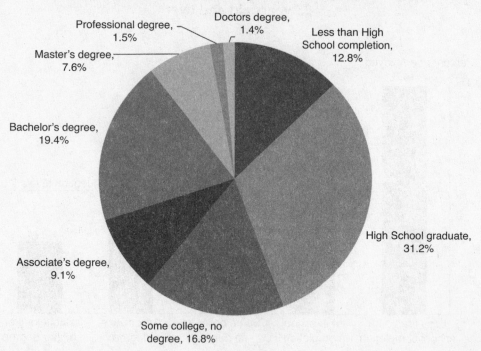

Educational Level Attained by Individuals 25 and older

Source: U.S. Census Bureau, Educational Attainment, last updated April 2011

To read a pie chart, students choose the element of the subject that interests them and compare its size to those of the other elements. Students must be careful not to assume that elements that are similar in size are equal. The exact percentage of each element will referenced either inside or outside the slice, or may be located in a key within the chart. Students should also notice the organization of the information. For instance, in the pie chart above the slices are organized by level of education attained, not by the percentage and are read clockwise as levels of education descend. The lowest level of education (less than high school completion), which is the starting point at the top of the chart, is next to the highest level (doctoral degree), which is the end point.

The chart above shows, for example, that among individuals 25 and older, those who completed high school represent the largest category, while those with doctoral degrees represent the smallest category.

Tables

A table is a method of organizing related information into rows and columns. Tables are useful because they can briefly summarize large amounts of information. To read a table, the column headings that run horizontally across the top of the table should be cross-referenced with the row headings that run vertically down the left side of the table.

Skill 30.3: Select a Representation of an Algebraic Expression, Equation, or Inequality that Applies to a Real-World Situation

As discussed previously, a helpful approach when attempting to solve a word problem is to translate the problem into an equation (or, sometimes, an inequality). For example, consider the following problem:

The Acme Taxicab Company charges riders $3 just for getting into the cab, plus $2 for every mile or fraction of a mile driven. What would be the fare for a 10-mile ride?

This problem can be translated into the following equation.

$$x = 3 + (2 \times 10)$$

The equation can be read as "the unknown fare (x) is equal to $3 dollars plus $2 dollars for each of the 10 miles driven."

Students should be attentive to phrases in word problems that are likely to indicate certain mathematical relationships and operations. (For example, the word "is" often suggests an equal sign, "product" indicates multiplication, and "difference" suggests subtraction). At the same time, students must understand the conceptual basis of the problem and not merely rely on key words as a basis for translating the problems into equations.

Skill 30.4: Demonstrate Knowledge of One- and Two-Step Linear Equations and Inequalities

One-step linear equations are those that can be solved by the application of a single operation. For example, consider the following equation:

$$x + 3 = 12$$

By subtracting 3 from each side of the equation, one determines that x is 9. This illustrates a one-step linear equation in which the single step is subtraction.

A two-step linear equation, as the name suggests, requires the application of two operations, or one operation twice. For example:

$$4x - 6 = 14$$

This equation must be solved in two steps. First, add 6 to each side of the equation. This step yields the following:

$$4x = 20$$

Now divide each side by 4, and the answer is found to be 5.

An important principle that these examples have in common is that whatever is done to one side of the equation must be done to the other side.

Skill 30.5: Apply the Commutative, Associative, and Distributive Properties to Show That Two Expressions Are Equivalent

Three important principles that govern the application of mathematical operations are the commutative, associative, and distributive properties.

- The commutative property holds that during addition and multiplication, the order in which one proceeds does not affect the sum or product. For example, $13 + 5 = 5 + 13$. And, $42 \times 9 = 9 \times 42$.

- The associative property holds that during addition and multiplication, the grouping of numbers added or multiplied does not affect the sum or product. For example, if one is adding 15, 6, and 3, it does not matter whether one adds the 15 and 6 first, or the 6 and 3 first (or the 15 and 3 first). Likewise, when multiplying 8, 10, and 4, one can multiply the 8 and 10 first, or the 10 and 4 first (or the 8 and 4 first).

- The distributive property holds that during multiplication when addition or subtraction is also involved, the multiplication step can be applied to each of the numbers being added or subtracted. For example, $21(3 + 7) = 21(3) + 21(7)$. To take another example, $16(9 - 2) = 16(9) - 16(2)$.

Competency 31: Knowledge of Data Analysis

As students get older they begin to go beyond the mere determination of single quantities to the analysis of patterns and relationships in sets of numbers. The focus of Competency 31 is on knowledge of data analysis tools and strategies.

Skill 31.1: Demonstrate Knowledge of the Concepts of Variability and Central Tendency

An ordered set of numbers is called a distribution, or a set. Often it is difficult to make sense of a distribution, since it is just a set of numbers, and so the scientist or mathematician will calculate a single number that represents the entire distribution in some useful way. Two kinds of numbers that are frequently used are measures of variability and measures of central tendency.

Variability

The single measure of variability, or spread, that students are introduced to is the range. The range corresponds to the difference between the largest and smallest numbers in a set. Thus, to determine the range of a set of numbers, one simply subtracts the smallest number in the set from the largest one. For example, in the set consisting of the numbers 15, 22, 26, 29, and 40, the range is 25 (i.e., 40–15).

Central Tendency

Measures of central tendency are single values that describe something "central" about a distribution or set of numbers. There are three main types.

1. *The mean* is the mathematical average of the distribution. To determine the mean, add the values in the set and divide by the total number of values. For example, the mean of 5, 7, 8, 12, and 18 is 10 (i.e., $(5 + 7 + 8 + 12 + 18) \div 5$).

2. *The median* is the value that falls in the exact middle of the distribution. To find the median, the distribution must be arranged in order from smallest to largest. For example, the median of 5, 7, 8, 12, and 18 is 8, because half of the other values are above 8 and half are below 8. In this example, there is an odd number of values (i.e., 5). If the distribution contains an even number of values, the median will be the mean of the middle two values. For example, for the distribution 6, 8, 10, 12, the median will be 9.

3. The mode is the most frequently occurring value in a distribution. For example, the mode of 3, 7, 7, 9, 11, 11, 15, 17, 17, 17, 21, and 22 is 17, because that value appears three times. A distribution may have more than one mode. Alternatively, a distribution may have no mode (e.g., if each value occurs only once).

Skill 31.2: Use Data to Construct and Analyze Frequency Tables and Graphs

Tables and basic graphs are discussed under Competency 30, Skill 30.2. Two other types of visual representations that are sometimes used are the box-and-whisker graph and the stem-and-leaf plot.

Box-and-Whisker Graph

The box-and-whisker graph displays the median, range, and quartiles of a distribution. (Quartiles consist of the highest, second-highest, second-lowest, and lowest 25% of a distribution.) The following box-and-whisker graph displays the scores of a class of students on a test for which the maximum score is 40.

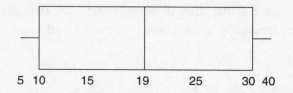

5 10   15   19   25   30 40

In this graph, the box represents the middle 50% of the scores. The "whiskers" extending from the left and right ends of the box represent the upper and lower quartiles. We can see from this graph that the median test score was 19, and the range was 35 (i.e., 40–5). We can also see that the upper quartile encompasses scores from about 30 to 40, while the lower quartile encompasses the scores between 5 and 10.

Stem-and-Leaf Plot

A stem-and-leaf plot is a relatively easy way to display an actual distribution. In this kind of plot, stems represent numbers in one place, and leaves represent all items with numbers in a lower place. For example, the following stem-and-leaf plot displays the ages of people attending a movie theater on a particular evening.

Stem	Leaf
3	0 0 3 3 5 8
4	5 6
5	6 7
6	2 2
7	3 4

Here, the stem column lists the numbers in the tens place, while the leaf column shows the numbers in the ones place. We can see, for example, that six audience members were in their thirties: two were 30, two were 33, one was 35, and one was 38. We can also see that the range is 44 (i.e., 74–30), and that there are three modes (30, 33, and 62).

Skill 31.3: Make Accurate Predictions and Draw Conclusions About Data

The purpose of problem-solving activities, such as data analysis, is to test predictions and draw conclusions. Doing so allows students to apply their mathematical skills as well as their higher-level thinking. For example, after studying the following graph, students may conclude that a new cigarette with 10 mg of tar would have between 0.7 and 0.8 mg of nicotine:

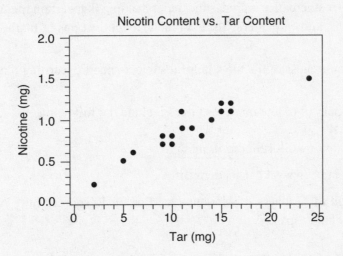

Competency 32: Knowledge of Instruction and Assessment

The focus of Competency 32 is on instruction and assessment specifically within the subject of mathematics.

Skill 32.1: Identify a Variety of Appropriate Instructional Strategies for Teaching Specific Concepts

Instructional strategies are discussed at length in prior chapters. Teachers should understand, however, that effective instruction in mathematics is, to an extent, subject-specific and requires pedagogical content knowledge.

Pedagogical Content Knowledge

Pedagogical content knowledge (PCK) consists of knowledge about instructional strategies within particular content areas. Whereas pedagogical knowledge refers to general principles of teaching and content knowledge refers to knowledge of subject, PCK is a combination of the two. PCK includes knowledge of how students learn particular subjects, what concepts are especially easy or difficult within particular subjects, and what kinds of strategies and examples are especially useful in teaching particular subject-specific concepts.

A simple example would be the understanding that students learn fractions more readily in the context of dividing actual manipulatives. Thus, the concept of half, for example, can be taught as students divide actual objects into parts or piles.

PCK with respect to mathematics includes the understanding that certain members of the community, such as bakers, musicians, and carpenters, discuss practical applications of math with students.

PCK also includes awareness of the most helpful subject-specific learning materials.

For example, some helpful online math resources include the following:

- Ask Dr. Math http://mathforum.org/dr.math/

- Kahn Academy http://www.khanacademy.org/

- National Council of Teachers of Mathematics Lesson Resources http://www.nctm.org/resources/default.aspx

Skill 32.2: Identify Ways That Manipulatives, Mathematical and Physical Models, and Technology Can Be Used in Instruction

Manipulatives

Manipulatives are movable materials that enhance students' understanding of a concept. These materials can be actual physical objects or virtual images on a computer screen.

Manipulatives foster active, engaged learning in the process of illustrating concepts in a concrete way. Some examples of manipulatives in math include the following:

- Plastic geometric shapes

- Number lines

- Place value cubes

- Tesselation blocks

The National Library of Virtual Manipulatives (http://nlvm.usu.edu/en/nav/vlibrary.html) provides a wealth of resources for numbers and operations, algebra, geometry, measurement, and data analysis and probability for students of a variety of levels. The following website also provides information and rubrics for a variety of resources: (http://school.discoveryeducation.com/schrockguide/eval.html).

Selection of Materials

The effective teacher carefully evaluates manipulatives, models, and computer technology before introducing them into the classroom. A checklist for selecting the materials could include criteria such as the following:

- Alignment with state curriculum standards

- Alignment with lesson goals

- Appropriate sequencing

- Appropriate pacing

- Meaningful student interaction

- Motivational impact

- Clarity of purpose

- Potential for individual or group use

When evaluating resources, teachers should also consider students' strengths and needs, learning styles or preferred modalities, and interests. The effective teacher evaluates resources well in advance of the lesson and before purchase whenever possible. The teacher also evaluates the materials as students use them. When students have finished using the materials, the teacher can assess material usefulness by considering students' achievement levels and/or by asking students to voice their opinions of the materials.

Technology

The effective teacher includes resources of all types in the curriculum planning process. Teachers should be familiar with the school library, the local library, education service center resources, and the libraries of any colleges or universities in the area.

Computer technology in particular plays a key role in math instruction. Calculators, smart phones, and computers with CD-ROM drives, DVD drives, and Internet access are among the many problem-solving tools available to students. However, their usefulness in classroom settings depends to a great extent on guidance from the teacher.

Teachers should carefully consider the appropriate place in the lesson for technology-based materials. If the material is especially interesting and thought-provoking, the teacher can use it to introduce a unit. For example, a travel video on coral reefs or snorkeling might be an excellent introduction to the study of ocean depths and how to graph them.

Because textbooks cannot stay up-to-date on numerical data such as batting averages and stock reports, newspapers and magazines as well as websites are useful resources for teaching mathematics. Some newspapers and magazines provide special programs to help teachers use their products in the classroom. Local newspapers may even be willing to send specialists to work with students or act as special resource persons.

Technology experts argue that tools such as the Internet provide so much content that today's teachers have a greater role than ever in helping students acquire process skills such as critical and creative thinking. Content changes and expands, but thinking processes remain salient and necessary, regardless of content.

Spreadsheets

Spreadsheets are especially useful in the math classroom. Teachers often keep grade books on spreadsheets because of the ease in updating information. Once formulas are in place, teachers can enter grades and have completely up-to-date averages for all students. Some spreadsheet programs also include charting functions that enable teachers to display class averages on a bar chart to provide visual comparisons of performance among various classes.

Spreadsheets are also useful for students. By means of spreadsheets, students can manage data and calculate measures of variability and central tendency, as described earlier. Students can use spreadsheets to enter and sort the data they collect. For example, students could enter population figures from different countries and then draw graphs—lines, bars, pies, and/or scatter plots—to convey the information in a written report, group project, or multimedia presentation.

Graphics and Presentation Software

Graphics or paint programs allow users to produce any type of chart, graph, or picture. In addition, many word-processing programs have some graphic functions. Students can use these programs to produce geometric shapes for analysis or for illustrating classroom presentations or individual research projects. For teachers, these relatively simple tools make it easy to create handouts and instructional materials with a very polished appearance.

Today's teachers also need to acquire and demonstrate skill in using presentation software (such as Microsoft PowerPoint) to prepare instructional lessons. Presentation software also makes it possible to provide students with instructional handouts and outlines to complement classroom instruction. In some situations and in some schools, Web authoring experience and skills will also prove useful.

Skill 32.3: Identify a Variety of Methods for Assessing Mathematical Knowledge, Including Analyzing Student Thinking Processes to Determine Strengths and Weaknesses

Teachers can determine students' needs through formal or informal assessment. Most standardized tests include an indication of which objectives the student did not master. Mastery of these objectives can be assisted with computer, online, or multimedia aids.

An acceptable testing environment requires the mathematics teachers to prepare students by emphasizing the critical knowledge they need to learn. This is accomplished by establishing a setting with clear instructions and fair tests for students to complete and giving feedback that praises correct responses and corrects errors and misunderstandings.

Additional assessment concepts are described in several earlier chapters.

End-of-Chapter Questions

1. Which of the following is not an integer?

    (A) -1

    (B) 0.3

    (C) 1

    (D) 7

2. Which of the following is a correct representation of the number 4,391 in scientific notation?

    (A) 4.391×10^3

    (B) $4 \times 10^3 + 3.91 \times 10^3$

    (C) 4.391×10^4

    (D) $4 \times 10^3 + 3.91$

3. Which of the following is the best estimate of the area of a circle whose radius is 9?

    (A) 50

    (B) 100

    (C) 250

    (D) 500

4. 20 pounds corresponds to approximately how many kilograms?

    (A) .9

    (B) 22

    (C) 44

    (D) 50

5. What is the volume of a box that is 2 feet deep, 2 feet wide, and 3 feet high?
   - (A) 7 cubic feet
   - (B) 12 cubic feet
   - (C) 27 cubic feet
   - (D) 54 cubic feet

6. What is x if $13x = y + 3$, and $y = 23$?
   - (A) 1
   - (B) 2
   - (C) 3
   - (D) 4

7. What property is reflected in the observation that 98×52 must equal 52×98?
   - (A) Commutative
   - (B) Associative
   - (C) Distributive
   - (D) Evaluative

Answer Key

1.	(B)	5.	(B)
2.	(A)	6.	(B)
3.	(C)	7.	(A)
4.	(A)		

FTCE Elementary Education K-6

Practice Test

This test is also on CD-ROM in our special interactive TestWare® for the FTCE Elementary Education K-6. It is highly recommended that you first take this exam on computer. You will then have the additional study features and benefits of enforced timed conditions and feedback that pinpoints the subtopics where you need to brush-up. See page 4 for instructions on how to get the most out of our book and software.

Answer Sheet

1. Ⓐ Ⓑ Ⓒ Ⓓ	29. Ⓐ Ⓑ Ⓒ Ⓓ	57. Ⓐ Ⓑ Ⓒ Ⓓ	85. Ⓐ Ⓑ Ⓒ Ⓓ
2. Ⓐ Ⓑ Ⓒ Ⓓ	30. Ⓐ Ⓑ Ⓒ Ⓓ	58. Ⓐ Ⓑ Ⓒ Ⓓ	86. Ⓐ Ⓑ Ⓒ Ⓓ
3. Ⓐ Ⓑ Ⓒ Ⓓ	31. Ⓐ Ⓑ Ⓒ Ⓓ	59. Ⓐ Ⓑ Ⓒ Ⓓ	87. Ⓐ Ⓑ Ⓒ Ⓓ
4. Ⓐ Ⓑ Ⓒ Ⓓ	32. Ⓐ Ⓑ Ⓒ Ⓓ	60. Ⓐ Ⓑ Ⓒ Ⓓ	88. Ⓐ Ⓑ Ⓒ Ⓓ
5. Ⓐ Ⓑ Ⓒ Ⓓ	33. Ⓐ Ⓑ Ⓒ Ⓓ	61. Ⓐ Ⓑ Ⓒ Ⓓ	89. Ⓐ Ⓑ Ⓒ Ⓓ
6. Ⓐ Ⓑ Ⓒ Ⓓ	34. Ⓐ Ⓑ Ⓒ Ⓓ	62. Ⓐ Ⓑ Ⓒ Ⓓ	90. Ⓐ Ⓑ Ⓒ Ⓓ
7. Ⓐ Ⓑ Ⓒ Ⓓ	35. Ⓐ Ⓑ Ⓒ Ⓓ	63. Ⓐ Ⓑ Ⓒ Ⓓ	91. Ⓐ Ⓑ Ⓒ Ⓓ
8. Ⓐ Ⓑ Ⓒ Ⓓ	36. Ⓐ Ⓑ Ⓒ Ⓓ	64. Ⓐ Ⓑ Ⓒ Ⓓ	92. Ⓐ Ⓑ Ⓒ Ⓓ
9. Ⓐ Ⓑ Ⓒ Ⓓ	37. Ⓐ Ⓑ Ⓒ Ⓓ	65. Ⓐ Ⓑ Ⓒ Ⓓ	93. Ⓐ Ⓑ Ⓒ Ⓓ
10. Ⓐ Ⓑ Ⓒ Ⓓ	38. Ⓐ Ⓑ Ⓒ Ⓓ	66. Ⓐ Ⓑ Ⓒ Ⓓ	94. Ⓐ Ⓑ Ⓒ Ⓓ
11. Ⓐ Ⓑ Ⓒ Ⓓ	39. Ⓐ Ⓑ Ⓒ Ⓓ	67. Ⓐ Ⓑ Ⓒ Ⓓ	95. Ⓐ Ⓑ Ⓒ Ⓓ
12. Ⓐ Ⓑ Ⓒ Ⓓ	40. Ⓐ Ⓑ Ⓒ Ⓓ	68. Ⓐ Ⓑ Ⓒ Ⓓ	96. Ⓐ Ⓑ Ⓒ Ⓓ
13. Ⓐ Ⓑ Ⓒ Ⓓ	41. Ⓐ Ⓑ Ⓒ Ⓓ	69. Ⓐ Ⓑ Ⓒ Ⓓ	97. Ⓐ Ⓑ Ⓒ Ⓓ
14. Ⓐ Ⓑ Ⓒ Ⓓ	42. Ⓐ Ⓑ Ⓒ Ⓓ	70. Ⓐ Ⓑ Ⓒ Ⓓ	98. Ⓐ Ⓑ Ⓒ Ⓓ
15. Ⓐ Ⓑ Ⓒ Ⓓ	43. Ⓐ Ⓑ Ⓒ Ⓓ	71. Ⓐ Ⓑ Ⓒ Ⓓ	99. Ⓐ Ⓑ Ⓒ Ⓓ
16. Ⓐ Ⓑ Ⓒ Ⓓ	44. Ⓐ Ⓑ Ⓒ Ⓓ	72. Ⓐ Ⓑ Ⓒ Ⓓ	100. Ⓐ Ⓑ Ⓒ Ⓓ
17. Ⓐ Ⓑ Ⓒ Ⓓ	45. Ⓐ Ⓑ Ⓒ Ⓓ	73. Ⓐ Ⓑ Ⓒ Ⓓ	101. Ⓐ Ⓑ Ⓒ Ⓓ
18. Ⓐ Ⓑ Ⓒ Ⓓ	46. Ⓐ Ⓑ Ⓒ Ⓓ	74. Ⓐ Ⓑ Ⓒ Ⓓ	102. Ⓐ Ⓑ Ⓒ Ⓓ
19. Ⓐ Ⓑ Ⓒ Ⓓ	47. Ⓐ Ⓑ Ⓒ Ⓓ	75. Ⓐ Ⓑ Ⓒ Ⓓ	103. Ⓐ Ⓑ Ⓒ Ⓓ
20. Ⓐ Ⓑ Ⓒ Ⓓ	48. Ⓐ Ⓑ Ⓒ Ⓓ	76. Ⓐ Ⓑ Ⓒ Ⓓ	104. Ⓐ Ⓑ Ⓒ Ⓓ
21. Ⓐ Ⓑ Ⓒ Ⓓ	49. Ⓐ Ⓑ Ⓒ Ⓓ	77. Ⓐ Ⓑ Ⓒ Ⓓ	105. Ⓐ Ⓑ Ⓒ Ⓓ
22. Ⓐ Ⓑ Ⓒ Ⓓ	50. Ⓐ Ⓑ Ⓒ Ⓓ	78. Ⓐ Ⓑ Ⓒ Ⓓ	106. Ⓐ Ⓑ Ⓒ Ⓓ
23. Ⓐ Ⓑ Ⓒ Ⓓ	51. Ⓐ Ⓑ Ⓒ Ⓓ	79. Ⓐ Ⓑ Ⓒ Ⓓ	107. Ⓐ Ⓑ Ⓒ Ⓓ
24. Ⓐ Ⓑ Ⓒ Ⓓ	52. Ⓐ Ⓑ Ⓒ Ⓓ	80. Ⓐ Ⓑ Ⓒ Ⓓ	108. Ⓐ Ⓑ Ⓒ Ⓓ
25. Ⓐ Ⓑ Ⓒ Ⓓ	53. Ⓐ Ⓑ Ⓒ Ⓓ	81. Ⓐ Ⓑ Ⓒ Ⓓ	109. Ⓐ Ⓑ Ⓒ Ⓓ
26. Ⓐ Ⓑ Ⓒ Ⓓ	54. Ⓐ Ⓑ Ⓒ Ⓓ	82. Ⓐ Ⓑ Ⓒ Ⓓ	110. Ⓐ Ⓑ Ⓒ Ⓓ
27. Ⓐ Ⓑ Ⓒ Ⓓ	55. Ⓐ Ⓑ Ⓒ Ⓓ	83. Ⓐ Ⓑ Ⓒ Ⓓ	111. Ⓐ Ⓑ Ⓒ Ⓓ
28. Ⓐ Ⓑ Ⓒ Ⓓ	56. Ⓐ Ⓑ Ⓒ Ⓓ	84. Ⓐ Ⓑ Ⓒ Ⓓ	112. Ⓐ Ⓑ Ⓒ Ⓓ

Answer Sheet *(continued)*

113. Ⓐ Ⓑ Ⓒ Ⓓ	141. Ⓐ Ⓑ Ⓒ Ⓓ	169. Ⓐ Ⓑ Ⓒ Ⓓ	197. Ⓐ Ⓑ Ⓒ Ⓓ
114. Ⓐ Ⓑ Ⓒ Ⓓ	142. Ⓐ Ⓑ Ⓒ Ⓓ	170. Ⓐ Ⓑ Ⓒ Ⓓ	198. Ⓐ Ⓑ Ⓒ Ⓓ
115. Ⓐ Ⓑ Ⓒ Ⓓ	143. Ⓐ Ⓑ Ⓒ Ⓓ	171. Ⓐ Ⓑ Ⓒ Ⓓ	199. Ⓐ Ⓑ Ⓒ Ⓓ
116. Ⓐ Ⓑ Ⓒ Ⓓ	144. Ⓐ Ⓑ Ⓒ Ⓓ	172. Ⓐ Ⓑ Ⓒ Ⓓ	200. Ⓐ Ⓑ Ⓒ Ⓓ
117. Ⓐ Ⓑ Ⓒ Ⓓ	145. Ⓐ Ⓑ Ⓒ Ⓓ	173. Ⓐ Ⓑ Ⓒ Ⓓ	201. Ⓐ Ⓑ Ⓒ Ⓓ
118. Ⓐ Ⓑ Ⓒ Ⓓ	146. Ⓐ Ⓑ Ⓒ Ⓓ	174. Ⓐ Ⓑ Ⓒ Ⓓ	202. Ⓐ Ⓑ Ⓒ Ⓓ
119. Ⓐ Ⓑ Ⓒ Ⓓ	147. Ⓐ Ⓑ Ⓒ Ⓓ	175. Ⓐ Ⓑ Ⓒ Ⓓ	203. Ⓐ Ⓑ Ⓒ Ⓓ
120. Ⓐ Ⓑ Ⓒ Ⓓ	148. Ⓐ Ⓑ Ⓒ Ⓓ	176. Ⓐ Ⓑ Ⓒ Ⓓ	204. Ⓐ Ⓑ Ⓒ Ⓓ
121. Ⓐ Ⓑ Ⓒ Ⓓ	149. Ⓐ Ⓑ Ⓒ Ⓓ	177. Ⓐ Ⓑ Ⓒ Ⓓ	205. Ⓐ Ⓑ Ⓒ Ⓓ
122. Ⓐ Ⓑ Ⓒ Ⓓ	150. Ⓐ Ⓑ Ⓒ Ⓓ	178. Ⓐ Ⓑ Ⓒ Ⓓ	206. Ⓐ Ⓑ Ⓒ Ⓓ
123. Ⓐ Ⓑ Ⓒ Ⓓ	151. Ⓐ Ⓑ Ⓒ Ⓓ	179. Ⓐ Ⓑ Ⓒ Ⓓ	207. Ⓐ Ⓑ Ⓒ Ⓓ
124. Ⓐ Ⓑ Ⓒ Ⓓ	152. Ⓐ Ⓑ Ⓒ Ⓓ	180. Ⓐ Ⓑ Ⓒ Ⓓ	208. Ⓐ Ⓑ Ⓒ Ⓓ
125. Ⓐ Ⓑ Ⓒ Ⓓ	153. Ⓐ Ⓑ Ⓒ Ⓓ	181. Ⓐ Ⓑ Ⓒ Ⓓ	209. Ⓐ Ⓑ Ⓒ Ⓓ
126. Ⓐ Ⓑ Ⓒ Ⓓ	154. Ⓐ Ⓑ Ⓒ Ⓓ	182. Ⓐ Ⓑ Ⓒ Ⓓ	210. Ⓐ Ⓑ Ⓒ Ⓓ
127. Ⓐ Ⓑ Ⓒ Ⓓ	155. Ⓐ Ⓑ Ⓒ Ⓓ	183. Ⓐ Ⓑ Ⓒ Ⓓ	211. Ⓐ Ⓑ Ⓒ Ⓓ
128. Ⓐ Ⓑ Ⓒ Ⓓ	156. Ⓐ Ⓑ Ⓒ Ⓓ	184. Ⓐ Ⓑ Ⓒ Ⓓ	212. Ⓐ Ⓑ Ⓒ Ⓓ
129. Ⓐ Ⓑ Ⓒ Ⓓ	157. Ⓐ Ⓑ Ⓒ Ⓓ	185. Ⓐ Ⓑ Ⓒ Ⓓ	213. Ⓐ Ⓑ Ⓒ Ⓓ
130. Ⓐ Ⓑ Ⓒ Ⓓ	158. Ⓐ Ⓑ Ⓒ Ⓓ	186. Ⓐ Ⓑ Ⓒ Ⓓ	214. Ⓐ Ⓑ Ⓒ Ⓓ
131. Ⓐ Ⓑ Ⓒ Ⓓ	159. Ⓐ Ⓑ Ⓒ Ⓓ	187. Ⓐ Ⓑ Ⓒ Ⓓ	215. Ⓐ Ⓑ Ⓒ Ⓓ
132. Ⓐ Ⓑ Ⓒ Ⓓ	160. Ⓐ Ⓑ Ⓒ Ⓓ	188. Ⓐ Ⓑ Ⓒ Ⓓ	216. Ⓐ Ⓑ Ⓒ Ⓓ
133. Ⓐ Ⓑ Ⓒ Ⓓ	161. Ⓐ Ⓑ Ⓒ Ⓓ	189. Ⓐ Ⓑ Ⓒ Ⓓ	217. Ⓐ Ⓑ Ⓒ Ⓓ
134. Ⓐ Ⓑ Ⓒ Ⓓ	162. Ⓐ Ⓑ Ⓒ Ⓓ	190. Ⓐ Ⓑ Ⓒ Ⓓ	218. Ⓐ Ⓑ Ⓒ Ⓓ
135. Ⓐ Ⓑ Ⓒ Ⓓ	163. Ⓐ Ⓑ Ⓒ Ⓓ	191. Ⓐ Ⓑ Ⓒ Ⓓ	219. Ⓐ Ⓑ Ⓒ Ⓓ
136. Ⓐ Ⓑ Ⓒ Ⓓ	164. Ⓐ Ⓑ Ⓒ Ⓓ	192. Ⓐ Ⓑ Ⓒ Ⓓ	220. Ⓐ Ⓑ Ⓒ Ⓓ
137. Ⓐ Ⓑ Ⓒ Ⓓ	165. Ⓐ Ⓑ Ⓒ Ⓓ	193. Ⓐ Ⓑ Ⓒ Ⓓ	221. Ⓐ Ⓑ Ⓒ Ⓓ
138. Ⓐ Ⓑ Ⓒ Ⓓ	166. Ⓐ Ⓑ Ⓒ Ⓓ	194. Ⓐ Ⓑ Ⓒ Ⓓ	222. Ⓐ Ⓑ Ⓒ Ⓓ
139. Ⓐ Ⓑ Ⓒ Ⓓ	167. Ⓐ Ⓑ Ⓒ Ⓓ	195. Ⓐ Ⓑ Ⓒ Ⓓ	223. Ⓐ Ⓑ Ⓒ Ⓓ
140. Ⓐ Ⓑ Ⓒ Ⓓ	168. Ⓐ Ⓑ Ⓒ Ⓓ	196. Ⓐ Ⓑ Ⓒ Ⓓ	224. Ⓐ Ⓑ Ⓒ Ⓓ
			225. Ⓐ Ⓑ Ⓒ Ⓓ

PRACTICE TEST

Read each question and select the option that best answers the question.

Language Arts

1. Phonemic awareness is a critical skill in reading because

   (A) it improves one's ability to read words and to spell.

   (B) it shows that letter–sound connections are completely consistent.

   (C) it supports recognition of syllables and morphemes.

   (D) it helps students hear when words begin with the same sound.

2. Effective phonemic awareness instruction includes

   (A) three or more types of phoneme manipulation at once.

   (B) manipulation of phonemes using letters of the alphabet.

   (C) teaching phonemic awareness for 30 minutes a day.

   (D) teaching phonemic awareness through synthetic phonics.

3. Which of the following most clearly reflects structural analysis?

   (A) hearing the difference between "bat," "bad," and "back"

   (B) articulating each syllable of the word "watermelon"

   (C) understanding that the /s/ sound is represented in more than one way

   (D) recognizing that "guarded" consists of the word "guard" plus the suffix "ed"

4. Characteristics of emergent literacy include

   (A) the realization that print carries a message.

   (B) the use of reading as a tool to learn.

   (C) the ability to read from multiple perspectives.

   (D) the understanding of specific words in texts.

5. Which of the following kind of book is preferable to use with early readers?

   (A) a book that introduces new themes and vocabulary words

   (B) a book that teaches students about practices in other cultures

   (C) a book that has many cultural references students will recognize

   (D) a book with complex ideas that the teacher can explain

6. Which of the following directly measures reading fluency?

   (A) multiple option tests

   (B) timed oral readings

   (C) sight-word analyses

   (D) running records

7. What is prosody?

   (A) the patterns of recurrent sounds in a language

   (B) the scientific study of reading comprehension

   (C) the rhythm, stress patterns, and intonations of speech

   (D) the sounds in a language that contribute to word meaning

8. Mrs. Williams wants to take some time to explicitly teach a reading strategy to her students. Which of the following should she do first?

(A) model the strategy

(B) explain the strategy

(C) write a description of the strategy on the board

(D) ask students to memorize the strategy

9. Which of the following poses a challenge for phonics instruction?

(A) Some students are visual learners.

(B) Many grapheme–phoneme connections are consistent across words.

(C) Phonics is a skills-based approach.

(D) Exceptions to phonics rules often occur.

10. Structural analysis involves the ability to

(A) understand linguistic organization

(B) identify missing words in passages

(C) apply rules of phonics when decoding

(D) break a word into parts or syllables

11. Which of the following is not part of the SQ3R as applied to a particular passage?

(A) surveying the passage

(B) asking the teacher for a brief summary of the passage

(C) brainstorming some questions that the passage is likely to answer

(D) reading the passage

12. Which of the following sentences is grammatically correct?

(A) Your unique excuses almost makes up for your missing assignment.

(B) Your unique excuses almost make up for your missing assignment.

(C) Your unique excuses makes up for your missing assignment.

(D) Your unique excuses will makes up for your missing assignment.

13. Which of the following sentences is grammatically correct?

(A) Neither Camden nor Paige am playing hockey.

(B) Neither Camden nor Paige is playing hockey.

(C) Neither Camden nor Paige had playing hockey.

(D) Neither Camden nor Paige were playing hockey.

14. Mr. Jackson is asking his students to read a brief essay and identify the theme. What level of comprehension is Mr. Jackson requiring of his students?

(A) creative

(B) critical

(C) interpretive

(D) literal

15. Mrs. Darnell is having her class read an expository text which contains many charts, pictures, and other graphics. Which of the following is the best way for her to support her students' comprehension of the text?

(A) encourage students to skip the graphics and focus their attention on understanding and reflecting on the text

(B) remind students that the purpose of the graphics is to maintain interest rather than convey essential information

(C) ask students to read the text first and to return to the graphics once they feel they have understood the main ideas

(D) help students understand the specific ways that the graphics support the details presented in the text

16. After reading her class a story about how one child helped keep his neighborhood clean, the teacher asks the class to brainstorm ways that they can keep their own neighborhood clean. What level in Bloom's Revised Taxonomy is primarily used for this activity?

(A) applying

(B) understanding

(C) creating

(D) remembering

17. Ms. Martinez is discussing the main character of a text with her students. Which of the following activities would best promote her students' thinking at the *evaluating* level of Bloom's Revised Taxonomy?

(A) asking students to look at various descriptions of the main character throughout the text and generate a summary description of the character's personality

(B) asking students to make a list of all the pages in which descriptions of the main character occur and note which of the other characters provided each description

(C) asking students to reflect on the author's treatment of the main character and whether it can be considered true-to-life or merely caricatured

(D) asking students to identify people they know whose attitudes and behaviors are similar to those exhibited by the main character

18. A text that describes contributors to World War I and then the main events of the war will most probably reflect which of the following types of organization?

(A) ordered list

(B) comparison

(C) cause and effect

(D) problem and solution

19. What type of assessment relies on predetermined criteria for student achievement?

(A) performance-based

(B) norm-referenced

(C) criterion-referenced

(D) portfolio

20. The results of what type of assessment are reported in percentile ranks?

(A) performance-based

(B) norm-referenced

(C) criterion-referenced

(D) portfolio

21. Which of the following is not part of emergent literacy?

(A) showing awareness of the directionality of print

(B) being able to decode words fluently

(C) recognizing where the title of a book is located

(D) understanding that words in books tell stories

22. Your school board is considering a proposal to lengthen the school day. You are encouraging your students to write to the board to express their views. You will be encouraging your students to use which mode of writing?

(A) persuasive

(B) narrative

(C) expository

(D) descriptive

23. A new novel about a fictional Native American girl who lived in the South during the pre-Colonial era represents which of the following genres?

    (A) traditional literature
    (B) fantasy
    (C) science fiction
    (D) historical fiction

24. Which sentence contains no punctuation errors?

    (A) You are my friend, however, I cannot afford to lend you any more money.
    (B) You are my friend; however, I cannot afford to lend you any more money.
    (C) You are my friend. However. I cannot afford to lend you any more money.
    (D) You are my friend however I cannot afford to lend you any more money.

25. Mr. Lee is discussing words such as "buzz," "hiss," and "splat" with his students. These words are examples of

    (A) parallelism.
    (B) kennings.
    (C) onomatopoeia.
    (D) homonyms.

26. Plot can be briefly defined as

    (A) the characters and setting of a story.
    (B) the fundamental theme of a story.
    (C) the main events of a story.
    (D) the twist that enlivens a story.

27. Which of the following descriptions contains a simile?

    (A) Patricia is like a bear.
    (B) Jill is practically a parrot.

    (C) Carolyn is more or less of a slug.
    (D) Nancy might be asleep.

28. All of the following would support the use of multicultural literature in the classroom EXCEPT

    (A) guiding students to think about the world from different perspectives.
    (B) informing students about the cultural contributions of different societies.
    (C) encouraging students to celebrate their own distinctive characteristics.
    (D) basing all readings on the works of 18th century European writers.

29. Why is monitoring important for helping students develop meaningful responses to literature?

    (A) Through monitoring, the teacher can check whether students are reading the right book.
    (B) Monitoring helps ensure that students understand what they are reading.
    (C) Having a class monitor helps maintain a classroom environment that is conducive to learning.
    (D) Teachers can modify inappropriate responses detected through monitoring.

30. Shonna likes to "write" about her family. She makes a long mark for her father, because he is the tallest one, a medium-sized mark for her mother, and small marks for herself and her brother. At what stage of writing does Shonna appear to be?

    (A) undifferentiated (stage 1)
    (B) differentiated (stage 2)
    (C) pictographic (stage 3)
    (D) biographic (stage 4)

31. Which of the following is the correct order of stages in process writing?

   (A) prewriting, editing, drafting, revising, publishing

   (B) drafting, prewriting, editing, revising, publishing

   (C) prewriting, drafting, revising, editing, publishing

   (D) drafting, prewriting, editing, publishing, revising

32. When planning an expository essay, which of the following should students consider?

   (A) audience, occasion, and purpose

   (B) means of introducing main character

   (C) methods of persuasion

   (D) approach to developing plot

33. Which of the following assessments gives you the best review of the needs of a student?

   (A) screenings

   (B) evaluations

   (C) diagnostic evaluation

   (D) progress monitoring

34. Generally speaking, rubrics are helpful in communicating

   (A) lesson content.

   (B) teacher expectations.

   (C) metacognitive strategies.

   (D) class goals.

35. A student whose scores on a standardized test of reading comprehension are in the 97th percentile is, with respect to reading comprehension

   (A) far above average.

   (B) slightly above average.

   (C) average.

   (D) far below average.

36. Which of the following would be most suitable for use in differentiating reading instruction?

   (A) rubrics

   (B) choral reading

   (C) running records

   (D) test of SAE proficiency

37. Ms. Riker administers a brief test of oral fluency each week and finds that students' scores tend to vary widely from week to week. Which of the following seems like the most plausible explanation for the variability in student scores?

   (A) The students are playing a trick on the teacher.

   (B) The test has very poor reliability.

   (C) The test has good reliability but poor validity.

   (D) The teacher does not know how to score the tests.

38. Mr. Samuels notices that one of his students, John, rubs his eyes a lot while reading. What should Mr. Samuels do?

   (A) ask John to stop rubbing his eyes

   (B) encourage John to get more sleep at night

   (C) try to find out whether John has a vision problem

   (D) remind John to keep his fingers away from his eyes

39. Which of the following is NOT essential to good penmanship?

   (A) posture

   (B) pencil position

   (C) paper position

   (D) type of paper

40. Which of the following teachers is engaging in active listening during a story retell by one of her students?

    (A) When the student pauses for more than a moment, the teacher asks "What's next?"

    (B) At the outset, the teacher reminds the student to cover the key points.

    (C) At several points, the teacher briefly paraphrases what the student just said.

    (D) As the student finishes, the teacher praises the retell.

41. Which of the following instructional approaches would best support the development of listening skills?

    (A) a multifaceted approach in which speaking, writing, and listening are integrated across various activities

    (B) a modular approach in which listening and speaking activities are implemented separately from writing

    (C) a graded approach in which listening activities are followed by speaking activities and then by writing

    (D) a student-specific approach in which speaking, writing, and listening are integrated for some but not all students

42. Which of the following can be a primary source?

    (A) a textbook

    (B) a letter

    (C) a movie review

    (D) a critical summary

43. Which of the following is most similar in meaning to the word "genre"?

    (A) theme of a story

    (B) setting of a story

    (C) response to story

    (D) type of story

44. Which of the following appears to violate the principles of fair use of copyrighted materials?

    (A) posting a photo from a website on the classroom wall

    (B) photocopying a textbook and selling it to students' parents

    (C) integrating several pages from a book into a slide show for students

    (D) asking students to write down their favorite passage from a play

45. Which of the following is not an example of a Web tool?

    (A) CD-ROM

    (B) wiki

    (C) message forum

    (D) blog

Social Sciences

46. Which of the following is best suited for summarizing historical cause–effect relationships?

    (A) photograph

    (B) drawing

    (C) timeline

    (D) spreadsheet

47. In order to illustrate relationships between math concepts and economics, Mr. Owen has decided to offer his class a savings program with the help of local banks. Once a week, students will make deposits into their savings accounts. Periodically, they will calculate interest at different rates and make notes on

how much the class is saving as a group. Mr. Owen's approach in this project is evidence that he understands the importance of

(A) focusing on Bloom's Revised Taxonomy at the level of remembering

(B) implementing elements of cooperative learning

(C) focusing on Bloom's Revised Taxonomy at the level of understanding

(D) integrating curriculum concepts across disciplines that support learning.

48. Which of the following lists reflects the correct chronological order of events?

    I.   Puritans arrive in New England

    II.   Protestant Reformation begins

    III.   Columbus sails across the Atlantic

    IV. Magna Carta is signed in England

(A) IV, III, II, I

(B) IV, III, I, II

(C) III, IV, II, I

(D) III, II, I, IV

49. The intellectual movement that encouraged the use of reason and science and anticipated human progress was called the

(A) American system.

(B) Mercantilism.

(C) Enlightenment.

(D) Age of Belief.

50. In American government, a system of checks and balances was developed to

(A) regulate the amount of control each branch of government has.

(B) make each branch of government independent from one another.

(C) give the president control over political decisions.

(D) give the Supreme Court control over political decisions.

51. Which of the following groups did not play a role in the settlement of the English colonies in America?

(A) Roman Catholics

(B) Puritans

(C) Mormons

(D) Quakers

52. Which of the following prohibited discrimination on the basis of race, color, or national origin?

(A) *Brown vs. Board of Education of Topeka* (1954)

(B) The Civil Rights Act (1964)

(C) *Serrano vs. Priest* (1971)

(D) Title IX of the Education Amendments (1972)

53. The Bill of Rights

(A) listed the grievances of the colonists against the British.

(B) forbade the federal government from encroaching on the rights of citizens.

(C) gave all white males the right to vote.

(D) specified the rights of slaves.

54. A teacher writes on the board, "All men are created equal," and asks each student to explain the meaning of the statement. The teacher's instructional aim is to

(A) determine whether students can reach consensus on the statement's meaning.

(B) ascertain how well students can defend their beliefs.

(C) provoke the students to disagree with the statement.

(D) engage the students in critical thinking as they express their opinions.

55. Studying various economic institutions promotes higher-order thinking skills. In Bloom's Revised Taxonomy, these skills are

(A) remembering and analyzing.

(B) evaluating and creating.

(C) understanding and application.

(D) creating and understanding.

56. Which of the following is considered the main economic institution in the United States?

(A) Food and Drug Administration

(B) Environmental Protection Agency

(C) National Education Association

(D) The Federal Reserve System

57. In what type of economy do individuals own the resources that are produced?

(A) mixed economy

(B) socialist economy

(C) command economy

(D) capitalist economy

58. Influenced by laissez-faire thinking, the theory of economic capitalism was developed by the father of economics, who is

(A) Adam Smith (1723–1790)

(B) John Kenneth Galbraith (1908–2006)

(C) Milton Friedman (1912–2006)

(D) Ludwig Erhard (1897–1977)

59. The ruling of the Supreme Court in *Brown v. Board of Education of Topeka* (1954) was that

(A) separate educational facilities could

offer equal educational opportunities to students.

(B) students could be placed in segregated tracks within desegregated schools.

(C) segregated schools resulted in unequal opportunities but caused no psychological effects.

(D) separate educational facilities were inherently unequal.

60. President Lyndon B. Johnson's "War on Poverty" resulted in the creation of all of the following EXCEPT the

(A) Peace Corps.

(B) Head Start program.

(C) VISTA program.

(D) Elementary and Secondary Education Act.

61. The Education for All Handicapped Children Act of 1975 mandated that schools provide free and appropriate education for all the following EXCEPT

(A) mentally handicapped children.

(B) physically handicapped children.

(C) socially-emotionally handicapped children.

(D) learning-disabled children.

62. Ms. Bailey is starting a unit on the history of the local community. She wants to encourage her fifth-graders to develop independent projects as part of their study. Which type of project would encourage the highest level of thinking among the students?

(A) giving students a list of questions about people, dates, and events and then having them put the answers on a poster, with appropriate pictures, to display in class

(B) giving students questions to pose older members of the community and then having them write articles based on the interviews and publish them in a booklet

(C) discussing the influence of the past on the present community and then asking students to project what the community might be like in 100 years

(D) using archived newspapers to collect data and then having students create a timeline that includes the major events of the community from its beginnings to the current date

63. Mr. Roberts's sixth-grade social studies class has surveyed student use of various types of video games. They designed a questionnaire and then administered it to all fourth-, fifth-, and sixth-grade students on campus. The students plan to analyze their data and develop a presentation to show at the next parent–teacher meeting. Which types of computer software would be helpful for this class project?

    I. Word processing

    II. Database

    III. Simulation

    IV. Graphing and charting

(A) I, II, III, and IV

(B) I, II, and IV

(C) I and III

(D) III and IV

64. The written history of Florida begins with the arrival of which explorer?

(A) Juan Ponce de León

(B) Hernando de Soto

(C) Pedro Menéndez de Avilés

(D) Tristán de Luna y Arellano

65. The Federal Emergency Relief Act, the Banking Act, and the Civilian Conservation Corps are associated with which of the following?

(A) World War II

(B) The Marshall Plan

(C) The Truman Doctrine

(D) The First New Deal

Questions 66 and 67 refer to the following scenario:

The social studies teachers of an inner-city school wanted to increase the relevance of their curriculum and to include units on economics throughout the world rather than just regions throughout the U.S. Ms. Dunn was asked to submit a proposal for the new curriculum, including related activities, sequencing, themes, and materials. In consultation with the other teachers in the department, a needs assessment was planned.

66. The teachers believed that the needs assessment would

(A) help the students make a connection between their current skills and new ones.

(B) reveal community problems that may affect the students' lives and their performance in school.

(C) promote a sense of responsibility for one's own learning among the students.

(D) engage students in learning activities and help them to develop the motivation to achieve.

67. The needs assessment revealed that student interests and parental expectations varied, that student exceptionalities were common, and that academic motivation was low. Which of the following would be most helpful in confronting these challenges?

(A) change the textbook and other reading materials

(B) relate the lessons to the students' personal interests

(C) create a positive environment to minimize the effects of negative external factors

(D) help students to learn and to monitor their own performance

68. What might Ms. Walker, a sixth-grade teacher of world history, do to challenge gifted students?

(A) ask them to write an extra report on the history of the Greeks

(B) allow them to tutor unmotivated students

(C) encourage them to plan learning activities of their own

(D) invite them to create a tightly organized and well-designed unit

69. Ms. Carter, a second-grade social studies teacher at a rural school, is often approached by parents about a program initiated by the school librarian who is active in the wildlife refuge program in the county. The librarian brings hurt or orphaned animals to the library to care for them during the day. Several parents are concerned about issues of hygiene as well as students with allergies. As a member of the site-based decision-making (SBDM) committee, Ms. Carter's best course of action is to

(A) tell the librarian to remove the animals at once.

(B) submit an agenda item to the principal to discuss the concerns at the next meeting.

(C) call the health department for a surprise inspection.

(D) praise the librarian for introducing students to the issues of wildlife preservation.

70. Which of the following would be the most effective way to evaluate students' efforts,

progress, and achievements with respect to an authentic activity?

(A) standardized tests

(B) teacher-made tests

(C) observations

(D) portfolios

71. Which of the following is the most effective way to evaluate mastery of specific objectives and content?

(A) self- and peer evaluations

(B) portfolios

(C) teacher-made tests

(D) observations

72. Which of the following assessments yields results that are reported in terms of percentiles, stanines, and scaled scores?

(A) portfolios

(B) teacher-made tests

(C) observations

(D) standardized tests

Questions 73 and 74 refer to the following scenario:

Students in Mrs. Ruiz's social studies class will be reading about an American they admire. Ms. Ruiz requests that the students use the library to find a magazine article about the person they have chosen and to work in pairs.

73. In assigning students to pairs, Ms. Ruiz attempts to match students whose learning preferences and characteristics are compatible. In choosing this approach, Ms. Ruiz

(A) encourages students to work with their friends.

(B) uses background information about students as a basis for differentiation.

(C) randomly assigns students to pairs in hopes they work together effectively.

(D) risks having incompatible students working together in pairs.

74. Before the class goes to the library, Ms. Ruiz asks the students to predict how they will find the information they will need for the assignment. By doing this, Ms. Ruiz is

(A) engaging the students in hypothetical thinking and inductive reasoning.

(B) saving time so that the students will be able to go straight to work once they get to the library.

(C) helping her students acquire good self-management skills.

(D) assisting the librarian by covering important information in class.

75. When a member of the House of Representatives helps a citizen from his or her district receive federal aid to which that citizen is entitled, the representative's action is referred to as

(A) casework.

(B) pork barrel legislation.

(C) lobbying.

(D) logrolling.

Questions 76–80 are based on the following scenario:

Ms. Doe has begun a two-week unit on Native Americans. To introduce the unit, she showed her fifth-grade class a movie on Native Americans in the twenty-first century. She encouraged students to ask questions about the movie and listened to what they had to say reflectively. The following day, Ms. Doe reviewed the use of encyclopedias, indexes, and atlases. She divided the students into groups and took them to the library, where each group was responsible for locating information on one topic. Topics included the topography of the land, the climate and wildlife, migration routes, and settlement areas.

76. Student engagement in the project can be attributed to which of the following?

(A) the teacher is using Direct Teaching Instruction.

(B) available resources and materials

(C) planning on the teacher's part

(D) effective use of cooperative learning strategy

77. Ms. Doe asked each group to prepare a presentation that included a written explanation of the assigned topic, a shadow box, and a sawdust map or models of Native American clothing. A pictograph was to be used in the telling of a legend or folktale. The presentation was concluded with a collage depicting the Native American way of life. Multiple strategies and techniques were used for

I. motivation of the group and its effects on individual behavior and learning.

II. allowing each student regardless of ability to participate in the project.

III. integrating the project with other subjects.

IV. developing a foundation for teaching American history.

(A) I, II, and III

(B) I and II

(C) III only

(D) IV only

78. After considerable planning and discussion with other teachers, Ms. Doe arranged a display of Native American artifacts and crafts

in the hallway, as well as a presentation for a general assembly, which included performances of Native American poetry, song, and dance, as well as instruction in games that had been played by Native American children. The planning of the assembly and its activities required

    I.   risk-taking by both the teacher and the students.

    II. stimulating the curiosity of the student body.

    III. recognizing individual talents among the students.

    IV. using the collaborative process of working with other teachers.

(A)   I only

(B)   II only

(C)   II and III

(D)   II, III, and IV

79. Ms. Doe also took her students on a field trip to a local museum of their choosing. The field trip

    I.   allowed the students to make connections between their current skills and those that were new to them.

    II. allowed external factors to create a learning environment that would take advantage of positive factors.

    III. allowed a sense of community to be nurtured among the students.

    IV. allowed the students to take responsibility for their own learning.

(A)   I and II

(B)   III only

(C)   IV only

(D)   III and IV

80. The choice of field trip locations was intended

    I.   to enhance the students' self-concept.

    II. to respect differences and enhance the students' understanding of society.

    III. to foster the view of learning as a purposeful pursuit.

    IV. as an example of using an array of instructional strategies.

(A)   II only

(B)   I and IV

(C)   II and III

(D)   III only

81. When developing a unit about the Erie Canal for elementary students, which of the following would be the best approach to informing students about assessment?

(A)   Explain to the students that since the unit covers many topics, many assessment tools will be used.

(B)   Explain each project in the unit to the students and then describe what they will be asked to do.

(C)   Give students a list of new vocabulary words that they will need to know for the final test.

(D)   Explain to the students that they will need to hand in their notebooks at the end of the unit.

82. Marxist philosophy includes all of the following EXCEPT

(A)   the assumption that economic factors determine history

(B)   the belief that class struggle occasionally occurs

(C)   the expectation that socialism is inevitable

(D) the theory that the true value of a product is labor

83. The industrial economy of the nineteenth century was based on all of the following EXCEPT

(A) the availability of raw materials.

(B) an equitable distribution of profits among those involved in production.

(C) the availability of capital.

(D) a distribution system to market finished products.

84. "Jim Crow" laws

(A) effectively prohibited blacks from voting in state and local elections.

(B) restricted American Indians to U.S. government reservations.

(C) restricted open-range ranching in the Great Plains.

(D) established segregated facilities for blacks and whites.

85. Which of the following is used to effect the release of a person from improper imprisonment?

(A) a writ of mandamus

(B) a writ of habeas corpus

(C) the requirement of search warrants

(D) the guarantee against self-incrimination

86. Which of the following best summarizes the Monroe Doctrine?

(A) The United States will not be subject to future colonization.

(B) The United States is a politically independent entity.

(C) The United States has the right to protect its political borders.

(D) The United States will accept

immigration on a limited basis.

87. Leaving a country because of its oppressive, legally-mandated racial segregation policies would be an example of exodus due to

(A) physical reasons.

(B) economic reasons.

(C) cultural reasons.

(D) political reasons.

88. Which of the following is not one of the main types of map projections?

(A) conic

(B) cylindrical

(C) interrupted

(D) meridial

89. The study of geography covers which of the following?

(A) the study of the U.S. Constitution

(B) the study of the age of exploration

(C) the study of knowledge of time, continuity, and change

(D) the spatial features and layout of the world

90. Which of the following is not a requirement to become a U.S. president?

(A) natural-born U.S. citizenship

(B) resident of the U.S. for at least 14 years

(C) member of major political party

(D) at least 35 years of age

Music, Art, Health, Physical Education

91. Mrs. Beck teaches elementary school music. She has found a song about helping others in which the range for the verses is about an octave and a half and the range for the chorus is six notes. Which of the following is the best approach for using this song with a combined first- and fifth-grade class?

    (A) All students will sing the verses and the chorus together.

    (B) Fifth-grade students will sing the verses and first-grade students will join in on the chorus.

    (C) First-grade students will sing the verses and fifth-grade students will join in on the chorus.

    (D) The range is not appropriate for first-grade or fifth-grade students.

92. Ms. Burke is trying to get her students to develop the correct "sound" when they sing. Which of the following similes would best achieve her goal?

    (A) Sing like a butterfly floating through the sky.

    (B) Sing like a soldier marching in a parade.

    (C) Sing like a bumblebee that is taking nectar back to the hive.

    (D) Sing like a lion who is proud and strong.

93. Mr. Keys told his students their tone sounded like a swarm of bees. Mr. Keys was referring to the students'

    (A) range.

    (B) timbre.

    (C) pitch.

    (D) volume.

94. Ms. Johnson's principal just told her that there is enough money in the budget for her to purchase some new harmonic instruments for her music program. Which of the following would be an appropriate choice?

    (A) tambourines

    (B) simple flutes

    (C) trumpets

    (D) autoharps

95. Which of the following is true of the music written below?

    (A) The music is written using shape notes.

    (B) The music is written in standard notation.

    (C) The music is written in simple music notation.

    (D) The music is written using harmonic music notation.

96. A school district is building a new K-5 elementary school that will serve approximately 500 students. What should the architects include in terms of art workspace?

    I.   6 art classrooms, 1 for every grade

    II. at least 55 square feet of workspace per student

    III. space that can be arranged in individual, small group, and large group configurations

    IV. natural as well as artificial lighting

    (A) I, II, III, and IV

(B) I, II, and III

(C) II, III, and IV

(D) I, III, and IV

97. Which of the following terms is related to musical dynamics?

(A) piano

(B) harmony

(C) timbre

(D) texture

98. Ms. Thomson plays the first few bars of the national anthem for her kindergarten class. What would be the best thing for her to say to help evoke an emotional response from the students?

(A) Do you like loud music or soft music?

(B) Raise your hand if you have heard this song before.

(C) What does this song make you think of?

(D) Is this a fast song or a slow song?

99. Which of the following is a true statement about colors?

    I. The primary colors are red, yellow, and blue.

    II. The secondary colors are green, orange, violet.

    III. The tertiary colors are black, white, and gray.

(A) I, II, and III

(B) I and II

(C) II and III

(D) I and III

100. Which of the following is an element of music?

(A) shape

(B) hue

(C) movement

(D) timbre

101. Mrs. Mitchell asked four of her students to each describe one element of music. Which student provided an incorrect answer?

(A) Luke defined timbre as tone.

(B) Lola said that dynamics are related to the volume of music.

(C) Amanda said rhythm involves different lengths of sounds.

(D) Jose said melody is the vertical aspect of notes.

102. Which of the following is an example of harmony?

(A) a chord

(B) a melody

(C) soft music

(D) loud music

103. Which of the following is a twentieth-century composer and an example of his music?

(A) Gershwin, *Rhapsody in Blue*

(B) Mozart, *The Magic Flute*

(C) Beethoven, *Moonlight Sonata*

(D) Handel, *The Messiah*

104. An art teacher is having her students experiment with different art styles. One student, who is using oils to paint flowers with light colors, thick layers of paint, and prominent brushstrokes asks, "Can you guess what style this is?" The answer is

(A) pop art.

(B) impressionism.

(C) fauvism.

(D) realism.

105. Which of the following art styles is arranged in order from earliest to latest, historically speaking?

    (A) Mesopotamian; Gothic; Baroque; Impressionist

    (B) Gothic; Mesopotamian; Baroque; Impressionist

    (C) Baroque; Impressionist; Gothic; Mesopotamian

    (D) Impressionist; Gothic; Mesopotamian; Baroque

106. Which of the following men was a twentieth-century American architect whose buildings (the Robie House and Fallingwater) were based on a philosophy of "organic architecture"?

    (A) Salvador Dali

    (B) Phillip Johnson

    (C) Jackson Pollock

    (D) Frank Lloyd Wright

107. What question would help Mr. Light's fifth-grade students develop analytical skills to evaluate musical performance?

    (A) Who likes Lady Gaga?

    (B) What musical instrument would you like to play?

    (C) Have you ever heard a violin?

    (D) What instrument(s) carried the melody in this song?

108. Which of the following questions would best help Ms. McNeill's fourth-grade students develop analytical skills to evaluate works of art?

    (A) What does Gothic architecture look like?

    (B) Which do you like more—painting or drawing?

    (C) Which artist best used shape and line to

show movement?

    (D) Did you think this was an effective use of timbre?

109. Mr. Sluder wants to incorporate music education into his third-grade class lessons. Which of the following activities would not support the goals of music education?

    (A) encouraging students to select an orchestral instrument to learn to play

    (B) asking students to write a poem to reflect their feelings about a piece of music

    (C) teaching students the basic elements of music

    (D) playing music from a variety of cultures and letting the class discuss how they are different

110. Mrs. Berry wants to meet the goals of art education in her fifth-grade class. Which of the following activities does not support the goals of art education?

    (A) going on a field trip to a local art museum to view a mixed-media exhibit

    (B) providing a variety of art tools and materials for students to use

    (C) assigning each student a different artist and asking for a two-page paper describing the artist's life

    (D) playing a game in which students view artworks and choose those with the best balance, line, or hue

111. Ms. Castille wants to encourage her students' analytical abilities in art. All of the following questions would meet that purpose EXCEPT:

    (A) Why do you think the artist created this sculpture?

    (B) Do you remember who painted *The Scream*?

(C) After looking at this painting, to what culture do you think it belongs?

(D) What aspects of art were used to create movement in this work?

112. Mrs. Kaye's music education lessons for her fourth-grade students will focus on skills development. What activity would help her achieve that goal?

(A) Students learn to sing *Three Blind Mice* as a round.

(B) Mrs. Kaye invites musicians to come to the class and play their instruments.

(C) Mrs. Kaye takes the students on a field trip to hear a high school band concert.

(D) Students take a test on music vocabulary.

113. Which of the following health problems is not related to lack of physical activity?

(A) Type 1 diabetes

(B) coronary artery disease

(C) hypertension

(D) osteoporosis

114. The U.S. Department of Agriculture's new food group symbol helps consumers think about food options by building a healthy plate. What should be true of a healthy plate of food?

(A) It should have about $1/3$ fruits and vegetables, about $1/3$ grains, and about $1/3$ proteins.

(B) It should have a variety of fresh vegetables.

(C) Whole milk should be chosen because it has more vitamins than skim milk.

(D) Whole grains should be avoided because they are difficult to digest.

115. Mr. Bridge's students have created posters about vitamins; however, the information on one poster is factually wrong. Which poster is it?

(A) Joe's poster: Vitamins are inorganic substances made by plants or animals.

(B) Janise's poster: Vitamins are either fat soluble or water soluble.

(C) Renee's poster: Your body stores fat-soluble vitamins, but not water-soluble vitamins.

(D) Gina's poster: Too much of the fat-soluble vitamins can be dangerous.

116. A student completed a paper on fats in the diet; however, the information in one of his paragraphs is incorrect. Which sentence is wrong?

(1) Some cholesterol is essential to the brain functions and to the production of certain hormones (2) Too much saturated fat causes the body to produce too much of the low-density lipoprotein (LDL) cholesterol. (3) Too much LDL cholesterol encourages the buildup of plaque in the arteries. (4) Thus, saturated vegetable fats are preferable to unsaturated fats found in meats or milk products.

(A) Sentence 1

(B) Sentence 2

(C) Sentence 3

(D) Sentence 4

117. Which teacher is encouraging students to be more aware of common health problems and associated risk behaviors?

(A) Mr. Zimmerman asks his students to make a list of their favorite foods, use grocery ads to research prices, and determine which grocery store has the best prices.

(B) Mrs. Leo provides her students with menus from various restaurants.

Students "place their orders" and then check published nutritional information to determine the calories and fat content of the meal.

(C) Ms. Clay's students are planning a multicultural dinner. They are researching authentic recipes, ingredients, and nutritional information for each dish.

(D) Mr. Gullet's students take a tour of the school cafeteria to see how meals are prepared.

118. Which of the following is true of weight and weight control?

(A) A person's weight is the best indicator of whether or not they are overweight or underweight.

(B) To lose weight, calories consumed must exceed calories burned.

(C) Quick weight loss is better because quick results help maintain motivation.

(D) Aerobic exercise is essential to successful weight loss because it increases metabolism and burns calories.

119. Which of the following is true of the human body?

(A) There are over 300 bones in the human body.

(B) Organs are groups of similar cells working together to perform a specific job.

(C) Connective tissues that hold bones together are called tendons.

(D) Muscle contractions are controlled by the nervous system.

120. Which of the following is true of the circulatory system?

(A) The carotid artery is the main artery in the heart.

(B) The top chambers of the heart are the

ventricles and the bottom chambers are the atria.

(C) In the aortas, the blood gives oxygen to tissues and absorbs a waste product containing carbon dioxide.

(D) Blood is oxygenated in the pulmonary artery.

121. At what age can children begin to dress themselves using zippers, buttons, and possibly tying shoes?

(A) 18 months

(B) Age 2-3

(C) Age 4-5

(D) Age 6-7

122. Mrs. Penny's students are learning to be independent and to control their environment. According to Erikson's theory of psychosocial development, her students are likely to be in

(A) preschool.

(B) elementary school.

(C) middle school.

(D) high school.

123. Mr. Novak overheard three of his middle school male students talking about going to the home of a fourth student to drink beer after school. According to Florida state law, what should Mr. Novak do?

(A) Talk privately to the boys about alcohol use and abuse.

(B) Contact the local police.

(C) Report what he heard to the proper school authorities.

(D) Contact the parents of each boy.

124. Which of the following statements is TRUE?

(A) Academic language is learned more quickly than social language.

(B) Social language is more abstract than academic language.

(C) Second-language learners need about five years to develop social language.

(D) Academic language has less context than social language.

125. Ms. Jackson finds that her students' negative beliefs about themselves are affecting their FCAT scores. What can Ms. Jackson do to help students "reprogram" their beliefs about themselves and what they tell themselves?

   I. Teach them to silently repeat sentences such as "I have worked hard to succeed and I will succeed."

   II. Teach them to imagine taking the FCAT test calmly and with confidence as the result of their preparation.

   III. Suggest that they get a good night's sleep and eat a healthy breakfast before the exam.

   IV. Provide peer tutors to give them extra practice on the test content.

   (A) I and II

   (B) II and III

   (C) III and IV

   (D) I, II, III, and IV

126. Which of the following scholars developed a theory of moral development with three levels: Preconventional Morality, Conventional Morality, and Postconventional Morality?

   (A) Piaget

   (B) Kohlberg

   (C) Erikson

   (D) Maslow

127. Which of the following is an example of a psychotic disorder?

   (A) autism

   (B) depression

   (C) schizophrenia

   (D) neuroses

128. Which student exhibits a risk factor for substance use or abuse?

   I. Phil is often in trouble for bullying other children.

   II. No matter what Suzette's teacher tries, Suzette seems distant and uninvolved with other students in the class.

   III. Belinda is dyslexic.

   IV. Paulina is very popular and enjoys karate.

   (A) I, II, and III

   (B) II, III, and IV

   (C) I, II, and IV

   (D) I, II, III, and IV

129. Mrs. Eckerd is aware of risk factors for school violence or other antisocial behavior; however, one of her students has exhibited a "trigger" that is making her pay closer attention. Which student is it?

   (A) Carlos, a student who gave a speech in which he talked about injuring his stepfather

   (B) Dave, a student whose grades are below average but whose attendance is acceptable

   (C) Rasheed, a student who just moved to the United States and speaks very little English

   (D) Marcia, a student whose parents just divorced and share custody of Marcia and her sister

130. West Elementary School is exploring what it can do to curb school violence and antisocial behaviors. What factors should be examined?

    I.   school design and use of space

    II. disciplinary procedures

    III. multicultural activities and views

    IV. parental and family perceptions of the school

    (A) I, II, III, and IV

    (B) I, II, and III

    (C) I, II, and IV

    (D) II, III, and IV

131. Twin Palms Elementary School has started a new "weekend backpack" program. Students who get free breakfast and lunch can get a backpack filled with nonperishable foods for the weekend. In terms of Maslow's hierarchy, this practice meets

    (A) the need for belonging.

    (B) the need for esteem.

    (C) physiological needs.

    (D) the need for self-actualization.

132. Mr. Pinkner is teaching his students how to be "good sports" when they lose a game. What domain does this lesson involve?

    (A) psychomotor

    (B) cognitive

    (C) affective

    (D) physiological

133. Ms. Jones has created a small service-learning project for her third-grade students. The students will be cutting hearts out of paper, decorating them, composing a four-line poem for each one, and then sending them to a local nursing home for Valentine's Day. This activity represents which domain or domains?

    I.   psychomotor

    II. cognitive

    III. affective

    (A) I, II, and III

    (B) I and II

    (C) II and III

    (D) I and III

134. It is the beginning of the school year and Ms. Robinson wants to focus on healthy eating as a theme for the entire year. Ms. Robinson wants to decorate her classroom to encourage her students to choose healthy options in eating. What could she do to achieve that goal?

    I.   Create a bulletin board consisting of pictures that illustrate the Healthy Plate logo.

    II. Have students draw pictures of what should be on a healthy plate and post them on a bulletin board.

    III. Hang commercial posters that show tips for healthy food options and leave them in place all year as reminders.

    (A) I, II, and III

    (B) I and II

    (C) II and III

    (D) I and III

135. Mr. Hebert is teaching his students about soccer. He has students use the Internet to locate information about soccer, identify the rules, and then fill in a world map showing the ten countries in which soccer is most popular. The focus of this project is on which domain?

    (A) psychomotor

    (B) cognitive

    (C) affective

    (D) self-actualization

Science

136. A student wants to create a science project to demonstrate chemical changes in matter. Which of the following might be part of the project's display?

    I. Pictures of a new nail and a rusty nail

    II. Pictures showing water and ice cubes made of water

    III. A picture of salt in a salt shaker

    IV. A picture of a fireplace log that is partially burned

    (A) I and II

    (B) II and III

    (C) III and IV

    (D) I and IV

137. Mr. Isaac wrote the following equation on the board: $CH_4 + 2\ O_2 \longrightarrow CO_2 + 2\ H_2O$. What is true of the equation?

    I. CH_4 is a reactant.

    II. $2\ O_2$ is a reactant.

    III. CO_2 is a reactant.

    IV. $2\ H_2O$ is a reactant.

    (A) I and II

    (B) II and III

    (C) III and IV

    (D) II and IV

138. Which of the following is true of matter?

    (A) Matter always has density.

    (B) Matter is always buoyant.

    (C) Matter can change physically but not chemically.

    (D) Matter only consists of one type of atom.

139. Ms. Post is teaching a lesson on force at a distance. Which of the following can she use as an example?

    (A) a lever

    (B) a screw

    (C) a magnet

    (D) a pulley

140. Which simple machine is correctly matched with its key concept?

    (A) wedge, bar and pivot

    (B) ramp, inclined plane

    (C) lever, wheel and rope

    (D) wheel and axle, inclined plane wrapped around a cylinder

141. A student made a display about magnets; however, one of the pictures on her poster is incorrect. Which picture is not an example of a magnet?

    (A) lodestone

    (B) compass

    (C) the planet Earth

    (D) the element iron

142. A principal is walking by Mr. Longman's classroom and hears him say, "Today we are going to be learning about the energy of moving molecules." What is the topic of Mr. Longman's lesson?

    (A) simple machines

    (B) heat

    (C) magnets

    (D) electrostatic force

143. What is true of energy?

    I. Energy is the ability of matter to move other matter or to produce a chemical change in other matter.

    II. Energy can be defined as the ability to do work.

    III. All energy is potential or kinetic.

    IV. Energy can be created or destroyed.

  (A) I, II, III, and IV

  (B) I, II, and III

  (C) I, II, and IV

  (D) II, III, and IV

144. Mrs. Bentley is demonstrating static electricity by rubbing two balloons together. What should Mrs. Bentley say in her explanation of the demonstration?

  (A) When I rub the balloons together, electrons move from one to the other.

  (B) Note how rubbing forms a simple machine that creates static electricity.

  (C) These balloons can be referred to as insulators.

  (D) Rubbing the balloons together releases atoms into the air.

145. Caitlyn is a fifth-grade student. She is writing a report about sound and has written the following paragraph; however, one sentence in the paragraph is factually incorrect. Which sentence is it?

Vibration, like when you play a guitar or trumpet, is what causes sound. Sound travels about 1,100 feet per second, but sound travels faster in cold weather. Sounds have highness or lowness, which is called pitch. Sound can be loud or soft, which is the intensity of the sound. Sound quality is how much an object vibrates.

  (A) Vibration, like when you play a guitar or trumpet, is what causes sound.

  (B) Sound travels about 1,100 feet per second, but sound travels faster in cold weather.

  (C) Sounds have highness or lowness, which is called pitch.

  (D) Sound quality is how much an object vibrates.

146. Mr. Berger has created an inquiry-based lesson using different convex and concave lenses. What should he expect students to discover about lenses?

    I. Lenses either curve in or curve out.

    II. Lenses either make what is seen through them look larger or smaller.

    III. Some lenses are thicker than others.

    IV. Thick lenses break light into colors but thin lenses do not.

  (A) I, II, and III

  (B) II, III, and IV

  (C) I, II, and IV

  (D) I, III, and IV

147. Mrs. Williford has created an inquiry-based lesson using different prisms. What should she expect students to discover about prisms?

    I. A prism breaks light into colors.

    II. If natural sun light passes through a prism, the resulting colors are in the sequence of red, orange, yellow, green, blue, indigo, and violet; however, if artificial light (e.g., from a light bulb) passes through a prism, the resulting colors are in the order blue, indigo, violet, green, orange, red, and yellow.

III. Two prisms in sequence result in white light.

(A) I, II, and III

(B) I and II

(C) II and III

(D) I and III

148. What is true of wavelengths?

(A) Most wavelengths are visible.

(B) The sun is the source of infrared light.

(C) Some wavelengths have medical uses.

(D) Some wavelengths, such as microwaves, are simple machines.

149. Which diagram correctly shows the three layers that compose the Earth?

(A)

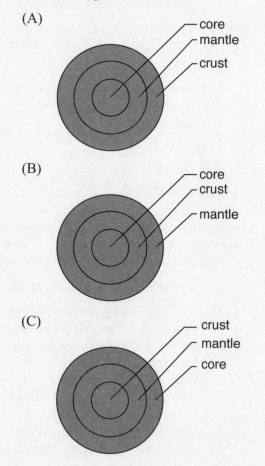

(B)

(C)

(D)

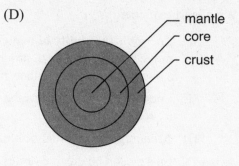

150. All of the following are examples of fossils EXCEPT

(A) an insect in a piece of amber found in South America.

(B) an arrowhead found in North America.

(C) a dinosaur bone found in Europe

(D) a leaf imprint in coal found in China.

151. Students are reviewing information about geologic maps. One student says, "I am thinking of imaginary lines on a map that run north to south. What am I thinking of?" The correct answer is

(A) poles.

(B) meridians.

(C) parallels.

(D) latitude.

152. Which of the following is TRUE of rocks?

I. Igneous rocks form from melted rock.

II. Erosion is the breaking down of rock into small pieces.

III. Sedimentary rocks can result from weathering.

IV. Under intense pressure, igneous or sedimentary rocks can turn into metamorphic rock.

(A) I, II, III, and IV

(B) I, II, and III

(C) I, III, and IV

(D) II, III, and IV

153. Ms. Jackson is having her fourth-grade students do a project on weather. First, she had them look up different kinds of clouds. Then, she had them observe the clouds at 8 a.m., 10 a.m., noon, and 2 p.m. each day, describe the weather at those times, and predict what weather will occur next. She is checking their observations on different dates and sees one that is clearly incorrect. Which one is it?

(A) September 3, 10 a.m.: I see light-colored stratus clouds in a blue sky. I predict that the weather will stay the same.

(B) September 8, noon: I see thin, wispy cirrus clouds. I predict a change in the weather.

(C) September 12, 2 p.m.: I see dark, flat stratus clouds. I predict sunshine for the rest of the day.

(D) September 14, 10 a.m.: I see white fluffy cumulus clouds. I predict good weather.

154. Which of the following would be the correct labels for the water cycle?

(A) A = evaporation, B = condensation, C = precipitation, D = collection

(B) A = condensation, B = evaporation, C = collection, D = precipitation

(C) A = collection, B = condensation, C = precipitation, D = evaporation

(D) A = precipitation, B = collection, C = evaporation, D = condensation

155. Which of the following is TRUE of the ways in which land and water interact?

(A) Percolation occurs most often in the water of a reservoir.

(B) Sink-holes can be natural or the result of human activities.

(C) Leaching occurs when water runs off the land too quickly to deposit sediment.

(D) The three main organic components of soil are sand, silt, and clay.

156. The correct order of planets from the sun is

(A) Mercury, Venus, Earth, Mars, Jupiter, Saturn, Uranus, Neptune

(B) Mars, Mercury, Earth, Venus, Jupiter, Saturn, Neptune, Uranus

(C) Mars, Venus, Mercury, Earth, Jupiter, Saturn, Neptune, Uranus

(D) Mars, Jupiter, Earth, Mercury, Saturn, Neptune, Venus, Uranus

157. What was the most immediate result of launching of the Soviet space satellite *Sputnik* on October 4, 1957?

(A) Congress established the Department of Defense in 1958 to focus on space exploration.

(B) The U.S. was afraid it was lagging behind in technology and took steps to change.

(C) The U.S. and Soviets worked collaboratively to win the space race.

(D) The U.S. had a manned lunar landing the following year.

158. Which of the following is true of the Earth's moon?

    I. It is the only moon in the solar system.

    II. It is a satellite of Earth.

    III. The moon's light comes from reflected light from the sun.

    IV. A lunar eclipse occurs when Earth blocks sunlight from reaching the moon.

(A) I, II, III, and IV

(B) I, II, and IIII

(C) II, III, and IV

(D) I, III, and IV

159. Which of the following statements is TRUE of the seasons in the Northern Hemisphere?

(A) The seasons change according to the distance of the Earth from the sun.

(B) The tilt and revolution of the sun cause the seasons.

(C) Days and nights are approximately equal in length on the vernal and autumnal equinoxes.

(D) A seasonal solstice occurs approximately every three months.

160. What is true of activities that differentiate living from nonliving things?

(A) The activities of living organisms include food getting, respiration, excretion, growth, and so on.

(B) To be classified as a living organism, life activities must occur on a daily basis.

(C) Cells, the smallest components in a living organism, are not in themselves considered as living things.

(D) Microbiology is the study of living things.

Use the following diagram to answer Question 161.

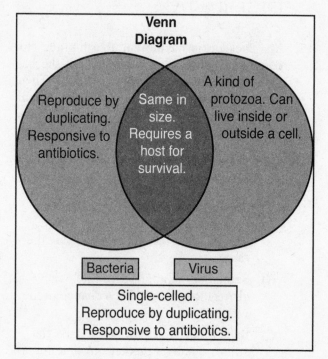

161. A student has created a Venn diagram, as shown above to compare and contrast bacteria and viruses. What, if anything, is incorrect?

(A) There are no factual mistakes in the diagram.

(B) The information about bacteria is correct; however, the information about viruses and the information about how viruses and bacteria are alike is incorrect.

(C) The information about bacteria and the information about viruses are correct; however, the information about how viruses and bacteria are alike is incorrect.

(D) The information about how viruses and bacteria are alike is correct; however, the information about bacteria and the information about viruses is incorrect.

162. What aspect of a plant cell distinguishes it most from animal cells?

    (A) nuclear membrane and endoplastic reticulum

    (B) chromosomes and mitochondria

    (C) nucleus and nucleosis

    (D) chloroplasts and cell walls

163. In plant cells, what allows the energy in sunlight to be converted to chemical energy and become biologically available?

    (A) phagocytosis

    (B) photosynthesis

    (C) fermentation

    (D) osmosis

164. The capacity to feel pain can be attributed to which part of the nervous system?

    (A) striated muscles

    (B) autonomic responses

    (C) exteroceptors

    (D) antibody molecules

165. Asexual animal propagation is most likely to occur in

    (A) fish.

    (B) reptiles.

    (C) fungi.

    (D) bacteria.

166. Mrs. Smith included the following short-answer question on an exam: *Describe the nitrogen cycle.* Which student response is correct?

    (A) To make food, green plants take in nitrogen from the air. The waste product that plants give off in the process is also nitrogen. When animals breathe in nitrogen to digest their food, they give off nitrogen as a waste product.

    (B) Nitrogen-fixing bacteria live in the soil and in the roots of legumes (e.g., beans, peas, and clover). Bacteria change the nitrogen in the air (that plants cannot use) into nitrogen materials that plants can use. After animals eat plants, they give off waste materials that contain nitrogen.

    (C) As the Earth cooled, water vapor, carbon dioxide, and nitrogen became components of the air. When the water vapor condensed, carbon dioxide and nitrogen remained. The plants reduced the amount of carbon dioxide in the air and increased the amount of oxygen in the air.

    (D) Nitrogen is essential for plant life. The plant needs nitrogen to make food, among other uses. A plant usually takes in more nitrogen than it needs. To get rid of excess nitrogen, the stomata of the leaves allow the nitrogen to pass out as water vapor. This evaporation of nitrogen from the plant is transpiration.

167. Precipitation that contains high levels of sulfuric or nitric acid is called

    (A) acid rain.

    (B) leaching.

    (C) pollution.

    (D) a temperature inversion.

168. Which definition and term is correctly matched?

    I. Biology is the study of the relationship between living things and their environment.

    II. A community is a group of populations that interact with one another.

    III. An ecosystem is a group of populations that shares a common pool of resources and a common physical or geographical area.

IV. A niche can be defined as a group of similar organisms.

(A) I and II

(B) II and III

(C) I and IV

(D) III and IV

169. A student has prepared two posters showing renewable and nonrenewable resources.

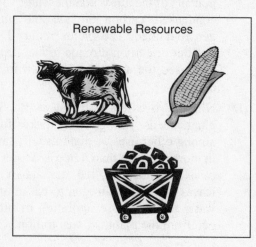

Renewable Resources

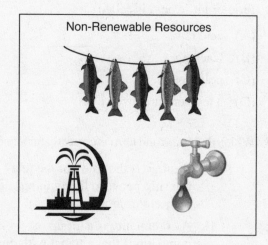

Non-Renewable Resources

What mistakes are in the posters?

I. Coal is not a renewable resource.

II. Water is a renewable resource.

III. Fish is a renewable resource

IV. Corn is not a renewable resource.

(A) I, II, and III

(B) II, III, and IV

(C) I, III, and IV

(D) II, III, and IV

170. Mrs. Brandt is teaching her fourth-grade students how to collect data. Which of the following classroom activities would be the best option for achieving that goal?

(A) Students will read a chapter in their science books about the scientific method.

(B) Mrs. Brandt will invite a science professor from a college to come talk to the class.

(C) Mrs. Brandt will put a weather-tracking chart on the wall for students to use every 2 hours for a week to record temperature.

(D) Students will watch a video showing how NASA scientists collect data on Skylab.

171. Mr. Bennett has created seven stations in his third-grade classroom and students are divided into pairs. At each station, Mr. Bennett has a different kind geologic material (e.g., a piece of granite, a piece of coal) as well as a scale and ruler. Each pair of students has a science notebook and pencil. Mr. Bennett tells the students that they will have 2 minutes at each station to learn as much as they can about the materials and take notes. What aspect of the scientific method is Mr. Bennett addressing?

(A) observations

(B) analysis of data

(C) creating a hypothesis

(D) testing a hypothesis

172. Mrs. Langley has created five stations in her classroom; each station contains the follow-

ing: Station 1, microscope; Station 2, thermometer; Station 3, scale; Station 4, ruler; station 5, barometer. She has divided students into groups. Each group has three different leaves. Students are instructed to find out as much as they can about their leaves at each station and record their findings. What aspect of the scientific method is Mrs. Langley most likely to be addressing?

(A) identify relevant variables

(B) identify necessary equipment and apparatus for measuring and recording the variables

(C) eliminate or suppress any other factors that could influence measured variables

(D) decide on a means of analyzing the data obtained

173. Ms. McCall has divided her third-grade students into groups of three. Each group gets three same-size balls that have differing weights. Students are to identify a testable question involving these materials. Which group has achieved this goal?

(A) Do smaller balls fall more quickly than larger ones?

(B) Do heavier balls move faster than lighter balls?

(C) What size ball rolls most easily across a floor?

(D) Is there a relationship between ball weight and size?

174. Ms. Lee is teaching her fifth-grade students how to use a microscope. Which of the following microscope activities would not be appropriate in meeting this goal?

(A) examining cotton fibers

(B) having students examine a leaf

(C) having students examine a strand of hair

(D) having students prick their fingers and examine a drop of blood

175. A student is weighing samples on a gram scale. The scale has an accuracy of 5 percent. If a sample weighs 100 grams, what is true of the actual value?

(A) It is still 100 grams.

(B) It could be 5 grams.

(C) The weight could be between 95 and 105 grams.

(D) The weight could be less than 95 or more than 105.

176. Mrs. Arton wants her students to learn to think scientifically. Which of the following is most likely to result in the deepest scientific understanding?

(A) Providing drills and practice preparation for the FCAT science exam

(B) Teaching students to design and do simple experiments

(C) Obtaining classroom subscriptions to science periodicals

(D) Asking student to locate examples of real-world science in newspapers

177. Ms. Martin uses a software program for saving and organizing grades. She is most likely to be using what kind of software?

(A) database

(B) word processing

(C) spreadsheet

(D) desktop publishing

178. Mr. Gholson is planning a lesson on geologic formation in oceans. What kind of software would be best for him to use?

(A) simulation

(B) digital atlas

(C) online database

(D) drill and practice

179. What are the components of a telecommunications system?

   (A) transmitter, channel, receiver

   (B) point-to-point, point-to-multipoint, broadcast

   (C) radio, television, telephone

   (D) computers, computer networks, and data communications

180. In terms of copyright, which term and definition are correctly matched?

   (A) Fair use doctrine: allows limited reproduction of copyrighted works for educational and research purposes

   (B) Brevity: use of software for less than 10 minutes

   (C) Spontaneity: the need for a teacher to use a work for a class within 24 hours of the time it was located

   (D) Cumulative effect: prevents citation of a source more than three times in a given document

Mathematics

181. $\sqrt{10,000} =$

   (A) 10

   (B) 100

   (C) 500

   (D) 1000

182. $(3^2)^3$

   (A) $\sqrt[3]{3}$

   (B) 3^5

   (C) 3^6

   (D) 3^7

183. $\frac{2}{3} \times \frac{3}{4} =$

   (A) $\frac{1}{4}$

   (B) $\frac{1}{3}$

   (C) $\frac{1}{2}$

   (D) $\frac{5}{2}$

184. Convert the decimal .875 to a fraction.

   (A) $\frac{2}{3}$

   (B) $\frac{7}{8}$

   (C) $\frac{4}{5}$

   (D) $\frac{8}{9}$

185. Convert the decimal .233 to a percentage.

   (A) 2.33%

   (B) 23.30%

   (C) 23.33%

   (D) 233.30%

186. Mr. Gleason is answering a question in math class. His answer is, "You do so by dividing the numerator by denominator." What was the question?

   (A) How do you change a fraction into a decimal?

   (B) How do you change a decimal into a fraction?

   (C) How do you change a fraction into a percentage?

   (D) How do you change a decimal into a percentage?

187. Mrs. Fortner told her class that the distance from the Earth to the sun is approximately 1.4959826×10^8 km. This number is equal to which of the following?

    (A) 14,959,826,000 km

    (B) 149,598,260,000,000,000 km

    (C) 14,959,826,000,000,000 km

    (D) 149,598,260 km

188. $8.94 \times 3.2 =$

    (A) 2.79375

    (B) 12.14

    (C) 28.608

    (D) 5.74

189. The numbers 3, 7, 11, and 13 are

    I.   integers.

    II. prime numbers.

    III. multiples.

    (A) I, II, and III

    (B) I and II

    (C) II and III

    (D) I and III

190. Students in fifth grade will buy a protractor and a compass for math class. Together they cost $7.59 (ignoring tax). The cost of the compass is $3.99 more than the protractor. Which of the following equations can be used to determine the cost of the protractor?

    (A) $x = \$7.59 - \$3.99$

    (B) $\$7.59 = x - \$3.99$

    (C) $\$7.59 = x + (x + \$3.99)$

    (D) $x = \$7.59 - \$3.99$

191. Mr. Thompson is grading papers. He sees that Elsa incorrectly solved the following four problems:

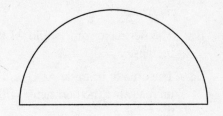

$$
\begin{array}{cccc}
18 & 95 & 73 & 22 \\
+23 & +18 & +27 & +99 \\
\hline
311 & 1013 & 910 & 1111 \\
\end{array}
$$

If Elsa continues to make the same mistake, what will be her answer to the problem $14 + 29$?

    (A) 313

    (B) 43

    (C) 53

    (D) 40

192. Assume that the following figure is half of a circle with a radius of 5. What is the area of the figure?

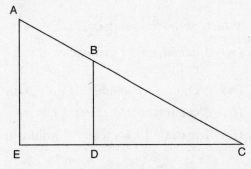

    (A) 78.5

    (B) 39.25

    (C) 157

    (D) 125

Use the following figure to answer Questions 193–195.

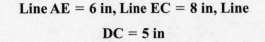

Line AE = 6 in, Line EC = 8 in, Line DC = 5 in

193. What is the length of segment *ED*?

    (A) 10
    (B) 3
    (C) 4
    (D) 6

194. What is the area of triangle *ACE*?

    (A) 19 square inches
    (B) 22 square inches
    (C) 24 square inches
    (D) 29 square inches

195. If line *AE* and line *ED* are increased by an inch, what will be TRUE?

    I.   The area of triangle AEC will increase

    II. The perimeter of triangle AEC will increase

    III. The area of triangle AEC will increase but the perimeter will be the same.

    IV. The perimeter of triangle AEC will increase but the area will be the same.

    (A) I and II
    (B) I and III
    (C) I and IV
    (D) II and III

196. Which of the following is TRUE?

    (A) 1 decimeter > 1 centimeter > 1 millimeter
    (B) 1 gram > 1 kilogram > 1 milligram
    (C) 1 centiliter > 1 deciliter > 1 liter
    (D) 1 meter > 1 kilometer > 1 millimeter

197. What could be used in converting gallons from customary units to metric units?

    (A) Kilogram
    (B) Kelvin
    (C) Centimeter
    (D) Liter

198. Which metric prefix and meaning are correctly matched?

    (A) deca -10^{-3}
    (B) centi -10^{3}
    (C) deci -10^{-2}
    (D) hecto -10^{2}

199. A truck container is 10 feet high, 10 feet wide, and 25 feet long. What is the volume of the container?

    (A) 2500 ft^2
    (B) 25000 ft
    (C) 2500 ft^3
    (D) 25000 ft^3

Use the following figure to answer Questions 200–202. $\overline{CD}$ is parallel to $\overline{EG}$

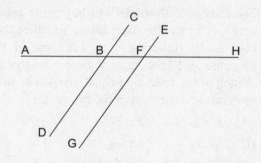

200. What angle is supplementary to ∠ABC?

    (A) ∠ GFH
    (B) ∠ EFH
    (C) ∠ DBF
    (D) ∠ DBC

201. ∠BFE and ∠EFH are what type of angle?

    (A) adjacent
    (B) complementary
    (C) congruent
    (D) vertical

202. Which of the following is TRUE of the figure?

    I. Line DC is a transversal.
    II. DBA and /ABC are consecutive angles.
    III. EFH is an exterior angle
    IV. Line DC intersects line GE

    (A) I and II
    (B) II and III
    (C) III and IV
    (D) I and IV

Use the following figure to answer Questions 203–204.

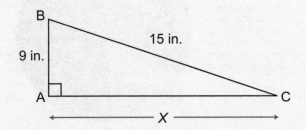

203. What is the length of side X?

    (A) 12 in
    (B) 13 in
    (C) 14 in
    (D) 15 in

204. If ∠ACB = 28°, what is the size of ∠CBA?

    (A) 92°
    (B) 72°
    (C) 52°
    (D) 62°

205. Which of the following figures depicts a tessellation?

    (A)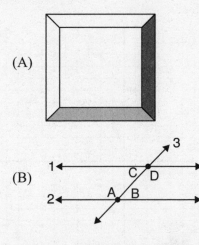

    (B)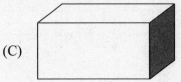

    (C)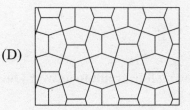

    (D)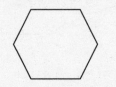

206. Given that the following hexagon is a regular polygon, what can be inferred?

    I. The sides are congruent.
    II. The figure is equiangular.
    III. The figure is symmetrical.

    (A) I, II, and III
    (B) I and II

(C)   I and III

(D)   II and III

207. In the following figure, which ordered pair is on the line?

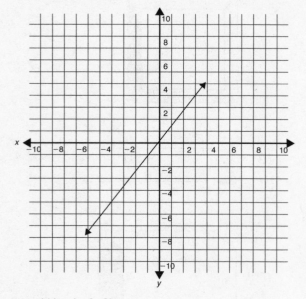

(A)   (−2, 2)

(B)   (−1, −1)

(C)   (1, 3)

(D)   (−1, 4)

Use the following line graph to answer Questions 208–209.

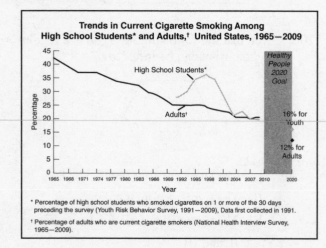

208. According to the graph, when was smoking for youths highest?

(A)   between 2004 and 2007

(B)   between 1995 and 1998

(C)   between 1989 and 1992

(D)   between 1998 and 2001

209. Between 1965 and 2009, the number of adults who are smokers has

(A)   decreased by about 20%.

(B)   decreased by 10%-15%.

(C)   increased by over 20%.

(D)   increased by 10%-15%.

Use the following graph to answer Questions 210–211.

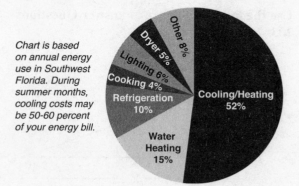

Chart is based on annual energy use in Southwest Florida. During summer months, cooling costs may be 50-60 percent of your energy bill.

210. If the portion of an individual's bill spent on water heating is $7.50, what is the cost of the total bill?

(A) $125

(B) $95

(C) $70

(D) $50

211. A homeowner's bill is $292. How much of that amount goes to dryer use?

(A) $14.60

(B) $18.55

(C) $22.30

(D) $24.60

Use the following bar graph to answer Questions 212–213.

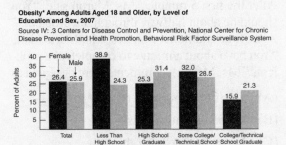

Obesity* Among Adults Aged 18 and Older, by Level of Education and Sex, 2007

Source IV: .3 Centers for Disease Control and Prevention, National Center for Chronic Disease Prevention and Health Promotion, Behavioral Risk Factor Surveillance System

*Defined as having a Body Mass Index (BMI) of 30.0 or more. Results are based on survey responses from 9 counties representing 89.1 percent of the Border population.

212. According to the graph, who is most likely to be obese?

(A) a male high school graduate

(B) a female who graduated from college

(C) a female who did not graduate from high school

(D) a male who completed technical school

213. At what level are obesity levels for males and females most similar?

(A) less than high school

(B) high school graduate

(C) some college or technical school

(D) college or technical school graduate

214. Ms. Essex gave a math test to 13 students who made the following scores: 100, 95, 95, 95, 95, 80, 75, 70, 65, 60, 55, 55, 45. Which of the following is TRUE of the test scores?

I. The mode is 95.

II. The median is 75.

III. The mean is 70.

IV. The range is 55.

(A) I, II, and III

(B) I, II, and IV

(C) II, III, and IV

(D) I, III, and IV

215. Mr. Sullivan has 23 students in his class; 12 are girls and 11 are boys. He is going to draw a name for a chance to eat lunch with the principal on Friday. What is the probability that the name he draws will be a girl?

(A) 12/23

(B) 11/12

(C) 11/23

(D) 23/12

Use the following stem and leaf plot to answer Questions 216–217.

Stem	Leaf
4	1 2 3
5	5 6
7	1 2 2 3

216. If the data in the stem and leaf plot represent the speed of a car, how many values are in the data set?

(A) 3

(B) 5

(C) 7

(D) 9

217. What is the mode in this set of data?

(A) 2

(B) 55

(C) 72

(D) 222

218. A spinner has 5 equal sectors colored yellow, blue, green, white, and red. After spinning the spinner, what is the probability of landing on blue?

    (A) 1 out of 2
    (B) 1 out of 3
    (C) 1 out of 5
    (D) 4 out of 5

219. A number from 3 to 13 is chosen at random. What is the probability of choosing an odd number?

    (A) 6 out of 11
    (B) 3 out of 11
    (C) 1 out of 13
    (D) 5 out of 11

220. A spinner has 5 equal sectors colored yellow, blue, blue, white and red. After spinning the spinner, what is the probability of landing on the color blue?

    (A) 2 out of 5
    (B) 4 out of 5
    (C) 3 out of 5
    (D) 1 out of 5

221. Given the following data set (12, 22, 38, 14, 24, 15, 39, 24, 16), which of the following stem-and-leaf plots correctly summarizes the data?

    (A)

1	2 4 5 6
2	2 4 4
3	8 9

    (B)

12	5 6 8
14	7 7
15	8 9

    (C)

1	1 2 3 4
2	2 2
3	8 0

    (D)

3	2 4 5 6
2	2 4 4
1	8 9

222. Ms. Martin is teaching math. She has given students 10 minutes to work four math problems. After the first 5 minutes, Ms. Martin said, "You should be about halfway through the problems." After four additional minutes, Ms. Martin said, "You have about a minute to complete the problems." Ms. Martin's comments were designed to

    (A) clarify the purpose of the task.
    (B) keep students on task.
    (C) foster higher-level thinking.
    (D) clarify teacher expectations.

223. Mr. Corzine wants his students to complete a math project consisting of a three-page paper, a poster, and a manipulative. What can Mr. Corzine do to clarify his expectations?

    (A) ask higher-order questions
    (B) divide students into cooperative groups
    (C) suggest additional sources
    (D) provide an assessment rubric

224. Which of the following assessments is summative?

    (A) an unannounced quiz that does not count toward GPA
    (B) an informal midterm progress report
    (C) the FCAT math test administered in standard fashion
    (D) an online drill and practice program that tracks student progress

225. Which request would foster thinking at the highest level of Bloom's Revised Taxonomy?

(A) Identify the formula you used to solve the third problem.

(B) Choose the three best examples of tesselation on this sheet.

(C) Solve the odd-numbered problems on page 22.

(D) Note which geometric figures are regular and which are irregular.

COMPETENCIES AND SKILLS

Language Arts and Reading	Question Number
1. Knowledge of the Reading Process	1, 2, 3, 4, 5, 6, 7, 8, 9, 10, 21
2. Knowledge of Literature and Literary Analysis	17, 18, 26, 27, 28, 29, 32, 37, 43
3. Knowledge of Writing Process and Applications	11, 12, 13, 14, 15, 22, 23, 24, 25, 36, 45
4. Knowledge of Reading Methods and Assessment	16, 19, 20, 30, 31, 33, 34, 38, 44,
5. Knowledge of Communication	39, 41
6. Knowledge of Information and Media Literacy	35, 40, 42
Social Science	
7. Knowledge of Time, Continuity, and Change (i.e., history)	48, 49, 51, 53, 60, 65, 82, 84, 90
8. Knowledge of People, Places, and Environment (i.e., geography)	52, 76, 77, 86, 87, 88, 89
9. Knowledge of Government and the Citizen (i.e., government and civics)	50, 59, 61, 75, 85
10. Knowledge of Production, Distribution, and Consumption (i.e., economics)	47, 55, 56, 57, 58, 83
11. Knowledge of Instruction and Assessment of the Social Sciences	46, 54, 62, 63, 64, 66, 67, 68, 69, 70, 71, 72, 73, 74, 78, 79, 80, 81
Music, Visual Arts, Physical Education, and Health	
12. Knowledge of Skills and Techniques in Music and Visual Arts	91. 92, 93, 94, 95, 96
13. Knowledge of Creation and Communication in Music and Visual Arts	97, 98, 99, 100, 101, 102
14. Knowledge of Cultural and Historical Connections in Music and Visual Arts	103, 104, 105, 106
15. Knowledge of Aesthetic and Critical Analysis of Music and Visual Arts	107, 108
16. Knowledge of Appropriate Assessment Strategies in Music and Visual Arts	109, 110, 111, 112
17. Knowledge of Personal Health and Wellness	113, 114, 115, 116, 117, 118

COMPETENCIES AND SKILLS *(continued)*	
18. Knowledge of Physical, Social, and Emotional Growth and Development	119, 120, 121, 122, 123, 124, 125, 126, 127
19. Knowledge of Community Health and Safety Issues	128, 129, 130, 131
20. Knowledge of Subject Content and Appropriate Curriculum Design	132, 133, 134, 135
Science and Technology	
21. Knowledge of the Nature of Matter	136, 137, 138
22. Knowledge of Forces, Motion, and Energy	139, 140, 141, 142, 143, 144, 145, 146, 147, 148
23. Knowledge of Earth and Space	149, 150, 151, 152, 153, 154, 155, 156, 157, 158, 159
24. Knowledge of Life Science	160, 161, 162, 163, 164, 165, 166, 167, 168, 169
25. Knowledge of the Nature and History of Science	170, 171, 172, 173, 174
26. Knowledge of the Relationship of Science and Technology	175, 176
27. Knowledge of Technology Processes and Application	177, 178, 179, 180
Mathematics	
28. Knowledge of Numbers and Operations	181, 182, 183, 184, 185, 186, 187, 188, 189, 190, 191
29. Knowledge of Geometry and Measurement	192, 193, 194, 195, 196, 197, 198, 199, 200, 201, 202, 203, 204, 205, 206, 207
30. Knowledge of Algebraic Thinking	208, 209, 210, 211, 212, 213
31. Knowledge of Data Analysis and Probability	214, 215, 216, 217, 218, 219, 220, 221
32. Knowledge of Instruction and Assessment	222, 223, 224, 225

Answer Key

Question	Answer	Competency	Question	Answer	Competency	Question	Answer	Competency
1	A	1	28	D	2	55	B	10
2	B	1	29	B	2	56	D	10
3	D	1	30	B	4	57	D	10
4	A	1	31	C	4	58	A	10
5	C	1	32	A	2	59	D	9
6	D	1	33	D	4	60	A	7
7	C	1	34	B	4	61	C	9
8	A	1	35	A	6	62	C	11
9	D	1	36	C	6	63	B	11
10	D	1	37	B	3	64	A	11
11	B	3	38	C	4	65	D	7
12	B	3	39	D	5	66	A	11
13	B	3	40	C	6	67	C	11
14	C	2	41	A	5	68	C	11
15	D	3	42	B	6	69	B	11
16	A	4	43	D	2	70	D	11
17	A	2	44	B	4	71	C	11
18	C	2	45	A	3	72	D	11
19	C	4	46	C	11	73	B	11
20	B	4	47	D	10	74	A	11
21	B	1	48	A	7	75	A	9
22	A	3	49	C	7	76	D	8
23	D	3	50	A	9	77	A	8
24	B	3	51	C	7	78	D	11
25	C	3	52	B	8	79	A	11
26	D	2	53	B	7	80	B	11
27	A	2	54	D	11	81	B	11

Answer Key (continued)

Question	Answer	Competency	Question	Answer	Competency	Question	Answer	Competency
82	B	7	109	A	16	136	D	21
83	B	9	110	C	16	137	A	21
84	D	7	111	B	16	138	A	22
85	B	9	112	A	17	139	C	22
86	A	8	113	B	17	140	B	22
87	D	8	114	B	17	141	D	22
88	D	8	115	A	17	142	B	22
89	D	8	116	D	17	143	B	22
90	C	7	117	B	17	144	A	22
91	B	12	118	D	17	145	B	22
92	A	12	119	D	18	146	A	22
93	B	12	120	D	18	147	D	22
94	D	12	121	C	18	148	C	22
95	B	12	122	A	18	149	A	23
96	C	12	123	C	18	150	B	23
97	A	13	124	D	18	151	B	23
98	C	13	125	A	18	152	C	23
99	B	13	126	B	19	153	C	23
100	D	13	127	C	19	154	A	23
101	C	13	128	A	19	155	B	23
102	A	13	129	A	19	156	A	23
103	A	14	130	B	20	157	B	23
104	B	14	131	C	20	158	C	23
105	A	14	132	C	20	159	C	23
106	D	14	133	A	20	160	A	24
107	D	15	134	B	20	161	B	24
108	C	15	135	B	21	162	D	24

Answer Key (continued)

Question	Answer	Competency	Question	Answer	Competency	Question	Answer	Competency
163	B	24	184	B	28	205	D	29
164	C	24	185	B	28	206	A	29
165	D	24	186	A	28	207	B	29
166	B	24	187	D	28	208	B	30
167	A	24	188	C	28	209	A	30
168	B	24	189	B	28	210	D	30
169	A	24	190	C	28	211	A	30
170	C	25	191	A	28	212	C	30
171	A	25	192	B	29	213	C	30
172	B	25	193	B	29	214	B	31
173	B	25	194	C	29	215	A	31
174	D	25	195	A	29	216	D	31
175	C	26	196	A	29	217	C	31
176	B	26	197	D	29	218	C	31
177	C	27	198	D	29	219	A	31
178	B	27	199	C	29	220	A	31
179	A	27	200	B	29	221	A	31
180	A	27	201	A	29	222	B	32
181	B	28	202	B	29	223	D	32
182	C	28	203	A	29	224	C	32
183	C	28	204	D	29	225	B	32

Answer Explanations

Language Arts

1. (A)

Phonemic awareness allows readers to connect sounds to letter patterns. As a result, phonemic awareness supports the ability to decode words during reading, and to spell words correctly. Thus, Option A is the correct answer.

2. (B)

Option B is correct because manipulation of letters can help students develop phonemic awareness. For children of this age, opportunities to learn through hands-on activities are a good way to engage student interest and promote learning.

3. (D)

Structural analysis is the division of words into parts during reading. An example of structural analysis is given in Option D, where decoding of the word is supported by recognition that it is a root word ("guard") combined with a past-tense suffix ("ed").

4. (A)

Emergent literacy includes the awareness that print consists of words that convey meaning, and thus Option A is correct. Options B, C, and D consist of more advanced knowledge and skills.

5. (C)

Effective instruction includes making connections to the background of the students by activating prior knowledge, and thus the strategy described in Option C is preferable. The other options would be more appropriate with more advanced readers.

6. (D)

Running records constitute direct, periodic assessments of individual students' fluency, and thus Option D is correct. Although the assessments described in Options A through C could be adapted to measure oral fluency, running records are designed to directly evaluate this skill.

7. (C)

"Prosody" refers to the rhythm, stress patterns, and intonations of speech. Thus, Option C is the correct answer.

8. (A)

Of the options given, the best approach would be to model the strategy first, and thus Option A is correct. Option B would be helpful after the strategy has been modeled, while the other options might be helpful depending on whether or not students possess the relevant abilities.

9. (D)

Option D is correct, because the many exceptions to phonics rules that early readers encounter can be confusing when attempting to apply phonics rules. In contrast, the other options describe phenomena that are not particularly challenging for phonics instruction.

10. (D)

Through structural analysis, unfamiliar words can be divided into familiar syllables and other units in order to facilitate decoding.

11. (B)

Surveying the passage before reading it, brainstorming some questions that the passage might answer, and then reading the actual passage are the first parts of the SQ3R strategy. Since asking the teacher for a brief summary is not part of this strategy, Option B is the correct answer.

12. (B)

The noun "excuses" requires the plural form of the verb "make," and thus Option B is correct. None of the other options uses the correct form of "make."

13. (B)

The "neither-nor" construction is singular and thus the associated verb must be singular. The verb must also be a third-person verb. Option B is the only one which satisfies both criteria by means of an appropriate verb.

14. (C)

Identification of theme is achieved at the interpretive level of comprehension since the integration of various details is required. Option C is thus the correct answer.

15. (D)

Since most of the graphics are likely to clarify, summarize, organize, or extend information in the text, the teacher should help students understand them. Thus, Option D is correct. The other options are counterproductive, in that they minimize the importance of graphics.

16. (A)

The teacher is asking students to *apply* the concepts they have learned to a new context. Doing so requires the use of application skills, and thus Option A is the correct answer.

17. (A)

Option A is correct because students would be exercising their synthesis skills by integrating the different descriptions of the main character. Options B and D would exercise lower-level skills, while Option C would exercise the highest level of thinking.

18. (C)

The text appears to discuss the causes of the war and then their effects in the emergence of the war, and thus Option C is the correct answer. An ordered list, a comparison, or a problem and solution organization would not be ideally suited for describing contributors to the war and their effects.

19. (C)

Criterion-referenced tests are used to measure student achievement with respect to pre-established criteria, and thus Option C is the correct answer. The other options are unlikely to rely on pre-established criteria for evaluating achievement.

20. (B)

Option B is correct because scores on norm-referenced tests can be converted to percentile rankings on the basis of normative data. Percentile rankings are not the main focus of the kinds of tests described in the other options.

21. (B)

Options A, C, and D all reflect rudimentary knowledge that can be considered part of emergent literacy. Fluent decoding is not part of emergent literacy but rather mature reading skills, and thus Option B is the correct answer.

22. (A)

Although the student letters may contain some personal narratives, some expository summaries of factual information, and/or some descriptive passages, the fundamental purpose of each letter is to persuade the school board to at least consider the writer's point of view. For this reason, Option A is the correct answer.

23. (D)

Option D is correct because historical fiction includes stories in which the characters are fictional.

The fact that the novel was written recently rules out Option A, while the fact that it is realistic rules out Options B and C.

24. (B)

The sentence consists of two clauses ("You are my friend" and "however, I cannot afford to lend you any money"). A semi-colon, rather than a comma, is required between clauses, because each clause could stand alone as a complete sentence. Thus Option B is the correct answer.

25. (C)

"Onomatopoeia" is the use of words that sound like the thing being described. Thus, Option C is the correct answer.

26. (D)

Option D is correct, because the main events of a story constitute the plot. Character, setting, theme, and narrative twists contribute to the plot of a story, but they do not themselves constitute the plot.

27. (A)

Option A is the correct answer, because similes are figurative descriptions that rely on words such as "like" to make comparisons. In Options B and C, the comparisons are made directly, while in Option D no comparison is made.

28. (D)

Guiding students to think from different perspectives, informing them about other cultures, and encouraging them to celebrate their own uniqueness are all approaches that could be integrated with and support the use of multicultural literature in the classroom. However, using only the works produced in 18th century Europe would limit the student's exposure to many cultures, thus, Option D is correct.

29. (B)

Although Options A, C, and D may be useful in classroom settings, they do not contribute to meaningful responses to literature. Understanding a work of fiction is a necessary condition for responding meaningfully to it, and thus Option B is correct.

30. (B)

The fact that the child is distinguishing between marks for different things indicates that she is beyond the undifferentiated stage, while the fact that the marks do not resemble their referents in specific details suggests that she has not yet reached the pictographic stage. Her use of marks for different things indicates that she is at the differentiated stage, and so Option B is the correct answer.

31. (C)

Only Option C reflects the correct order of stages, which consist of prewriting, drafting, revising, editing, and then publishing.

32. (A)

Options B and D are incorrect because character and plot are not typically considered in expository essays, while Option C is incorrect because persuasion is not the primarily goal of expository writing. Option A is correct because it describes elements that should be considered when planning an expository essay.

33. (D)

Progress monitoring, option D, is used to assess students' academic performance and evaluate the effectiveness of instruction.

34. (B)

A rubric conveys teacher expectations for an assignment and summarizes the criteria by which each element of the assignment will be evaluated, and thus Option B is the correct answer. Lesson content, metacognitive strategies, and class goals may be briefly noted in the rubric, but only as reminders rather than in an informative way.

35. (A)

The 97th percentile would mean that the student scored above approximately 97% of peers who took the same test. Thus, Option A is correct.

36. (C)

Rubrics, choral reading, and tests of SAE (Standard American English) proficiency are not designed to differentiate among students in terms of reading instruction. Option C is the correct answer, because running records would be consistently and directly useful in the process of differentiation.

37. (B)

Although Options A, C, and D may be possible in theory, they are each extremely unlikely. The test appears to have poor reliability, because student answers are not consistent over short periods of time, and thus Option B is correct.

38. (C)

Options A, B, and D reflect strategies that may be useful in some circumstances. However, one of the many causes for students rubbing their eyes is eyestrain, because they either need glasses or a new prescription, and thus Option C is correct.

39. (D)

Good posture, good pencil position, and good paper position are among the essential elements in good penmanship. However, the type of paper has very little to do with penmanship; thus, Option D is the correct answer.

40. (C)

Option C is correct because paraphrasing what a speaker just said is an essential part of active listening. Although Options A, B, and D may be helpful, they do not reflect active listening.

41. (A)

Option A is the correct answer because listening, speaking, and writing are interdependent developments, and thus each skill can benefit from activities that incorporate the others. The other options are not ideal because at least one of these skills is separated from the others.

42. (B)

A letter can be a primary source when it describes an event first-hand, while textbooks, reviews, and summaries are necessarily secondary sources. Thus, Option B is correct.

43. (D)

A genre is a particular type of written work, therefore, option D is correct.

44. (B)

The activities described in Options A, C, and D each involve minimal use of published materials for strictly educational purposes and are thus consistent with fair-use policy. Profiting from photocopies of published materials is likely to be a violation of copyright law, and so Option B is the correct answer.

45. (A)

Wikis, message forums, and bogs are all Internet-based. A CD-ROM is a physical disc rather than a web tool, and thus Option A is correct.

Social Sciences

46. (C)

Although in theory a photograph, drawing, or spreadsheet could be used to illustrate historical cause-effect relationships, a timeline is better suited for doing so. Thus, Option C is correct.

47. (D)

Option D is correct, because option D illustrates the relationship of math and economics. Options A and C do not apply because they are the lowest levels of Bloom's Taxonomy, and this task utilizes the higher levels of thinking, such as analysis, synthesis and evaluation. "B" is not correct because this is not a group project.

48. (A)

The Magna Carta was signed in 1215, Columbus's voyages began in the fifteenth century, the Protestant Reformation occurred in the sixteenth century, and the Puritans came to America in the seventeenth century. Thus Option A is correct.

49. (C)

Option C is the correct answer because the Enlightenment was prominent for its emphasis on reason and science as a basis for action, as well as a belief in the capacity of human progress. Reason, science and anticipation of progress played a role in the other options but were not among their central defining features.

50. (A)

The statements in Options B, C, and D are somewhat inaccurate. Checks and balances allow each branch of government to limit the actions of the other branches, and thus option A is correct.

51. (C)

Roman Catholics, Puritans and Quakers all played a role in English colonization of America. Option C is correct because Joseph Smith founded Mormonism in 1830, well after the period of English colonization.

52. (B)

All of the options address discrimination. However, the Civil Rights Act of 1964 prohibited discrimination on the basis of race, color, or natural origin, and thus the correct answer is Option B.

53. (B)

Options A, C, and D are each factually incorrect. The correct answer is Option B, because the Bill of Rights indicates numerous ways that Congress may not make laws abridging citizens' rights and liberties.

54. (D)

Option D is correct because the teacher hopes to engage the students in critical thinking through expression of opinions and the realization that classmates will have different interpretations of the statement. The other options describe scenarios that the teacher may or may not implement.

55. (B)

Remembering, understanding and applying are the three lowest levels in Bloom's Revised Taxonomy, followed by analyzing, then evaluating and creating. Thus, Option B is correct.

56. (D)

Option D is correct because the Federal Reserve System is the central bank of the United States.

Option A is not correct because it deals with public health issues. B is not correct because it deals with environmental issues. C is not correct because The National Education Association (NEA), which represents public school teachers, is the largest professional organization and largest labor union in the United States.

57. (D)

In capitalist economies, individuals own the resources that are produced, in contrast to mixed, socialist, and command economies. Thus, Option D is correct.

58. (A)

Option A is the correct answer because Adam Smith, referred to as the father of economics, developed a theory of economic capitalism well before the work of the economists listed in the other options.

59. (D)

Options A, B, and C are each inconsistent with the ruling of *Brown v. Board of Education of Topeka*. In this ruling, the Supreme Court stated that "Separate educational facilities are inherently unequal and violate the equal protection clause of the Fourteenth Amendment," and thus Option D is correct.

60. (A)

President Johnson was responsible for the creation of Head Start, VISTA, and the Elementary and Secondary Education Act. However, the Peace Corps was established by President John F. Kennedy, and thus Option A is the correct answer.

61. (C)

The Education for All Handicapped Children Act of 1975 provided for children with mental and physical handicaps, as well as those with learning disabilities. However, it did not provide for socially or emotionally handicapped students, and so Option C is correct.

62. (C)

Option C is correct, because the activity would require students to analyze how prior causes have produced current effects and then to predict what future effects might be based on what they have learned about cause–effect relationships.

63. (B)

Word processing, database, and graphing and charting software would all be useful, and thus Option B is the correct answer. Simulation software would be useful in this context, since the students' main purpose is to collect and analyze data.

64. (A)

Ponce de León led the first known European expedition to Florida in 1513. His arrival represents the beginning of the written record of Florida, and thus Option A is correct.

65. (D)

Option D is the correct answer because the Federal Emergency Relief Act, the Banking Act of 1933, and the Civilian Conservation Corps represent achievements of President Franklin Delano Roosevelt's First New Deal.

66. (A)

A needs assessment could in theory provide information of relevance to Options B, C, and D. However, the needs assessment would more directly help students make the connection between their current skills and those that will be new to them, and so Option A is the best choice.

67. (C)

Options A, B, and D could conceivably have a slight impact on these challenges. However, Option C is the best approach because a positive environment must be created to minimize the effects of negative external factors.

68. (C)

Giving gifted students the opportunity to guide their own learning activities is a good way of challenging them academically, as described in Option C. The other options describe activities that are not intrinsically challenging.

69. (B)

Option B describes a procedure in place at the campus level to deal with this type of issue, as action is clearly needed but the teacher is not authorized to act on her own. The teacher may not be authorized to ask the librarian to remove the animals or to call the health department, and praising the librarian would be counterproductive.

70. (D)

Portfolios are purposeful collections of work that exhibit the efforts, progress, and achievement of students and enable teachers to document teaching in authentic settings. Thus, among the available options, Option D would be the best approach to evaluation of this sort.

71. (C)

Teacher-made tests are designed to evaluate the specific objectives and specific content of a course, and so Option C is correct. The other options would not be ideal for evaluating mastery of course objectives and content, although they are useful in other ways.

72. (D)

Standardized tests rate student performance against the performance of other students and report the scores in terms of percentiles, stanines, scaled scores, and other descriptive statistics. Portfolios, teacher-made tests, and observations do not ordinarily yield this kind of information, and so Option D is the correct answer.

73. (B)

Options A, C, and D only provide descriptive information for the teacher's assignment of students to pairs. Option B is correct because it is the only choice that describes the rationale for the teacher's actions.

74. (A)

Each of the options describes a potential benefit of the prediction activity. However, Option A is the best choice because it reflects the academic purpose of this activity.

75. (A)

The term "casework" is used to describe the activities of members of Congress on behalf of individual constituents, and thus Option A is the best answer. The other options describe actions that are not usually carried out on behalf of specific individuals.

76. (D)

Option D is the correct answer because students are grouped and given a specific task to complete. Option A is not correct because in this scenario students are interacting with each other. Options B and C are not correct because materials and planning are preliminary steps prior to student engagement.

77. (A)

Option A is correct, because multiple strategies were planned for the motivation of the students, and each student was able to participate in some way regardless of ability. Moreover, the unit was integrated into other subjects through library assignments, reading, writing, and so on.

78. (D)

Option D is the correct answer. Working collaboratively with other teachers, the teacher was able to identify the talents of the students, stimulate their curiosity, and plan the assembly, and in the process no risks were taken.

79. (A)

The external factors of the field trip could create positive motivation and allow the students to make connections between old and new skills, but no mention is made of community involvement or of means of giving students responsibility for learning. Thus, Option A is the correct answer.

80. (B)

Option B is the correct answer, because the teacher showed respect for the children by allowing them the option of field trips. and it is one of an array of instructional strategies that she used.

81. (B)

Although Options A, C, and D might be helpful, Option B is the one that would give students the most information about teacher expectations and the criteria for evaluation.

82. (B)

Options A, C, and D each describe a key element of Marxism. However, Marxism also holds that class struggle is ongoing, and so Option B is the correct answer.

83. (B)

The industrial economy of the nineteenth century was based on factors such as availability of raw materials and capital, as well as a distribution system for finished products. However, it was not based on an equitable distribution of profits among all those who were involved in production, and thus Option B is correct.

84. (D)

In the 1880s and 1890s, the U.S. Supreme Court struck down desegregation laws and upheld the doctrine of segregated facilities for blacks and whites. These laws became known as "Jim Crow" laws, and so Option D is the correct choice.

85. (B)

A writ of habeas corpus is a court order that directs an official who is detaining someone to produce the person before the court so that the legality of the detention may be determined. This is part of due process, as guaranteed by the Bill of Rights, and thus Option B is correct.

86. (A)

Option A is correct because the Monroe Doctrine consisted of a statement that Americans would henceforth not be considered as subjects for future colonization by European powers.

87. (D)

Although citizens are likely to experience physical, economic, and cultural consequences of segregation, legally-mandated segregation would be an example of a political reason for leaving a country, and so Option D is the correct answer.

88. (D)

The four main types of map projections are conic, cylindrical, interrupted, and plane. There is no such thing as a meridial projection, and thus Option D is correct.

89. (D)

Geography includes the study of spatial features and layout of the world. A, B and C are not correct because they cover historical concepts.

90. (C)

U.S. presidents must be natural-born citizens, residents of the U.S. for at least 14 years, and at least 35 years of age. Option C is correct, because membership in a political party is not required to be president.

Music, Art, Health & Physical Education

91. (B)

Option B is correct because older students have a greater vocal range than younger students. Older students, but not younger ones, would be capable of singing the verses of the song.

92. (A)

Vocal quality should sound like it is "floating out" and not forced, and thus Option A is the best choice. The other options describe metaphors that might induce children to force their sound when they sing.

93. (B)

Option A is incorrect because range refers to the number of different notes (high-low), Option C is incorrect because pitch refers to whether or not a note is in tune, and Option D is incorrect because pitch refers to loudness. Option B provides an acceptable synonym for tone.

94. (D)

Option A is incorrect because a tambourine is a rhythm instrument, Option B is incorrect because simple flutes are melodic instruments, and Option C is incorrect because trumpets are orchestral instruments. Option D is correct because autoharps are harmonic instruments.

95. (B)

Option B is the correct choice, because the music is written in standard notation rather than in one of the notations described in the other options.

96. (C)

Options A, B, and D are incorrect because they include statement I, which is incorrect because only one art classroom would be needed. Thus, Option C is the correct answer.

97. (A)

Option A is correct because a "piano" note is one that is played quietly. Option B is incorrect because harmony refers to vertical relationships in notes, Option C is incorrect because timbre refers to tone, and Option D is incorrect because texture refers to the context in which simultaneous sounds occur.

98. (C)

Option C is the best answer because it asks students to relate their experiences to music. Options A and D are incorrect because they are asking about elements of music, while Option B requires students to indicate if they have heard a song and thus elicits recall, not feelings.

99. (B)

Option B is correct because statements I and II correctly list the primary and secondary colors, respectively. Options A, C, and D are incorrect because they include statement III, which fails to acknowledge that tertiary colors are those that fall between primary and secondary colors.

100. (D)

Option D is correct because timbre is a quality of tone. Options A, B, and C are incorrect because they are elements of art rather than music.

101. (C)

Options A, B, and D each consist of an accurate statement about music. Option C is correct because the student is mistaken: melody is the horizontal, not the vertical, aspect of notes.

102. (A)

Option A is correct because chords can reflect harmony. Option B is incorrect because melody is the horizontal aspect of music and harmony involves the vertical aspect of music, while Options C and D are incorrect because volume and speed of music have no relationship to harmony.

103. (A)

Option B is correct because Gershwin's *Rhapsody in Blue* is a famous 20th century composition. Option B is incorrect because Mozart was an eighteenth century composer, Option C is incorrect because Beethoven composed in the late 1700s and early 1800s, and Option D is incorrect because Handel was an 18th century composer.

104. (B)

Option A is incorrect because pop art combines consumerism and art, Option C is incorrect because fauvism features harsh colors and flat surfaces, and Option D is incorrect because realism is a more rustic style. Option B is correct because the student appears to be using an impressionist approach.

105. (A)

Mesopotamian art represents the Ancient Era, Gothic art was created in the Middle Ages and followed by the Baroque period, while Impressionism was a later, 19th century development. Thus, Option A is correct.

106. (D)

Option D is the correct answer. Option A is incorrect because Salvador Dali was a twentieth century Spanish artist, Option C is incorrect because Jackson Pollock was a twentieth century American artist, and Option B is incorrect because although Phillip Johnson was a twentieth century American architect, his architecture is considered sleek and modern as opposed to Wright's *organic architecture*.

107. (D)

Option D is correct because the students have to listen to the song and break down what they hear in order to analyze which instrument(s) carry the melody. Options A and B are questions of preference, not analysis, while Option C is a recall question and does not involve analysis.

108. (C)

Option C is correct because the question asks the student to analyze the art element of shape and line in evaluating best depiction of movement. Option A is incorrect because it involved comprehension, Option B incorrect because it involves preference, and Option D is incorrect because it involves evaluation of a musical element.

109. (A)

Option B meets the goal of encouraging responsiveness to music, Option C meets the goal of promoting understanding of music and music structure, and Option D meets the goal of increasing listening awareness.

Option A is correct because choosing an orchestral instrument to play is not a goal of music education at this age.

110. (C)

Option A meets the goal of providing opportunities to examine many art forms, Option B meets the goal of providing opportunities to develop and extend art abilities, and Option D meets the goal of promoting the ability to analyze and enjoy forms based on informed judgments. Option C is correct because writing a research paper is not a goal of art education.

111. (B)

Options A, C, and D each present questions that would promote the use of analysis. Option B is correct because it presents a simple recall question rather than one that exercises analytical skills.

112. (A)

Although Options B, C, and D can be beneficial, they do not focus on skills development. Option A is the correct answer, because learning to sing rounds is an appropriate skill for grades 3-5.

113. (B)

Coronary artery disease, hypertension, and osteoporosis have all been linked to lack of regular physical activity. Type 1 diabetes is not caused by lack of physical activity, and so Option B is correct.

114. (B)

Option B is correct because it summarizes one aspect of a healthy plate. Option A is incorrect because half of the plate should be fruits and vegetables with ¼ of the plate having grains and ¼ of the plate having lean proteins, Option C is incorrect because low-fat or skim milk has as many vitamins as whole milk and contains less fat than whole milk, Option D is incorrect because whole grains are healthier than grains that have been processed.

115. (A)

The statements in Options B, C, and D are all correct, unlike the statement in Option A. Vitamins by definition are required for normal functioning and growth.

116. (D)

Options A, B, and C consist of accurate sentences. Option D presents an incorrect sentence – the sentence should read, *Thus, unsaturated vegetable fats are preferable to saturated fats found in meats or milk products* – and thus this option is the correct answer.

117. (B)

Option B is correct because of the focus on nutritional information. Options A, C, and D consist of activities that do not include attention to nutrition.

118. (D)

Option D is correct because aerobic exercise is essential to weight loss for the reasons given. Option A is incorrect because body-mass index is the best indicator of a healthy weight, Option B is incorrect because to lose weight, calories burned must exceed calories consumed, and Option C is incorrect because slow weight is more permanent.

119. (D)

Option A is incorrect because there are just over 200 bones in the human body, Option B is incorrect because tissues are groups of similar cells working together to perform a specific job, and Option C is incorrect because connective tissues that hold bones together are called ligaments. Option D provides a correct statement about the role of the nervous system in muscular contractions.

120. (D)

Option D is correct because blood is oxygenated in the pulmonary artery. Option A is incorrect because the main artery in the heart is the aorta, Option B is incorrect because the top chambers of the heart are the atriums and the bottom chambers are the ventricles, and Option C is incorrect because blood gives up oxygen and nutrients to tissues and absorbs a metabolic waste product containing carbon dioxide in the pulmonary artery.

121. (C)

Although there will be variability among children in the age at which they begin to dress themselves, most children can perform simple activities such as using zippers and buttons at around ages 4–5. Thus, Option C is correct.

122. (A)

Preschool students have reached Erikson's "initiative vs. guilt" stage, in which they learn to be independent and to exert control over their environment. Thus, Option C is the correct answer.

123. (C)

Option C is the correct answer. Florida state law requires that school personnel report suspicions of use, possession, or sale of any controlled substance, model glue, or alcoholic beverage to the appropriate school authorities.

124. (D)

Option A is incorrect because academic language is learned less quickly than social language, Option B is incorrect because social language is less abstract than academic language, and Option C is incorrect because second language learners need about five to seven years to develop academic language and about two years to learn social language. Option D is the best choice because there tends to be less of a meaningful context for academic language learning.

125. (A)

Option A is correct because statements I and II involve affirmation and visualization. The other options are incorrect because Statement III addresses physiological preparation and Statement IV does not directly provide a means of addressing negative beliefs.

126. (B)

Option B correctly identifies Lawrence Kohlberg as the scholar who described moral development in terms of Preconventional, Conventional, and Postconventional reasoning. Although Piaget, Erikson, and Maslow each discussed moral development, their ideas are less well-known and are not grounded in Kohlberg's levels.

127. (C)

Option C is correct because schizophrenia is considered a psychotic disorder. Autism and depression are not ordinarily psychoses, while neuroses, or neurotic disorders, are by definition different from psychotic disorders.

128. (A)

Option A is the correct answer, because statements I, II, and III indicate risk factors (aggressiveness, failure to bond, disability and academic failure). The student in statement IV is less likely to be at risk, because she has developed social relationships and activities.

129. (A)

Option A is correct owing to the discussion of injuring another person. Although the students described in the other options may have problems that foster drug or alcohol use, they do not exhibit any behaviors that warrant immediate attention.

130. (B)

Statements I, II, and III identify factors that should be examined in an effort to curb violence and antisocial behavior, and thus Option B is correct. The other options are incorrect because they include statement IV, which is not among the main contributing factors to school violence and antisocial behavior.

131. (C)

Food is a physiological need, and thus Option C is the correct answer. The other options describe higher-level needs in Maslow's Hierarchy.

132. (C)

Option C is correct, because being a "good sport" concerns feelings and attitudes. Option A is incorrect because psychomotor skills involve large or small muscle activities, Option B is incorrect because the cognitive domain relates to thinking, and Option D is incorrect because it does not correspond to a domain.

133. (A)

Option A is correct because the project involves all three domains – the affective domain because a service is performed for others, the psychomotor domain because small motor skills are used to cut out the paper hearts, and the cognitive domain because thinking is required to create the poem.

134. (B)

Having a bulletin board and displaying student work can be helpful, as can the use of commercial posters, and thus Option B is the best choice. Keeping the poster in place throughout the year may result in students getting used to them and failing to take note of their content.

135. (B)

Students are completing tasks that involve thinking at various levels, and thus the correct answer is B. The tasks involve very little by way of psychomotor, affective, or self-actualization activities.

Science

136. (D)

Option D is correct because chemical changes such as rusting and burning alter the molecular structure of matter. Statement II shows a physical change because the pictures show water in different forms, while statement III does not show a chemical or a physical change.

137. (A)

Reactants are materials to the left of the arrow, while materials to the right of the arrow are products. Thus Option A is correct.

138. (A)

Option A is correct because matter is anything with mass and volume. Option B is incorrect because matter sinks in liquids or gases if it is denser than the material that surrounds it, Option C is incorrect because matter can change physically or chemically, and Option D is incorrect because matter can contain many types of elements (as in the case of compounds, solutions, or mixtures).

139. (C)

Options A, B, and D are incorrect because they exemplify mechanical force. Option C is correct because magnetic force acts at a distance.

140. (B)

Option B is correct because a ramp consists of an inclined plane. Option A is incorrect because a wedge is a variation of an inclined plane, Option C is incorrect because a lever is a bar and pivot, and Option D is incorrect because a wheel and axle are two circular objects of different sizes.

141. (D)

Although iron attracts magnets, iron is not a magnet, and so Option D is correct. Options A, B, and C are magnets.

142. (B)

Option B is correct because heat consists of the heat of moving molecules. Option A is incorrect because simple machines involve the energy of objects based on position, while Options C and D are incorrect because magnets and electrostatic forces are at-a-distance forces.

143. (B)

Option B is correct because statements I, II, and III are each true. However, statement IV is false because energy can be transformed but it cannot be created or destroyed.

144. (A)

Option A is the best choice because it contains a statement that partially explains static electricity. Option B is incorrect because rubbing balloons together is not an example of a simple machine, Option C is incorrect because insulators hold electronics tightly and would not produce static electricity, and Option D is incorrect because rubbing the balloons together transfers electrons but does not release atoms into the air.

145. (B)

Although sound does travel about 1,100 feet per second, it travels faster in warm, not cold, weather, and thus Option B is the correct answer. The sentences in Options A, C, and D are factually correct.

146. (A)

Option A is the correct answer because statements I, II, and III are true of lenses. Statement IV is not true, because prisms break light into color.

147. (D)

Options A, B, and C are incorrect because statement II is not true. Option D is correct, because the colors are always in the order red, orange, yellow, green, blue, indigo, and violet.

148. (C)

Option C is correct, because X-rays are wavelengths that have medical uses. Option A is incorrect because only about 10% of wavelengths are visible, Option B is incorrect because the sun is the source of ultraviolet rather than infrared light, and Option D is incorrect because simple machines are mechanical but wavelength energy is not.

149. (A)

Option A is the diagram that correctly shows the layers that compose the Earth. The other diagrams consist of incorrect labels for the three layers.

150. (B)

The insect in amber, the dinosaur bone, and the leaf imprint are all fossils. Option B is correct because an arrowhead is not a fossil but rather an artifact made by humans.

151. (B)

Option B is the correct answer. Option A is incorrect because poles are at the top and bottom of the Earth where meridians meet, Option C is incorrect because parallels run east to west, and Option D is incorrect because latitude is measured by parallels.

152. (C)

Statements I, III, and IV are true, and thus Option C is correct. Statement II is incorrect in that it is weathering that breaks down rock into small pieces; erosion is what transports rock or sediment to new areas.

153. (C)

Options A, B, and D contain correct predictions. The student in Option C is incorrect, however, because dark, flat stratus clouds indicate rain.

154. (A)

Option A correctly identifies the labels for the picture. Options B, C, and D name parts of the water cycle but do not link them accurately to their representations in the picture.

155. (B)

Option B is a correct statement about sinkholes. Option A is incorrect because percolation occurs when water passes through an aquifer, Option C is incorrect because leaching occurs when water percolates through an aquifer, and Option D is incorrect because the sand, silt, and clay are mineral-based, not organic materials.

156. (A)

Only Option A lists the planets in the correct order.

157. (B)

Option B is the best answer of the available options. Option A is incorrect because Congress established the National Aeronautics and Space Administration (NASA) in 1958 to coordinate space research and development, Option C is incorrect because the Americans and Soviets competed against each other in the space race, and Option D is incorrect because although the U.S. completed a manned lunar landing, this did not occur until 1969.

158. (C)

Statements II, III and IV are true. Statement I is false because other planets also have moons, and thus Option C is the correct answer.

159. (C)

Option C is correct because it accurately defines the equinoxes. Option A is incorrect because the distance of the earth from the sun has no effect on the seasons, Option B is incorrect because the tilt and revolution of the arth, not the sun, causes the seasons, and Option D is incorrect because the solstices occur only twice a year, every six months.

160. (A)

Option A is the correct answer because it lists some of the critical activities that distinguish living from nonliving things. Option B is incorrect because to be classified as a living organism, life activities must occur at some point in the organism's lifespan, Option C is incorrect because cells, the smallest components in a living organism, are surely considered as living, and Option D is incorrect because biology, not microbiology is the study of living things.

161. (B)

Option B is correct in that the information about characteristics that both viruses and bacteria share is not accurately depicted. Bacteria are larger than viruses and do not require a host for survival and reproduction; moreover, a virus is not a protozoan and it can only live within a cell.

162. (D)

The cell components in Options A, B, and C are found in both plant and animal cells. Option D is correct because chloroplasts and large central vacuoles distinguish plant cells from animal cells.

163. (B)

Option B is the correct answer. Option A is incorrect because phagocytosis occurs when the cell membrane engulfs and stores particles too large to pass through the cell membranes in vacuoles until the particles are digested, Option C is incorrect because fermentation is an energy producing process that occurs in yeast and other cells in the absence of oxygen, and Option D is incorrect because osmosis is diffusion of water across a semi-permeable membrane.

164. (C)

Option C correctly lists exteroceptors as

the type of neurons that register pain. Option A is incorrect because muscles are not part of the nervous system, Option B is incorrect because the autonomic system controls involuntary processes (e.g., heartbeat) in the body, Option D is incorrect because antibody molecules are part of the lymphatic system.

165. (D)

Options A and B are incorrect because asexual animal propagation occurs most often in single-celled animals, while Option C is incorrect because fungi are not animals. Option D is the correct answer, because bacteria reproduce asexually.

166. (B)

Option B provides a correct summary of the nitrogen cycle. The other three options are incorrect because they contain misstatements of fact.

167. (A)

Option A is the correct answer. Option B is incorrect because leaching is the extracting of a substance from a solid by dissolving it in a liquid, Option C is incorrect because pollution refers to any material added to an ecosystem that disrupts its normal functioning, and Option D is incorrect because temperature inversion occurs when cold air is next to the ground with warm air lying on top, thereby allowing pollutants to remain concentrated in one area.

168. (B)

Statements II and III each provide an accurate definition, and thus Option B is the correct answer. Statement I is incorrect because ecology is the study of the relationship between living things and their environment, while statement IV is incorrect because a group of similar organisms is a population.

169. (A)

Option A is correct because coal is not renewable but water and fish are renewable. Statement IV is incorrect, in that because corn is a renewable resource, it is correctly placed in the poster.

170. (C)

Options A, B and D could be helpful, but they are incorrect answers to this question because they do not allow the students to collect data. Option C is preferable because it would provide students with an authentic, hands-on opportunity to collect data.

171. (A)

Option A is correct because students are only asked to learn about materials. Option B is incorrect because students were not asked to draw conclusions about what they observed, while Options C and D are incorrect because students were not asked to make or test any predictions about the materials.

172. (B)

Option B is correct, because Mrs. Langley has provided the students with different measuring devices that they will then use to find out different kinds of information. Options A and C are incorrect because the task is not experimental and does not involve variables, while Option D is incorrect because students are not asked to analyze their findings.

173. (B)

Option B is the correct answer. Options A, C, and D include the size of the ball as a variable, but the balls were actually the same in size.

174. (D)

In order to meet health and safety requirements, students should avoid using bodily fluids of any kind, and thus Option D is the correct answer. The other options would not ordinarily pose health or safety risks.

175. (C)

Five-percent accuracy means that the range for the actual value could be plus or minus 5%, and thus Option C is the correct answer.

176. (B)

Options A, C, and D are all likely to promote scientific understanding. However, hands-on activities are likely to result in the deepest science learning, and thus Option B is the correct answer.

177. (C)

Option C is correct because a spreadsheet would be most helpful for saving and organizing grades. Option A is incorrect because databases organize both text and numerical data, Option B is incorrect because word-processing programs are used to write and edit text, and Option D is incorrect because desktop publishing programs permit integration of text and graphics to produce more complex publications.

178. (B)

Option A is incorrect because simulation programs speed up or slow down processes, Option C is incorrect because online databases are used for research, and Option D is incorrect because drill and practice programs are used to practice recall of concepts.

179. (A)

Transmitters, channels, and receivers are the basic components of telecommunications systems, and thus Option A is the correct answer. The lists in each of the other options are incorrect.

180. (A)

Option A presents an accurate definition of fair use doctrine. Option B is incorrect because brevity generally refers to quantity of text, Option C is incorrect because spontaneity refers to the need for a teacher to use a work without undertaking the normal time to obtain copyright permission, and Option D is incorrect because the cumulative effect test refers to copying material for only one class, from a single author, and no more than nine times during a term.

Mathematics

181. (B)

Finding the square root of 10,000 means finding the number that, when multiplied by itself, equals 10,000. In fact, $100 \times 100 = 10,000$.

182. (C)

Because the exponent on the outside of the parenthesis indicates multiplication, the exponents 2 and 3 can be multiplied to equal 6.

183. (C)

To solve the problem, you multiply the numerators (2×3) and the denominators (3×4). The answer is 6/12. To simplify, divide the numerator and the denominator by 6. The answer is 1/2.

184. (B)

To convert a decimal to a fraction, write the decimal as a fraction with the denominator a power of 10 (875/1000) and then reduce to lowest terms.

185. (B)

To convert a decimal to a percentage, shift the decimal point two places to the right and add the percent symbol (%).

186. (A)

If you are dividing a numerator by denominator, you must be starting with a fraction. Since there was no mention of percentages, you are changing the fraction to a decimal.

187. (D)

The number 1.4959826×10^8 means that the decimal place moves 8 places to the right. Since there are only 7 digits, a 0 is added to form the answer.

188. (C)

The easiest way to find the answer is to estimate by multiplying the whole numbers in the problem (3×8). The answer should be a little higher than that product. Thus 28.608 is the best option.

189. (B)

The 3, 7, 11, and 13 are integers (Statement I) as well as prime numbers (Statement II) with no multiples. Statement III is not true because the multiples of any whole number are the results of multiplying that whole number by the counting numbers.

190. (C)

x would be the price of the protractor and ($x + 3.99$) would be the price of the more expensive item.

191. (A)

Elsa is failing to carry a "1" in both places. Elsa is treating $14 + 29$ as if the problem were $1 + 2$ and $4 + 9$ with the result written as 313.

192. (B)

The formula for computing the area of a circle is $A = \pi r^2$. So, for a full circle, the expression would be $A = 3.14\ (5^2)$ or 78.5. Since the figure is a half circle, the answer is 78.5 divided by 2 or 39.25.

193. (B)

Line DC is a segment of line EC. Thus, Line EC (8) - Line DC (5) = Line ED (3).

194. (C)

A right triangle can be visualized as half of a rectangle. Since the formula for the area of a rectangle is $A = l \times w$, the formula for the area of a triangle would be half of that or A = (l × w)/2. In this figure, A = (line EC × line AE)/ 2 or A = (6 × 8)/2. 48/2 simplifies to 24.

195. (A)

An increase in length of the line segments will increase both the perimeter and the area.

196. (A)

Option B is incorrect because 1 kilogram > 1 gram > 1 milligram. Option C is incorrect because 1 liter > 1 deciliter > 1 centiliter. Option D is incorrect because 1 kilometer > 1 meter > 1 millimeter.

197. (D)

Gallons are customary units of volume and liters are metric units of volume. Option A is incorrect because kilograms are used to measure mass. Option B is incorrect because Kelvin measures temperature. Option C is incorrect because centimeters are a unit of length.

198. (D)

Option A is incorrect because deca- is 10^1. Option B is incorrect because centi- is 10^{-2}. Option C is incorrect because deci- is 10^{-1}.

199. (C)

The formula for computing the volume of a rectangular prism is l × w × h. Here, 10 ft × 10 ft × 25 ft = 2500 cubic feet.

200. (B)

Supplementary angles = 180°. Since ∠ABC is an obtuse angle, the supplementary angle will be acute. Options A and C are incorrect because they describe obtuse angles. Option D is incorrect because it describes a straight angle.

201. (A)

Option B is incorrect because, together, the angles are supplementary, not complementary angles.

Option C is incorrect because in order to be congruent, the angles would need to have the same measure and they do not. Option D is incorrect because vertical angles are opposite each other, not adjacent.

202. (B)

Statement I is incorrect because a transversal must cross two lines. Statement IV is incorrect because the two lines are parallel rather than intersecting.

203. (A)

The problem is solved using the Pythagorean theorem ($a^2 + b^2 = c^2$) as follows:

$$9^2 + x^2 = 15^2$$
$$81 + x^2 = 225$$
$$x^2 = 225 - 81$$
$$x^2 = 144$$
$$x = \sqrt{144} = 12$$

204. (D)

The total number of degrees in a triangle is 180°. The size of the missing angle is found by the following calculation: 180° − 90° − 28° = 62°.

205. (D)

A tessellation is a collection of plane figures that fill the plane with no overlaps and no gaps.

206. (A)

All of the options describe characteristics of regular hexagons.

207. (B)

Only (−1, −1) is on the line.

208. (B)

Smoking rates among high school students were evidently highest between 1995 and 1998.

209. (A)

The number of adults who smoke decreased about 20%.

210. (D)

If 15% is $7.50, 5% is $2.50. Thus, 5% × 20 = 100% and $2.50 × 20 = $50.00

211. (A)

5% of $292 = $14.60.

212. (C)

The bar graph shows that 38.9% of females who did not graduate from high school are obese.

213. (C)

The bar graph shows a difference of 3.5% between males and females who completed some college or technical school.

214. (B)

The mode is 95 because it occurs most frequently. The median is the seventh score, which is 75. The range is the difference between the highest and lowest scores, which is 100 − 45 = 55.
The mean is not 70, but rather 75.77.

215. (A)

The probability that the name will be a girl equals the number of ways the event can occur (12 girls) divided by the total number of possible events (23 students) so the probability is 12/23.

216. (D)

The data derived from the chart consist of the following values: 41, 42, 43, 55, 56, 71, 72, 72, and 73.

217. (C)

The value that occurs most often in the values 41, 42, 43, 55, 56, 71, 72, 72, and 73 is, in fact, 72.

218. (C)

The probability of blue is the number of ways to land on blue (1) out of the total number of colors (5).

219. (A)

The 6 odd numbers between 3 and 13 are 3, 5, 7, 9, 11, and 13. The probability of an odd number being chosen is the number of possible odd numbers (6) out of the total possible numbers (11).

220. (A)

The probability of blue being selected is the number of ways to land on blue (2) out of the total possible numbers (5).

221. (A)

The numbers in the first column are the digits in the tens place in each of the two digit values (1, 2, 3). The numbers in the second column are the values from the ones place.

222. (B)

Ms. Martin's comments are designed to help students manage time in completing the assignment.

223. (D)

An assessment rubric would let students know what Mr. Corzine expects and how the project will be graded.

224. (C)

Unlike formative (ongoing) assessments such as those in Options A, B, and D, summative assessments are given at the end of a learning period such as the FCAT.

225. (B)

The level in question is the evaluation level. Option A is incorrect because it reflects the remembering level. Option C is incorrect because reflects the applying level. Option D is incorrect because it reflects the understanding level.

Index

A

Abstract art and architecture, 192
Abstract expressionism, 193
Abuse
  recognizing, 230
  sexual, 219–220
Acid rain, 273
Active listening, 75
Adams, John, 116
Addition, 289
  word problems, 291
Additive identity property, 299
Africa
  kingdoms and cultures of, 96
African Americans
  children's literature and, 50–51
Civil Rights Movement, 131–133
  contribution to Americans society,
    89–90
  Ku Klux Klan and, 125
Air masses, 254
Air pollution, 272
Algebra, 316–322
  algebraic expression, 320–322
  equations, 317
  functional relationships, 316–317
  graphs, 317–320
  linear equations and inequalities,
    321–322
  properties to show equivalency, 322
Alliteration, 40
Alphabetic principle, 17–18
Amendments, to Constitution, 153–154
American Revolution, 113–115
  beginnings of, 113–114
  Boston Tea Party, 114
  Sugar and Stamp Act, 113–114
  war for independence, 114–115
Americas
  age of exploration, 104–107

ancient civilizations of, 96–97
English interests in New World,
    107–108
Ancient period
  art from, 187, 188
  music from, 183
Anecdotal records
  for reading assessment, 66
Angles, 310–311
Animal cells, 264
Antagonist, 44
Apostrophe, 40, 62
Aquifers, 253
Aquinas, Thomas, 98
Area, 302–303
Art
  analytical skill development, 194
  art materials for, 179
  art room requirements, 178–179
  assessment strategies, 198, 202
  curriculum, 199–201
  elements and principles of, 181
  historical periods of art, 186–193
Article of Confederation, 151
Assessment
  art, 198, 202
  mathematics, 328–329
  music, 195
  reading, 63–73
  science and technology, 279–280
  social studies, 164–169
  writing, 59–60
Assimilation, 49–50, 91
Associative property, 299, 322
Assonance, 40
Atomic bomb, 128–129
Atoms, 237–238
Audience, writing process and, 58
Auditory learners
  assessment and, 72
  phonics method and, 20

Authoritarian government, 149
Autism, 218
Autobiographies, 37
Automaticity, 25
Aztecs, 96, 105–106

B

Babylonian captivity, 94
Backdrop setting, 43
Bacteria, 264
Balboa, 105
Balkans, 136
Banking Act, 126
Bantu, 96
Bar graph, 318–319
Baroque period
  art from, 187, 189–190
  music from, 184
Bathos, 40
Bill of Rights, 116, 153
Biographies, 37
Black death, 98
Bloom's taxonomy, 32
Books, parts of, 35
Boston Tea Party, 114
Box-and-whisker graph, 323–324
Buddhism, 96
Buoyancy, 236
Bush, George H. W., 135
Bush, George W., 136
Byzantine empire, 95

C

Calcium, 206
Calvin, John, 99
Camp David Accords, 134
Cape Canaveral, 143
Capitalist economies, 163
Capitalization, 61–62

Carbon dioxide-oxygen cycle, 272
Carter, Jimmy, 134
Cause-and-effect writing, 34
Cause-effect analysis, 87–88
Cells, 264
Central tendency, 322–323
Characterization, 44–45
Chemical energy, 249
Chiasmus, 40
China, ancient Chinese empires, 96
Chinese Exclusion Act, 124
Christians/Christianity
    crusades, 98
    early Christian era music and art,
      184, 188
    Reformation, 99
    scholasticism, 98
Chronological order writing, 34
Circles, 303–304
Circuits, 243
Circulation, 269
Circumference, 303–304
Citizenship. *See* Government and
    citizenship
Civilian Conservation Corps, 126
Civil Right Movement, 131–133
Civil Rights Act, 122
Civil War, 119–122
    beginnings of, 121
    Dred Scott decision, 120
    election of 1860, 120
    Emancipation Proclamation,
      121–122
    in Florida, 141–142
    Homestead Act, 121
    Kansas-Nebraska Act, 120
    Missouri Compromise, 119
    Morrill Land Grant Act, 121
    reconstruction, 122
    secession, 120
Classical music, 184
Classroom management, 217
Classroom tests for reading assessment,
    68–69
Clinton, Bill, 135–136
Clouds, 254–255
Cloze test, 33

Colonial America
    beginnings of, 112–113
    English interests in New World,
      107–108
    Enlightenment in, 112–113
    French and Dutch settlements, 108
    Great Awakening, 112
    growth of slave trade, 111
    Jamestown settlement, 109–110
    religion in, 112
    Roanoke, 108
    Salem witch trials, 111
    Virginia settlements, 110–111
Colons, 62
Columbus, Christopher, 104–105
Command economies, 162
Commas, 62
Commercial Revolution, 101
Communication knowledge, 73–79
    listening and speaking strategies,
      74–79
    penmanship, 73–74
Communication skills for social
    development, 213
Communism, 130–131
Commutative property, 322
Comparison writing, 34
Composite, numbers, 298
Compounds, 237
Compound word rule, 22
Computer-related technology, 82–83
Concave lens, 240–241
Conceit, 40
Conduction, 258
Conductor, 241
Confederate States of America,
    120–122
Confederation, 149
Confessions, modern children's fiction,
    48–49
Conflict
    conflict resolution, 215
    in literature, 43
Confucius, 96
Congress, 154–155
Congruency, 306
Constitution, United States, 116
    amendments, 153–154

Article of Confederation, 151
Bill of Rights, 153
    compromise in establishing, 152
    contents of, 152–153
    judicial principles and, 159–160
    origins of, 151–152
    rights of citizens and, 159
Contextual clues, 22
Continental drift, 251
Convection, 258
Conversions
    measurements, 314
    numbers, 286–287
Convex lens, 240–241
Coordinate system, 307–308
Cortez, Hernando, 105–106
Counting numbers, 284
Creative level of comprehension, 31
Criterion-referenced test, 69
Critical-thinking skills development,
    32–33
Crusades, 98
Cuba, 123
    Cuban missile crisis, 132
Cultural pluralism, 91–92

D

Data analysis
    central tendency, 322–323
    frequency tables and graphs,
      323–324
    predictions and draw conclusions,
      324–325
Dead metaphor, 40
Decimals, 284, 286
Decoding skills, 17–25
de León, Juan Ponce, 139
De Luna, Tristán, 139–140
Density, 236
Descartes, René, 100
Descriptive writing, 33, 57
Desert Shield, 135
Developing reading stage, 24
Dew, 257
Diffusion, 265
Digestion, 270
Digestive system, 268

Directionality of print, 35–36
Distributive property, 299, 322
Divisibility, 300
Division, 290
 word problems, 292–293
Double-entry journal, 27
Drafting stage, 56
Dred Scott decision, 120
Dynamic character, 44

E

Earthquakes, 251
Earth science, 250–263
 composition of Earth, 250
 continental drift and seafloor
  spreading, 251
 earthquakes and volcanoes, 251
 Earth's tilt and seasons, 261–262
 land and water interactions,
  253–254
 moon, 260–261
 plate tectonics, 250
 radiation, conduction, convection,
  257–258
 renewable and nonrenewable
  resources, 262
 rock types and weathering, 252–253
 soil formation, 252
 solar system, 258
 space exploration, 258–260
 storms, 255
 sun's effect on Earth, 262–263
 water cycle, 256
 weather, 254–257
Ecology, 271–272
Economics
 consumer decision making, 163
 defined, 161
 economic institutions, 161–162
 economic interdependence among
  nations, 164
 limited resources, 161
 market economies, 162
 production through distribution and
  consumption, 162–163
 resources and production of goods,
  164
 supply and demand, 163
 types of, 162–163
Ecosystems, 271
Editing stage, 56
Egypt, ancient, 93
Eisenhower, Dwight, 131, 143
Electoral college, 156–157
Electrical energy, 248
Electricity, 241–243
 circuits, 243
 electron transfer, 242
 insulators and conductors, 241
 laws of electrostatic attraction and
  repulsion, 242–243
 static and moving electricity, 242
Electromagnetic wave spectrum,
 246–247
Electrons, 237–238
Electron transfer, 242
Electrostatic force, 239
Elements, 236–237
Elision, 40
Emancipation Proclamation, 121–122
Emergency Banking Relief Act, 126
Emergency Quota Act, 124
Emergent literacy, 34–36
Emergent reading stage, 24
Emotional health
 factors in, 212–216
 problems and support for, 216–219
Encoding skills, 17–25
Energy
 kinetic, 248
 light, 247
 potential, 248
 sound, 244
 types of, 243, 248–249
Engels, Friedrich, 102
England
 American Revolution, 113–115
 colonial America, 107–113
 feudalism in, 97–98
 interests in New World, 107–108
 War of 1812, 117
Enjambment, 40
Enlightenment, 100
 colonial America and, 112–113
Environment
 acid rain, 273
 adaptation with clothing, food,
  shelter, 146
air pollution, 272
 carbon dioxide-oxygen cycle, 272
 ecology, 271–272
 ecosystems, 271
 nitrogen cycle, 272
 tools and technology affect on, 146
Episodic plots, 43
Equations, 317
Estimation, 297–298
Europe
 age of exploration, 102–107
 black death, 98
 crusades, 98
 Enlightenment, 100
 French Revolution, 100
 Holy Roman Empire, 97–98
 medieval Europe, 97
 Napoleonic era, 101
 Reformation, 99
 Renaissance, 98–99
 scholasticism, 98
 Thirty Years' War, 100
Evolution, 270–271
Excretory system, 268–269
Executive branch, 155–156
Exploration, Age of, 102–107
 Balboa, 105
 beginnings of European, 102
 Columbus, 104–105
 Cortez, 105–106
 early challenges for, 103
 effects of European-American
  contact, 107
 main elements of, 104
 Pizarro, 106
 Spanish interest and settlements in
  new world, 106–107
 technical innovations aiding, 103
Exponents, 287
Expository writing, 57–58

F

Fables, 47

Factors, 298
Fairy tales, 47
Fantasy, 37
Fat, dietary, 204
Federal government, 149, 158
Federalist era, 116
Feet, poetic term, 40
Fermentation, 266
Fetal alcohol syndrome, 222
Feudalism
    in England, 97–98
    in Japan, 95
Fiction
    modern children's fiction, 48–49
    traditional children's fiction, 47–48
Fictional narrative, 57
Fifteenth Amendment, 122
Figurative language, 46
First aid, 228–229
Flat character, 44
Florida
    American possession of, 140–141
    Civil War and Reconstruction,
        141–142
    demographics of ethnic and racial
        diversity of, 138
    early history, 139
    early twentieth century, 142
    eighteenth century, 140
    first European explorers and, 139
    first European settlements, 139–140
    origin of reservations, 141
    post-war immigration and
        migration, 142
    slavery in, 141
    space program and, 142–143
Fog, 257
Folktales, 48
Food choices, 203
Forces, 239
Formal assessment
    for reading assessment, 68–71
Formative evaluation, 65
Fractions, 284, 285–286
France
    French Revolution, 100
    Napoleonic era, 101
    settlements in New World, 108

Frank, Anne, 129–130
Freedman's Bureau, 122
French Revolution, 100
Frequency tables, 323–324
Fronts, 254
Functional relationships, 316–317

G

Gases, 237
Genre art, 190
Geography
    compare/contrast major regions of
        world, 148–149
    economic, cultural, physical,
        political forces in migration,
        146–148
    essential elements of, 143–144
    map and graphic skills for, 145
    people adaptation to environment,
        146
    statistics for human and physical
        characteristics, 145
    transportation and communication
        in economic development, 148
Geometry, 301–316
    angles, 310–311
    area, 302–303
    circumference and circles, 302–303
    geometric properties and problem
        solving, 305–306
    ordered pairs, 307–308
    perimeter, 301–302
    points and lines, 310
    symmetry, congruency, similarity,
        transformation, 306–307
    three-dimensional shapes, 309
Gore, Al, 136
Gothic art, 188–189
Government and citizenship
    citizen rights and documents that
        guarantee, 159
    Constitution, 151–154
    electoral college, 156–157
    federal, state and local government,
        157–158
    legal system, 159–160

legislative, executive and judicial
        branches of, 154–156
    rights and responsibilities of citizen,
        151
    structure, purpose and function of
        government, 148–149
Grant, Ulysses S., 122
Grapheme, 19, 23
Graphic aids, 31
Graphic organizers, for reading fluency,
        27
Graphophonemic awareness, 17
Graphs, 317–320
Gravitational force, 239
Gravity, 236
Great Awakening, 112
Great Britain
    American Revolution, 113–115
    colonial America, 107–113
    War of 1812, 117
Great Depression, 125
Greece, ancient, 94
Guam, 123
Guided imagery, 77

H

Hail, 257
Hamilton, Alexander, 116
Hardware, computer, 82–83
Harmonic instruments, 176
Health. *See* Physical education and
        health
Health care reform, 135
Heat, 238–239
    radiation, conduction, convection,
        257–258
Heat transfer, 238–239
Hebrews
    Babylonian captivity, 94
    Palestine and, 93–94
Heredity, 270–271
Hierarchy of needs, 227–228
Hinduism, 96
Hiroshima, 128–129
Historical fiction, 37
Hitler, Adolph, 129
Holocaust, 129–130

Holy Roman Empire, 97–98
Homestead Act, 121
Homonyms, 40
Hoover, Herbert, 125
Hyperbole, 41
Hyphens, 62

I

Identity vs. role confusion stage, 211–212
Igneous rocks, 252
Immigration
  assimilation and, 91
  earliest Americans, 137
  economic, cultural, physical, political forces in migration, 146–148
  Florida demographics, 138
  fundamental immigration questions, 137
  national immigration trends, 138
  post-war immigration, 142
  restrictions on, and discrimination, 124
Impressionism, 187, 191
Incas, 96–97, 106
India, ancient empires, 96
Industrialism, 123
Industrial Revolution, 101
Industry vs. inferiority stage, 211
Informational and media literacy, 79–83
  current technology in educational setting, 82–83
  multimedia literacy, 81–82
  multimedia resources, 80–81
  primary sources, 80
  professional and ethical process for collection information, 82
  secondary sources, 80
Informational text structures, 33–34, 37
Initiative vs. guilt stage, 211
Insulator, 241
Integers, 284, 285
Integral setting, 44
Internal voices, 214–215

Interpretive level of comprehension, 30
Intimacy vs. isolation stage, 212
Iran
  hostage crisis, 134
  Iran-Contra scandal, 135
Iran-Contra scandal, 135
Iraq
  Persian Gulf crisis, 135
Iron, 206
Islam
  Islamic civilization in middle ages, 95
  Sharia, 95
Italics, 63

J

Jackson, Andrew, 118, 140, 141
Jacksonville, Florida, 140, 141
Jamestown settlement, 109–110
Japan, feudalism in, 95
Jefferson, Thomas, 116–117
Jeffersonian Era, 116–117
Jet stream, 254
Jews
  holocaust, 129–130
Jones, Frederick McKinley, 90
Judicial branch, 156, 159–160
"Just Read, Florida" reading formula, 18–19

K

Kansas-Nebraska Act, 120
Kennedy, John F., 132
Kennedy, Robert, 132
Kennings, 41
Khrushchev, Nikita, 132
Kinetic energy, 248
King, Martin Luther, Jr., 131, 132
Korean War, 130–131
Ku Klux Klan, 125
Kuwait
  Persian Gulf crisis, 135

L

Labor unions, 127

Laden, Osama bin, 136
Language Arts and Reading, 17–83
  communication knowledge, 73–79
  informational and media literacy, 79–83
  literature and literary analysis, 36–54
  reading methods and assessment, 63–73
  reading process, 17–36
  writing process, 55–63
Language cues, 23
Language Experience Approach, 63
LAPS, 77
Latimer, Lewis H., 90
Latinos
  contributions to American society, 90
Laudonnière, René Goulaine de, 140
Learning styles
  reading assessment and, 72
Lee, Robert E., 122
Legal system, 159–160
Legends, 48
Legislature, 154–155
Leitmotivs, 41
Lenses, 240–241
Lever, 245
Life science, 263–273
  animals/humans organ systems, 267–269
  environmental issues, 271–273
  heredity, evolution, natural selection, 270–271
  infectious agents, 263–264
  living vs. nonliving things, 263
  plant organelles, 266–267
  plant physiological processes, 265–266
  plant vs. animal cells, 264
Light
  invisible, 247
  properties of, 240
  visible, 247
Lincoln, Abraham, 120–122
Linear equations and inequalities, 321–322
Line graph, 317–318

Lines, 310
Liquids, 237
Listening and speaking strategies, 74–79
  guided imagery, 77
  LAPS, 77
  listening and media centers, 76
  listening guides, 77
  listening skills, 75
  oral storytelling, 78
  partner retells, 77–78
  playing listening games, 76–77
  promoting voice, 79
  RAP, 78
  reading aloud, 76
  SLANT, 77
  speaking skills, 75–76
  think, pair, share, 78
Listening guides, 77
Literacy
  emergent, 34–36
  multimedia literacy, 81–82
Literal level of comprehension, 30
Literature and literary analysis, 36–54
  characteristics and elements of genres, 36–42
  characterization, 44–45
  encouraging students to respond to literature, 54
  figurative language, 46
  modern children's fiction, 48–49
  motifs, 45
  multicultural literature, 49–54
  nonfiction, 37
  novels, 37–38
  plot, 43
  poetry, 38–42
  rhyme schemes, 39
  short stories, 38
  style, 46
  theme, 42
  traditional children's fiction, 47–48
Litotes, 41
Local government, 157–158
Locke, John, 100
Locus of control, 213–214
Luther, Martin, 99

M

Madison, James, 116–117
Magellan, 105
Magna Carta, 97–98, 152
Magnesium, 207
Magnetic force, 239
Manhattan Project, 128
Manifest destiny, 118–119
Mapping, reading comprehension and, 28
Market economies, 162
Marshall, George C., 130
Marshall, John, 117
Marshall, Thurgood, 131
Marshall Plan, 130
Marx, Karl, 102
Marxism, 102
Mass, 235
Mathematics, 283–329
  algebra, 316–322
    algebraic expression, 320–322
    equations, 317
    functional relationships, 316–317
    graphs, 317–320
    linear equations and inequalities, 321–322
    properties to show equivalency, 322
  assessment, 328–329
  data analysis
    central tendency, 322–323
    frequency tables and graphs, 323–324
    predictions and draw conclusions, 324–325
  geometry, 301–316
    angles, 310–311
    area, 302–303
    circumference and circles, 302–303
    geometric properties and problem solving, 305–306
    ordered pairs, 307–308
    perimeter, 301–302
    points and lines, 310
    symmetry, congruency, similarity, transformation, 306–307
    three-dimensional shapes, 309
  instructional strategies, 325–329
  measurement, 313–316
  numbers and number sense, 283–301
    conversions, 286–287
    divisibility, 300
    equivalent forms, 289
    estimation, 297–298
    exponents, 287
    integers, 285
    kinds of numbers, 284
    number representations, 283–284
    number sequences, 300
    number theory concepts, 298–300
    operations, 284, 289–290
    order of operations, 300–301
    ratios, proportions, percents, 288
    scientific notation, 287–288
    word problems, 290–298
McGuffey Readers, 19
McKinley, William, 123
Measurement, 313–316
Mecca, 95
Mechanical energy, 248
Medieval art, 187
Melodic instruments, 176
Melting pot, 91
Menéndez de Avilés, Pedro, 140
Mesolithic period, 92–93
Mesopotamia, 93
Metamorphic rocks, 252
Metaphor, 46
Metonymy, 41
Mexican War, 119
Middle ages
  Europe during, 97
  Islamic civilization in, 95
Middle Stone Age, 92–93
Migration
  economic, cultural, physical, political forces in, 146–148
Minerals, 204–207
Missouri Compromise, 117–118, 119
Mixed economies, 163
Mixture, 237
Modern children's fiction, 48–49

Mohammed, 95
Monroe, James, 117
Monroe Doctrine, 117
Moon, 260–261
Moore, James, 140
Morgan, Garrett A., 90
Morgan, J. P., 123
Morphemic cues, 23
Morrill Land Grant Act, 121
Motifs, 45
Motion, 249–250
Motor-skill development, 209–210
Multicultural literature, 49–54
  assimilation and pluralism, 49–50
  example of African American
    children's literature, 50–51
  guidelines for selecting, 49
  poetry, 52
  promoting multiculturalism, 50
  sexism, 52–54
  use of, 51–52
Multimedia literacy, 81–82
Multimedia resources, 80–81
Multiples, numbers, 298
Multiplication, 289–290
  word problems, 292
Multiplicative identity property, 299
Muscular system, 268
Music
  analytical skill development,
    193–194
  appropriate varieties of, 173
  assessment strategies, 195
  cultural differences in, 183
  curriculum for, 196–197
  elements of, 180
  harmonic instruments, 176
  historical periods of, 183–186
  melodic instruments, 176
  reading music notation, 176–178
  rhythmic instruments, 175
  singing techniques, 174
  styles of music, 182
Muslims
  Islamic civilization in middle ages,
    95
MyPlate.gov, 204
Mysteries, 37

Myths, 48

N

Nagasaki, 129
Napoleonic era, 101
National Aeronautics and Space
  Administration (NASA), 143, 259
  creation of, 131
National Industrial Recovery Act
  (NIRA), 126
Native Americans
  conflict with colonists, 109–111
  origins of reservations, 141
Natural selection, 271
Nazis, 129
Needs, hierarchy of, 227–228
Neglect
  recognizing, 230
Neoclassicism, 190
Neolithic period, 93
Nervous system, 268
Neurotic disorders, 218
Neutrality Act, 127
Neutrons, 237–238
New Deal, 125–127
New Stone Age, 93
Niagara Movement, 124
Nitrogen cycle, 272
Nixon, Richard M., 133–134
Nonfiction, 37
Nonrenewable resources, 262
Norm-references tests, 70
Novels, 37–38
Nuclear energy, 249
Numbers and number sense, 283–301
  conversions, 286–287
  divisibility, 300
  equivalent forms, 289
  estimation, 297–298
  exponents, 287
  integers, 285
  kinds of numbers, 284
  number representations, 283–284
  number sequences, 300
  number theory concepts, 298–300
  numerical properties, 298–299
  operations, 284, 289–290

order of operations, 300–301
  ratios, proportions, percents, 288
  scientific notation, 287–288
  word problems, 290–298
Nutrition, 203–207
  fat, dietary, 204
  food choices, 203
  vitamins and minerals, 204–207

O

Obama, Barack, 137
Old Stone Age, 92
Onomatopoeia, 41
Operation Just Cause, 135
Operations, 289–290
Oral storytelling, 78
Ordered list, 33
Ordered pairs, 307–308
Osceola, 141

P

Paleolithic period, 92
Panama Canal, 123, 134
Parables, 47
Paradox, 41
Parallelism, 41
Paris, Treaty of, 115
Parliamentary government, 150
Partner retells, 77–78
Pathogens, 263
Pathos, 41
Pearl Harbor, 128
Penmanship, 73–74
Pensacola, 140, 141
Percents, 288
Performance-based assessment, 71–72
Perimeter, 301–302
Periods, 62
Persian Gulf crisis, 135
Personal narrative, 57
Personification, 46
Persuasive writing, 58
Philippines, 123
Phoneme, 19, 23
Phonemic awareness, 18
Phonics, 19–21

advantages of, 20
disadvantages of, 20
methods of instruction for, 20–21
Phosphorus, 206
Photosynthesis, 265
Physical education and health, 202–232
   common health problems, 208–209
   curriculum design, 231–232
   goal setting for health and wellness,
      207–208
   identifying signs of sexual abuse,
      219–220
   importance of physical fitness,
      202–203
   motor-skill development, 209–210
   nutrition, 203–207
   problem identification for physical,
      social and emotional health,
      216–219
   psychosocial development stages,
      210–212
   resources for health information,
      224
   safety and injury prevention,
      227–230
   social and emotional health factors,
      212–216
   substance use and abuse, 221–224
   violence prevention strategies,
      225–227
   weight, 207–208
Physical science, 235–281
   atoms, 237–238
   electricity, 241–243
   elements, compounds mixtures,
      236–237
   energy types, 243–244, 248–249
   forces, 239
   light, 240
   motion, 249–250
   optics, 240–241
   physical properties of matter,
      235–236
   physical vs. chemical changes, 236
   potential and kinetic energy,
      248–249
   solids, liquids, gases, 237
   sound, 244

temperature and heat transfer,
      238–239
   work, 245–246
Picaresque theme, 42
Pie chart, 320
Pizarro, Francisco, 106
Plants
   cells of, 264
   diffusion and photosynthesis, 265
   organelles, 266–267
   respiration, fermentation,
      reproduction, 266
Plate tectonics, 250
Plot, 38, 43
Pluralism, 49–50
Pocahontas, 109–110
Poetic terms, 40–41
Poetry, 38–42
   forms of, 42
   multicultural literature, 52
   poetic terms, 40–41
   rhyme schemes, 39
Points, 310
Polk, James, 119
Polygons, 311
Portfolios, for reading assessment, 67
Portugal, age of exploration and,
      103–104
Potassium, 206
Potential energy, 248
Prefixes, 22
Prehistorical period, 92–93
   art from, 187–188
President of United States, 155–156
Prewriting stage, 56
Primary sources
   advantages of, 80
   defined, 80
   evaluating for historical perspective,
      89
Primes, 298
Print, directionality of, 35–36
Problem-and-solution writing
   organization, 34
Problem behavior patterns, 217–218
Progressive plots, 43
Progress monitoring, 71
Proportions, 288

Prosody, 26
Protagonist, 44
Protons, 237–238
PROVE, 29
Psychotic disorders, 218
Public Works Administration, 126
Publishing stage of writing, 56
Pueblos, 107
Puerto Rico, 123
Pulley, 246
Punctuation, 62–63
Puritans, 108, 112
Purple patch, 41
Purpose, in writing process, 59

Q

Quotation marks, 63

R

Radiant energy, 249
Radiation, 257
Rain, 257
Raleigh, Walter, 108
Ramp, 245
RAP, 78
Ratios, 288
   word problems, 293–294
Reading aloud, 76
Reading comprehension, 28–31
   assessing, 33
   creative level of, 31
   critical level of, 30–31
   interpretive level of, 30
   literal level of, 30
   mapping and webbing, 28
   PROVE, 29
   puzzles, riddles, think-alouds, 29
   SQ3R, 28–29
   study plans, 28
Reading methods and assessment,
      63–73
   anecdotal records, 66
   checklists, 66
   classroom tests, 68–69
   criterion-referenced test, 69
   diversity and, 73

formal assessment, 68–71
formative evaluation, 65
informal assessment, 65–68
learning styles and assessment, 72
norm-references tests, 70
percentile scores, 70
performance-based assessment, 71–72
portfolios, 67
progress monitoring, 71
reliability and validity of, 70–71
running records, 65–66
summative evaluation, 65
Reading process, 17–36
alphabetic principle, 17–18
automaticity, 25
contextual clues, 22
critical-thinking skills development, 32–33
decoding and encoding skills, 17–25
emergent literacy, 34–36
graphic organizers, 27
informational text structures, 33–34
"Just Read, Florida" reading formula, 18–19
language cues, 23
multiple representations of information for variety of purposes, 31
phonemes and graphemes, 23
phonemic awareness, 18
phonics, 19–21
prosody, 26
reading comprehension, 28–31
reading fluency, 25–27
reading strategies, 24–25
stages of reading development, 23–24
structural analysis, 21–22
vocabulary acquisition, 27–28
word structure, 21–22
Reagan, Ronald, 134–135
Realism, art, 187, 191
Realistic fiction, 37
Realistic novels, 48
Reconstruction, 122, 141–142
Rectangles, 302–303
Rectangular solids, 309

Reformation, 99
Refraction, 240
Refrains, 41
Reign of Terror, 100
Religion
in colonial America, 112
Great Awakening, 112
Renaissance, 98–99
art from, 187, 189
music during, 184
Renewable resources, 262
Reproduction
animal, 270
plant, 266
Reservoirs, 253
Respiration
animal, 269
plant, 266
Reversal of fortunes theme, 42
Revising stage, 56
Rhyme schemes, 39
Rhythmic instruments, 175
Ribault, Jean, 140
Roanoke, 108
Rockefeller, John D., 123
Rocks, 252
Rococo style art, 190
Rolfe, John, 110
Romances, 48
Romanesque style art, 188
Romantic period
art from, 187, 190–191
music from, 185
Rome, ancient, 94
Roosevelt, Franklin D., 125–127
Roosevelt, Theodore, 123
Round character, 44
Running records
for reading assessment, 65–66
Runoff, 253
Rural Electrification Administration, 127

S

Safety and injury prevention
common injuries, symptoms and treatments, 229–230

first aid, 228–229
hierarchy of needs, 227–228
recognizing abuse and neglect, 230
school safety, 227
for teaching science, 275–277
St. Augustine, Florida, 106, 139, 140
Salem witch trials, 111
San Mateo, 140
Santa Fe, New Mexico, 107
Satire, 49
Scaffolding, 23
Scholasticism, 98
School safety, 227
Science and technology
assessment, 279–280
earth science, 250–263
composition of Earth, 250
continental drift and seafloor spreading, 251
earthquakes and volcanoes, 251
Earth's tilt and seasons, 261–262
land and water interactions, 253–254
moon, 260–261
plate tectonics, 250
radiation, conduction, convection, 257–258
renewable and nonrenewable resources, 262
rock types and weathering, 252–253
soil formation, 252
solar system, 258
space exploration, 258–260
storms, 255
sun's effect on Earth, 262–263
water cycle, 256
weather, 254–257
instructional strategies, 279–280
laboratory equipment for, 274
life science, 263–273
animals/humans organ systems, 267–269
animals/humans physiology, 269–270
environmental issues, 271–273
heredity, evolution, natural selection, 270–271

infectious agents, 263–264
living vs. nonliving things, 263
plant organelles, 266–267
plant physiological processes, 265–266
plant vs. animal cells, 264
physical science, 235–281
atoms, 237–238
electricity, 241–243
elements, compounds mixtures, 236–237
energy types, 243–244, 248–249
forces, 239
light, 240
motion, 249–250
optics, 240–241
physical properties of matter, 235–236
physical vs. chemical changes, 236
potential and kinetic energy, 248–249
solids, liquids, gases, 237
sound, 244
temperature and heat transfer, 238–239
work, 245–246
safety procedures for teaching, 275–277
scientific method, 273–274
technology and, 277–278
Science fiction, 37
Scientific notation, 287–288
Scientific Revolution, 101
Screw, 246
Seafloor spreading, 251
Seasons, 261–262
Secession, 120–121
Secondary sources, 80
Sedimentary rocks, 252
Self-efficacy, 213
Self-esteem, 213
Semantic cues, 23
Semicolons, 62
Seminole War, 141
Sequence writing organization, 34
Setting, in literature, 43–44
Sexism, literature and, 52–54

Sexual abuse
identifying signs of, 219–220
reporting suspicions of, 220
Sharia, 95
Sherman, William, 122
Short stories, 37, 38
Similarity, 307
Simile, 46
Sinkholes, 253
Skeletal system, 267
SLANT, 77
Slaves/slavery
beginning of slave trade, 104
colonial times and growth of slave trade, 111
Constitution and, 152
Dred Scott decision, 120
early antislavery movement, 118
Emancipation Proclamation, 121–122
in Florida, 141
Missouri Compromise, 117–118, 119
New World and, 107
Smallpox, 106, 107
Smith, Adam, 100, 163
Smith, John, 109
Snow, 257
Social environment of school, 218–219
Socialism
Marxism, 102
Utopian, 101–102
Socialist economies, 163
Social science, 87–169
assessment methods for teaching, 169
cultural contributions of Africa, Americas, Asia, Middle East and Europe, 89–90
cultural contributions to Florida, 139–143
economics, 161–164
exploration, settlement and growth, 102–107
geography and people, places, environment, 143–149
government and citizenship, 149–160

historical events and cause-effect analysis, 87–88
immigration and settlement patterns in United States, 137–138
instruction and assessment in, 164–169
physical and human geographic factors in major historical events, 90–92
prehistorical period through nineteenth century in Eastern and Western civilizations, 92–102
primary sources for historical perspective, 89
resources for teaching, 164–169
United States history, 107–137
Social Security Act, 127
Social skills, 212–216
Sodium, 206
Software, computer, 83
Solar system, 258
Solids, 237
Sound, 244
Space exploration, 131, 258–260
early years of, 258–259
Florida and space program, 142–143
other achievements, 260
quest for the moon, 259
space race, 259
Spain
age of exploration and, 104–106
Spanish-American War, 123
Spanish interest and settlements in new world, 106–107
Spanish-American War, 123
Speaking skills, 75–79
Speculative writing, 58
Speech-to-print match, 36
Spelling
conventions of, 60
steps for learning to spell new word, 61
Sputnik, 259
SQ3R, 28–29
Squares, 302–303
Standard American English (SAE), 63
State government, 158
Static character, 44

Stem-and-leaf plot, 324
Stereotyping
    in characterization, 45
    in fairy tales, 47
Storms, 255
Stress management, 215–216
Structural analysis, of words, 21–22
Substance use and abuse, 221–224
    fetal alcohol syndrome, 222
    Florida state law concerning, 224
    legal requirements and, 218
    prevention of, 223–224
    resources for teaching about, 224
    risks for, 221–222
    signs and symptoms of, 222–223
    treatment of, 224
Subtraction, 289
    word problems, 291–292
Suffixes, 21, 22
Sugar Act, 113
Summative evaluation, 65
Sun, 262–263
Supply and demand, 163
Supreme Court, U.S.
    Dred Scott decision, 120
    legal system and, 159–160
    Marshall court, 117
    women on, 160
Surrealism, 192
Survival of the unfittest theme, 42
Symmetry, 306
Synechdoches, 41
Syntactic cues, 23

T

Tallahassee, 141
Taoism, 96
Temperature, 238–239
Temple, Lewis, 89
Theme, 42
Thermal energy, 248
Think, pair, share, 78
Thirty Years' War, 100
Three-dimensional shapes, 309
Traditional children's fiction, 47–48
Traditional economies, 163
Transformations, 307

Transitional reading stage, 24
Triangles, 302–303
Twentieth century art, 187

U

Unitary government, 149
United States history, 107–137
    American Revolution, 113–115
    Carter's presidency, 134
    Civil Right Movement, 131–133
    Civil War, 119–122
    Clinton's presidency, 135–136
    colonial times, 107–113
    Cuban missile crisis, 132
    discrimination, 124–125
    early antislavery movement, 118
    Federalist era, 116
    Great Depression, 125
    industrialism, 123
    Jacksonian democracy, 118
    Jeffersonian Era, 116–117
    Korean War, 130–131
    labor unions, 127
    manifest destiny and westward
        expansion, 118–119
    Marshall court, 117
    Mexican War, 119
    Missouri Compromise, 117–118,
        119
    Monroe Doctrine, 117
    New Deal, 125–127
    Obama, 137
    Persian Gulf crisis, 135
    progressive reform and social
        change, 123–124
    Reagan's presidency, 134–135
    space exploration, 131
    Spanish-American War, 123
    terrorism and September 11, 2001,
        136
    Vietnam War, 133
    War of 1812, 117
    Watergate, 133–134
    World War II, 127–130
Utopian Socialists, 101–102

V

Variability, 323
vc/cv, 22
v/cv, 22
Venn diagrams, 27
Vietnam, 131, 133
Vietnam War, 133
Violence prevention strategies, 215,
    225–227
Virginia settlements, 110–111
Viruses, 264
Viscosity, 236
Visual learners
    assessment and, 72
    phonics method and, 20
Vitamins, 204–207
Vocabulary acquisition, 27–28
Voice, promoting, 79
Volcanoes, 251
Volume, 235
Voting Rights Act, 132

W

Wagner Act, 127
War of 1812, 117
Washington, George, 115–116
Water cycle, 256
Watergate, 133–134
Weather, 254–257
Weathering, 253
Webs, graphic organizer
    reading comprehension and, 28
    reading fluency and, 27
Web tools, 83
Wedge, 245
Weight
    health and wellness, 207–208
    losing, 208
    as physical property of matter, 235
Westward expansion, 118–119
Wheel and axle, 246
Wilson, Woodrow, 124
Wind, 254
Woods, Granville T., 89
Word problems, 290–298
Word structure, 21–22

Work, machines and, 245–246
Works Progress Administration (WPA), 127
World War I, 124
World War II, 127–130
    American entry into, 128
    end of, 128–129
    holocaust, 129
Writing
    penmanship, 73–74
    types of, 33–34, 57–58
Writing process, 55–63
    audience, 58
    capitalization, 61–62
    conventions of, 60–63
    descriptive writing, 57
    developmental stages of, 55–56
    drafting stage, 56
    editing stage, 56
    expository writing, 57–58
    fictional narrative, 57
    Language Experience Approach, 63
    language groups and conventions, 63
    occasion and, 59
    personal narrative, 57
    persuasive writing, 58
    prewriting stage, 56
    publishing stage, 56
    punctuation, 62–63
    purpose and, 59
    revising stage, 56
    rubrics for assessing writing, 59–60
    speculative writing, 58
    spelling, 60–61

Z

Zinc, 206